The Accelerated Schools

Resource Guide

AUTHORS

Wendy S. Hopfenberg

Henry M. Levin

Christopher Chase

S. Georgia Christensen

Melanie Moore

Pilar Soler

Ilse Brunner

Beth Keller

Gloria Rodriguez

ILLUSTRATIONS

Christopher Chase

Substantial discounts on bulk quantities of Jossey-Bass books are available to corporations, professional associations, and other organizations. For details and discount information, contact the special sales department at Jossey-Bass Inc., Publishers. (415) 433-1740; Fax (415) 433-0499.

For international orders, please contact your local Paramount Publishing International office.

The paper used in this book is acid-free and meets the guidelines for permanence and durability of the Committee on Production Guidelines for Book Longevity of the Council on Library Resources.

Library of Congress Cataloging-in-Publication Data

The Accelerated schools resource guide / Wendy S. Hopfenberg . . . [et al.].
    p. cm. — (The Jossey-Bass education series)
    Includes bibliographical references and index.
    ISBN 1-55542-545-3
    1. Educational acceleration.   2. School management and organization—United States.   3. Educational innovations—United States.   I. Hopfenberg, Wendy S., [date].   II. Series.
LB1029.A22A22   1993
371'.04—dc20
                                         93-15387
                                            CIP

FIRST EDITION
HB Printing   10 9 8 7 6 5 4 3 2   Code 9348

Please Read

This resource guide has been created to serve as a reference manual for establishing and supporting accelerated schools. It is not a substitute for the training and coaching that your school will need. In order to launch and sustain an accelerated school, this resource guide should be used in conjunction with full staff training by a certified accelerated schools coach.

Contents

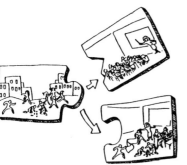

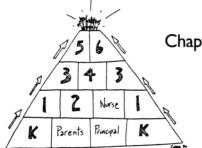

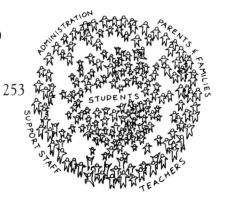

The Accelerated Schools
Resource Guide

Prologue

The Accelerated Schools Project was established to bring "at-risk" students into the educational mainstream by the end of elementary school. Because of the early success of accelerated elementary schools, the needs of early adolescents, and many requests from middle schools, we later began working with middle schools as well. Instead of slowing down student learning with remediation, the idea was to enhance their academic growth through challenging and stimulating activities. Instead of lowering expectations for these children, the goal was to treat them as gifted and talented students by

by

Henry M. Levin

identifying and building on their strengths. Instead of treating a school as a collection of individual programs and staff members with individual goals, the objective was to create a schoolwide unity of purpose that would encompass all children, staff, and parents. Instead of using state- and district-mandated "canned" curriculum packages as solutions to learning challenges, the goal was to incorporate the entire staff into a governance and decision-making process around the unified purpose of creating powerful learning experiences for *all* children.

These ideas were melded into a process that incorporates an integrated approach to school curriculum, instructional strategies, and organization— a process by which parents, students, teachers, support staff, administrators, district offices, and local communities could work together to reach their shared vision. Schools that were launched on the basis of these goals and this process were named *accelerated schools*. The first accelerated elementary schools were established in 1986–87, and by 1993–94 the movement had grown to about 500 elementary and middle schools in thirty-five states. What these school communities have achieved is remarkable, both in their individual accomplishments and in altering the very premises of educating the so-called at-risk population. What they have demonstrated is that *all* students can do high-quality academic work, can engage in collaborative and individual inquiry and research, can communicate effectively, and can meet high standards.

The ideas for the accelerated school had their origin in work that I did in the late sixties and in the seventies on urban schools. In this work on the finance and organization of schools, I searched for more effective ways of educating children from the inner cities. I was obsessed particularly by the inequalities in funding and educational outcomes for minorities and children from poverty backgrounds. Up until the early eighties, I limited my research to the outer workings of schools, evaluating the financing arrangements, organizational incentives, and other external conditions affecting their success. I avoided the inner workings—that is, the details of teaching and learning. As an economist specializing in the economics of education, I saw curriculum and instructional strategies as being beyond the purview of my expertise.

All of this changed in the eighties, when I was confronted with the plethora of national reports calling for educational reform for college-bound youngsters. These reports said nothing about students in at-risk situations with high dropout rates or the improvement of elementary schools. I was struck by the absence of concern for those populations for whom we had dedicated the War on Poverty.

Curiosity led me to inquire into what had happened to so-called disadvantaged or at-risk student populations. I found that the national reports omitted them for matters of convenience, not for lack of severity of their situation. Sadly, the War on Poverty had not been won when it came to these children. By 1984 I had prepared a demographic study for Public/Private Ventures in Philadelphia, which showed that these students were a large and increasing portion of the student population and were still at great risk of school failure (Levin, 1985, 1986). Moreover, I found that existing educational reforms were unlikely to do much for these students, because the reforms focused primarily on raising high school standards for college-bound students rather than on improving the preparation of students who were dropping out under existing standards.

At this point, I plunged into a study of the internal practices of schools attended by at-risk students. I buried myself in the Cubberley Library at Stanford University to review reams of research on at-risk students and school practices as well as evaluations of purportedly effective programs. I undertook scores of interviews with teachers, parents, principals, central office administrators, state and federal education authorities, and academics with expertise on the subject. Finally, I visited schools around the country with high concentrations of at-risk students to observe existing practices.

From these activities, I came to a startling conclusion: the inevitable consequences of existing educational practices used with students in at-risk situations actually undermined the future success of these students. Even though these students started school behind other students in academic skills, they were placed in instructional situations that slowed down their progress. They were stigmatized as remedial students or slow learners and assigned boring and repetitive exercises on worksheets. Their parents were often uninvolved in the school, and school staff were given little or no opportunity to provide more challenging and successful approaches. School districts, with the support of the publishers, had saddled schools with "teacher-proof" approaches that consisted of low-level textbooks in combination with student workbooks full of dull and tedious exercises. Rarely did I see opportunities for problem solving, enrichment, or applications of knowledge that drew upon student experiences and interests.

To me the solution seemed obvious: instead of slowing down these students—with the inevitable consequence of getting them farther and farther behind—we needed to *accelerate* their progress to bring them into the educational mainstream. Accordingly, I drew on research on learning and effective organizations to design and implement a process whereby schools could accelerate the learning of students in at-risk situations. It became clear that schools implementing such a process would have to draw on the talents of all of their staff, students, and parents and would have to be based on effective approaches to gathering information, making decisions, and building incentives for success at all levels. Finally, I found the appropriate learning approach in the enrichment strategies used for gifted and talented students—the design of creative approaches that build on strengths.

As these ideas percolated, I began to talk with colleagues at Stanford about the accelerated model. Fortunately, such distinguished colleagues as Ed Bridges, Bob Calfee, Larry Cuban, Milbrey McLaughlin, and Mike Smith were willing to lend a sympathetic ear and confirm or challenge my observations and conclusions. During this time, I had a group of talented graduate students, including Brenda LeTendre, Bob Polkinghorn, John Rogers, and Claire Smrekar, who indicated an interest in pursuing an idea that had by then officially become the Accelerated Schools Project (Levin, 1987a, 1987b, 1988).

Accelerated schools represent an attempt to create schools that deepen the learning of all students, bring them into the educational mainstream by the end of elementary school, and continue that advancement in middle school and beyond. The full transformation of a school takes five or six years, but there are major gains even in the first year. An important goal of the Accelerated Schools Project is to provide the best educational and life options for *all* students while also clearly reducing the dropout rate, drug use, and the number of teenage pregnancies in secondary schools as a by-product.

Accelerated schools are built on a unity of purpose among the entire school community in creating practices and activities that are dedicated toward accelerated progress. They establish an active school-site decision-making process with responsibility for results, and active participation in decisions by all school staff as well as parents, with reliance on small-group task forces, a schoolwide steering committee, and schoolwide governance groups. Instead of focusing on weaknesses, accelerated school staff and parents use a pedagogy constructed on the strengths and cultures of the children (and indeed all members of the school community), with a heavy reliance on relevant applications, problem solving, and active and "hands-on" learning approaches as well as an emphasis on thematic learning that integrates a variety of subjects into a common set of themes. Finally, parental involvement both at home and at school is central to the success of an accelerated school.

In 1986–87 we established collaborative relations with two pilot schools in the San Francisco Bay Area: Daniel Webster Elementary School in San Francisco and Hoover Elementary School in Redwood City. Both had very high concentrations of at-risk students and some of the lowest achievement scores in their districts. In each school, we spent time getting to know the staff and students and the few parents who were around, as well as informing the staff about the notion of creating an accelerated school. Ultimately, both schools voted unanimously to establish a collaborative project with Stanford around accelerated schools.

We began by sharing with the school communities the research that we had done on students in at-risk situations and the rationale behind creating accelerated schools with a unity of purpose, schoolwide empowerment and responsibility, and a commitment to building on strengths—our three principles. We also outlined a process of getting started and a system of organization and governance based on full-staff involvement, parental participation, and informed decision making. In addition to providing an early version of accelerated schools training and a system of governance, we formed Stanford teams for each school that visited on a weekly basis. The teams met with and trained groups of staff, observed classes, participated in school meetings and discussions, and met with the principals for planning, coaching, and troubleshooting. In addition, the teams collected data on all school activities and attended major school events.

By 1987–88 other schools asked to join the Project, on the basis of articles they had read or information they had received at professional meetings, and by the fall of 1990, about fifty-four schools were involved. These included two self-initiated state networks of accelerated schools in Illinois and Missouri and Hollibrook Elementary School, an extraordinary school in Houston. Recognizing the tremendous task of trying to work with a large number of schools on a nationwide basis, we began to develop the concept of satellite centers. The idea behind these centers was to build regional capacity to launch and support accelerated schools.

Fortunately, the Chevron Corporation provided generous funding to establish such satellite centers in Houston, Los Angeles, New Orleans, and San

Francisco. Each satellite center staff received training from Stanford before beginning to work with a pilot school in its area. Some three years later, these satellite center efforts have resulted in two statewide networks—in Louisiana and Texas—and a considerable increase in the number of accelerated schools in their areas. In addition, we have added an elementary school satellite center in Las Vegas. The Edna McConnell Clark Foundation, which initially supported our development of a middle school model, provided funding for us to launch middle school satellite centers in Massachusetts, Colorado, and Wisconsin, as well as to extend the elementary satellite capabilities of the Louisiana and Texas sites to include middle schools.

In addition to initiating regional satellite centers, we have also begun to build the capacity of school districts and states to support accelerated schools. Indeed, we see this as the next major step: building systemic support for accelerated schools by creating a capacity throughout the educational system to support such schools (Levin, 1991). We began this task in the summer of 1992 by training a group of district and state education officials; these officials will work with pilot schools in their respective regions and eventually begin launching and supporting additional schools.

This *Accelerated Schools Resource Guide* has been a major undertaking for the Accelerated Schools Project. Although we have a separate acknowledgments section to recognize all of the wonderful input that we received in putting it together, I would like to express my personal gratitude to that group. Support for the *Resource Guide* came from the Lucille and David Packard Foundation and the Edna McConnell Clark Foundation. I wish to apologize to these foundations for the long gestation of this work. At first we thought that it would be a straightforward activity to be accomplished in a relatively short period of time. As we began to work more intensively and with a greater number of schools, however, we continually pushed the accelerated schools model forward. Taking our own accumulated and embedded knowledge and sharing it in a written format required considerable discussion among us. Moreover, we found that we benefited from extensive feedback from teachers, principals, students, support staff, district office staff, and parents in accelerated school communities.

During preparation of the *Resource Guide*, we drew on all of our Project activities, including training funded by the Smart Family Foundation, our work with middle schools funded by the Edna McConnell Clark Foundation, and the work with satellite centers funded by Chevron. Accordingly, I wish to thank those funding entities for supporting our work more generally. Finally, I wish to thank the members of our Core Team—Wendy Hopfenberg, Ilse Brunner, Beth Keller, and Pilar Soler—and an extraordinary team of graduate students and support staff. They are the heart, soul, and brains of the Accelerated Schools Project. They have repeatedly demonstrated that a talented, creative, and hard-working team can create miracles. I have been blessed to have them as colleagues.

With respect to this *Resource Guide* I want to pay special tribute to Wendy Hopfenberg for accomplishing the herculean tasks of conceptualizing a framework and establishing a process for creating the *Guide*, coordinating a large group of authors and contributors, writing considerable portions herself, and editing all of this work into a unified whole. What is especially notable is her wonderful combination of competence, humor, and grace in meeting these demands.

Stanford, California   Henry M. Levin
August 1993

Accelerated Schools Project Statement

The National Center for the Accelerated Schools Project provides leadership and coordination in the development and implementation of accelerated schools across the country in the areas of project growth, training, research, dissemination, and evaluation. In addition, the National Center serves as a clearinghouse in all areas relating to the Project. Every member of the staff at the National Center works directly with satellite centers, accelerated schools networks in districts and states, and accelerated schools. Our ongoing work in schools and districts is crucial to our constantly evolving understanding of how to best launch and support accelerated schools around the country. Our involvement with these schools and districts allows us to develop and test our latest innovations in training, evaluation, coaching, and troubleshooting and, most important, to experience directly the workings of the accelerated schools process. The National Center staff includes a team of professional staff members and doctoral students who are involved in a number of project activities, including the following:

- Launching and supporting schools to test new ideas and stay in regular contact with accelerated schools

- Initiating and supporting the progress of satellite centers at universities, state education agencies, district offices, and nonprofit organizations, with ongoing coaching and troubleshooting

- Training district and state personnel as accelerated schools coaches, providing ongoing follow-up and support, and working with districts and states to transform their institutions

- Developing, implementing, evaluating, and refining training strategies and materials

- Developing publications, including the *Accelerated Schools Newsletter* and this *Accelerated Schools Resource Guide*

- Conducting research on accelerated schools and sharing our findings through articles and conferences throughout the country

- Providing networking opportunities through annual retreats of satellite centers, trainers, and schools and through regional and national conferences

- Establishing a data collection center and serving as a clearinghouse for information on accelerated schools, districts, and satellite centers

- Developing an assessment model and synthesizing evaluation strategies based on our own experience and the experiences of satellite centers and trainers

- Obtaining resources to continue training and capacity-building at a national level

If you would like more information about any of these activities, please contact the National Center for the Accelerated Schools Project at CERAS 109, School of Education, Stanford University, Stanford, CA 94305-3084, (415) 725-1676.

The Authors

The authors of *The Accelerated Schools Resource Guide* have a broad range of personal and professional experience with a clear common denominator: a strong commitment to improving education for *all* children. We have taught at all levels, from elementary to graduate school, in school communities as diverse as public schools in Boston and Washington, D.C., Catholic schools in Iowa, Wisconsin, Washington, and northern California, and community colleges and private universities in California and Wisconsin. We have also taught children and adults in Japan, Mexico, China, Venezuela, and Spain. Our experiences in the field of education have taken us beyond the classroom as well. We have worked as principals, vice-principals, assistant superintendents, directors of curriculum, and directors of research institutes. Some of us have initiated program-development efforts in large urban school systems; directed educational enrichment programs for inner-city youth; coordinated adult education and literacy programs in rural areas of foreign countries; worked on fiscal and policy analysis for state legislatures; developed and marketed higher educational programs; and chaired evaluation committees of educational efforts throughout the country. We have experience in nonschool settings as well; we have been health educators, tenant educators, tutors, and community organizers. Several of us have also worked in the private sector, in publishing, management consulting, private hospitals, and research organizations.

As we worked together to create this guide, we were pleased to discover that our process of collaboration mirrored the accelerated schools process in many ways. Our common vision of a comprehensive *Resource Guide* for accelerated schools in all stages of implementation provided us with a clear and unified purpose that directed our work. Each of us had a unique vision of what the guide could be, however, and our process of collaborative decision making ensured that the finished product represents all of our distinctive contributions. Because we functioned as such an interdependent team throughout the writing process, it is difficult to pinpoint where one person's words end and another's begin. Creating the guide in this way was possible because we built on each other's strengths, in terms of past experiences as well as personal qualities. Together, we are pleased to share the product of our collaboration—*The Accelerated Schools Resource Guide*—with you and your school community.

Acknowledgments

The Accelerated Schools Resource Guide is the product of amazing collaboration among educators involved with accelerated schools in all parts of the country. The ideas and words on these pages reflect an incredible array of experiences and ideas from our friends inside and around accelerated schools. The Accelerated Schools Project, as described in this *Resource Guide*, is a continuously evolving effort. While every single person involved with the Project helps to push the model further, we would like to pay special thanks to the following individuals whose ideas and input have helped make this written embodiment of the Project possible.

For their early work on the Accelerated Schools Project, we thank Brenda LeTendre, Pia Moriarity, Rose Owens-West, Bob Polkinghorn, and John Rogers. We also thank these individuals, as well as Gail Meister, for their contributions to the guide in terms of case studies and early writings for the Project. We also appreciate the time and contributions of Robin Avelar, Norma Francisco, Deirdre Kelly, and Marc Vantressa during the first years of the Project. We are grateful to Ursula Casanova, Shawn Horst, David ibnAle, Joe Kahne, Carolyn Krohn, Kit Lively, Jonathan Matthews, Patrick Phillips, Lisa Richardson, Claire Smrekar, Dorothy Steele, and Carolyn Tucher for their work on earlier versions of this guide. We offer special thanks to teachers Jackie Dolan, Amy L. Meyer, Joan Moss, Connie Posner, and Barbara Ruel for their contributions and careful reviews and edits in the areas of powerful learning. We thank Paula Gill for her help in editing each chapter and her work on the References and Resources section. Finally, we offer thanks to Christine Finnan and Jane McCarthy for their time, contributions, edits, and reviews at many different points in the *Resource Guide's* development.

Many, many members of accelerated school communities gave of their time and experiences to enrich the *Resource Guide*. Teachers, parents, students, support staff, administrators, district office personnel, and local community members responded to our requests for stories about what life in accelerated schools is like. Their contributions are not only fun to read; they are the true gems in this guide. We would like to thank John Baker, Julia Bell, Robert Benn, Francesca Bertone, Alison Beskin, Michael Bom, Juanita Brewer, Marla Brower, Valerie Butler, Gorette Cardosa, Judith Carter, Gene Chasin,

Oscar Chinas, Marilyn Chinnis, Glenda Coching-Yap, Doris Cross, Pat Dell, Jack DiCarlo, Jackie Dolan, Cynthia Dudley, Yvette Dunavant, Sandra Dutra, Mary Dwight, Kris Estrada, Elaine Farace, Maria Eugenia Fernandez, Adrian "Al" Foreman, Bert Galindo, Carol Henderson, Kathy Hoffman, Lavon Horton, Frank Howseman-Cabral, Anthony Jackson, Valerie Johnson, Janet Katzenburger, Chris Krzemniski, Susan Lake, Fran Laplante, Marvin Levine, Vira Lozano, Gloria Luna, Kathy Lynn, Lynne Mahan, Leslie McIlquham, Hope Marquez, Marian Mentavlos, Amy L. Meyer, Joan Moss, Betty Mundinger, Steve Novotny, Michael O'Kane, Ann Oplinger, LeAda Orrell, Mima Parsons, Claire Pelton, Lynn Pickering, Connie Posner, Barbara Ruel, Ken Saltzberg, Consusion Sanchez, Willie Santamaria, Andrea Santiago, Sherry Schmidt, Camilla Schneider, Kathleen Shimizu, Eugenia Singleton, Alice Smith, Joan Solomon, Jennifer Spotorno, Suzanne Still, Jesse Tello, Neto Torres, Bob Tyson, Kelly Vaughn, Greg Washington, Michael Weir, Carol Weiss, and Julia Wilhelmsen. Without them, the guide would not have been possible.

Claudette Sprague provided administrative support and encouragement throughout the writing process, as did our undergraduate assistants, Matt Gloier, Cara Henderson, David ibnAle, Andy Katz, and Elena Lejano.

The
Accelerated Schools
Resource Guide

Introduction:

A Guide to the Guide

Imagine a school in which all children perform at or above grade level, regardless of their background or family situation. Imagine a school that treats all children as gifted and talented students and builds on their talents through enrichment strategies, independent research, scientific experiments, writing, music, art, and problem solving. Imagine a school in which opportunities and support are provided to help all parents participate in their children's education, both at school and in the home. Imagine a school in which all members develop a vision of the kind of school that they would want for their own children, work toward that dream, and achieve it over a five- or six-year period. Imagine a school in which the entire school community, including staff, parents, and students, collaboratively makes major decisions about curriculum, instructional strategies, and school organization. Imagine a school where ideas count, where students, staff, and parents work together in an exciting environment. Let your imagination go as far as it will, and you've discovered the accelerated school.

In 1993–94, some 500 accelerated schools serving about 250,000 students in thirty-five states are at various stages of the accelerated schools process. Some of these schools are taking stock of the current situation in their school. Others are developing shared visions of the dream school that they want for their students. Others are comparing their current situation to their dream situation and determining the challenges that they want to explore more fully. Some schools are beginning to work within new governance structures that will allow their entire community to participate in school decisions. In other schools, groups of parents, staff, and students are mastering the Inquiry Process, a group problem-solving and decision-making process that allows entire school communities to tackle their major challenges effectively. Still others have completed these processes and are implementing and evaluating solutions that have emerged from the Inquiry

Process. Through a combination of training followed by practical applications, these schools are all accelerating the academic progress of students, the professional growth of staff, and the effectiveness of parents in the development of their children.

An accelerated school is a school that has been transformed through the accelerated schools philosophy and process to bring all of its students into the academic mainstream. The emphasis in this process is to establish a blend of theory and practice in which every dimension of the school is transformed, rather than focusing on incremental and piecemeal changes. The initiation and practice of the accelerated schools philosophy and process, as well as continuous reflection on implementation efforts, is at the heart of the school transformation.

Purpose of the *Resource Guide*

This *Resource Guide* has been created to serve as a sourcebook on the accelerated school. It is not a substitute for the training and coaching that your school will need. Rather, it provides background and supportive information that can be used in conjunction with training to launch and sustain an accelerated school.

This guide is the product of both research and practice. Indeed, it is a diary of the evolving Accelerated Schools Project. Because the ideas stemming from all of our direct work with schools have led to the continual growth and development of the Project, there was a reluctance on our part to commit all of our findings to a publication. Since each day brings new information and lessons, we felt that there was much more to learn before inscribing ideas on paper. But the request for a sourcebook on accelerated schools was a pressing one. We finally had to bite the bullet and put what we had learned together in a systematic guide, with the comfort of knowing that we will be able to update it in future editions.

The appropriate use of the *Resource Guide* can best be understood by considering the development of expertise in any field. The accelerated schools philosophy states that the school is the center of expertise. Expertise is obtained through training, study, practice, reflection, and reformulation. It requires considerable hands-on experience and active learning. Reading a physics book does not make a physicist, although it can give a picture of what physics is about and what physicists have concluded about different aspects of the physical world. If one wishes to be a physicist, one must not only study the texts and scientific articles that characterize that field; one must also *do* physics. That is, to learn how to be a practicing physicist, one must receive training in physics, undertake experiments, and engage in actual research.

Likewise, we view this *Resource Guide* as an informative picture of the background, philosophy, and processes of the accelerated school. But a school does not become an accelerated school simply because its members read a book. It becomes an accelerated school when all parties involved receive training and apply the ideas as a school, work closely with colleagues on acceleration, and receive support under the watchful eye of an experienced accelerated schools coach. This is the spirit in which we ask you to use this guide. (Please contact the address listed in the Accelerated Schools Project Statement at the beginning of the book about receiving accelerated schools training).

Audience

This publication has been written for a number of educational audiences. It is devoted primarily to staff in elementary and middle schools who are committed to transforming their own schools into accelerated ones. Of particular concern is the creation of accelerated schools for children in "at-risk" situations. (Chapter One, "Children in At-Risk Situations," provides a discussion of what we mean by this term.) However, it is important to note that the accelerated schools philosophy and process is aimed at creating the best schools for *all* children. The *Resource Guide* is also addressed to those concerned with elementary and middle school education more generally, such as parents and students, accelerated schools coaches, the staffs of district and state education agencies, college and graduate students studying to be teachers and administrators, and local community members.

We have emphasized the applicability of the guide for both elementary and middle school audiences. We began with the purpose of creating accelerated elementary schools in 1986. Our premise was that if we could bring all children into the educational mainstream by the end of elementary school, the middle schools and high schools could build on those results. Unfortunately, we found that this view was overly optimistic. Many middle schools serving students from accelerated elementary schools did not have adequate opportunities or expectations for these students. The result was that accelerated elementary school graduates found themselves in schools built on remediation and traditional drill-and-practice strategies rather than accelerated ones and therefore were not able to build meaningfully on their previous experiences.

Accordingly, we conducted research on how to apply accelerated schools ideas to the middle school and launched our first middle school in the autumn of 1990. Since that time, we have expanded the number of middle schools and the development of the middle school accelerated model with excellent results. The overall principles of acceleration and the general outlines of their application apply equally well to both elementary and middle schools. Because middle schools are usually larger than elementary schools and are departmentalized, and because many of the needs of adolescents differ from those of younger children, the applications of accelerated practices may differ somewhat. At one point, we envisioned separate versions of the *Resource Guide* for elementary and middle schools, but the overlap between them was so substantial that we decided to provide a single guide. At this time, we have not launched accelerated high schools, although we believe that the general ideas are applicable at that level too.

Reading the Guide

In this guide, we attempt to provide a comprehensive and systematic picture of the accelerated schools philosophy and process that can be used to transform traditional schools into accelerated schools. We hope that it inspires readers to improve the situation of students in at-risk situations by creating schools in which they will succeed. Primarily, however, we view the guide as a reference manual for school communities and accelerated schools coaches who have committed themselves to accelerated schools and have arranged to participate in training.

While the *Resource Guide*'s length might deter you from reading it in one sitting, it certainly provides a comprehensive overview of accelerated schools and could be read from beginning to end. Because each of the chapters has an important purpose and necessary order, we would like to provide some sense of how we view each of the chapters and suggest which ones need to be read together. Chapter One, "Children in At-Risk Situations," provides a rationale for having accelerated schools. In this chapter, we offer our own definition of students in at-risk situations, describe how the traditional educational system has treated these students, and outline the dire consequences of such practices.

Chapters Two through Four outline the accelerated schools philosophy and process, so we urge you to read these chapters together before beginning any of your school's transformation activities. Since the philosophy and process are so very comprehensive and interrelated, each of these chapters builds on the one before and after it. Chapter Two, "What Are Accelerated Schools?" offers an overview of the entire accelerated schools model and describes the accelerated schools philosophy in detail, including the overall goal of providing all children with the education we would want for our own children, the accelerated schools principles and values, and our beliefs about powerful learning.

Chapters Three and Four encompass the nuts and bolts of the accelerated schools process. In Chapter Three, "Getting Started," we provide detailed descriptions of the getting-started steps—that is, how to build the capacity to make informed decisions collaboratively. This chapter includes how to take stock, develop a schoolwide vision, set priorities, and create accelerated schools governance structures. In Chapter Four, "The Inquiry Process," we discuss the crucial nature of effective problem solving in an accelerated school. We then provide an analytical description of the accelerated schools Inquiry Process—the method accelerated schools use for *collaboratively* and creatively addressing their school's priority challenge areas. This chapter is full of examples, case studies, and tips for effectively following the ever-challenging Inquiry Process.

We view Chapter Five, "Group Dynamics and Meeting Management," as an "enabling" chapter for the processes described in Chapters Three and Four. Because the entire accelerated schools process necessitates so much group work, it is important for your school community to have a sense of productive group processes. In this chapter, we show how the accelerated schools principles and values relate to effective collaboration as well as offer specific strategies for working together most effectively.

Chapters Six through Ten are quite different from the first five chapters. While the first five chapters give a sense of how to implement the accelerated schools philosophy and process, Chapters Six through Ten describe the changes in teaching, learning, and family involvement that have occurred in accelerated schools as a result of using the accelerated schools philosophy and process. These chapters are designed to give a sense of what's possible. Remember, the accelerated schools model is not a cookie-cutter approach, and these examples are not meant to form a blueprint; your school community will come up with your own wonderful stories and examples by using the philosophy and process to forge and work toward your own unique vision. You may notice that we have included several Inquiry Process case studies in Chapters Seven through Ten. Because using the Inquiry Process becomes a habit in accelerated schools, we wanted to share *how* accelerated schools have actually come up with many of the examples highlighted in these chapters.

In Chapter Six, "Creating Powerful Learning Experiences," we discuss our beliefs about powerful learning strategies, which can most simply be thought of as what we presently do for gifted and talented children. We also offer a way of thinking about the accelerated schools philosophy as actual criteria that you can use in designing powerful learning experiences. In Chapters Seven, Eight, and Nine, we look at powerful learning through the lenses of the three different dimensions of learning: the *what* of powerful learning (curriculum), the *how* (instructional strategies), and the *context* (ways the school is organized to enable the what and the how to occur). Rich vignettes from actual accelerated schools form the backbone of these three chapters.

In Chapter Ten, "Family and Community Involvement," we offer a host of examples of how families and communities become involved in their accelerated school communities. Like the chapters on powerful learning, this chapter draws heavily on examples from real accelerated schools.

Finally, in Chapter Eleven, "How Will I Know If My School Is Accelerating?" we offer our thoughts on a process to assess your progress as an accelerated school. To ensure that your school is well on its way to reaching the ultimate goal of excellent student outcomes, you'll need to assess how well you're using the accelerated schools philosophy and process to reach that goal. Indeed, regular assessment is an important part of the accelerated schools process. How well did you take stock? How well are you using the Inquiry Process? Are the three accelerated schools principles becoming internalized by all members of the school community? In addition to outlining an assessment model, we have provided a set of reflection questions at the end of Chapter Eleven to stimulate discussion and reflection among the school community. We suggest that you use these questions on a regular basis. For your convenience, we have also included many of these questions throughout the guide.

Involvement of Accelerated Schools in Producing This Guide

Too much of the education literature consists of abstractions that are hard to envision in practice. To as great a degree as possible, we have tried to balance the presentation of theory with real experiences of those people who actually "live" in accelerated schools. Indeed, we could not have written this guide without the accelerated school communities with which we work. The first major contribution of our colleagues in accelerated schools was their collaboration in the development of the accelerated schools model. Our ideas became real as we worked with members of our pilot school communities to implement them. In surmounting the challenge of implementation (the hard part!), accelerated school community members have not provided just the learning ground; they have also contributed wonderful ideas and strategies to the evolving model. The second (and more visible) contribution of accelerated schools teachers, support staff, students, parents, administrators, district personnel, and local community members in this guide are their examples of actual practices and experiences described through vignettes and quotations. We appreciate everyone's openness, honesty, willingness to risk, and collegiality in making these contributions.

When we began writing this guide in 1989, we asked all of the then-existing accelerated schools to contribute anything that they thought would be helpful in showing how the philosophy and processes of accelerated schools were being implemented in their schools. We're grateful to the schools that participated. Despite this broader participation, there are several schools that are referred to often in this guide. For the most part, these are the pilot schools in the San Francisco Bay Area, with which we are most familiar because of their proximity and our continuing contacts with them. However, our on-site visits and extensive discussions with our colleagues in other sites have shown that these schools are representative of the types of practices found in other accelerated schools around the country.

As your school engages in the process of transformation into an accelerated school, we extend an open invitation to you to share *your* experiences with us. We're eager to hear your stories, your experiences, and the insights of all of the members of your school community. We want to include everyone's ideas in what is essentially a democratic and ever-evolving approach to school improvement. For that reason, we feel that this guide is not finished; it is a collaborative work that will continue to develop.

We need your input in order to publish future editions of the guide. Specifically, we would like to hear accounts of changes occurring in accelerated schools across the country. These accounts might include case studies, drawings, newsletters, and photographs. We also invite you to send us short essays, stories, poems, and songs that celebrate, analyze, explain, epitomize, or illustrate the different aspects of accelerated schools. These contributions will be considered not only for future editions of the *Resource Guide* but also for publication in the *Accelerated Schools Newsletter* and a future publication focusing solely on the experiences of real accelerated schools that we hope to publish annually. Finally, we would like to receive suggestions on how to improve the presentation of the material in this guide and what you'd like to see included in subsequent versions.

Next Steps

We have attempted to make this document as comprehensive as possible. However, given both space and time limitations, there are a number of areas on which we have not done as much as we would have liked. We plan to produce comprehensive documents on each of these subjects that will be incorporated into the next version of the *Resource Guide*.

As an example, one area of great importance to accelerated schools is assessment and evaluation. As Chapter Eleven illustrates, we view three levels of assessment as necessary in accelerated schools: assessing the degree to which a school is implementing the accelerated schools philosophy and process, assessing the degree to which school decisions emerging from the accelerated schools process are implemented in classrooms and throughout the school, and assessing the outcomes of accelerated schooling in terms of the quality of student learning, parent participation, student and teacher attendance, school activities, projects and project outcomes, and so on. Only if the accelerated schools process is fully implemented and the decisions emerging from that process are translated into practice will we expect to see the desired outcomes. Thus all three levels of assessment must be considered when evaluating whether a school is accelerating the education of its students.

In addition, we are concerned about evaluating the effectiveness of the National Center for the Accelerated Schools Project and the regional satellite centers in launching and supporting accelerated schools. Although these assessments have been initiated, they have not advanced far enough to report in this guide. They will be incorporated into a future edition, however, along with a more fully developed assessment model.

We recognize that educational reform cannot be limited to individual schools; it must extend to the school districts and state education agencies that support schools. This broader view has been a recent focus of the National Center for the Accelerated Schools Project as we have explored ways of transforming the operations of entire school districts and states. To this end, officials from various school districts and state education agencies across the country were trained during the summer of 1992 to launch and support accelerated schools in their areas. As we deepen our relationship with these agencies and come to a better understanding of how they function and how they can best transform themselves to support accelerated schools, we will incorporate our findings into future editions of the *Resource Guide*.

As the accelerated schools movement continues to expand through district and state centers, we must not forget that the school is the center of expertise in the transformation process. This means that schools use articles, consultants, and other resources to expand their own expertise, not that "outside experts" tell them what to do. The accelerated schools process is designed to help school communities develop a rich understanding of the challenges that they face and the strengths that they can build on to address those challenges. The accelerated schools training you receive and this *Resource Guide* should also be used in that spirit. We provide a process to assist a school in building expertise that will lead to acceleration for all students. But in the final analysis, the school community must look to itself for answers, not to this guide. While we offer the necessary training and guidance, it is you who must transform your school.

We sincerely hope that what follows helps you in your quest to create an accelerated response to the educational challenges that face your school today.

CHAPTER **1**

Children in At-Risk Situations

Education is a national concern. Schools across the country are eager to improve themselves, and the Accelerated Schools Project has put forth a philosophy and process to help them do so. Because many students attend schools that face some of the toughest challenges, we are particularly concerned with providing support for them. Before discussing our philosophy and process, however, we would like to share our definition of "at-riskness."

We define at-risk students as those students who are unlikely to succeed in schools as schools are currently constituted because they bring a different set

of skills, resources, and experiences than those on which school success is traditionally based. Children who come in with certain kinds of backgrounds are in for a tough time. An at-risk student, then, is one caught in a mismatch between the experiences that he or she has in the home, family, and community, on the one hand, and what schools expect for success, on the other. Because there is nothing at risk about the child, it's more accurate to refer instead to the at-risk situation in which a child is caught. Perceiving at-riskness as a human trait suggests that children are defective or in need of repair or remediation. But children are not the problem: at-riskness has to do with the *situation* in which we place children. As educators, we can change that situation.

1.1. How Many Children Are in At-Risk Situations, and Who Are They?

Recent estimates show that about fourteen million children, or *one-third* of all elementary and secondary students, are considered at risk. Although these children come from all racial and economic backgrounds in our society, most are white children from monolingual, English-speaking backgrounds (Waggoner, 1991). However, children in at-risk situations are disproportionately concentrated among families that are in poverty, families headed by single parents, non-English-speaking families, minority families, and migrant families from the rural areas of Latin America and Asia. This does not mean that all children whose families fit into one or more of these categories are in at-risk situations; rather, it means that a *disproportionate* number of these children are in situations where they are at risk of educational failure. Even more disturbing than the current statistics is the fact that the number of children in at-risk situations may rise considerably in the future for several reasons:

- First, a large portion of the at-risk adult population is of childbearing age, and birthrates among this population tend to be high.

- Second, the United States is experiencing a wave of immigration that will rival the great immigrations of the nineteenth and early twentieth centuries, with most of the immigrants coming from the poorest regions of Latin America and Asia, equipped with little formal education.

- Third, the rate of poverty has risen in the United States, especially among children. In 1969 only one in seven preschool children was in poverty. In 1989 one in four was in poverty, and among African American children the number was one in two. If this trend continues, our educational institutions will be serving four million more children who live in poverty in the year 2020 than in 1987 (Natriello, McDill, & Pallas, 1990).

All of these statistics suggest that the number of children caught in at-risk situations will grow enormously. In many schools and school districts and in some states, such as California, students in at-risk situations already constitute the majority of the student population.

1.2. Educational Failure and Social Consequences

The mismatch between the skills and experiences many students bring to school and what schools expect of them leads to disastrous consequences for these children. Conventional schools base their programs on the expectation that students come to school equipped with the following:

- Proficiency in English, including a background in interrogative language use

- Parents with the time, energy, and resources to support student achievement

- Sound health care, including a nutritious diet

- Ability and desire to respond and interact within the predominantly white, middle-class culture

- Physical and psychological well-being

Because so many children do not come to school equipped with this "standard" set of resources on which the traditional school bases "success," they fall farther and farther behind over time. By the sixth grade, they are about two years behind grade level on standardized achievement tests. Such children enter middle school with the attitude that they are "slow learners," "lacking in motivation," and "just plain failures." Combine these feelings with a traditional school setting that does not identify or build on these children's strengths, and with the natural stresses that accompany adolescence, and these youngsters become highly susceptible to drug use, juvenile crime, teen pregnancies, and dropping out (Carnegie Council on Adolescent Development, 1989). If perseverance and determination prevail and the students complete high school, they are generally four years behind by the time they graduate.

Just as the home-school mismatch often leads to problems throughout students' school careers, academic failure often leads to problems in adulthood. A study of test scores for nineteen- to twenty-three-year-olds highlights these links (Berlin & Sum, 1988). Among the young adults who scored in the bottom fifth of the population on a test of basic skills,

- Forty-six percent were in poverty.

- Forty percent were unemployed.

- Fifty-two percent had dropped out of high school.

- Fifty-three percent received public assistance.

- Fifty-nine percent were unwed parents.

- Thirty-seven percent had been arrested within the previous year.

As the population of children in at-risk situations grows, so will the population of undereducated adults, unless we can turn the tide. A large and growing population of poorly educated and disadvantaged adults will contribute to a poorly trained work force, a deterioration in higher education, and increases in the costs of public assistance and criminal justice. Thus the failure to educate students caught in at-risk situations will affect not only these populations but our entire society.

These challenges arise at a time when the United States is already struggling to compete in the international economic system and to maintain a high standard of living. Our society is in the midst of transition. Due to a multitude of technological advancements, an increasing demand for worker participation and initiative, and the effects of a globalization of the market-place, the jobs of the future will require a different set of skills and competencies than the jobs of the past. In order to properly prepare *all* of our children for this shift in the demands and requirements of the workplace, schools must emphasize a much richer set of skills than just the standard competencies in reading, writing, and arithmetic. The jobs of the future—even entry-level service positions and assembly-line manufacturing jobs—will require a variety of skills, such as facility in critical thinking and problem solving, good communication skills, and the ability to work in groups or teams (Levin & Rumberger, 1989).

1.3. How Most Schools Have Dealt with Students in At-Risk Situations

Most children arrive at school full of excitement and curiosity; they are eager to learn. But as the weeks pass, many youngsters start showing a pattern of failure. Their achievement slips, discipline problems emerge, and their eagerness wilts as self-esteem starts to decline. Class sizes are too large to permit the individual attention that each student needs. The curriculum does not sustain the interest of the children, but the standard materials and activities adopted by the school district can't easily be modified. High student turnover prevents the type of long-term attention these students need. And if children live in a world of poverty, violence, drugs, and other problems, they must often deal with being afraid, anxious, and suspicious—emotions not particularly conducive to learning.

The organization of most schools makes it hard for educators to improve the situation for their students. Teachers and principals often are not provided with the authority, training, or resources to make headway on the challenges they face. Principals typically find that they have to spend a great deal of time dealing with emergency situations created by fights and other disciplinary problems and complying with mandates from the district and the state. Teachers and support staff feel isolated from each other and do not have many opportunities for collegial support. Low test scores and other problems create the reputation of a "loser school," further undermining the self-esteem of a hard-working school staff. This situation provides no winners. Instead, all parties are frustrated:

- *Teachers* feel stressed and unappreciated, and they are frustrated by the lack of student progress and parental support. They want to do a good job but feel constrained by all of the rules, regulations, and mandates and by a top-down curriculum that doesn't seem to be working.

- *Principals* spend so much time handling emergencies and complying with district policies that they have little time or energy for instructional leadership.

- *Parents* feel left out and don't know how they can change things. As a result, they blame the school for the problems of their children.

- *Students* are passive recipients of information that doesn't seem relevant to their lives. They want to learn and to succeed, but they feel bored and frustrated by a system that doesn't work for them.

- *Taxpayers* complain about a waste of their resources.

- *Business leaders* worry about whether they can compete when their workers are increasingly drawn from an undereducated, at-risk population.

If we are to relieve this pathos, we must understand what created the situation. Over the years, as the educational system worked to address the challenges of educating all students, a series of well-meaning efforts led to an unfortunate set of circumstances for students in at-risk situations. What we've ended up with is a lot of very good people working in a system that doesn't allow them to use their talents to address the needs of students in at-risk situations.

If you step back and look at this system from afar, you'll notice a set of common practices (with accompanying well-meaning rationales) and unfortunate consequences. Here's how the educational system for at-risk students has seemed to operate:

- *Practice 1.* Identify students in at-risk situations and label them as slow learners or as remedial or Chapter I students.

  Rationale. These children must be separated out and grouped with similar students who aren't adequately prepared for school and can't keep up with the standard curriculum.

- *Practice 2.* Set few or no goals for students in at-risk situations, beyond making sure that they get into remedial classes.

  Rationale. The best way to help students who are lagging is to place them in remedial settings where their educational experiences can accommodate their poor foundations. To set other goals is to be unrealistic.

- *Practice 3.* Slow down the pace and reduce the educational challenge.

   Rationale. Although other students can walk and run through the curriculum, students in at-risk situations must learn to crawl before they can walk. Many of them try to walk or even run anyway. This is called "acting out," which leads to more time on their hands and knees learning to master the crawl.

- *Practice 4.* Use drill-and-practice exercises as the principal educational strategy so that slow learners devote much of the school day to completing worksheets containing low-level repetitive exercises in all curriculum areas. Innovative applications or learning situations that draw on students' own experiences and cultures require higher-order problem solving, which these students aren't ready for.

   Rationale. Ever since the invention of the ditto machine, it's been possible to reproduce reams of drill-and-practice exercises to make sure that slow learners really learn their basic skills. Until they master these simple tasks, there's no point in providing more enriched experiences (which are "too advanced" for them anyway).

- *Practice 5.* Delegate the design, preparation, and selection of curriculum and instructional policies and materials to specialists in state departments of education, to central district offices, and to publishers in order to ensure remote control of classroom activities.

   Rationale. In order to ensure consistency and "quality," school and classroom practices are prescribed. Mandated materials come with a teaching guide that's in perfect alignment with student textbooks, workbooks, and tests to ensure perfectly standardized delivery.

- *Practice 6.* Treat parents as a problem rather than a part of the solution.

   Rationale. Students are at risk because their parents don't care about their education and have little to offer them. Far from helping their children, the parents are responsible for the poor educational preparation and the behavioral problems of their children.

Unfortunately, the consequences of the traditional educational system are dire:

- Many students are stigmatized as slow learners. This label effectively reduces the learning expectations of teachers, parents, and the students themselves and undermines the children's self-esteem.

Further, students who are quarantined with other students who are lagging see few successes or role models among fellow students.

- Once students are placed in a remedial setting, they're unlikely ever to leave.

- Students in at-risk situations get bored with the slow pace of remedial instruction and their lack of progress. School seems arduously tedious, and the gap between them and other students grows ever wider.

- A heavy concentration on "drill-and-kill" exercises, following directions, and passive listening makes school joyless. This approach discourages active participation and fails to build on the experiences and strengths of the child. The child becomes increasingly bored and restless and gets farther and farther behind mainstream peers.

- Teachers and support staff are forced into using routine educational practices and complying with educational decisions made without their input. They feel powerless to intervene even when things are obviously not working, and they're often unaware of the educational consequences of their own activities. Staff talent that might be used to improve matters is ignored in a system where most important decisions are made at the higher levels, away from the schools.

- Parents feel helpless to assist their children educationally, and the children lose a major ally in acquiring an education.

....

Identify ways in which the traditional educational system has set the agenda of your school. What practices are present in your school that do not benefit students in at-risk situations? You may want to break out into groups and dramatize for each other how these practices show up in your school.

Exercise

....

1.4. What's Wrong Here?

The fact that children in at-risk situations do poorly in school and get farther and farther behind the educational mainstream the longer they are in school should hardly be surprising. These are exactly the consequences that one should expect from educational experiences that are plodding and without substance, that are based on low expectations for and the stigmatization of such students, that disregard and discourage the potential support of parents, and that treat teachers as assembly workers who are there to follow packaged practices that have proven to be ineffective.

What is wrong is the very premise on which compensatory and remedial education is based: that there is something fundamentally flawed about certain students. Acting on that premise, educators seek to remediate or repair the defects, always concentrating on children's weaknesses or flaws rather than on their strengths and capabilities for learning. Yet that premise will inevitably lead to a second-rate education and the production of "second-rate" human beings as self-fulfilling prophecies that are brought to fruition.

1.5. The Premises of Acceleration

The best way to view children caught in at-risk situations is simply to view them as children—with the same characteristics and potential of *all* children. These children have the same curiosity, desire to learn, imagination, and need for love, support, and affirmation as all children. Moreover, schools must recognize that many of the experiences that these youngsters bring from home—while perhaps different from what's found at school—are integral to their understanding of the world and to their way of learning. It is our responsibility as educators to change the mismatched situation to reduce the risk of failure. Because the schooling process represents one side of that mismatch and the school's connections to parents constitute a central part of the other side, the school has considerable potential for alleviating the situation. Eliminating the mismatch calls for empowering school communities so that they can define a unity of purpose centered on the success of *all* children, make important educational decisions together regarding the children, and build on strengths.

That is the purpose of the accelerated school.

CHAPTER 2

What Are Accelerated Schools?

An accelerated school is where the whole community and school push education a step further to make it more fun and advanced for all students.

Chris Krzemniski, Eighth Grade Student, North Middle School, Aurora, Colorado

Accelerated schools are communities of staff, parents, students, district office representatives, and local community members working together to create the *best* schools for *all* children so that every child has the opportunity to succeed as a creative, critical, and productive member of our society. Adults in accelerated school communities work to create for *all* children the kind of schools they would want for their *own* children. We call these schools *accelerated* schools because children in at-risk situations have to learn at a faster rate, not at a slower rate that drags them farther and farther behind. A comprehensive enrichment strategy, rather than a remedial one, offers the greatest hope for reversing the present educational crisis of so many children in at-risk situations.

Accelerated schools give school communities an opportunity to break out of traditional molds:

- Instead of labeling certain children as slow learners, *accelerated schools have high expectations for* all *children.*

- Instead of relegating students to remedial classes without setting goals for improvement, *accelerated schools have a vision and clear goals for making all children academically able.*

- Instead of slowing down the pace of instruction for students in at-risk situations, *accelerated schools create powerful learning experiences to accelerate the progress of all children.*

- Instead of providing instruction based on drill-and-kill worksheets, *accelerated schools offer stimulating instructional programs based on problem solving and interesting, relevant applications.*

- Instead of simply complying with "downtown" decisions made without staff input, *accelerated school communities systematically define their own challenges and search out unique solutions that will work for them.*

- Instead of treating parents as a problem, *accelerated schools build on the strengths of their students' parents and families.*

At first it may seem strange to talk of acceleration for children in at-risk situations. Acceleration is a strategy usually reserved for "gifted and talented" students—those who perform at the very top. Yet accelerated schools believe that *all* children are gifted and talented and should be treated as such. It's interesting to ponder why we channel so much enrichment to help top students develop their talents further when we slow down the learning of children who need acceleration most.

> **Fairbanks Elementary School involved parents in the accelerated schools process from the beginning. At back-to-school night, the principal, Joyce Creemer, gave a presentation to parents about what Fairbanks becoming an accelerated school would mean for their children. She explained that an accelerated school considers all children gifted and builds on their strengths. A concerned father in the audience raised his hand and said, "My son isn't gifted. In fact, he's in the low classes. What's going to happen to him?" The principal replied, "Your son *is* gifted, and he has so much to contribute to his class and to this school. An accelerated school community believes that all children can learn and creates powerful learning experiences for everyone." The father beamed with pride and a new sense of possibility for his son.**
>
> Fairbanks Elementary School, Springfield, Missouri

Acceleration is not only the right thing to do—it works! Indeed, accelerated schools across the country have shown tremendous gains in children's achievement and self-esteem.

- Before becoming an accelerated school, the achievement of Chapter I students at Burnett Academy, San Jose, California, was below the district average; after the first year of the Accelerated Schools Project, achievement of the same students exceeded the district average, and more students were on the honor roll. Burnett Academy eliminated ability grouping; all classes are now grouped heterogeneously. All sixth grade students take accelerated math, all seventh grade students take pre-algebra, and all eighth grade students take algebra. Now most eighth graders graduating from Burnett go on to take geometry in high school, rather than pre-algebra or general math as they did in previous years.

- In its second year as an accelerated school, Hollibrook Elementary School, Houston, Texas, had dramatic achievement gains, with students scoring above the district average in mathematics at all grade levels—with particularly large gains for students from the lowest socioeconomic groups and those with limited English proficiency. In its third year, fifth grade students gained two grade levels in reading and language arts and performed one year above grade level in mathematics on the standardized tests. Student expulsions decreased from five to zero. Dramatic increases were also shown in teacher and student self-esteem and morale.

- By the end of its second year as an accelerated school, the students at Hoover Elementary School, Redwood City, California, had moved from the 10th percentile in mathematics achievement to the 27th percentile.

- At Memminger Elementary School in Charleston, South Carolina, the number of fifth graders scoring at or above the national average increased, elevating that group's combined composite score from the 34th to the 61st percentile in all areas—reading, language arts, and mathematics—in Memminger's first year as an accelerated school.

- Fairbanks Elementary School, Springfield, Missouri, implemented a "no-pull-out" approach for Chapter I students in its first year as an accelerated school. At the end of that year, 39 percent of the school's Chapter I math students and 36 percent of its Chapter I reading students tested out of the program. A self-esteem assessment given during that year showed increases in every grade level between fall and spring.

- At Briar Crest Elementary School, St. Louis, Missouri, student attendance went from the lowest in the district to the highest during its second year as an accelerated school.

- At Hermes School, East Aurora, Illinois, the Illinois Goal Assessment Plan (IGAP) scores showed a fifty-four-point increase in third grade language arts and a thirty-one-point increase in mathematics after two years of accelerated schooling. Attendance has been at 95 percent for the last three years.

While these schools have tremendous pride in their gains on standardized measures, they are not striving for test-score gains. Rather, these accelerated school communities have begun to work on creating powerful learning experiences for *all* children; they are striving to reach their shared visions. The test scores go up, but they rise as a *by-product* of the collaborative and creative efforts of accelerated school communities.

2.1. No Package for Change! A Philosophy and a Process

The Accelerated Schools Project represents a *philosophy* and a *process* for transforming conventional schools into accelerated schools—schools in which powerful learning experiences become daily occurrences for all members of a school community. The integrated *philosophy* of accelerated schools centers on three interrelated principles and on the overall goal of creating the types of schools we want for our own children for all children. The accelerated schools values support the three principles as well as our beliefs about powerful learning. The *process* is a systematic set of practices for "getting from here to there"—from conventional schools to accelerated schools.

2.1.1. Overall Goal

For too long, we have set our educational goals far too low for children caught in at-risk situations. We have been satisfied if a particular school enrolling "at-risk" children was performing a bit better than "typical" schools enrolling such students. However, few educators would consider even this "better" school for children in at-risk situations as a prospective school for their own children. We believe that *if a school is not good enough for our own children, it is not good enough for any child.* Creating schools for *all* children that we would want for our own children is the overall goal toward which all accelerated schools strive.

2.1.2. Three Central Principles

Accelerated schools are premised on three interrelated principles that are largely absent from traditional schools: *unity of purpose, empowerment coupled with responsibility, and building on strengths.* Active practice of these three principles serves as a vehicle for becoming an accelerated school. All three principles are important, because they enable schools to respond creatively and collaboratively to their particular community's needs. Clearly, a school that adopts acceleration has to break some old habits, which is never easy. Moving from old ways to acceleration takes a lot of reflection, careful planning, unprecedented levels of cooperation, and a real internalization of the three underlying principles. But many educators who have tried it say that it's worth the hard work.

You can't fit into this whole accelerated process if you don't have the ability to say, "Yeah, maybe I should change some things. Maybe I can do something different. Maybe I should try this out." People who are very rigid in their beliefs will probably have a difficult time working in

the accelerated schools process. You've got to be able to change. You can't stay static, because there's no one right way of doing anything. You rethink how you do things; you rethink what's important; you rethink your way of working with your peers. One of the best values is people opening up and being able to make changes and being willing to try to do something different. And if it flops, it flops . . . and then you try something else. People are willing to change.

Jackie Dolan, Teacher, Daniel Webster Elementary School, San Francisco, California

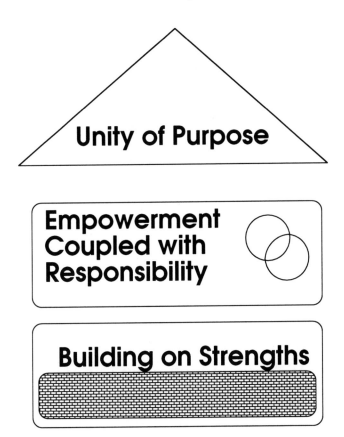

Accelerated Schools Principles

Unity of Purpose

Empowerment Coupled with Responsibility

Building on Strengths

The following paragraphs are more detailed explanations of each principle.

Unity of Purpose. The first principle, unity of purpose, refers to a striving among parents, teachers, support staff, students, administrators, the district, and the local community toward a common set of goals for the school that become the focal point of everyone's efforts. Clearly, a central element of that unity of purpose must be the desire to transform the school into an accelerated one that will make children academically able as soon as possible so that they can fully benefit from their further schooling experiences and adult opportunities.

The all-inclusive process of defining a common purpose is extremely important in and of itself. By including from the start all of the parties (parents, teachers, students, support staff, school site and district administrators, and the local community) involved in the planning and design of educational programs, the implementation of those programs, and the evaluation of those programs, the school can ensure more cohesive educational efforts and a greater commitment to those efforts. Unity of purpose stands in contrast to disjointed planning, implementation, and evaluation of educational programs—disjointedness caused when various members of the school community have differing educational goals and expectations of students.

Traditional elementary and junior high school structures offer us little opportunity or incentive to work together on a schoolwide level to construct and fulfill a vision of success for the entire school. Rather, we work largely in isolation from each other. For example, teachers see their roles as providing the best instruction they can in their own classrooms and departments. Those who perform highly specialized roles in the school—working with Chapter I, bilingual education, or special education, for example—are often isolated and have little opportunity to coordinate with the "regular" teachers.

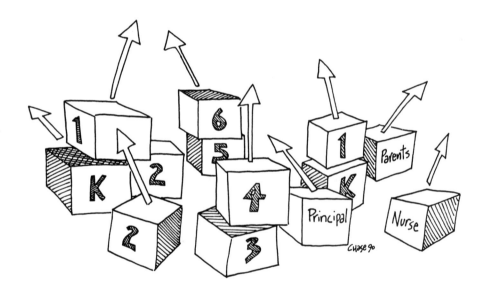

In contrast, all staff in an accelerated school collaborate to reach their shared vision—from science teacher, to bilingual teacher, to custodian, to vice-principal, to Chapter I teacher, to special education teacher. Moreover, accelerated schools work to transform the traditional structure, which offers few precedents for substantial parent and student collaboration, into an environment that depends on the participation of all members in the school community.

Unity of purpose is much more than a vision statement or even the process of forging a vision. Forging your vision and even taking stock are just the beginning of developing a unity of purpose. Unity of purpose is something that *emerges* in an accelerated school community over time. It comes to life through the active and collaborative process of working toward a shared vision and is exhibited by the various parties collaborating in the educational process.

We "see" a sense of unity of purpose when we walk through an accelerated school. We see teachers of all grade levels and subject areas excitedly discussing collaborative efforts; we see support staff, administrators, and teachers working together; we see students engaged in powerful learning experiences with a sense of how their current lesson relates to their next lesson, their next school year, and their real lives.

We see a team effort at our school. We've stopped hearing my *and instead we hear* our *when something goes well.*

Alice Smith, Office Staff, J. Will Jones Elementary School, Houston, Texas

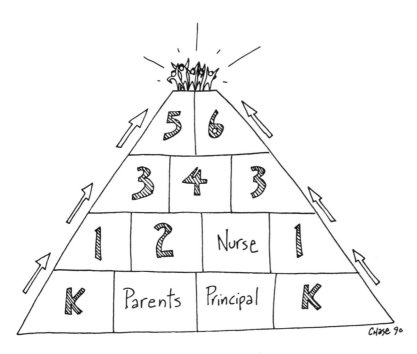

CHASE 90

In the following example, we see how unity of purpose plays out in the collaborative decision-making process:

At Burnett Academy, the Family Involvement Cadre proposed to establish a parent room on campus in an empty classroom. Although many departments were highly intent on using the last spare classroom for other projects, the school community discussed the issue at a school-as-a-whole meeting and unanimously voted to have the spare classroom serve as a parent room. Those who had wanted the space for other reasons felt that the parent room was a higher priority in terms of the school community's shared vision and goals.

Burnett Academy, San Jose, California

Empowerment Coupled with Responsibility. The second principle, empowerment coupled with responsibility, refers to the ability of *all* participants in a school community to (1) make important educational decisions, (2) share responsibility for implementing those decisions, and (3) share responsibility for the outcomes of those decisions. The purpose is to break the present stalemate among administrators, teachers, support staff, parents, students, the district office, and the community, in which the participants tend to blame each other as well as other factors "beyond their control" for the poor educational outcomes of students.

You know, I think that schools should pay more attention to the most effective business organizations. Anytime they've sold the employees stock in their own corporation, they've always had better production. And anytime you give the teachers say-so in what they're going to do in their building, naturally you're going to have more enthusiasm and better education for their kids. The big thing is that it makes you accountable.

Sherry Schmidt, Teacher, Hollibrook Elementary School, Houston, Texas

Unless all of the major actors have the shared power and responsibility for developing a common set of goals (and influencing the educational and social processes to realize those goals), desired improvements will probably not take place or be sustained. Accelerated schools build an expanded role for all groups to participate in and take responsibility for the educational process and educational results.

Such an approach requires a shift to school-based decision making, with heavy involvement from teachers, support staff, parents, children, and the community; it also offers some new roles for administrative leadership.

Everyone is working hard on those challenges they've decided are priorities. Because we all created our vision, determined our priorities, and chose the area of greatest personal interest, there's tremendous commitment to each specific change and overall school improvement. The outcomes rest upon our collective shoulders, and we're prepared to assume the responsibility.

Alison Beskin, Principal, Sheppard Elementary School, Santa Rosa, California

Among the areas for which site-based decision making is most crucial are curriculum, instructional strategies, materials, schedules, personnel, and the ability to allocate and organize resources. While state and local regulations and guidelines may place some limits on each of these areas for purposes of accountability and uniformity among schools, it's important that the *major* share of decisions be made at the school site. Also, many of the limitations are perceived rather than real. Once accelerated schools begin to communicate with their district and state education offices, they're usually able to move ahead in areas where obstacles once stood in their way.

District office involvement in accelerated schools not only helps remove existing limitations but helps prevent new limitations from arising. Once district office personnel become personally involved with accelerated schools, they can respond to their needs through the provision of requested support services in the areas of information, technical assistance, staff development, and assessment. Districts and schools can jointly draw up an appropriate system of student and school assessment that can be used as a basis for accountability.

Empowerment coupled with responsibility emerges in different ways for various members of each school community. For some, it's a scary proposition.

> **As a teacher, being empowered in the way we are now is kind of scary at first. At the beginning, you have some doubts. You're really not sure if what they're saying is going to be true. And it's also very scary because you're going to be held accountable for the decisions that you make. It's not like, "We did this because you said to, and so if it doesn't work, it's your fault." If something goes wrong, it's the person who's handling the class or making the decisions who's responsible. That can be very scary. And it took a while to adjust to that. But I think that once everyone saw how much better it was to be empowered, people were no longer apprehensive. And it's not as if you're going at it all alone. You've got a group of people there for support, and everybody works together. No one's left out on their own.**
>
> Marla Brower, Teacher, Hollibrook Elementary School, Houston, Texas

For others, empowerment has been so long in coming that they at first move in a way that *divides* rather than *shares* power.

> **When we first became an accelerated school, I think that many of the teachers were so ready to give their say of how things should be that they came on like gangbusters; they viewed power as it always has been—a zero-sum game, with the haves and have-nots. Over time, we discovered that empowerment means *shared* responsibility for decision making.**
>
> Connie Posner, Teacher, Burnett Academy, San Jose, California

Of course, empowerment also extends to students. Students in an accelerated school make decisions and serve on governance structures.

> **The accelerated schools process is a good way for students to tell the school what it should be like. Now we can tell what's on our minds.**
>
> Adrian "Al" Foreman, Seventh Grade Student, North Middle School, Aurora, Colorado

Students also experience empowerment coupled with responsibility in their academic lives, by helping to choose what they will study, participating actively in classes and school, and taking responsibility for long-term projects.

Building on Strengths. The third principle, building on strengths, refers to sharing and utilizing all of the human resources that students, parents, school staff, districts, and local communities bring to the educational endeavor. In the quest to place blame for the lack of efficacy of schools in improving the education of students in at-risk situations, it's easy to exaggerate the weaknesses of the various participants and ignore their strengths.

> **The idea of building on strengths has been one of the most motivational forces behind the project. It changes the way we perceive each other and our students, parents, and community. Instead of seeing problems, we see potential. For example, before the project, teachers often would sit around and complain about the kinds of students and kinds of problems in the classroom. Now they're much more positive when they talk about students and parents.**
>
> Ann Oplinger, Principal, Memminger Elementary School, Charleston, South Carolina

Both families and teachers are largely underutilized sources of talent in most schools. Families can be powerful allies in the educational process, because they love their children deeply and want them to succeed. And it's often parents and family members who know the strengths of their children best. Accelerated schools establish a partnership with families and communicate their importance to the educational process. Teachers bring the gifts of insight, intuition, and instructional and organizational acumen. These qualities are largely dormant in schools that exclude teachers from the decisions that they ultimately must implement.

> **One thing that we did in our faculty meetings was to have people think about where they felt their expertise was. And we also asked that when you came to a faculty meeting, you should bring something that you've done in your class that worked really well—share it with everybody else. So that way we all began to look within ourselves. Now we give in-service training to each other, and we do it on the strength that we know we have in teaching. So we sometimes have faculty meetings during the year in different teachers' classrooms. And that teacher might spend half an hour presenting to her peers something she's done in her room that's worked really well. And we come in and look around and see her room. You know, most teachers don't get to visit fellow teachers. You're in your room and the door is closed. You don't know where your colleagues have their strengths. That's just the way it's always been. And so by having these kinds of exchanges, we find our strength as a faculty.**
>
> Jackie Dolan, Teacher, Daniel Webster Elementary School, San Francisco, California

Schools often overlook the strengths of children in at-risk situations, because they perceive these children as lacking the learning behaviors associated with conventional success in school. Instead, schools should view these children as having a wealth of assets that can be used to accelerate their learning. Educators can then identify and build on the gifts of each child. Actively showing high expectations is one way to build on the strength of everyone's inner desire to succeed.

> **An important part of building on children's strengths is simply raising our expectations for them. It was never a matter of, "Well, maybe you can do it." It was just an attitude that you brought into your class: "You *will* do it, and there's really no question, and I know you can do it." And the kids just amazed us all. They rose to the level of our high expectations . . . on test results, on the papers they turned in. They just did it. I don't know; it's kind of hard to say why. Expectations—they just rose up and met them.**
>
> Valerie Johnson, Teacher, Hollibrook Elementary School, Houston, Texas

From the student's perspective, high expectations can accomplish wonders; they can even be responsible for a total change of life direction. Greg Washington, who moved to San Jose from southern California last year to live with his uncle, shares how the expectations at his new school changed his life:

> **No one really cared about school or anything [in the old area]. So that depressed me. It didn't motivate anyone, and if it motivated them, it motivated them to do bad things. So I moved up here. I picked Burnett because they said it was a good program—challenging work. So I said, "All right, I'll go." I met Mr. O'Kane [principal] and Ms. Farace [vice-principal], and they told me, "Well, we're going to put you in algebra." I was like, "I can't do this work. It's too hard. I was doing first-grade math last year in seventh grade." But after the first week, I was doing it all. It was hard at first, but then after awhile, it came to me easily. I started getting A's and a scholarship. Now I'm going to go to high school and get A's there too. It changed my life. Now I like school. I want to finish and go to college—maybe play basketball. That's how it should be.**
>
> Greg Washington, Eighth Grade Student, Burnett Academy, San Jose, California

In addition to actively exhibiting high expectations for all students, building on students' strengths and unique talents means broadening the types of teaching strategies we utilize. Curriculum mandates have traditionally focused on lecture and "book-learning" strategies, yet we all have ideas about many other ways to teach and learn—orally, kinesthetically, artistically, and so on. Children's learning strengths can include an interest and curiosity in oral and artistic expression, the ability to learn through the manipulation of appropriate materials (as stressed by Montessori), a capability to delve eagerly into intrinsically interesting tasks, and a capacity for learning how to write without first having to master the language-decoding skills necessary for learning how to read. And we can think about each child's interests, experiences, culture, and need for human interaction—as well as their aptitudes—as strengths that can be used to accelerate their learning.

We build on our kids' strengths rather than harping on their weaknesses. We do a lot of oral language, focusing on our students' backgrounds and letting them know how important that is. We try to make them feel important so that they're not afraid to try and to do other things. It's the opposite of saying, "This is the status quo, and you have to fit into this mold." We go with where they come from and use that and their background in teaching them. We tend not to do as many paper/pencil tasks, ditto sheets. And even though our kids don't do much paper/pencil work, our students' standardized test scores have gone up. And I think it comes with the language: talking about things more, getting them the vocabulary that they're missing.

Marla Brower, Teacher, Hollibrook Elementary School, Houston, Texas

People ask me all the time how I deal with those students who just don't want to learn, or who refuse to cooperate, or who just can't learn—they put it a lot of different ways—and I always tell them, "He learned how to tie his shoes, didn't he? He can get himself dressed in the mornings. He speaks the Spanish language; he had to learn that. How can you say that this child can't learn?" You just have to keep trying and trying to reach every student on his or her own terms. There's always something in a child's mind! Now there will always be those children who may take two years before you see them really blossom, and your job as a teacher is to be patient and keep finding out that student's other strengths. I suppose somewhere there may be a child who will never show any growth, but that's never happened to me; I've never seen one. Even in extreme cases of a child not functioning at school, as a teacher you have to assess the situation before you assess the child. Maybe he needs a different teacher, a different group of kids, help with a problem at home. You can't assume that there's something wrong with the child.

Maria Eugenia Fernandez and Valerie Johnson, Teachers, Hollibrook Elementary School, Houston, Texas

I learned how to listen to the students in another way. I used to compare students' abilities by how they wrote their stories, but now they've shown me that there are other ways to communicate. Many of them do a wonderful job of describing their stories through pictures.

Consusion Sanchez, Teacher, J. Will Jones Elementary School, Houston, Texas

Like the strengths of students, families, and teachers, the strengths of administrators are also underutilized in the traditional school setting. School-based administrators are often placed in "command" roles and asked to meet the directives and standard operating procedures of districts rather than to work creatively with parents, staff, and students. Similarly, the strengths of support staff, who are almost never asked to offer their input, are underutilized in conventional schools.

Communities have considerable resources, including youth organizations, senior citizen groups, businesses, and religious groups, that should be viewed as major assets for the schools and the children of the community.

> **When people retire, we can tap their resources. I bring my mother to school once a week to help teachers grade papers. She loves working around the kids. Kids relate to her like their grandmother. Other teachers want her to come into their rooms.**
>
> Lynn Mahan, Teacher, Burnett Academy, San Jose, California

The strengths of all of these participants are a major set of resources for creating accelerated schools. As you could probably tell from reading the descriptions and vignettes that accompanied our discussion, the three principles are highly interrelated and interdependent.

Exercise

- Pair your students and give each one a colorful piece of paper. Have them interview each other about their strengths, asking the following questions: What things do you like to do? What things do you do best? If you could teach someone how to do something that you know how to do, what would it be?

- Next, have the students share their partner's strengths with the class. Make sure everyone's strengths get mentioned, including your own!

- Have each student place his or her own "strength brick" into a "wall of strengths" that you create on one side of your classroom. This wall will serve as a visual reminder of the wealth of knowledge, experience, and ability you have in your class.

- Point out to the class the different strengths students have. Praise your students for using untraditional abilities such as intuitive reasoning, finding creative solutions to old problems, drawing or painting, writing poetry or raps, doing dramatizations, inventing jokes, developing dance routines, and so on.

- Establish an environment in your classroom in which multiple strengths and abilities are truly valued. Update the wall of strengths as your students develop and grow.

This exercise deals with building on strengths. What kind of activities could you design that would bring the other two principles—unity of purpose and empowerment coupled with responsibility—to life for your students?

2.1.3. The Values of Accelerated Schools

Accelerated school communities share a set of values, beliefs, and attitudes that contribute to creating a culture for growth, creativity, and accelerated learning. These values undergird every aspect of the accelerated schools philosophy, process, and daily practices. As an accelerated school develops, the following values emerge, guiding the actions and interactions of people in the community:

- *Equity.* All students can learn and have an equal right to a high-quality education. Is our school the kind of school that we would want for our *own* children?

- *Participation.* Everyone participates in the accelerated schools transformation process—students, parents, and certified and classified staff. Everyone's ideas count. Students participate in learning and decision making; teachers, support staff, parents, administrators, community members, and district office representatives participate in decision making and the creation of powerful learning experiences.

- *Communication and collaboration.* All members of the school community work together and share ideas. Children engage in active and group learning. Their thoughts, feelings, and interests are

[To his students:] You're getting the best, because you deserve the best.

Bert Galindo, Teacher, Burnett Academy, San Jose, California considered important, and students are given the opportunity to express and communicate these thoughts to their community. The entire school community collaboratively works toward a shared purpose by meeting with, talking with, and learning from each other's experiences.

The Values of Acceleration

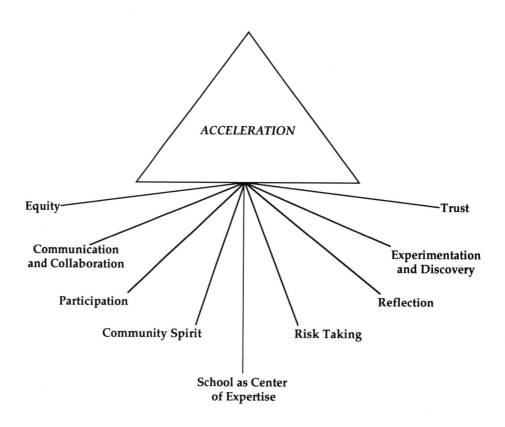

- *Community spirit.* School staff, parents, students, district office representatives, and the local community are all part of the school community. When they succeed, they do so together, because they've built strong connections with each other—all in the service of the children.

- *Reflection.* In transforming a school, we need time to reflect, to do research, to work together, to share ideas. Children engage in problem-solving exercises that develop over time and require an interpretive approach to curricula. The entire school community constantly scrutinizes the world of the school and addresses challenges to school improvement.

- *Experimentation and discovery.* When members of a school community decide that what they are presently doing is not effective (either for themselves or for the children or both), they change. In changing, we have to take some risks and try some experiments, but they are *informed* risks and informed experiments. All staff, parents, and students explore, design, and implement experimental programs after communicating about and reflecting on the school's challenges and participating in discovery exercises.

- *Trust.* Trust is essential. Teachers, parents, support staff, administrators, district office representatives, community members, and students come to believe in each other, support one another, and focus on each other's strengths.

- *Risk taking.* All parties are encouraged to be entrepreneurial in their efforts. While some new programs may fail, the ones that succeed are the keys to lasting school improvement.

- *School as center of expertise.* The members of the school community recognize that they possess the vision and the talent they need to make their dreams a reality. The school is a professional community with the expertise to create the best programs for its children, staff, and parents. As a school uses the accelerated schools process, the community itself decides how to do research and when to hire consultants.

Many of the values of the Accelerated Schools Project stem from the work of John Dewey, an educational philosopher who believed that a democratic education implies faith in the potential of both children and adults to understand, and to some extent shape, the world around them (Dewey, 1915, 1916). Individuals begin to realize this potential, Dewey argued, when, as members of groups, they take active roles in *inquiring into shared problems* (Dewey, 1938b). This process of collaborative inquiry serves as the vehicle for decision making in an accelerated school. Chapter Four, "The Inquiry Process," describes this process in great detail. John Dewey's thoughts about education and experience have also influenced the way we've come to think about powerful learning (Dewey, 1929, 1938a).

2.1.4. Powerful Learning: *What, How,* and *Context*

Our conception of powerful learning is based on the premise that the education we use with "gifted" children works well for *all* children. With this fact in mind, accelerated school communities create situations in which every school day encompasses the *best* things we know about children and learning.

Accelerated school communities work together to create powerful learning situations that will motivate students to grow and succeed. In accelerated schools, children see meaning in their lessons and perceive connections between school activities and their real lives. They learn actively and in ways that build on their own strengths. Accelerated school communities work together to create powerful learning experiences that provide opportunities for all children to develop their natural talents and gifts. These learning experiences often require imaginative thinking, complex reasoning, and relevant content. In such situations, children actively construct and discover the learning objectives rather than passively going through textbooks and filling out worksheets. At the same time, this type of learning environment requires organization and support; thus adults are challenged to create a safe environment for learning that extends far beyond the classroom into every aspect of the school, home, and community. If we think about our own powerful learning experiences and what made those experiences so powerful, we will come up with some similar themes.

> **Powerful learning is complete and total *emotional*, *physical*, and *intellectual* involvement in what you're doing, the problem you're solving, etc. It's launching yourself fearlessly into risk taking because it's okay to try and perhaps fail. And it's lasting, because it affects every fiber of your being and changes your perceptions forever.**
>
> Connie Posner, Teacher, Burnett Academy, San Jose, California

The Accelerated Schools Project does not set forth a recipe or checklist of features for creating powerful learning experiences. Rather, each accelerated school creates and chooses its own ever-growing set of powerful learning experiences based on its unique needs, strengths, resources, and vision. The creation of powerful learning experiences results from both collaborative and individual efforts through an interactive process that we call "big wheels" and "little wheels."

The "big wheels" refer to the formal accelerated schools processes (taking stock, forging a vision, setting priorities, creating governance structures, and using the Inquiry Process—described fully in Chapters Three and Four) and are designed to assist entire school communities in transforming their schools into places where powerful learning occurs frequently and consistently. By collaboratively focusing on the larger challenges and concerns of the community, a social infrastructure supportive of day-to-day powerful learning emerges.

The "little wheels" are the spin-offs of the collaborative big-wheel activities and take shape as small, creative experiments by all members of the school community. The little wheels give people an immediate opportunity to make changes in their own environment, whether it be designing a new unit based on summer travels or trying out a more user-friendly attendance procedure. The entire accelerated schools process creates an environment in which we're free to try such innovations.

While individuals and small groups experiment with new and stimulating learning experiences, the accelerated schools processes will move forward as well—perhaps more slowly, but ever so surely and productively.

We see every powerful learning experience as having three dimensions: *what* is taught (the content or curriculum), *how* the content is taught (instructional strategies), and the *context* in which one galvanizes all available resources to achieve the *what* and *how*. (Context refers to time, personnel, funding, materials, physical space, and other resources that shape the social and organizational environment of the school.)

We see these three dimensions as being *completely and necessarily integrated*. A change in what we teach necessitates a change in how we teach it and the context that supports it, and vice versa. For example, if you wanted to make what you teach more interdisciplinary, it would be difficult to teach using rigidly defined subject-area textbooks, forty-five-minute blocks of time, and a predominantly teacher-directed instructional strategy. Interdisciplinary content lends itself to more active instructional strategies and more flexible uses of time.

The triangle below summarizes the integrated nature of powerful learning.

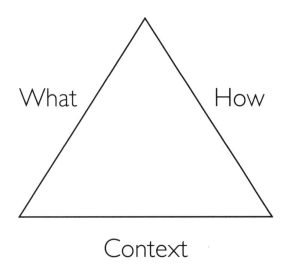

Many past educational reforms have represented piecemeal changes that only focus on one specific side of the triangle. For example, it's not uncommon to read about a reform that talks only about restructuring (base of the triangle), or a new math series (left side), or a new instructional strategy (right side). Because schools tend to make these changes separately and independently, the changes have relatively little impact on the overall school program or student learning.

The accelerated schools philosophy views this piecemeal approach as unfruitful (though well-meaning) in terms of bringing about long-term

> *I feel a sense of freedom, in the classroom, to express myself and use my talents. Accelerated schools has given me more courage to reach out, to provide more for the students, and to try new ideas.*
>
> Consusion Sanchez, Teacher, J. Will Jones Elementary School, Houston, Texas

improvements. Instead, we favor a comprehensive approach in which all three elements of powerful learning work dynamically together on behalf of students, school staff, and parents. Accelerated school communities work to create schools where students *want* to be—schools with powerful learning experiences for *all* students, both inside and outside the classroom. We've found that when students' needs are met, the needs of parents, staff, and administration are met as well.

The three dimensions of powerful learning are so closely interrelated that it's often difficult to tease the *what*, the *how*, and the *context* apart. The following example of a learning experience from an accelerated school demonstrates this phenomenon. As you read this description, you might reflect on how the choice of context and the form of instruction influence the curriculum.

At Daniel Webster, three third grade classrooms individually explored the art, culture, science, and history of a specific Native American tribe and then came together to construct an elaborate Native American museum. In one of these classes, the teacher built on her own interest in and knowledge of the Lakota Sioux in order to introduce her students to the art, technology, and culture of the tribe. The children gave Native American names to partners, compared the tribe's culture and technologies to those of modern Western society, and engaged in many of the daily activities of the Lakota people. The experience was capped off when the children learned dance and music from their teacher's mentor, who's a Lakota Sioux, in preparation for their actual participation in a real Native American powwow.

Daniel Webster Elementary School, San Francisco, California

These third graders immersed themselves in several distinct learning *contexts*—from simulations of daily activities to the construction of a museum to full participation in a real powwow. In turn, each of these contexts required a different form of instruction (the *how*), including reading, modeling, discussion, hands-on experience, and learning through discovery. Each situation also impacted *what* was learned by students. In addition to knowledge of Native American culture, art, and technology, other lessons were learned that would not be reflected in standard teaching and testing practices. The children learned, for example, that they have much in common with people in other communities, that one's culture is valuable and important, and that one's culture can be shared and celebrated with people beyond the immediate community.

Constructing powerful learning situations requires creativity, an openness to risk, and a willingness to share responsibility with students. It also requires that you think through all dimensions of a powerful learning situation—the *what*, the *how*, and the *context*. If you've never created learning opportunities like this before, you may want to start slowly and work with a group of your peers. We hope that as you begin to build on strengths—your own and those of your students and colleagues—you'll be able to find new highs in teaching and learning. In Chapters Six through Nine, we more fully explore the concept of powerful learning and its three dimensions.

2.1.5. The Process of Becoming an Accelerated School

As you can tell, an accelerated school is not just a conventional school with special programs grafted onto it. Rather, the entire school and its operations are transformed into a vital environment. The focus is on the school as a whole rather than on a particular grade, curriculum, approach to teacher training, or other, more limited strategy.

The next few chapters are devoted to the process of becoming an accelerated school—a process whereby the school community develops its own capacity to make important educational decisions together in order to create the best possible school for all students. The school community begins by taking a deep look into its present situation. It then forges a shared vision for the future, including the views of all members. By comparing the vision to the initial situation, community members come up with priority challenge areas for inquiry. Through the creation of accelerated governance structures and the practice of the Inquiry Process, accelerated school communities work systematically toward reaching their visions.

2.2. A Visit to Two Accelerated Schools

Before turning to a full description of the accelerated schools process, let's take a look at two real accelerated schools—one elementary and one middle school—via profiles from the *Accelerated Schools Newsletter*. First we'll take a visit to Houston, Texas, to see the Hollibrook Elementary School; then we'll travel to San Jose, California, to visit Burnett Academy, a middle school.

2.2.1. Hollibrook Elementary School

Hollibrook Accelerated Elementary School in Spring Branch Independent School District of Houston is situated in a neighborhood that's dominated by several large government-subsidized apartment complexes. The school sprawls across several acres and is a maze of hallways, corridors, temporary classrooms, and outside walkways. A new cafeteria and wing are under construction at the rear of the property.

As students begin to arrive on campus, most come on foot from the surrounding neighborhood. Over thirty-five countries of national origin are represented here, with more than 90 percent of the students coming from Hispanic immigrant families. More than 85 percent of the students enter the school speaking no English, and many have never been to school before. Ninety-one percent of the students are on the free and reduced lunch and breakfast program at school.

Hollibrook is a school that by all rights should not be successful. It is very large—over 1,000 students and 100 staff members. Its children are poor and don't speak English. Before the Accelerated Schools Project, they performed in the bottom 25th percentile on district-administered standardized tests. Student turnover amounted to 104 percent, with many students cycling in and out several times during the course of the year. Both student and staff morale were low, and discipline and vandalism were major concerns. Few parents or family members came to school to attend PTA meetings or conferences. The new principal, Suzanne Still, and her teachers decided that something drastic had to be done to improve things at school. After a year of careful study, discussion, and reflection, the vehicle of change they selected in 1988 was the Accelerated Schools Project.

In adopting the accelerated schools philosophy and process, the school expanded its definition of community and the roles that each member of the community plays in the decision-making process. The Hollibrook family—composed of teachers, staff, administrators, students, parents, and the local community, began the process of acceleration by taking stock of the present situation and formulating a unified vision of what Hollibrook should be in the future. The unity of purpose that began to emerge from these activities induced changes that have made a dramatic difference in the lives of Hollibrook students and faculty.

The school community prioritized its areas of challenge and selected several for immediate attention. Task forces (known as *cadres*) were established for each of these priority areas, which included school improvement, staff development, curriculum, and parent involvement, and they began to meet weekly to discuss the challenges and to utilize an early version of the Inquiry Process to define and solve them. In addition to the cadres, the governance structure also included a steering committee and the school as a whole decision-making body. Decision making at the school was informed by research and school data, with the children as the central focus. After several years of participation in the process of acceleration, Hollibrook can look with pride at many notable successes.

The goal of broadened community participation is exemplified at Hollibrook. As a result of the efforts of the Parent Involvement Cadre, which sponsored teacher home visits and outreach projects, parents and family members are now a visible presence at Hollibrook. They serve on task forces, serve as volunteers, and attend training sessions to strengthen their ability to help their children academically. Family attendance at meetings and conferences has soared to 94 percent. The local community has also become actively involved in the school. Fifteen volunteers from a local oil company volunteer one day a week in classrooms around the school. Local businesses contribute time, materials, and labor to a number of other projects.

The unified efforts of the school community have borne considerable fruit in creating an inviting and productive educational environment and program. As we enter the front door of the school, we're struck by the warm, inviting atmosphere. There are large plants, sofas, and easy chairs arranged in comfortable groupings throughout the vestibule. There are books and magazines in abundance, including several bins of books labeled, "Free—help yourself." The walls are covered with banners that have slogans such as, "Encouraging parents to actively participate in the education of their children," "Students working and striving to demonstrate mastery on or above grade level by the completion of the fifth grade," and "Further enhancing a campus climate which is orderly and academically focused." Yet another one says, "SWEAT!" The principal tells us that this one comes from the quote by Thomas Edison that creativity is 1 percent inspiration and 99 percent perspiration. (High expectations are the norm here at Hollibrook, as in other accelerated schools.) Elsewhere on the walls is an abundance of student artwork and writing samples.

Many parents accompany their children inside the building, where they're greeted warmly by the office staff, whose desks are right out in the foyer so that they can be accessible. Some parents go on to the parent room, where there are comfortable chairs, a pot of coffee, playpens for toddlers, and a wide array of materials and equipment, including a sewing machine and typewriter. The school social worker also has her desk in the parent room, and there are signs in English and Spanish advertising workshops she's offering for parents. Some parents work as volunteers in the building and go on to their posts. One mother learning how to use the computer is busy printing out some banners she's designed. Her excitement at her accomplishment is evident.

As we pass by the clinic, we see that it's filled with an assortment of teddy bears. The nurse explains that all sick or injured children are assigned a teddy bear to talk to and to help "make better" while they receive her assistance. Because of this (and other warm and inviting features of the school), students have renamed it "Huggibrook Elementary."

Another room along the hallway looks like a miniature North American home, with a completely furnished living room, kitchen, and dining room.

The teacher inside explains to us that this is the newcomers' center, where students newly arrived from Central and South America learn English in a setting that also enables them to learn about the customs and culture of their new country. The older bilingual children spend time in the room as tutors for the new children and help them to adjust to their new home. The teacher tells us that it doesn't take long for students to become comfortable enough to be placed in regular classrooms. The entire school is language-centered—an essential feature of an accelerated school.

Let's follow a group of students into their room and visit for a while. This particular third grade room is a ship, and students must cross a gangplank to enter. There are nautical artifacts everywhere and sailor hats for all. This week the students have sailed to Antarctica. There's a giant simulated continent on the floor, complete with icebergs, stuffed penguins, and toy seals. All subjects have been taught this week with an emphasis on this continent and its characteristics. Student math problems have focused on temperatures of air and water, distances from place to place on the continent, and sizes and weights of animals found there. Student writing has taken the form of letters from Antarctica to the people back home. Two little girls have written a letter to their principal. "Dear Mrs. Still," it begins. "We are sailing around Antarctica. We miss you very, very much. We are sailing on the SS *Discovery*. We learned about penguins. It is very, very cold in Antarctica. We will write from our next port. Hugs and kisses from Rosa and Blanca."

There's a trunk in the room containing artifacts that might be found on Antarctica. There are gloves, snow goggles, a parka, boots, a compass, a shortwave radio, some books written by Antarctic explorers, and some freeze-dried foodstuffs along with cooking utensils. One group of students is studying the objects in the trunk and using them as catalysts for stories about life in the cold.

One boy has written and illustrated a colorful book called *All About Penguins*. The teacher has had it laminated so that he can show it off proudly. One page reads, "Penguins' enemies are sea lions, fur seals, and killer whales and the most dangerous is the leopard seal." It's beautifully illustrated with pictures of penguins and all their enemies.

These third grade students are all actively engaged in their academic tasks. Some are working in small groups with a student as facilitator. Others are working with the teacher or teacher's aide. There are also two student observers from the local university's teacher education program in the room. They're down on the floor working with students who are producing a map of Antarctica. Another group of students is working on a math worksheet entitled "Penguin Power Math." Although there's much activity in the room, the noise level isn't very high and no one seems to be distracted by other groups. Students are so eager and engrossed that they scarcely notice visitors in their midst. This focus on thematic learning and active and interactive teaching and learning illustrates the enormous success of the Staff-Development and Curriculum Cadres that have focused on the improvement of teaching and learning at the school.

Let's leave our wonderful ship, the SS *Discovery*, and walk down the hall to another third grade classroom. As we peek in this room, we see that it has a Hawaiian motif. There are posters of Hawaii, flower leis, pineapples, grass skirts, and flowers typically found on the islands. A papier-mâché volcano in the corner of the room serves as a learning center for math and science activities. Students in this room have a goal—to take a trip to Hawaii. They started out in second grade by selling popcorn in the cafeteria at lunchtime. This was so successful that they invited a stockbroker to visit and help them set up a corporation called Only Popcorn. They sold shares, held stock-holders' meetings, and decided to establish a franchise with the fifth grade. Some of the profits were used to pay for a field trip to NASA; students had their way paid and were treated to lunch as well. Prior to the trip, students called up fast-food restaurants and checked out menu prices before deciding where they would stop for lunch. Problem solving and higher-order thinking skills—hallmarks of an accelerated curriculum that treats all students as gifted and talented—are in evidence in this classroom and in many others across the school.

The teacher and students of this second grade class became so close during the year that they decided to stay together as a family. The teacher moved with them to the third grade, where the corporation continues, and the goal is a graduation trip to Hawaii. These students, who started out speaking only Spanish in second grade, are now communicating fluently in English. They're busy tallying up the previous day's receipts from popcorn sales. All have a task: some get out supplies and equipment for today's sales, some work on the daily accounting ledgers, and others plot the weekly sales curve. All are actively and productively engaged.

The teacher tells us that the scores on standardized tests for these students have shot up dramatically, in some cases more than two years of growth in just one year. There's little student turnover in this room. Parents want their children to stay in the school, and whenever a student has to transfer, everyone feels the loss. We find out that other teachers at every grade level like the idea of staying with their own students, and a number of them have voluntarily moved with students to the next grade. Pods have been formed to create "schools within schools" so that students feel connected to a school family.

As we leave this room, we find ourselves near a stage whose open curtains reveal a small grocery store. There are freezers, cans and boxes of food on shelves, fruits and vegetables with scales, a cash register, and even a flower cart. Our guide explains that this is the consumer math class, with items donated by a local grocery store. Students learn English as well as math as they run the store. As our guide tells us, "At this school, we fill the students up with language. Every teacher is a language teacher, and every subject area has a language component. Even the cafeteria workers and the custodians help in the task." Students in the grocery store are busy playing many roles—shopper, stocker, checker, weigher. All are on task and involved as the fifth graders do inventory and the third graders make comparative graphs of the sugar content in various cereals to determine which would be most nutritious.

Farther down the hall are the kindergarten classrooms. We find teachers team-teaching here. Bilingual classes are paired with English-speaking classes, and children play together as well as learn together. We hear lots of English and lots of Spanish spoken. The teachers proudly tell us that each group is learning the language of the other. In one room, we see a mix of Spanish and English speakers actively involved with their teachers using colored bears, lollipops, plastic spoons, and tops as they delve into the concept of "greater than/less than"—in both languages simultaneously. Spanish words are written in black, and English words are written in red. Children are learning to speak, read, write, and think in both languages.

We also notice a number of older students in the room. Each of these students is reading to a younger child or playing reading and language games with him or her. We find out that this is the cross-age tutoring program; all the older kids have a "little buddy" that they work with on a regular basis. This not only has an academic payoff for each group, but there are social benefits as well: there's no more teasing of younger students by older students, and the younger students are no longer afraid to walk in the halls of this big school building alone.

As we leave the kindergarten wing, we see a school bus drive up and unload a group of students who have been on a field trip to a local middle school. The principal tells us, "They had no idea what a middle school was, so we put them on buses and take them there for an orientation. That way they know what to expect when they get there. We also take them to a high school and a university so that they can see what the future will hold for them. How can you aspire to go to college if you have no idea what that means? Our children have such a limited experiential background that many of them have never been out of their own neighborhoods. We try to enrich their backgrounds and broaden their conceptions of the possibilities life can hold for them. These are the kinds of experiences that middle-class kids take for granted. We're building bridges to the middle class for our kids."

Today is Friday, and after lunch something special happens throughout the entire school. Fabulous Friday begins! The principal tells us that Fabulous

Friday was designed for several purposes. One was to enable the children to experience an enriched curriculum that would expose them to the kinds of activities and materials that middle-class kids have regular access to. Another was to enrich the academic skills of students through exciting and innovative course offerings. Fabulous Friday is run like a mini-university. Students register for courses, listing a first and second choice. Students from all grade levels are integrated into these classes. The older students go to the kindergarten and first grade classrooms to pick up their "little buddies" and escort them to their Fabulous Friday class. The course offerings are extensive, and every adult in the building teaches one.

Some of the classes in session today include beginning swimming, bowling, scuba diving, the history of rug making, art, counted cross-stitch, baby-sitting, tumbling for tots (for the pre-K classes), camping, mystery writers, eating around the world, sign language, secret codes and spy stories, and book making. At a given signal, students pass quickly and quietly through the hallway to their classes. Vans wait outside to take the bowlers and swimmers to their destination. The rest of the afternoon is spent in these special classes, which are four weeks in duration. All have an academic focus as well as an activity base.

When the school day comes to an end, several groups of teachers gather together in grade-level team meetings to plan for the coming week. The mood is light and relaxed in every group we visit. Teachers are sharing what worked and didn't work this week and what they'd like to accomplish next week. Several groups talk about going out together for something to eat—a Friday ritual at the school. The principal tells us that she can't keep teachers away from the school. They'd be up there on weekends if they could get in.

As visitors, we're overwhelmed by what we've seen and heard in the building today. The one thing that we all noticed is how happy the teachers and students seem to be and how actively engaged everyone is in the academic work at hand—important features of an accelerated school. The school is a pleasant place to be and feels inviting to everyone. Parents and community volunteers are an integral part of the school. Teachers have input into all important decisions, including the hiring of new faculty. While the principal tells us that things are certainly not perfect here yet, they seem to be well on their way. Student and teacher attendance rates attest to the fact that this is a school where people want to be. One teacher who's eligible to retire this year doesn't plan to: "I've been waiting twenty years for a good year like this one. I'm not going to leave now!"

The efforts and hard work of the entire school community at Hollibrook have yielded enormous dividends. Student and teacher surveys document dramatic increases in self-esteem and morale. Student mobility rates have come down from 104 to 47 percent. Incidents of vandalism are down by 78 percent. Student expulsions decreased from five in 1988–89 to zero in 1989–90. The PTA meetings now attract from 600 to 800 people. In addition to these important changes, test scores on standardized tests have soared. In 1988 the fifth graders at Hollibrook scored at the 4.8 grade level (composite scores) on the SRA standardized tests used in Texas. They scored at the 3.7 level in reading and language arts. In early spring of 1991, fifth graders achieved a composite score of 5.8, and reading and language arts scores rose to 5.2 and 5.6 respectively—a gain of almost two grade levels in just two and a half years. Even more remarkable, students scored a year above grade level in mathematics (6.6). Other scores across grade levels have been equally impressive.

The principal of Hollibrook sums up their experience: "The faculty, with focused vision and effort, turned Hollibrook around in a fashion that's true to the Cinderella fairy tale. However, this is no fairy tale. The results are due to the valiant efforts of the staff, the students, the parents, and the community. There was no infusion of funding to make the difference. It wasn't the purchasing of new gadgets or textbooks or the adoption of new programs from publishers. The staff wasn't replaced. Scores reflecting improved student achievement weren't accomplished by exempting the less capable, remediating those who were behind, or adding a magnet gifted program to bring in the more capable children from across the district. The Hollibrook story is remarkable because the school community has defied all odds—defied conventional wisdom—and succeeded as a direct result of collectively embracing the philosophy, principles, and process embedded in the Accelerated Schools Project. The Hollibrook family embraces every aspect of the Accelerated Schools Project with enthusiasm and passion. We've become a productive and happy community of learners busy and involved in the act of teaching and learning."

(Accelerated Schools Newsletter [1991, Summer], 1[3])

2.2.2. Burnett Academy

Burnett Academy is an inner-city public school located in San Jose Unified School District in California; it has a student body that's 62 percent Hispanic, 10 percent African American, Filipino, and Asian, and 28 percent Caucasian, many of whom are non-English speaking Portuguese students. Approximately 60 percent of the school's students are on the free or reduced lunch program.

"Good morning, Burnett Bears!" booms an enthusiastic voice over the loudspeaker. "Today is Tuesday, January 21. Congratulations, seventh grade boys' basketball team, on the great win last night! Today at lunch there will be a student council meeting. . . ."

Such announcements aren't surprising in a middle school, where the diversity of activities makes schoolwide announcements a must. What's different about Burnett's morning routine is that the enthusiastic voice heard by all is that of a student, not an office administrator. What's even more unique about this situation is that the students themselves decided that they would like to take over this responsibility.

Everyone is more involved in Burnett these days. What used to be "just the workplace" for teachers and staff and "just school" for Burnett's now 860 students in sixth, seventh, and eighth grades is becoming a vital community of learners, all working toward a common vision. One of the most notable and important changes in Burnett since it began the process of acceleration is the participation of the whole school community in making important decisions that will lead to their common vision. In all areas of the school, teachers, support staff, administrators, students, parents, and the local community are contributing their energies, opinions, and expertise to solve challenges confronting Burnett. Neto Torres, sixth grade counselor, explains: "We've done a lot of great things in the last year and a half, but I think it's the communication that makes everything happen. Accelerated schools gave us a way of communicating. Before, if I had an idea, I wouldn't really have a mechanism for putting it out into the school community. The accelerated schools process gave us a way of bringing all of the ideas of everyone together."

The First Year. Burnett's entire school community voted to become an accelerated school in June of 1990. Following full-staff training sessions at Stanford in the late summer, all members of the Burnett school community, including teachers, administrators, support staff, students, parents, and members of the local community, spent the fall of 1990 creating a vision of their dream school and taking stock of their present situation. The taking-stock research process allowed the school community to discover unknown strengths as well as many challenge areas. In January 1991, all members of the school community compared their taking-stock findings to their ambitious vision and set initial priorities for change. This process of setting priorities produced Burnett's five cadres: School Interactions, Curriculum, Instruction, Family and Community Involvement, and Culture. After all the staff members (and student and parent representatives) divided themselves among the five cadres, facilitators were chosen for each group. Each facilitator also serves on the steering committee, along with administrators, support staff representatives, department heads, and a student council representative.

During the first year, the school community spent much of its time developing the capacity to make decisions as a group. Through the cadres, teachers, administrators, support staff, students, and parents explored problems using the Inquiry Process. The entire school community was enthusiastically involved in Burnett's process of change, and real changes were taking place. At the end of the first year, teachers reported feeling more professional and excited about improving their teaching and working with other teachers; classified staff felt more like equal partners in the school's transformation; and students had more confidence that the staff really cared about them. In more quantitative terms, the number of students on the honor roll increased, and the achievement of Chapter I students rose from below district average to far exceed it.

In May, as Burnett neared the end of its first year as an accelerated school, the district broke some bad news: major budget cuts and layoffs were in store for the following school year; music, art, and library programs would be discontinued districtwide. Burnett was hit hard. The school community reacted at first with shock, anger, and confusion. Many speculated as to whether the school would be able to continue the process of acceleration. An emergency steering committee meeting was called by several teachers to discuss emotions, concerns, and strategies for confronting the budget crisis. Committee members decided that the accelerated schools process gave them a vehicle for addressing the budget crisis together. Each cadre developed strategies, which they then funneled to the steering committee to synthesize and delegate for action. Their theme for dealing with the budget situation became the school's watchword: no *one* of us is as smart as *all* of us. Among other things, it was decided that Burnett would remain an accelerated school the following year, whether there were thirty-five or ten teachers. In the end, five teachers—vital members of the Burnett community—were laid off. Morale wasn't destroyed, however; all of the laid-off individuals continued to operate as part of the school team through their last moments as staff members at Burnett. Two of these teachers even volunteered to help train another middle school in the accelerated schools process the following summer.

The beginning of the 1991–92 school year brought a precipitous 47 percent increase in enrollment and a 300 percent increase in the number of non- and limited-English-speaking students. Despite these overwhelming challenges, Burnett continues to accelerate, primarily because of everyone's dedication to their shared vision:

Burnett Academy is a cooperative partnership of students, parents, staff, and community working together to create an environment in which:

- All students have the freedom, right, and responsibility to learn.

- All students can succeed and celebrate their own and others' successes.

- All students develop a love of learning, inquisitiveness about the world around them, and resourcefulness in meeting life's challenges; they are problem solvers, critical thinkers, and communicators.

- All students are prepared, both academically and emotionally, for high school, college, and beyond; they know their choices and can achieve their dreams.

- All students connect the past, the present, and the future by applying their academic knowledge to the world around them and learning through experience.

- All students have the freedom to take risks in a safe and nurturing environment.

- All students appreciate and build on the strengths of many cultures.

- All students exhibit democratic values, ethics, and principles in their daily activities and interactions.

- All students find opportunities to express their individual needs and talents through a variety of artistic, musical, technological, athletic, social, and intellectual outlets.

- All students experience happiness, friendship, fun, self-confidence, and well-being during their years at our school.

Burnett's vision, a synthesis of the ideas of over 2,000 students, teachers, support staff, administrators, parents, and community members, permeates the school and is a part of everyday life. The entire campus has a spirit of extremely high expectations, as exhibited by the move to heterogeneous grouping in all classes. Teachers experiment with new classroom innovations. The lunchroom conversations of staff members center around making the school the best it can be for all students. In one counselor's office, each component of the vision is displayed across an entire wall. She refers to it each time she speaks to a student or parent. The school as a whole recently voted to set aside a day for students to rewrite the vision in their own words, and these new signed vision statements are on display in the cafeteria. "In setting goals, all schools in the district are required to come up with a mission statement," says principal Mike O'Kane. "Often these end up in a drawer. The difference with accelerated schools is the *process* of getting to the mission statement. Even if both the conventional and accelerated schools missions end up the same, the fact that there's been input from all levels makes a difference in how it's carried out. This involves a lot of trust, and we all have to keep working at it."

If you ask a student at Burnett what being an accelerated school means to him or her, she might say, "Classes are harder now. I have to take algebra!" Or "We're all working together and have a lot of input." Or she might take you by the arm and lead you into the cafeteria to show you the vision quilt hanging over the stage. "There's my class's piece up there in the corner. See it? Everyone in the class worked together to come up with a picture or something to describe our vision of our accelerated school. Every class in the school has a piece up there. We put them all together on December 13 last year." You might say, "Wow! I'm surprised you can remember the date. What was so special about December 13?" "Oh," she'd reply, "that was our vision celebration!"

It isn't surprising that everyone in the school community can remember the vision celebration vividly, even after a year. An early-release day was set aside for the first ever schoolwide assembly to celebrate the school's vision and to share the vision with the local community. The festivities began in the cafeteria, where live music from the jazz band pumped the emotions of students, faculty, staff, parents, and community members sky high as they entered. One of the most moving parts of the day came when several students addressed the entire assembly, speaking about what the vision meant to them. It was the first time that Hispanic students had ever addressed the Burnett community. Their speeches were eloquent, moving teachers and fellow students alike. Following the speeches, students from each class paraded to the front of the cafeteria to present their class's vision quilt pieces, which would later be sewn together. The music teacher and several students led the school community in an "accelerated rap" about Burnett. Spirits were very high as the entire school marched along the one-mile parade route to present the vision to the county supervisor and mayor. Led by the jazz band and mounted police officers, the Burnett school community marched through the streets of San Jose, stopping traffic and the San Jose Light Rail, proclaiming their ambitious vision for the nineties.

Beyond the spirited pronouncements and written statements, the vision serves as a filter for all activities that take place at Burnett. As one teacher and cadre facilitator, Mike Weir, commented, "If an activity doesn't lead us to our shared vision, then perhaps it's not an idea worth embracing."

Governance and Decision Making. Burnett's governance and decision-making process works well; cadres and the steering committee meet regularly and carefully use the Inquiry Process. The school-as-a-whole meetings allow for systematic participation of the *entire* school community. The process, which was developed more fully in Burnett's second year of acceleration, works as follows: cadres make their recommendations to the steering committee, where they're discussed and refined. These proposals are then included in the daily school bulletin so that all members of the school community can reflect on the proposals before discussing and voting on them at their monthly school-as-a-whole meetings. In this way, the steering committee serves primarily as a clearinghouse of information for cadre and staff concerns before the school as a whole votes on items that involve schoolwide changes in curriculum, instruction, or organization.

The ideas that are put before the school as a whole are the result of careful exploration and reflection by the cadres. The Burnett Family and Community Involvement Cadre was formed to address the issue of involving parents in the education of their children, both at school and at home. Last spring this cadre tackled stage 1 of the Inquiry Process—defining the problem—and produced a list of hypotheses addressing why parents weren't more involved at Burnett. Parents were asked for their input on obstacles to parent involvement and ideas for overcoming these obstacles. Some of the hypotheses confirmed by the parents were these: parents don't always know where to take their concerns; some parents are reluctant to criticize the school when they feel something is wrong or needs improving; parents feel like second-class citizens when they come to the school. Focusing on these confirmed hypotheses, the cadre worked on generating ways to make parents feel more welcome and informed.

After brainstorming ideas, cadre members have embarked on several initiatives—all approved by the steering committee and the school as a whole—to meet their focus area described above, including a weekly parent newsletter, parent seminars, and a parent room. One of the biggest achievements was making the dream of a parent room a reality. Based on the parents' feeling that they were often in the way and out of place, the parent room was conceived as a comfortable space in which parents could relax, consult with other parents or teachers, work on a project, or do just about anything. After the cadre presented the idea to the steering committee, the school as a whole voted unanimously to turn a highly sought after spare classroom into the Burnett parent room. Giving the room to the parents of Burnett students is yet another example of the way in which the Burnett staff places the good of the whole school above the good of individual parts.

"This whole process has given all segments of the school energy, input, and control—it's really succeeding," says Frank Howseman-Cabral, vice-principal. "It's offering an opportunity for leadership to develop within the ranks. People are sharing and feeling good about it—and successful." He and other school staff are quick to point out that this newfound empowerment goes beyond the steering committee and cadres. Burnett's chapter of the California Junior Scholarship Federation (CJSF) learned "on the job" about the value of the Inquiry Process following the Oakland firestorm last fall. CJSF, a student service organization, wanted to do something to assist the hundreds of people left homeless by the blaze, so they proposed to Fran Laplante, the group's adviser and the seventh grade counselor, that they collect clothes and blankets to send to the victims: "At first I thought, 'Oh, that's a good idea.' But then I started thinking about what we do in our cadres, about how we solve problems by first trying to find out exactly what the problem is before jumping to the solution-generating stage. So I asked the students how they knew that clothes and blankets would help the situation. Of course, they didn't know that. Then we discussed how they could find out what might be useful for the fire victims. Finally we decided to call the Oakland Red Cross, who told them that the people needed food: they had plenty of clothes and blankets already donated. The students were so pleased! They felt much more of a direct connection with the people they were setting out to help, because they'd bothered to find out what they really needed."

Burnett classes and the student council have also become actively involved in taking an "inquiring" approach to shared concerns.

Accelerated Learning for All Children. Burnett's office is a hub of activity, busy with teachers, support staff, administrators, parents, and students bustling in and out. Staff come in at least twice a day to check their mailboxes or confer with colleagues. This morning staff arriving in the mailroom pick up the *Daily Bulletin*, the school newsletter, and check the large cadre bulletin board for the latest cadre meeting minutes.

Today staff members find new minutes from the previous day's meeting of the Instruction Cadre, which mention that cadre members will be giving a brief presentation to the steering committee at its next meeting and ask that the cadre be placed on the upcoming school-as-a-whole agenda to present its findings. Last spring this cadre began to inquire into the most effective teaching strategies and learning styles of the Burnett staff and students by examining some of the school's taking-stock data and by asking the people most affected by the teaching at Burnett: the students. Cadre members from each department and grade level spent time with their own classes doing an exercise on students' most powerful learning experiences. Students got into small groups, discussed times that they felt they'd really learned something, and came up with a list of the elements they considered crucial to creating such powerful learning experiences.

Using that classroom exercise, the student surveys, and taking-stock data as a springboard, the cadre spent the first half of this year organizing a comprehensive program to improve instruction. The first part of the cadre's program proposal is the creation of a data base that would contain instructional strategies that have been successful for both teachers and students and individual teachers' strengths and interests (so that people can contact each other for suggestions and ideas). In addition, the program proposes the organization of peer visits and peer coaching based on the instructional needs of teachers, visits to other schools' classrooms, the videotaping of teachers for self-study, a video library of lessons that proved exceptionally successful with students, staff presentations of effective lessons at school-as-a-whole meetings, and a periodic newsletter with "tips for teachers" developed by Burnett staff.

Gloria Luna, a humanities teacher serving on the cadre, is implementing in her classroom many of the innovative teaching strategies that the group researched, even though the school as a whole hasn't yet voted to adopt them schoolwide. In accelerated schools, individual teachers' initiatives and innovations often occur simultaneously with larger schoolwide initiatives and can fuel the process of whole-school change. Most recently, she and the two other seventh-grade humanities teachers, Lynn Pickering and Lynne Mahan, worked together to incorporate some creative cooperative learning projects into their unit on archaeology/geography. "We started working together last year to design the humanities curriculum," says Luna, "and this year we've totally pulled together. We share everything, every piece of our individual curricula, even if we've worked hours on it. We try to empower each other."

Earlier this week, students in Luna's class sorted through a bag of trash she brought in from her own home. Like archaeologists at a dig, they were to analyze each piece of trash and come up with a valid hypothesis as to the characteristics and makeup of her household. Today the classroom is abuzz with activity; students are in small groups busily cutting pictures from magazines and drawing on construction paper. Their assignment: an atomic bomb has wiped the United States off the face of the earth, and the only remnant of our civilization is a time capsule. Using only seven items (pictures or drawings of which are to be pasted on a large piece of construction paper next to an explanation of what these items symbolize), each group must decide what they would include to best represent our society. One group is huddled around a boy sketching a representation of the Constitution; in another group, a young girl explains why she thinks a photo of her family should be included. "Remember," calls out Luna as she makes her way from group to group, "that you want whoever finds this to be able to tell as much as he or she can about our history. What did we value?"

Walking down the hallway, we see that Lynn Pickering's class is engaged in a similar activity. Each of six small groups is sorting through a bag of trash that Pickering has "rigged" to represent six different families. Each group must hypothesize together about what each item tells them: How many people lived in the house? Did they have pets? What kinds of activities did they like to do? "Look, you guys," shrieks one of the students, waving a crumpled credit card bill in the air. "They spent $500 one day on clothes at Nordstrom!" Based on their observations and analysis, each group will write a report to be presented to the class. "Learning is more fun now," says Brandy, a seventh grader. "We do things besides just reading from textbooks."

Hands-on learning that builds on a rich array of both teacher and student talents takes many forms at Burnett. Mike Weir's seventh grade aerospace engineering class has just finished a two-week lighter-than-air-craft unit. After designing and constructing their own hot-air balloons, students are launching the projects today on the schoolgrounds. Other teachers have brought their classes out to watch the launch and see which team's balloon stays in the air the longest.

Several buildings over, Robert Benn is using the theme of astronomy to integrate instruction about physical science, life science, and earth science. Teams of four students have designed a team logo, or mission patch, and will be working together throughout the semester just as astronauts do on a mission control base. "The way that science works in real life is that you have to work with different people," explains Benn. "And their skill may be something completely different than yours; you might have a good artist, you might have someone who's good at numbers or good at finding patterns, and you need to be able to work with them and get the product done." Today students are working on designing travel posters with a twist: these posters lure viewers to faraway planets such as Saturn, Neptune, and Jupiter. One student who's drawn a colorful ring around Saturn promises that, as a tourist, you'll be able to hang glide for a "long, long, time." After school Benn heads the Young Astronauts Club, a national student organization designed to incorporate space, science, and math curricula. Twelve students are currently members, three of these students are in the special education program; all are enthusiastically working together on building rockets, to be followed by a space station model.

Many of these classroom offerings reflect the hard work of the Curriculum Cadre. Burnett's old schedule offered classes in language arts, social studies, math, and physical education, along with one semester of science paired with one semester of computers. Now students are offered classes in humanities, math (all students take algebra by the eighth grade), and physical education, along with one semester of science paired with one semester of aviation/aerospace and elective courses based on student preferences. Despite the severe budget cuts that took away Burnett's arts program, teachers have volunteered to teach Saturday classes in drama, music, and chess. Staff members have also been actively involved in grant writing. Burnett's recent aviation and aerospace grant, for example, funds Lab 2000, a technology lab equipped to offer students learning experiences in such areas as computer graphics, desktop publishing, flight simulation, laser communications, aerodynamic design, and satellite communications.

The desire to serve the needs of all students was the springboard for one of the most challenging and innovative decisions implemented this year by the school community: the elimination of all tracking. Every student in each grade level and in all subject areas now studies the same curriculum in heterogeneous classes. "If you make the lessons creative enough and gear them toward the highest-level student," says Pickering, "then you really help the lower-end students by acknowledging that every child can contribute, but maybe not in the conventional way. They end up feeling a lot more tuned in and a part of everything. When you plan a lesson, you ask yourself, 'How am I going to get everyone to do it and benefit from it?'" In addition to teachers' efforts in the classroom and the work of the Instruction Cadre, the school developed a peer-tutoring program to help students having trouble in subjects such as algebra. In the future, the school hopes to match sixth grade tutors with any ESL students having a hard time adjusting to the school community.

Yvette Dunavant, eighth grade student-body president and a member of the School Interactions Cadre, explains what accelerated learning has meant for the students at Burnett: "Everyone's treated equally here. We're *all* in high classes now."

Communication Beyond Traditional Boundaries. Throughout the school, lines of communication continue to expand and interconnect as staff, teachers, administrators, and students work together on issues that affect the whole school. Elaine Farace, vice-principal, comments on her experience: "For me the biggest change has been what seems to now be the philosophy of the whole school: everything influences something else. We no longer consider only parts or segments; individuals and departments no longer work in isolation. Frank [Howseman-Cabral] isn't just in curriculum, and I'm not just handling guidance and discipline. And it makes a lot of sense, because classroom instruction affects classroom discipline, and classroom discipline affects classroom instruction. All of those things are so interrelated. And because we're all working together on those things, the interdependency is more clear, I think, to everyone. One little wheel affects another little wheel, and that affects the whole."

This holistic approach has brought with it a greater sense of empowerment and responsibility, as Steve Novotny, an aeronautics/aviation instructor explains: "Two years ago, I wouldn't have cared what the math department was doing. That was their business; I just worried about my classroom. Now I want to know everything that's going on in the school. And if I don't agree with something, I feel like it's my place to say that." More and more teachers are breaking the mold of teacher isolation and reaching out to other staff members and colleagues for guidance and support. Kris Estrada, the writing lab instructor, says, "Teachers often tend to think that all the problems in the classroom are on their shoulders, and if they have to look outward for help, it's almost a weakness. With the accelerated schools Inquiry Process, a natural part of it is reaching outward for information and help to try and solve the problem, so the responsibility is shared, as well as the rewards."

Not only are teachers expanding the boundaries of their jobs and their responsibilities, but support staff also have an increased role in the functioning of the school. Hope Marquez, a campus assistant and member of the Family Cadre, is officially responsible for reporting student misbehavior on campus and organizing school cleanup crews made up of students who've been sent out of class for misbehaving. Affectionately called Grandma by the students as well as her colleagues, Hope is primarily concerned about the children. She says, "The most important thing is to get the kids to stay in school. We're doing everything we can to let them know that there's something going on here, something they can be interested in. I try to talk to the students *and* the parents. I talk to them in Spanish and try to get them to see what *accelerated schools* means and what we're doing in all of these meetings. Getting parents to appreciate and know what's going on will help them encourage their kids to stay in school. We really want to involve them." At the last school-as-a-whole meeting, Hope was named an honorary English teacher. Although she's not certificated and she doesn't teach a formal class, Hope works every day to build the language skills of the children she works with. Whether she's teaching a new English word to a Spanish-speaking student or correcting the grammar of someone who already speaks English, Hope's work goes beyond discipline, and the school community has recognized her for it.

Burnett's heightened sense of shared responsibility and its improved communication are exhibited not only in day-to-day relations between students, staff, and parents but also in school initiatives that involve the entire community. Last year the Egg Drop Contest, originally designed by aerospace teacher Steve Novotny as a class activity, blossomed into what will now be an annual schoolwide and community event. Contestants each designed and built a contraption that held eggs and protected them from breaking when the container was dropped off a two-story building. Almost every child entered, many as part of a team. In an effort to drum up materials for the event, Novotny walked door to door within the community asking for support. "I found out that there's tremendous community support. . . . To my surprise, when I said, 'I'm a teacher at Burnett,' people's eyes lit up and they listened because I was a teacher. As more and more people began buying into the project, we all had more and more responsibility to make it great." Neighborhood restaurants donated free dinners, General Electric representatives served as judges, and community businesses and organizations donated a total of $3,000 toward prizes and materials. Almost every member of the school community became actively involved in the event.

From the vision celebration, to classroom innovations, to the Egg Drop Contest, the Burnett community is actively providing opportunities for all students to learn and prosper. As eighth grade humanities teacher Connie Posner says, "We all are taking much more responsibility for the students. Every child is everyone's child."

(Accelerated Schools Newsletter [1992, Winter], 2[1])

CHAPTER 3

Getting Started

How have we typically gone about improving our schools? Many of us are probably thinking back to the one- and two-hour after-school staff-development sessions we've attended—those good and not-so-good workshops at which we were trained to use a new "package" of instructional strategies or curricular materials. Staff developers, publishers, and consultants who facilitate such workshops assume that once we go through the training, we'll be equipped to fully utilize the new curriculum, materials, or instructional approaches. Rarely does someone provide follow-up observation and reinforcement.

As each year goes by and new sets of educational changes and staff-development workshops are introduced with little follow-up or integration into the larger school context, we don't seem to be able to attain the deep, long-lasting results we're looking for. Why not? Because teachers, support staff, parents, and students are rarely involved in choosing the new approaches, and there's little attempt to ensure that the approaches meet the needs of a particular school. In addition, the approaches sometimes come and go so quickly that there's inadequate time to fully understand or implement them.

In contrast, the accelerated schools model is neither a set of packages nor a cookie-cutter approach of piecemeal changes for a school. The Accelerated Schools Project sets out a systematic *process* through which individual school communities build a unity of purpose, undertake responsibility for decision making and the consequences of those decisions, and build powerful learning experiences for all students based on their individual strengths.

To initiate this process, each school undertakes a sequence of interrelated activities over the course of four to five months. At the end of this period, the school has both the organization and the capacity to pursue its own

Take stock.

Forge a vision.

vision. The organization takes the shape of smoothly functioning governance groups, while the capacity emerges from the exciting processes of taking stock, developing a shared vision, setting priorities, and learning how to use the Inquiry Process. Through the Inquiry Process, members of the school community pursue their vision by identifying and defining educational challenges, looking for alternative solutions, implementing a plan, and evaluating the outcomes of the plan.

Before delving into schoolwide challenges using the Inquiry Process (see Chapter Four), there are four important steps a school must take to initiate the accelerated schools process: (1) take stock, (2) forge a vision, (3) set priorities, and (4) create governance structures. These four steps are the "getting from here to there" steps. They involve all members of the school community (teachers, other staff, principal, parents, central office members, students, the local community) to ensure coordination and harmony in planning, implementation, and evaluation of accelerated schools educational efforts. If central office representatives help your school design its vision, for example, they'll share your goals and therefore act as advocates and liaisons in helping you cut through red tape during the planning and implementation of, say, a new discovery method of teaching mathematics. And if central office representatives are active participants in the planning and implementation phases of such projects, they'll better understand what it is that they're later asked to help evaluate.

Set priorities.

Create governance structures.

The flowchart that follows illustrates these four "getting started" steps and how the accelerated philosophy underlies all of them. The roadmap that follows the flowchart also depicts an accelerated school's first year of transformation.

As a school works its way through its first year of acceleration, there are a number of milestones along the way. The entire school first decides together that it wants to become an accelerated school; full buy-in is crucial to such an all-inclusive process. Then the entire staff and representative parents, students, district office staff, and local community members go through an initial training session. Sometimes called a *launch*, this training session generally occurs over two tc three days before school starts. This training gives the school community an opportunity to get acquainted with the accelerated schools philosophy and overall process; time is spent understanding and beginning to internalize what's meant by the three principles, powerful learning, and the underlying values and goals of acceleration. The school also gets started on taking stock at this training. Within a month, the school begins working on the vision.

It takes three to four months to do a thorough job of taking stock and reporting the findings to the school community. The task of involving all the stakeholders in the creation of the vision takes approximately two months (and wraps up with a great celebration).

Accelerated Schools

1. Philosophy

The schools we want for children in at-risk situations should be the same schools we want for our <u>own</u> children.

Powerful learning experiences are provided for all children through the integration of curriculum, instruction, and organization.

Accelerated school communities share a set of values, beliefs, and attitudes.

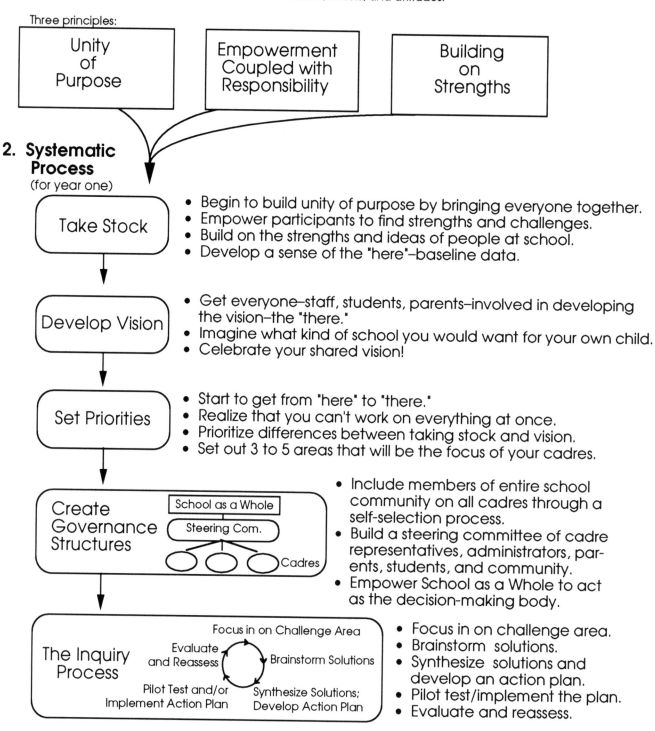

Three principles:

| Unity of Purpose | Empowerment Coupled with Responsibility | Building on Strengths |

2. Systematic Process
(for year one)

Take Stock
- Begin to build unity of purpose by bringing everyone together.
- Empower participants to find strengths and challenges.
- Build on the strengths and ideas of people at school.
- Develop a sense of the "here"–baseline data.

Develop Vision
- Get everyone–staff, students, parents–involved in developing the vision–the "there."
- Imagine what kind of school you would want for your own child.
- Celebrate your shared vision!

Set Priorities
- Start to get from "here" to "there."
- Realize that you can't work on everything at once.
- Prioritize differences between taking stock and vision.
- Set out 3 to 5 areas that will be the focus of your cadres.

Create Governance Structures

School as a Whole
Steering Com.
Cadres

- Include members of entire school community on all cadres through a self-selection process.
- Build a steering committee of cadre representatives, administrators, parents, students, and community.
- Empower School as a Whole to act as the decision-making body.

The Inquiry Process

Focus in on Challenge Area
Evaluate and Reassess
Brainstorm Solutions
Pilot Test and/or Implement Action Plan
Synthesize Solutions; Develop Action Plan

- Focus in on challenge area.
- Brainstorm solutions.
- Synthesize solutions and develop an action plan.
- Pilot test/implement the plan.
- Evaluate and reassess.

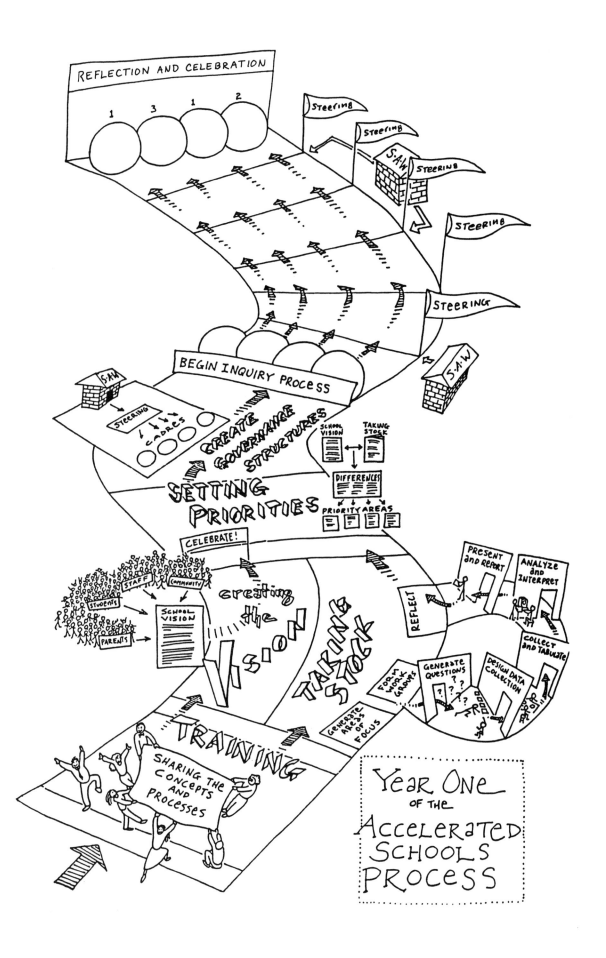

Once the vision is complete and the taking-stock data are analyzed, the school can take another day to set priorities. After that, the governance structures and the Inquiry Process are formally put into place after training. Then, you're ready to roll along in your cadres. Have a great trip! (Before getting started on your trip, you may want to refer to Chapter Five, "Group Dynamics and Meeting Management," to ensure that your "getting started" efforts run as smoothly as possible.)

> **With the accelerated process, everyone can now see the "light at the end of the tunnel." Mutual cooperation and utilization of all participants' strengths enable us to focus on our main objective—i.e., the growth of *every child*. The entire group wants "our school" to be a "dream school" and a real-life, positive experience for all.**
>
> Marvin Levine, Teacher, Arnone School, Brockton, Massachusetts

Let's start our detailed discussion of getting started at the beginning—with taking stock.

3.1. Taking Stock

Before your school begins to dream about where it wants to go, it's important that you step back and look at where it is now. Think of your school change-effort as a journey to your vision. Before setting out on any journey, one determines a path—a task that requires both a destination and a starting point. If a family called a travel agent and said, "We want to go to Chicago," for example, the travel agent couldn't book tickets without also knowing where the family was beginning their trip. A trip from Vancouver to Chicago would certainly take a very different path than one from Miami to Chicago.

In traveling from "here to there" in an accelerated school, taking stock is the "here." It's the fullest picture of the *present* situation at your school in all of its many, varied, and complex dimensions. You might think that your school already has a firm handle on where you are. Indeed, you may have gone through district or state reviews of your school's present situation. If so, these experiences can be used to facilitate taking stock. However, taking stock in an accelerated school is a much more in-depth process than most school communities have ever gone through together.

> **Once we started working in our groups, we were forced to do some serious thinking—more than was required for the PQR [Program Quality Review]. The PQR tended to be more objective; taking stock emphasized *our values*, the things that were important to *us*. We hadn't really given much thought to that before.**
>
> Connie Posner, Teacher, Burnett Academy, San Jose, California

Taking stock differs from more traditional school assessments in a number of ways:

Typical School Assessments	*Taking Stock*
• Small committee does all the work.	• Total school community is actively involved.
• Focus is on weaknesses.	• Focus is on areas of strength and challenge.
• Focus areas and questions are determined from the outside.	• Focus areas and questions are determined by the school community.
• Final document is intended for outsiders' use.	• Final document is used as a tool for the school community.
• Initiator asks for recommendations before challenges are understood.	• Report serves as a comparison point for setting priorities and provides baseline data for cadres to use in the Inquiry Process.

Taking stock is important because school communities accomplish the following:

- Learn about the school in all of its facets.

- Begin to work together on a schoolwide effort.

- Begin to take responsiblity for school challenges.

- Recognize the school's strengths.

- Create baseline data from which change will be measured.

The actual process of taking stock is all-inclusive in two important ways. First, *everyone* in the school community is included in the effort. The views of teachers, students, parents, support staff, administrators, district personnel, and the community all constitute crucial pieces of a school community's picture of its present situation. Second, beginning accelerated school communities take stock of *all* facets of the school. These facets may include students, the curriculum, instructional strategies, family involvement, achievement, school organization, assessment, school history, the local community, demographics, and the feelings of all members of the school community. But these are just potential areas of exploration. When your school community takes stock, *you* determine all of the facets that *you* want to explore in order to get a comprehensive view of your school community.

The facets that you choose then come together to make up one big picture of the school's present situation. You might think of the different facets as pieces of your school's unique puzzle or as components of a three-dimensional picture that's able to capture both the tangible and intangible aspects of your current school situation with great depth and perspective.

Once you've chosen all of the different facets that you wish to explore, you look at the many aspects of each facet that further illustrate the present situation. For example, if one facet is "curriculum and instruction," you might ask questions such as these: Do children sit in rows and always work independently of each other? Are lots of children retained each year? Is your curriculum fresh and creative, or do you use pretty much the same lessons year after year? What are the predominant teaching strategies? Where are test scores strong? Where are they weak?

The process of taking stock incorporates a unity of purpose, empowerment and responsibility, and building on strengths. School communities work together to provide a comprehensive picture of their school, its strengths, and its challenges in order to move toward a unified vision. This activity culminates in a report that the entire school discusses and deliberates. The information that you gather will be interesting to look back at as you move forward. And once you begin to "accelerate," you'll collect new information along the same lines. You'll experience a great feeling of accomplishment when you compare your baseline data with your later accelerated data. Moreover, the information that you collect as you take stock will be like a treasure chest of data for your inquiry cadres as they begin to research the underlying causes of your priority challenge areas.

The process of taking stock takes approximately four months. This may sound like a lot of time, yet when all members of the school community get involved in the process, the time flies. All members of the school community become extremely excited about taking responsibility for their school and learning more about it.

Taking stock involves gathering a lot of data. We wrote a student survey. Every kid in this school, pre-K through grade 5, took it. We analyzed it, disaggregated it, and looked at it again. We put together a parent survey; we looked at teacher perceptions. We looked at our kids' achievement data. We gathered our archival data from every which way: demographic data, data that we never thought of collecting before, even down to how many kids were visiting the clinic each day.

We spent about a month collecting data in groups. Then each group presented its data to the whole faculty and staff, and we moved all of the charts and everything into the teachers' lounge. We chewed on

Suzanne Still, Former Principal, Hollibrook Elementary School, Houston, Texas

3.1.1. How Can Your School Take Stock?

The gathering of the baseline data for taking stock should incorporate the participation of *all* staff, students, and central office personnel and as many parents and community members as possible. Taking stock is an in-depth research project, and while it's both interesting and important, it can be quite challenging to pull off logistically. For these reasons, we outline here some steps that other accelerated schools have used to streamline the process. You're certainly welcome to try other strategies. (We're always open to new ways to streamline the process, so let us know what you find!)

Step 1. With all staff and representative students, parents, district office representatives, and community members present, start by brainstorming what facets or areas of the school you'd like to take stock of. Remember, you're trying to get as full a picture as possible of your present situation. You'll probably come up with thirty or more areas at first. Because you'll need to research each area, your school community should group similar areas into six to eight clusters.

Step 2. Once you've come to consensus about which six to eight clusters make up your school's present situation, you should establish a committee to take stock of each one. Have all staff and representative parents and students choose which committee they want to work on. Each of the committees should include a mixture of teachers, classroom aides, other classified staff, parents, students, and district office and community representatives, if possible. One committee might be responsible for exploring the area of instruction; another committee might look into parents; another, school history; another, school climate—and so on, depending on the areas you've chosen to focus on. (Each committee should receive all of the thoughts that were generated under each cluster area—the original thirty or more facets—to use as a starting point.) Each committee should pick a representative to serve on the taking-stock coordinating committee—a clearinghouse committee (described further in step 6 below) made up of representatives from each area.

Step 3. Your taking-stock committees should outline a list of questions that will begin to define your *present situation.* An appropriate "here and now" question in the area of family involvement, for example, would be, "How many parents attend back-to-school night [or attend conferences]?" An inappropriate taking-stock question in the same area would be, "How can we involve more parents in our school?" This is inappropriate because it asks for a *solution* rather than a *description of a current situation*; it's a "solution dressed in question's clothes." Questions that ask for what our school "should have" or "needs" are similarly inappropriate at this stage of the process. Thus "What are our scores in reading?" is appropriate, and "What kind of reading strategy should we use to improve reading?" is inappropriate—another solution in question's clothes. During stage 2 of the Inquiry Process, you'll begin to search for solutions—but only once your problems are well defined and understood.

Listed below are some questions that might help you in gathering baseline information. Look at them to get an idea of appropriate taking-stock questions but don't feel bound by them. *It's important that you create your own*; however, if some of these make sense for you, feel free to use (or revise) them. Once you begin the process, you'll think of lots more information to gather than these sample questions would provide. As you can see, baseline information covers everything about a school, not simply test scores.

- *School history.* When was the school built? Was it originally an elementary school or a middle school? Why was it built?

- *Students.* How many children enter your school at grade level? How many bilingual students do you have in your school? How many non-English-speaking students do you have? What languages do they speak? What ethnic/cultural groups are represented in your school? What socioeconomic levels are represented in your school? Are students in classes with an equal mix of cultures? How many students does your school retain each year? What's the student attendance rate? What are your students' challenges? What are your students' strengths? What type of expectations do the students have for themselves? For their futures? What types of expectations do staff have for the students? What about parent expectations?

- *Achievement.* How many of your students leave your school achieving on grade level? How do your students fare when they go on to middle school (high school)? What are your overall test scores? Disaggregated scores? How do your scores compare with the national average and with similar schools in the district? In what particular areas do students achieve higher, lower, and at grade level? How do the different ethnic populations at your school compare in their achievement?

- *Curriculum and instruction.* Describe the school's curriculum, programs, and instructional approaches. What teaching styles are most prevalent? What type of expectations do staff members exhibit for students? Do staff members encourage active learning? Are students grouped heterogeneously? If not, how often does a student move from one group to another? How extensive is tracking in your school (and within classes)? Where do the different demographic/ethnic groups fall in these tracks? Do teachers typically use a lecture format? Do teachers do any interdisciplinary teaching? Do staff members ever pilot new programs? How often do students write? How often do they make presentations?

- *School organization.* How many students are in your school? Has this changed lately? Are community organizations involved at the school site? How do you interact with the central office? What type of schedule do you use? Does it allow for creative instruction?

    Governance and staff relationships: Do teachers talk among themselves about school-related issues? Where and when do staff members meet to talk? Are staff meetings fruitful? Do teachers give input on major school decisions regarding curriculum and instruction? How about support staff? Do teachers feel that the principal listens to their ideas? Are parents or students ever involved in major decisions?

    Resources: How good is your library? Are the supplies you need readily available? Do you use textbooks? Have you updated your texts lately? How do they compare with the most innovative teaching materials? What technology is available in your school? How often do students have access to your resources?

- *School climate.* How comfortable do your students feel at your school? How comfortable do parents feel at your school? How are your students behaved? Do you have a system for dealing with behavior problems? Are teachers free to try new ideas? Is there any forum for teachers to explore new approaches? Are all cultures validated? Are students able to function productively after lunch? What subjects do you teach after lunch? Would all staff members of the school choose to send their *own* children to the school they teach in?

- *Parents and community.* Are parents involved? How? When? Does your school have a plan for involving parents? Are parents from each of the major representational groups involved? Is parent involvement equal among grade levels? Do parents come to conferences? Do parents clearly support their children's education? Do you provide any type of training for parents in skills that they'd need to be supportive? Does the school provide multiple opportunities for two-way communication? Who makes up your community (people, businesses, government, and public and private agencies such as Rotary Club, Boy and Girl Scouts, YMCA, churches, and so on)? What resources do you take advantage of? What resources are there that you *could* take advantage of?

Each school community member should also write a single page describing how he or she feels about the school.

In formulating taking-stock questions, steer clear of *why* questions— questions that attempt to explain underlying reasons for the present situation. In taking stock, we want to learn about the current situation as it is. Later, the Inquiry Process will help us to understand the reasons why. Good "here and now" taking-stock questions are generally in the *present tense* and often begin with *what, when, how, who,* or *where.* They ask about what is rather than what should be or what's needed.

Step 4. After developing questions, each taking-stock committee should look back over the brainstormed questions to make sure that they help clarify the present situation—the here and now. Did any solutions dressed in questions' clothes sneak in? Test yourself: Which of these is appropriate, and which hints of a solution?

- Should we use cooperative learning?
- What teaching styles are predominant at our school?

Your school's committees should also think about what it is they want to learn from their brainstormed questions and make sure that the questions will yield the information they're looking for. Sometimes a second reading helps questioners become more specific in what it is they're after. For example, which of these questions is more useful?

- Do all departments receive equal funding?
- How much funding does each department receive?

Step 5. Once each group has come up with a set of questions for their area, they should decide *who* they want to ask each question of and *how* they want to get each question answered. In terms of *who* to ask the questions of, each taking-stock committee should look at each of their questions and determine if they want to ask the question to staff, students, parents, the community, the district, or some combination of the above groups. The committee should notate the party(ies) they want to ask the questions of next to each individual question. Some questions will be directed to only students, while others might go to students, staff, and parents in order to get a comparative perspective.

In terms of *how* to find the information for each question, taking-stock committees can use lots of different strategies to gather baseline information. For example the committees can:

- *Conduct interviews.* Talk to school staff, parents, the community, and central office staff about your school's history; what do parents, teachers, students, think about your school?

- *Create surveys.* Design and send out a survey on student, teacher, and parent attitudes toward the school.

- *Look through test scores.* Analyze where students are strong and weak academically. Look at disaggregated scores as well. What patterns do you see?

- *Reflect on instructional styles.* Visit classrooms; what types of instructional strategies do you use most often? Your colleagues?

- *Look through data in your very own school office.* How many students are eligible for free lunch? How many students live with their parents?

- *Take a walk around the school.* What is the atmosphere in the office? How about the cafeteria?

Notate the strategy that your committee wants to use to answer each question at hand. Then divide the questions up into survey and nonsurvey questions.

Step 6. Each committee should choose a representative to serve on a taking-stock coordinating committee. Because each of the six to eight committees will have questions that they want to ask of staff, parents, and students—and because nobody wants to bombard a group with eight separate surveys or interviews!—the coordinating committee's first task is to streamline the groups' survey questions onto master surveys for each population type: all of the committees' questions to staff on a master survey for staff, all of the committees' questions for parents on a master survey for parents, and so on.

**Taking-Stock
Coordinating Committee**

- Achievement
- Organization
- Climate
- Community
- Curriculum Instruction
- Family Involvement

The coordinating committee should also check for overlap in nonsurvey questions and get the lists back to the committees *as soon as possible* so that they can begin their nonsurvey research.

The integration of all taking-stock questions isn't an easy task, but it definitely teaches the value of teamwork: one person would have quite a difficult time accomplishing it, but a group can surmount it with success. In order to accomplish the logistical challenge of streamlining the data collection effort, committee representatives should meet with the school administrator(s) (and any other staff who have some flexibility in their schedules) to go over their survey questions, nonsurvey questions, and survey audiences. It's important to include the principal and other nonclassroom personnel in the coordinating committee meetings, because they probably have the broadest purview of the school community. They can help coordinate the gathering of information so that there's no doubling of efforts.

Give each question (whether survey or nonsurvey) a code that reveals which taking-stock committee asked it. Then, when the results come back, they can be directed to the appropriate committee for analysis. Here's an example of how the sample codes for taking-stock areas and sample questions as coded by the coordinating committee might look:

Sample Committee Codes	Sample Questions
ach = achievement	Would you send your child to Dewey elementary? (cl)
cl = climate	How do you use test scores? (c&i) (ach)
c&i = curriculum and instruction	How many parents attended back-to-school night last year? (fi)
fi = family involvement	
co = community	
o = organization	

Gathering Input from Parents

Several accelerated schools have found that many parents don't want to respond to a written survey (especially at the onset of a school's journey into acceleration, when they may not know the purpose of the taking-stock survey). Yet Rancho Milpitas Middle School in Milpitas, California, had a 90 percent return rate on parent surveys. Here are the steps that school community took to ensure such a high return rate.

- The staff devoted the entire back-to-school night to explaining to parents the accelerated schools philosophy and process and the parents' role in making acceleration a reality.

- The principal wrote a column in the parent newsletter that included information on accelerated schools and on the taking-stock and forging vision processes.

- Students filled out their surveys at school the same day that parents received theirs, so as to keep the subject on both of their minds.

- Science teachers coordinated the sending out and receiving of the parent survey, which eased the coordinating committee's task.

- The school set an early deadline for returning the surveys.

- The staff helped "psych up" the students about the importance of bringing back their parents' surveys.

- The school sent home number 2 pencils and a Scantron answer sheet to facilitate parents' response.

Other schools have had different ideas for encouraging parental survey responses: some have used shortened surveys; some have conducted phone interviews with parents; some have asked the students to interview their parents; some have built parent phone trees; some have held community meetings.

Rancho Milpitas Middle School used an effective method to streamline questions onto master surveys. Each taking-stock committee representative reported to the coordinating committee meeting with questions typed out in a large font and triple-spaced. Each of the eight representatives had questions on a different color paper (to differentiate the committees from each other). Next to each question, the committees had noted how they wanted to find the information and, where relevant, whom they wanted to ask. The coordinating committee then cut up the pages into individual questions and separated the strips of paper into two piles: survey and nonsurvey questions.

The coordinating committee first went through all of the nonsurvey questions, looking for areas of overlap. If they found total overlap, committee representatives negotiated which committee would do the research. For example, both the family involvement committee and the curriculum committee had a question about how many parents came to teacher conferences. The coordinating committee decided that the family committee would do the research and share it with the curriculum committee. If there was partial overlap, the relevant committees tried to take different approaches to gathering the information. If there was no overlap, the coordinating committee glued the question (and accompanying notations) onto a piece of chart paper labeled with the appropriate committee's name. After about an hour, the eight pieces of chart paper were covered with the taking-stock committees' nonsurvey questions. Each committee received fewer of their questions back than they turned in, because of the streamlining of overlapping questions.

The coordinating committee next turned its attention to the rest of the strips (all survey questions) and four boxes in the middle of the table. One box was for parents, another was for students, the third was for staff, and the last was for the district office and local community. Committee members distributed the survey questions into these boxes, controlling for overlap. For instance, if both the curriculum and family involvement committees asked two questions about communicating with parents about homework issues, the coordinating committee would help rewrite the questions so both committees' interests are addressed while also streamlining the questioning. This would avoid creating a parent survey of deterring length. Also, whenever a question was meant for more than one population/box, one of the committee members copied it (using the color-coded paper) and put the strips into the appropriate boxes. This task took about two hours.

At the next meeting of the coordinating committee, members drafted surveys for each of the population groups based on the questions in the box. In order to keep the information organized by taking-stock com-

mittee, the survey drafters coded each question according to each committee's name.

Rancho Milpitas Middle School, Milpitas, California

While the coordinating committee is working on the master surveys, the individual taking-stock committees should be busy doing their nonsurvey research (through data gathering, interviews, records analysis, visitations, and so on). Many taking-stock committees assign roles (such as facilitator, recorder, reporter, closure person) so that their meetings run efficiently and no one person ends up overloaded with work. Many also divide the non-survey questions among the members so that it's clear who will do the research.

Step 7. After the taking-stock coordinating committee has finished drafting the master surveys, committee members should send them back to the full school community for approval.

Step 8. Members of the coordinating committee should arrange for translating the master surveys into the languages of the students and parents (if necessary), copying them, and sending them out to the appropriate parties. Children, members of the central office staff, and volunteer parents are all wonderful resources for helping to translate the surveys!

Step 9. As surveys come back, volunteers from the school community (especially those with computer and data analysis expertise) should team up to compile and tabulate the responses. Once the survey responses are compiled, the volunteers should return each taking-stock committee's survey questions and responses for the committees to analyze.

Step 10. Each of the taking-stock committees analyzes and reflects on survey and nonsurvey responses and prepares to present their findings to the school as a whole. Each committee should prepare a presentation of approximately twenty minutes. We encourage the taking-stock committees to create visuals and handouts for their presentations.

Setting up short-answer survey questions in a manner that allows the answers to be recorded on Scantron computer sheets is a great time-saver when it comes to compiling the responses.

Analyzing Taking-Stock Results

Your taking-stock data is very personal to your school community. While you look for strengths and celebrate them, you need to be open to your challenges. Once you recognize your challenges honestly, you will have taken a full step toward solving them. With this said, consider the following taking-stock result: 70 percent of our students feel safe at our school. Is this good (because it's far above 50 percent)? Some might say yes. Yet if your school has 500 students, this statistic means that a full 150 students *don't* feel safe at your school. Look at your results critically. Celebrate the strengths but accept responsibility for the challenges.

Step 11. Schedule at least three hours for the committee presentations. The school community should review, reflect on, and digest the findings of all the committees (both the summaries and the raw data). Discuss the findings without setting priorities or reaching toward solutions. It's helpful to make the data available for people to reflect on at their leisure after the presentations. *Remember, the whole taking-stock effort is designed to help your school gain a full picture of its present situation.* The data will be crucial to compare to your vision in setting priorities. The data will also be extremely useful as cadres begin to explore their challenge areas, so keep your findings in a safe place!

> **I'd always believed that it isn't fair to hold these kids back, to expect less of them, and I know other teachers felt the same way. We thought our school was handling the problem very well, but when we started looking at the classrooms, looking at the curriculum, we discovered that a really high percentage of the special education students were Hispanic, and only 3 or 4 percent of the kids in the geometry classes were Hispanic. There was really a problem. The things we did well, we tended to keep on doing. The things we did badly, we ignored. It's easy to sharpen the talents we already have, but if you're really going to make changes, you have to identify and take responsibility for your weaknesses.**
>
> Connie Posner, Teacher, Burnett Academy, San Jose, California

The steps described above are definitely not carved in stone. They're a composite of methods that existing accelerated schools have found to be successful. But every accelerated school finds new and creative ways to take stock of itself. As these are implemented and perfected, they too will become helpful tools. For example, some accelerated schools are beginning to experiment with ways to involve an increasing number of parents and students more actively in the taking-stock process:

> **At Washington Junior High, the school community has designed an entire interdisciplinary unit around taking stock. The students will become action researchers and learn about the entire accelerated schools process, taking-stock question formulation, interviewing strategies, data analysis, and presentations. The students will each interview their parents as part of the unit. Along with facilitating the students' studies, the staff will formulate and research their own questions.**
>
> Washington Junior High, Conroe, Texas

We look forward to hearing how this unit goes and sharing it in future editions of the *Resource Guide*.

During the taking-stock phase, many individuals in the school community begin longing to make changes immediately. While long-term, schoolwide

A Time Capsule!

Your taking-stock information can also serve as a time capsule: it can be put aside and taken out periodically in the future to see how the school has changed since it began to accelerate. Perhaps you might even include a brief videotape in your time capsule, along with interviews with staff, students, and parents, and so on.

changes require group decision making through the Inquiry Process (see Chapter Four), there's no reason that an individual teacher, parent, staff member, or administrator can't start the little wheels turning. You may find that reflecting on the information you gathered in the taking-stock process will alter what you do every day.

> **We took the sample taking-stock questions and decided to ask all of them, and gradually we came up with our own. Little by little as we thought about it, we began to look at the whole process—what is it that we're trying to do in this school? What is it that I'm trying to do with my classroom? What do I want these youngsters to know? Other teachers asked themselves these questions too. I know because we talked about it; everyone became more evaluative of his or her own teaching. When we started to synthesize really meaningful questions, it made a difference in my classroom. I started looking for ways to accelerate the students even more than I had before.**
>
> Connie Posner, Teacher, Burnett Academy, San Jose, California

3.1.2. Taking-Stock Reflection Questions

Were *all* members of the school community meaningfully involved in all aspects of the taking-stock process? How did the committees generate questions? What areas of school life were investigated? What were your taking-stock committee names? How was the taking-stock information gathered? How effective was the taking-stock coordinating committee at fulfilling its tasks and communicating with the rest of the school? What was the response rate on the master surveys for the various groups? How did the taking-stock committees follow through on the nonsurvey research? Were the reports generated by each taking-stock committee thorough and clear? How did the school community feel about the findings? Was there widespread agreement among the members of the school community about the big picture of the here and now? What strengths were found in the school community through the taking-stock process? What challenges were identified? Did the taking-stock process yield some surprising information? How did the taking-stock process and report build a sense of ownership of and responsibility for the school? What evidence is there that the school community has begun to develop a unity of purpose, collective empowerment, and recognition of strengths and opportunities to build on them?

3.2. Forging a Shared Vision

The vision is the *there* in "getting from here to there." Many schools begin forging their vision while they're taking stock so that the processes run simultaneously. These two processes are the "ingredients" for setting priorities.

Creating a shared vision means thinking about what you want the school to become. *Think about the school that you'd design for your own child.* Think about your dreams, the school's strengths, who you are, and where you want your school to go. Developing a vision involves thinking creatively and boldly. Your vision is both your inspiration and your destiny. By working together and using the accelerated schools process, you *will* reach it.

Everyone participates in forging your school's vision—teachers, parents, administrators, students, support staff, central office staff, secretaries, custodians, cafeteria workers, central office personnel, and community members—because everyone shares responsibility for helping children. These diverse people will also all pull together to make that vision come true.

The process of getting everyone to agree on a vision isn't as hard as it may sound. Chances are you already discuss "the way things should be" over lunch or in faculty meetings and talk at home with your family about what you'd like for your school. In an accelerated school, however, *all* participants talk *together* about what they want for the school, and then they make it their daily work to create that dream—*together.*

When we built the vision, we were saying what we wanted for the future. I want to see people getting along. You know, with all these wars and stuff. And that's what building a vision is all about anyway, people working together.

Michael Bom, Eighth Grade Student, Burnett Academy, San Jose, California

One of the first things that we did was to develop our vision statement. Everyone who had any connection to the building had an opportunity to participate in that process. We got an opportunity to say what we thought our school should be about. And what came out of that, I think, is that everyone had a sense that they had a part in creating what the accelerated school here is going to look like. That was a really positive experience.

Janet Katzenburger, Teacher, Missouri Accelerated Schools Network

The most exciting part of creating the vision was getting parent and student input. One way we elicited input from parents was through a parent forum. Parents and staff worked together in small cooperative groups in order to develop ideas. Each group then reported out to everyone. It was thrilling to watch unsure, tentative parents slowly blossom when they saw we were *really* valuing their input. The best student ideas came by forming small discussion classes one week in P.E. classes. This information was so different from student input typically gleaned from impersonal and simplistic surveys. The task of completing these often diminish student responses. However, by asking students questions directly and allowing discussion time, we got excellent ideas from *everyone*. Students were able to experience their contribution to the school vision, which made our celebration more meaningful and personal.

Ann Oplinger, Principal, Memminger Elementary School, Charleston, South Carolina

By involving all the various members of the school community in developing a vision, you ensure that every single person in that community has a real feeling of *ownership*. Every time individuals in your school community look at the vision, they'll see their ideas, their dreams reflected; therefore,

---

Vision: Students with a Future

Here's the vision statement forged by the Hoover Elementary School community in Redwood City, California. Underlying it is a large list of goals that characterize the vision. While the vision statement is a summary of the larger dream that the staff, students, parents, and community have constructed for their school, the goals should also be reproduced in their entirety for the record.

Through the combined efforts of our school, home, and community resources:

- Our students will develop a strong sense of self built on successful experiences in academic and social pursuits at Hoover School.

- Our students will acquire the cognitive skills which will enable them to participate successfully in the educational mainstream through extensive emphasis on language development, literacy, and critical-thinking skills.

- Our students will broaden their experiential base to increase their knowledge and understanding of the world around them through participation in an expanded curriculum.

- Our students will develop interpersonal skills that will enable them to interact productively with children and adults of varied economic and/ or cultural backgrounds through instructional programs that promote multicultural appreciation and cooperative learning.

- Our students will develop a sense of responsibility and respect for their physical well-being through participation in a developmental health and physical education program.

the vision will make sense to all involved, making it more likely to move from words on paper into *action*. Involving everyone also ensures coordination in planning, implementation, and evaluation of all future efforts. Central to any vision should be bringing students into the educational mainstream in the best sense of that notion. This means making the students academically able, of course, but it also means helping them develop holistically—enabling them to reach in artistic, social, and creative directions as well.

3.2.1. How to Go About Creating Your Vision

I thought the vision process would be kind of "hippy-dippy," even though I'm a child of the sixties. I thought, Don't we all know why we're here? Don't we all want the same things for the kids? I tended to think we were all on the same wavelength and that the vision stuff was just fluff. What I've discovered is that going through that process and involving everyone is vital. It's become a benchmark for us.

Elaine Farace, Former Vice-Principal, Burnett Academy, San Jose, California

The vision that you develop will be unique to your school. It should be based on what you desire, not what you think is presently possible. If you think big, you'll accomplish more as an accelerated school than if you think small. One of the major goals of accelerated schools is to close the achievement gap and get all students into the academic mainstream. But what are your other goals?

There are many ways to compile the school community's dreams into a shared vision. Because the vision should reflect the ideas of everyone, you'll need to devise strategies for obtaining the vision ideas of all staff, all students, as many parents as possible, and any other interested parties that you feel are appropriate (for example, representatives of the district and/or the community). You may want to use the creative interplay between small and large groups to maximize participation at both an "intimate" and a more public level. The all-inclusive process of developing a vision—whatever means you employ—also helps you interact and coordinate with all members of the school community at subsequent stages of the acceleration process.

The following outline of steps that you can take to develop a vision might help you get started:

Step 1. Before any scheduled meeting of the staff, students, and/or parents, all participants should reflect on their personal visions. We all carry around in our heads a vision of what we think our school should be like. In forging a shared vision for an accelerated school, parents, teachers, and other involved adults must first ask themselves, "What type of school do I want for my *own* child?" Students should ask themselves, "What type of school do I want for myself?"

Step 2. In an initial meeting of all staff and representative parents and students (perhaps at training or soon after), your school community should begin to forge a vision of a school. Schedule the initial vision-setting meeting to last for at least two to three hours so that people will have time to give the discussion a lot of serious thought. At that meeting, you might assign all participants to small groups and encourage them to share their personal visions/ideas. Individuals in the groups should think about the following issues:

- Features of the school that they would want to attend or have their own children attend

- What they would like today's students to be like when they leave the school

- How their school would look if it were to work well for everyone

- What their school would be like six years from now if they had the school of their dreams

- Features of the school that they would want to work in

These topics should generate some lively discussion—and disagreement! Someone in each group should write down *every* suggestion on chart paper and post them for large-group discussion. (People can also *draw* depictions of their dream school to share with others!) Back in the large group, a facilitator should encourage everyone to look for common threads among these small-group visions so that the resulting goals will be solidly based and reflect the thinking of the whole group. After all, you'll be living with these ideas for some time. If they're poorly conceived, they won't serve you well over the long haul. At this point, you don't need to attempt to summarize all the many ideas into a single statement.

Step 3. The entire group should decide who all the major constituent groups of the school are and devise strategies to get their input into the vision. Each member present then self-selects onto one of the constituency-group committees. (People don't necessarily need to serve on the committee representing their own particular constituency group. A parent can serve on the committee working out ways to obtain student input, for example—or vice versa.)

3a. The people who choose to serve on the student vision committee need to devise ways to obtain input from every single student in the school. All the students should contribute their personal dreams for themselves and their school to the vision-forging process. This can be accomplished through student surveys or class discussions and classroom vision statements that become part of a schoolwide vision. Accelerated schools have come up with very creative ways of involving students in creating the vision statement.

> **At North Middle School, most of the students who participated in the initial accelerated schools training joined the committee to obtain student vision ideas and took responsibility for creating a student newsletter, which went out on the first day of school. The newsletter shared student perceptions about the accelerated schools approach and the vision in particular. They described the vision as a way to get their "dream" school. They invited students to a "*big*" meeting and also included a survey form on vision ideas for those who could not come to the meeting.**
>
> North Middle School, Aurora, Colorado

Because forging a dream school is an extremely positive way to bring students into the acceleration process, many accelerated schools build on the vision through creative activities inside and outside the classroom all year long.

In addition to having each class write their collective vision ideas down on paper, Burnett Academy had each class democratically create a vision illustration on a patch of material. Each class's patch of material was sewn together into a vision quilt, which was used in their vision celebration.

> **My class got really excited about making the vision quilt. They wanted our class piece to look so nice! Everyone brainstormed about what we wanted our design to be, and they came up with a drawing of stairsteps with children, in a circle, helping each other up the stairs. At first each vision piece was displayed in the library and you would see kids pointing to their class's work. They were obviously very proud. That was theirs! This year all the pieces have been sewn together into one quilt hanging in the cafeteria. Now it's obvious that their contribution is there, and they know it.**
>
> Gloria Luna, Teacher, Burnett Academy, San Jose, California

3b. The parent vision committee needs to devise ways to obtain the ideas of as many parents as possible for the vision statement. Accelerated school communities have obtained parent input in a variety of ways—among them, including a vision question on parents' taking-stock surveys, interviewing parents, questioning parents at back-to-school night, forming telephone trees, holding special vision event nights, and going out into the community.

3c. Another committee should be working on ways to obtain ideas about the school vision from the local community, including the school district.

3d. If the *entire* school staff didn't attend the initial vision-setting session, another committee needs to figure out a way to incorporate vision ideas from the rest of the staff as well (all support staff, secretaries, custodians, and any others).

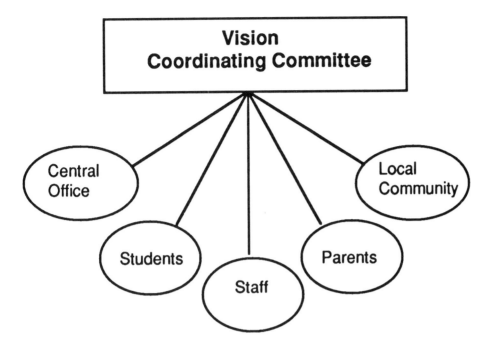

Vision Coordinating Committee

Central Office

Students

Staff

Parents

Local Community

We really struggled over the words. We had ideas from everyone—parents, students, and staff—and we had to try to incorporate literally thousands of ideas, attitudes, and feelings. We had pages of stuff!

Connie Posner, Teacher, Burnett Academy, San Jose, California

Step 4. Parent, student, community, and staff representatives should form a vision coordinating committee that first helps coordinate the efforts of the vision committees in their quest to obtain input from all constituency groups. Once everyone has contributed vision ideas, the vision coordinating committee synthesizes and summarizes all of the ideas from the various groups. After compiling all of this information, a few people from the coordinating committee can get together over a computer and hammer out a draft of the large-group vision, incorporating the staff, student, parent, and community vision pieces.

Step 5. The vision coordinating committee should then give the draft vision statement to the school community as a whole to review and reach consensus on.

Step 6. Once members of the school community have agreed on a vision statement, they should display and *celebrate* their vision. Research shows that if people see the vision statement enough and say it enough, they begin to internalize it and make it happen! You can post the vision statement everywhere—in each classroom, on the cafeteria walls, in the schoolyard, on T-shirts, perhaps even on a small placard on each teacher's, staff person's, and student's desk.

To celebrate their visions, accelerated schools hold schoolwide celebration rallies that get everyone in the school community—staff, students, parents, district representatives, and community members—committed to making the vision a reality.

Burnett Academy's Vision Celebration

On December 13, 1990, all students and staff members as well as many parents filed into the cafeteria for the first-ever whole-school assembly at Burnett Academy in San Jose, California. The school's jazz band, the Downtown Upbeats, played a variety of songs as the cafeteria filled up with people. The energy was contagious—balloons lined the walls, which had student-made signs all over them. Nadia Coggins, student-body president, and Mike O'Kane, principal, welcomed everyone to the ceremony. The following is a summary of the key events:

- Yesenia Lozano, a seventh grade student, spoke to the school about her experience on the vision-writing committee.

- Nadia Coggins, student-body president, read the entire vision statement to the school community.

- Music teacher and band leader, Dave Anderson, and several of his students led the entire school community in a rap about Burnett Accelerated School.

- The Deputy Assembly members (part of the student government) paraded posters proclaiming Burnett's vision ideas for the nineties while the band played.

- Six students spoke individually about what the vision meant to them. (This was particularly striking, because it was the first time in the school's recent history that Hispanic students had addressed the entire school.)

- A slide show of students and faculty was accompanied by a Janet Jackson song about having a vision and dreams.

- Students from each first-period class paraded to the front of the cafeteria to present their class's vision quilt pieces.

At that point, the *entire* school community (all 700 members) marched off to proclaim Burnett's vision publicly, led by the jazz band and accompanied by mounted police officers who stopped traffic and the San Jose Light Rail for the group. The first stop was the county supervisor's office steps, where Ron Gonzalez, the county supervisor, spoke eloquently to the students. The second stop was City Hall, where Susan Hammer, the mayor-elect, spoke to the students. The principal presented a framed copy of Burnett's new vision to both the supervisor and the mayor-elect.

Step 7. Remember to revisit your vision statement periodically to keep it alive. As your school makes progress, you'll probably wish to revise the vision. In addition, any new staff, students, and parents should contribute revision suggestions when they join your school community.

> At the beginning of Burnett Academy's second year as an accelerated school, the principal, Mike O'Kane, suggested that the school form a "kickstart" committee in order to pull all of the new students, parents, and staff into the accelerated schools process and to keep the vision alive. The kickstart committee began by orienting new staff while the Family Involvement Cadre worked with new parents. Then they got all students involved in rewriting the vision in their own words. The kickstart committee stayed active throughout the year through the creation of schoolwide vision-related events: students drew, painted, rapped, sang, danced, and acted out the vision in various events with parents and the community. All of these events helped give continued meaning to the accelerated schools philosophy and process for the entire school community.
>
> Burnett Academy, San Jose, California

The vision statement serves as a guide for all members of the school community as they seek to transform their school. Once it has been created, it's up to every single person in the school community to internalize the vision and ensure that it becomes reality. The vision's first step off the paper and into reality is its foundation as a basis for setting priorities and as an organizer for school activities.

> Before we were an accelerated school, we were just going through our daily routines and doing our work. Day by day, we didn't tend to all get together and really look for that vision. But now, we are looking at that vision, and we are assessing the vision, and we are assessing ourselves in the activities that go on. Are they really related to the goals? And so this vision is within us so that every time we come to work, it is on our minds, and with that we tend to find lots of ways to achieve the vision. To be there where we want to be.
>
> Willie Santamaria, Former Principal, Daniel Webster Elementary School, San Francisco, California

With that said, it's now time to start seeing how each member of the school community can make the vision come alive—in the classroom, in the office, in the schoolyard, at home, and in the community.

> In looking back over our first year of building capacity as an accelerated school, several seemingly little things were instrumental in bringing students and staff, parents and community together in learning how to journey collectively toward a vision:
>
> In October, one teacher began planning, educating, and involving the entire school community in turning an overgrown unclaimed bird sanctuary at George Cox into a "butterfly garden."

Having the vision statement has been a unifying experience for the entire staff. Every staff member (teachers, instructional aides, office staff, etc.) knows that we're all striving to reach a common goal that will have positive effects for everyone in the school.

LeAda Orrell, Special Education Teacher, Burnett Academy, San Jose, California

In February, the account clerk, while standing in line at the bank, read a customer's T-shirt and approached him about it. On the shirt, a colorful butterfly was emerging from a brown chrysalis. The slogan read, "You can fly but the cocoon has to go." In the spring, at our vision celebration parade around the school, every adult wore such a T-shirt, including the man who sold them to us.

The message we communicated to one another and the community was a powerful one of change both in our vision and on our shirts. Unity of purpose, empowerment, and building on strengths were no longer just nice phrases but words embodied with strong feelings of ownership. These action words represented who we were and what we wanted to become.

In May of 1992, monarch butterflies emerged from jars and milkweed at George Cox. Perched on tiny fingers and watched by excited and hopeful eyes, these wonderful creatures of God took flight—and so did we!

Judith A. Carter, Assistant Principal, George Cox Elementary, Gretna, Louisiana

3.2.2. Vision Reflection Questions

Creating the Vision. Were all members of the school community meaningfully involved in the visioning process? How did the various members contribute to the vision? How did your school community synthesize all the ideas of the various constituents into the vision statement? How does the vision address the dreams of parents, staff, and students? How about the district and community? How was the vision made known to all staff, students, parents, and local community members? Did the whole school community celebrate the vision? How so?

Keeping the Vision Alive. How is the vision being kept alive? What connection do individuals within the school community have with the vision? How does this play out in their actions? What connection does the vision have with group decisions? Are decisions evaluated in terms of how they will lead to achieving the vision? How does the vision continue to address the dreams of the entire school community? How does the vision contribute to a framework for action? What goals does the vision suggest for the school community?

For more mature accelerated schools, how often have you revisited the vision to see if it continues to address your dreams? How have you incorporated the views of new members of your school community into the vision?

3.3. Setting Priorities

Once the school has taken stock of its current situation and forged its vision for the future, it's ready to set specific priorities. Priorities are the primary

challenge areas that need to be addressed in order to "get from here to there." The school will need at least a half day (and possibly a full day) to complete this part of the process. The setting-priorities day should begin with a brief review of the taking-stock report and the vision. Then staff and representative parents and students should break up into small groups to identify all of the places where the present reality (as revealed in the taking-stock information) falls short of the vision.

The process of agreeing on priorities usually generates very animated discussions that get to the heart of the school community's concerns. The dynamics of the discourse are themselves useful, because they engage all participants in the realization that they are responsible for change and for choosing those areas where they will begin. Ultimately, all of the school's priorities will be handled, but only the highest priorities will be addressed initially. By focusing efforts on three to five priorities at a time, accelerated schools are able to make more long-lasting changes. As a school community successfully addresses these initial priorities, others will take their place.

3.3.1. How to Set Priorities

To help the school community prepare for setting priorities, each taking-stock committee should make enough copies of all of its survey and non-survey results (in both raw data and summary form) for *all* participants. Each participant should also have a copy of the vision. Participants should receive all of this information ahead of time, for reflection and informal discussion. Because setting priorities involves comparing lots of data from the taking-stock process (including numbers and feelings) and lots of thoughts from the vision, it's quite a task. If it feels sort of tedious, you're doing it right! One strategy for setting priorities is outlined below:

1. Number off into small groups, making sure that each group includes members from the different taking-stock groups.

2. Get people into their groups.

3. Have each group compare the vision to the entire package of taking-stock information and identify all of the differences on a piece of chart paper. Brainstorming about the differences between "here" and "there" can easily produce a list of forty or fifty items. Groups work for at least one hour.

    As an example, suppose part of your vision focuses on appreciating and building on the cultures of each school community member. You may find responses on the student, parent, and staff surveys about culture. Do the surveys uncover similar feelings on the topic? If so, what are they? If not, how do they differ? Some of the information

Priorities are challenge areas, not solutions. After you finish prioritizing your challenge areas, you'll use the Inquiry Process to understand them and to come up with ways to address them. For now, beware of solutions in a challenge area's clothes!

The Process of Setting Priorities

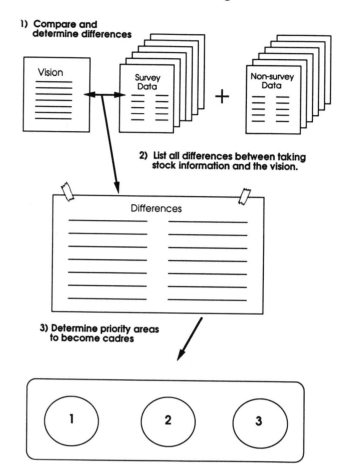

1) Compare and determine differences

Vision

Survey Data

+

Non-survey Data

2) List all differences between taking stock information and the vision.

Differences

3) Determine priority areas to become cadres

1   2   3

gathered from the taking-stock committee that looked at your community and demographics may also be pertinent. List all the differences that you can identify.

4. The forty or fifty differences discovered are far too many areas for any school community to address in any systematic or focused way, so each small group should pick the five differences its members see as most important and put them onto chart paper.

5. Post all chart-paper listings of the small groups' five most important differences between the vision and the taking-stock information. Some may be overlapping; that is fine at this stage.

6. Ask the large group if anyone sees anything that he or she feels needs to be added to any of the groups' work.

7. As a large group (led by an accelerated schools trainer), look at all of the posted charts and start clustering similar items onto summary charts. Each time something is recorded under a cluster heading on the new summary charts, cross it off the original chart paper. Make

sure each item is transferred. If some fit more than one cluster, decide where they fit best and record them only once.

8. Take a look at both the clustered areas and items in each cluster and make sure that they're *challenges* and not solutions. If there are more than three to five areas, give all participants three stickers to put beside the three individual items that they feel are of highest priority. Look at where the dots are clustered. Try to eliminate the items with the fewest dots through discussion and reclustering. *Note that the size of your staff will determine the number of areas you can address.* A small staff should not choose more than three priority areas, and a large staff should not have more than five. At the end of the setting-priorities session, have the participants discuss and decide which items *within* each cluster area are most important. This step is important because it allows the school to democratically give the cadres an initial direction to pursue.

It's perfectly natural and expected that the process of setting priorities will bring about some conflict. Your school community will be choosing areas on which it will focus for approximately the next year. You need to choose priorities that you feel merit attention over a long period—priorities that you can live with. One way to ensure that everyone is comfortable with the priorities is to encourage participants to reflect on them for a few days (and allow time for revision) before the cadres are established.

As your school community settles on the top three to five priorities, you set the stage for establishing the new governance structure for your school. At the heart of decision making and governance are self-selected *cadres* of participants addressing each of the priorities. You might wind up with cadres to tackle the clustered challenges of curriculum, culture, and family involvement, for example. Each school will be different. The important thing is that the clustered priorities represent your school's greatest *challenges*. Each cadre should receive not only its general assignment but also all the items listed under the cluster heading so that participants have an initial focus as they begin the Inquiry Process. For example, the cluster *curriculum* is broad, but if mathematics was listed as an important concern within that cluster, the cadre will know to focus on math first.

As cadre members begin to explore their challenge area using the Inquiry Process, members sometimes change the cadre's name. For example, one Parent Involvement Cadre changed its name to Family Involvement Cadre once members realized that a large number of their students didn't live with their parents.

Once your cadres successfully address the first set of priority areas, your school community will choose the next priorities on which to work. Thus all charts, all notes, all ideas, and all concerns should be saved for later reference.

3.3.2. Setting-Priorities Reflection Questions

What process did your school community use to compare its vision with all of the information gathered in the taking-stock process in order to set priorities? Were all participants in the school community involved in this process? How thorough was the process of identifying all of the challenge areas? How did the school select initial priorities from the full list of challenge areas? Was there widespread agreement among the members of the school community as to the priorities? In what ways will these challenge areas eventually lead your school community to the vision? How were the challenge areas not included in the initial priorities recorded for future action?

For more mature schools, how are you assessing which priority areas have been addressed and shifting emphasis toward other challenge areas that need to be addressed?

3.4. Setting Up School Governance Structures

Governance, which refers to the communication and decision-making processes of institutions, is handled very differently in accelerated schools than conventional schools. You've heard of school-based management, school-based decision making, and school-based budgeting. Unfortunately, these words don't often spring into real action. You probably know of schools supposedly practicing site-based decision making where it's the principal who makes most of the decisions, letting the staff have only a token bit of say. In an accelerated school, the *whole school community really does set the agenda and make decisions together*. A well-run school depends on the ideas of every single person.

> **There were times in some of the schools I've been in before where teachers wouldn't voice an opinion because they knew that their administrator was going to say, "No, I'm going to make that decision, and that's that." But accelerated schools governance is quite different. It gives an opportunity for everyone's visions to be respected.**
>
> Jackie Dolan, Teacher, Daniel Webster Elementary School, San Francisco, California

Earlier in this guide, we talked about the three principles of acceleration. These three principles relate to every aspect of accelerated schools governance:

- *Unity of purpose* gives the school a focus toward which to direct its collaborative work.

- *Building on strengths* acknowledges that all staff, parents, students, and administrators have unique strengths that complement and further build on each other in creating an accelerated school.

- *Empowerment* places the *responsibility* for education back at the school site, in the hands of all involved. Because the school site is the place where education really happens, it makes sense that those responsible for educating the next generation are charged with responsibility for the educational process and its outcomes.

Moving from old, established ways to acceleration may seem terribly daunting at times. Keep in mind that you can take only one step at a time. As long as you're stepping in the direction of your vision, you're making very important progress. Accelerated governance structures and the Inquiry Process will help your school move toward your vision in a *systematic* way, allowing for the input of feelings, data, and experience.

3.4.1. Levels of Governance

Let's look now at the governance model of the accelerated school. We've found that three levels of participation enable schools to tackle, in a democratic but systematic way, the range of issues that they need to address: the cadres, the steering committee, and the school as a whole (SAW).

Accelerated Governance Structures

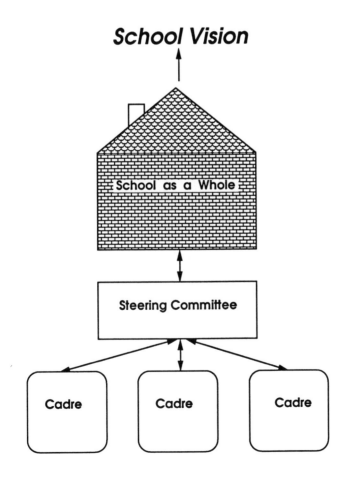

School Vision

School as a Whole

Steering Committee

Cadre   Cadre   Cadre

Teachers, support staff, parents, administrators, students, community members, and district office representatives serve at each of these governance levels.

> **Many accelerated schools have had school-site councils, leadership teams, or steering committees before becoming accelerated schools. They've found that streamlining previous groups into the accelerated schools governance structures works most efficiently. Burnett Academy, for example, streamlined the previous steering committee (made up of department heads) with the new accelerated schools steering committee; it now includes all cadre facilitators as well as the department heads.**
>
> Burnett Academy, San Jose, California

Cadres. The small groups that inquire into the school's most important areas of concern—the school's priority challenge areas, where the school's present situation falls short of its vision—are known as *cadres.* Cadres are composed of teachers, support staff, administrators, parents, students, district personnel, and community members who self-select to serve on them after the priorities-setting stage.

Cadre members don't start by suggesting solutions to a broadly defined challenge area. Rather, they use the Inquiry Process to refine the larger challenge area into a clearly understood set of problems. Once the cadre understands the underlying causes of a challenge area, cadre members search for and pilot-test solutions and then evaluate the results of those solutions.

While most priority challenge areas involve continuing, long-term challenges (such as mathematics or family involvement), some may involve short-term challenges. For example, after your cadres have been formed, an episodic challenge may occur, such as the planning of new facilities. If this happens, your school should form an ad hoc cadre for the duration of the task to ensure that you take a systematic, reflective look at everything you do and that all efforts lead to the realization of your school vision.

Steering Committee. The steering committee consists of cadre representatives, administrators, representative support staff, students, parents, community members, central office staff members, and members of any other group that you feel should be represented. The steering committee serves at least six purposes. Its first and most important role is to *ensure that the cadres and the entire school are moving in the direction of the school vision.* As the steering committee conducts all of its business, members keep an eye out to make sure that discussions, practices, and proposals lead toward the vision.

Second, the steering committee *serves as a clearinghouse of information* so that cadres and all other groups in the school communicate and coordinate with one another rather than operating in isolation. For example, a Family Involvement Cadre might recommend a family math program to better involve parents in the school work of their children; Math Cadre members may have considered recommending a similar proposal for achievement reasons. Through the steering committee, the two cadres can consult together and support each other's efforts in piloting the project, instead of doubling efforts. Similarly, one cadre might present a set of analyzed achievement findings that would save another cadre a lot of time.

Third, the steering committee *serves as a communication vehicle for disseminating information to cadres and the school as a whole.* In order to keep information flowing so that everyone is aware of everything that's going on (which fosters collaboration and general good feeling), steering committee members report what goes on in their cadres/departments to the steering committee and then report back to their respective groups about what takes place at the steering committee meeting. Thus steering committee members are up to date on the happenings of their accelerated school; they're familiar with information handled by the groups they represent on the steering committee as well as information shared by other groups at steering committee meetings.

Fourth, the steering committee *monitors the progress of cadres and all other groups in the school to ensure that they stay on track with the Inquiry Process.* As various cadre representatives discuss and report their progress, everyone keeps the Inquiry Process in mind; in other words, they help each other think systematically. Thus one cadre may restrain another from jumping to a premature solution before fully understanding its problem. The steering committee also helps keep cadres moving so that no one gets "stuck."

Fifth, the steering committee *helps cadres and other groups develop and refine recommendations for consideration by the school as a whole.* Cadres report their progress regularly to the steering committee, as we've noted. In addition, once the cadres get to the point of suggesting pilot action plans, they present these as proposals for the steering committee members to discuss together. After discussing such proposals and helping to refine them, the steering committee jointly recommends them to the school as a whole for voting/consensus. Other groups also present proposals that need to go to the school as a whole for approval to the steering committee. The steering committee doesn't vote on proposals itself. Rather, it's a clearinghouse for school-as-a-whole agenda setting.

Sixth, the steering committee *helps the administration deal with incoming information to the school and helps disseminate this new information to the cadres.* Suppose, for example, that a new policy comes in from the central office or that the school has an important issue to deal with that doesn't fit neatly into any one cadre area. By working through the steering committee, the school can see how different cadres may combine their efforts to deal with the incoming information or simply share the information with cadre members (saving the school a full-blown school-as-a-whole meeting).

Additionally, the steering committee, like the cadres, can spark friendships and foster collaboration among school community members in various cadres who are interested in similar ideas.

School as a Whole (SAW). The school as a whole refers to all administrators, all teachers, all support staff, and parent, student, central office, and community representatives. The SAW is required to approve all decisions that have implications for the entire school. It must approve decisions before cadres begin implementation of pilot programs, for example.

3.4.2. The Creation and Workings of the Various Governance Structures

Once you've set your priorities, you can create your accelerated schools governance structures. You first form task forces or *cadres* around each priority. You can accomplish this by asking every staff member and representative parents, students, and district office and community members to decide which priority challenge area they want to work on. Your priority areas are long-term projects stretching over months, so it's important that people think seriously about where they want to devote their time and energy. And because the variety of your school community's perspectives is important to understanding your challenges, we suggest that, if possible, you balance your cadres by department and grade level and by certified and noncertified staff.

The formation of the steering committee stems directly from the cadres. The steering committee consists of cadre representatives, administrators, and representative support staff, students, parents, community members, and central office staff, as well as members of any other groups (such as departments or teams) that you feel need to be represented so that communication is smooth and efficient in your school.

The school as a whole, as we have noted, is everyone in the school community—all staff and administrators, as well as representative parents, students, district office staff, and community members.

The governance structure combined with the Inquiry Process and the school vision work together to give the school community the framework and direction needed to bring all children into the educational mainstream. They also instill a sense of security and involvement in the ever-changing educational world in which we live.

We recommend that the cadres meet weekly, the steering committee meet *at least* twice a month, and the SAW meet monthly. Cadres should report their progress in the Inquiry Process at each steering committee and SAW meeting, with the steering committee serving as the clearinghouse for setting the school-as-a-whole agenda.

> **At Burnett Academy, when cadres have a proposal for the school as a whole, the steering committee discusses and refines the proposal and then distributes the proposal in writing *before* the next SAW meeting so that people have an opportunity to discuss and reflect on it before voting.**
>
> Burnett Academy, San Jose, California

Communication is key. Each of the governance groups should set (and circulate) meeting agendas ahead of time, and each should take (and distribute) minutes. Agendas, minutes, and updates from all governance levels should be posted in a frequented public space in the school. Although taking minutes is time-consuming, it provides an important record of your efforts. Minutes are important for more than archival reasons, though. Suppose you identify a problem, brainstorm solutions, implement a solution, and evaluate it as unsuccessful. Your minutes from one meeting may help you figure out why you implemented what you did, while minutes from another may offer additional brainstormed solutions, allowing you to implement another option without beginning the whole process again. (Please refer to Chapter Five, "Group Dynamics and Meeting Management," for an extensive discussion of strategies for making meetings effective.)

3.4.3. Governance Reflection Questions

Cadres. What cadres were formed? What is the membership of each? How does the membership reflect the total school community? Are teachers, support staff, parents, students, administrators, and the community represented on each cadre? Are the cadres meeting weekly? If not, are they meeting at least biweekly so that they can thoroughly address their challenge areas and develop an action plan? Are all the cadres following the Inquiry Process? Are they having any difficulties? Are they incorporating the participation of all members? Do all members take responsibility? How well are they using productive group processes to ensure continuity from meeting to meeting? How are participants prepared for their roles as facilitator, recorder, closure person, and so on? How are agendas created? Do the cadres report on how they're doing and where they are in the Inquiry Process at least twice a month to the steering committee and once a month to the school as a whole? Do cadres seek ratification from the steering committee and the SAW on decisions and proposals? Do all participants receive agendas and minutes in a timely manner? Are agendas and minutes also posted regularly in a public place? How well do cadres follow through with implementing and assessing decisions or plans of action? How do the cadres

You know, it makes me feel good to know that with all this chaos (budget cuts, layoffs, increase in student population, etc.) we still have our cadres and steering committee and school as a whole. I feel like we're stable because of it.

Valerie Butler, Teacher, Burnett Academy, San Jose, California

91

keep in touch with the district and obtain district assistance or advice on implementation? How do the members build on the strengths of the school community, work toward a unified purpose, and provide a real opportunity for shared decision making coupled with responsibility?

Steering Committee. What is the membership of the steering committee? Are all cadres represented? Are teachers, support staff, parents, students, administrators, the district office, and the community represented? Was the whole school involved in determining the composition of this group? How often does the steering committee meet? Does it meet at least twice a month so that it can discuss schoolwide issues and make sure that the cadres and the SAW are using the Inquiry Process in moving toward the vision? Is the steering committee using the Inquiry Process? Do all steering committee members actively participate? Do all members take responsibility? Are they using productive group processes to ensure continuity from meeting to meeting? How are participants prepared for their roles as facilitator, recorder, closure person, and so on? How are agendas created? Are ad hoc committees formed in response to short-term problems? If so, how are they coordinated through the steering committee? Do all participants receive agendas and minutes in a timely manner? Are agendas and minutes also posted regularly in a public place? How does the steering committee keep in touch with the district and obtain district assistance or advice on implementation? How do the members build on the strengths of the school community, work toward a unified purpose, and provide a real opportunity for shared decision making coupled with responsibility? For more mature accelerated schools, is the steering committee helping cadres set new priorities as solutions to earlier priorities are successfully implemented?

School as a Whole. Is there full participation of all teachers, support and classified staff, administrators, and representative parents, students, district office, and community members in SAW meetings and decisions? How often is the SAW meeting to discuss schoolwide issues and approve major decisions? At least once a month? How are SAW decisions made? How are members of the school community informed about the activities of the steering committee and cadres? Is the communication between cadres, the steering committee, and the SAW smooth, regular, and effective? Do cadres regularly report verbally to the SAW? Does the SAW use the Inquiry Process? Do all SAW members actively participate? Do all members take responsibility? Does the SAW use productive group processes to ensure continuity from meeting to meeting? How are agendas created? Do all participants receive agendas and minutes in a timely manner? Are agendas and minutes also posted regularly in a public place? How does the SAW follow through with implementing and assessing decisions? How does the SAW keep in touch with the district and obtain district assistance or advice on implementation? How do the members build on the strengths of the school community, work toward a unified purpose, and provide a real opportunity for shared decision making coupled with responsibility?

What's to Come

In the following chapter we provide a detailed description of the Inquiry Process, which is the vehicle that all governance groups and individuals in an accelerated school use to address their challenges. The Inquiry Process is a systematic decision-making process that allows for the input, creativity, and collaboration of all members of an accelerated school community. It helps groups understand the underlying causes of their challenges so that they can address them most successfully.

CHAPTER 4

The Inquiry Process

In the previous chapter ("Getting Started"), we described the processes of taking stock, forging a vision, setting priorities, and creating governance structures to support inquiry into your school's priority areas. As you remember, the cadres are the small governance groups that collaboratively inquire into these challenge areas. One might say that they're the school's problem solvers. Before you set out to address your school's challenges, let's turn to a general discussion of problem solving.

4.1. Solving Problems

Problem solving is one of those educational buzzwords that has pretty much lost any real meaning because it is so overused. That's too bad, because the process of identifying problems and solving them is the key to innovative education in an accelerated school.

The thought of tackling the complicated challenges of a school can be daunting at first—and with good reason. It means a community must look closely—and with brutal honesty—at the underlying causes of the school's challenges. Then school community members must address those causes and evaluate the success of their efforts. What a gargantuan task! How can anyone possibly do that? School staff aren't supposed to work together with parents and students to do that kind of thing!

Well, accelerated schools are set up to encourage entire school communities to think critically and creatively about education. After all, the school site is a center of expertise. The way to start solving the challenges of a school is to call on the skills that we use to solve problems in our everyday life. Outside the classroom, most of us use systematic thinking skills to solve problems all the time. Imagine that your car won't start. What do you do? First you try to figure out what the problem is. *Why* won't the car start? (*Is the battery dead? Am I out of gas? Or does the problem seem more complicated?*) Clearly, understanding the cause of the problem has great implications for what solution you eventually choose. Putting gas in the car if it has a dead battery, for example, won't solve your problem.

To determine why the car won't start, you would first look closely at a multitude of plausible explanations for the problem at hand. Then you'd try to see which of the plausible explanations was actually the one (or more) causing the car not to start. Once you figured this out (possibly with the help of a mechanic), you'd consider ways to fix your car and evaluate those potential solutions. Now, with all of this information in mind, you would choose a solution and see how it worked.

In our everyday lives, problems that may seem overwhelming at first (such as a car that fails to start) turn out to be complicated but manageable. You know where to get expert help when you need it and how to locate and take advantage of other resources that exist. The problem-solving process is demanding but familiar; we've already managed to tackle problems more challenging than this in our lives.

But solving the complex and institutionalized problems of a whole school community can be much more intimidating. Most of us have not been trained to look beyond our offices, classrooms, or homes. Traditional school structures keep us isolated and focused on our individual assignments, jobs, or students. And even within this small, restricted universe, we operate on overload. When we begin to face schoolwide issues, there are no clear guideposts pointing out a single, true, unassailable path to follow. But, we *can* do it. The process is much the same as for unraveling most everyday problems.

The keys are these:

- Explore the problem fully and try to determine why the problem exists.
  My car won't start. Is it the battery? Am I out of gas? Is it the starter?

- Confirm or disprove causes of the problem.
  I looked at my gas gauge, and it seems I have gas. The AAA service person thinks that the starter is defective.

- Search for solutions.
  Fix the car? Buy a new one? A used one? Take a bus?

- Look at the consequences of your proposed solutions.
  What can I afford? Which car will be more reliable? Will walking to and from the bus be a hassle?

- Choose a solution and try it.
  I'll take the bus and try to think about the positive effect my choice will have on my health and the natural environment. I'll also try to sell my car for its parts.

- Evaluate your success and reassess.
  The walk to and from the bus stop is relaxing on beautiful days but depressing in bad weather. Getting up earlier isn't a problem. I got $1,500 for my car.

Of course, it would be facile to pretend that transforming a school is as easy as fixing your car! Changing your school is more complicated and will take much more time—at least several years—*but you don't do it alone.* The process of acceleration brings together the resources of everyone in the school community. It also offers an opportunity to establish collegial working relationships in a new way and thereby build the capacity of your community to collaboratively solve problems and make decisions. It takes lots of cooperation, trust, and mutual respect, as well as the courage to collectively face your school's problems head-on. But think of the rewards: your jobs will be much richer, and you'll have more latitude to enrich the lives of the children you teach and interact with.

Exercise

Break into groups of four or five people. In your groups, pretend you're new to a town, have begun a new job, and have placed your toddler in a child-care center. The problem is that every evening when you pick your child up, he's nervous and anxious. What would you do? After all members of the group have shared their thoughts, try to think about how your approaches fit with the key steps to problem solving described above.

4.2. What Is Inquiry in an Accelerated School?

A big part of being an accelerated school is learning to work together in order to face and solve your school's challenges. Accelerated schools use a systematic approach to solving problems that we call the *Inquiry Process*. It's a way of recreating your school from the ground up, of transforming the school into a vibrant community of learners. It's exactly the opposite of traditional "teacher-proof" education, in which someone from the state or district comes in and dictates what you must do and how you must do it. The Inquiry Process sets up a way of working together on-site so that you can look critically at your school's challenges with the support of the whole school community.

But inquiry into what? Inquiry into the relationship between your present situation and the way you'd like things to be at your school. Inquiry into the relationship between challenges and dreams. In more specific terms, inquiry into the priority areas where your taking-stock information fell short of your vision.

This may sound like an overly ambitious undertaking. The whole idea of educators, parents, children, and other community members asking questions, sharing perspectives, and working collaboratively toward a common vision sounds utopian and idealistic. Everybody knows how schools are supposed to operate: as educators, you're expected to cover certain material by such and such a date; moreover, you're expected to have all the answers, not ask the questions. Yes, you share concerns with other teachers in the halls and at lunch, but you usually try to tackle classroom problems in isolation. You know that the issues are bigger than that, of course. You know that persistent discipline problems, for example, neither begin nor end in the classroom. Sometimes you feel that you've tried everything. (So do colleagues at your school and at other schools all across the country.)

The situation isn't much easier from the perspective of others in the school community. As an administrator, you're expected to come up with solutions for all the major problems facing the school. You're expected to enforce rules, evaluate the performance of teachers, and take responsibility for raising student test scores. As a member of the support staff, you're usually expected to do only what you're asked to do; unfortunately, your input about how something could be done better is rarely sought.

As parents and family members, you struggle on your own to solve your family's problems. You may not know what's going on in your children's schools or what you can do to support their education.

As a local businessperson or church leader, you're distracted by many of your own challenges. You're expected to worry only about your business or congregation, not about the educational difficulties facing children in the local school.

Finally, as a student, you're expected always to listen to adults and to do what you're told. Unfortunately, adults are often much too busy or distracted to listen to you. In the classroom, you're usually expected to do your work by yourself and not to talk to other students. How much you're interested in a lecture or an assignment isn't considered important or relevant. You must complete all work, even if you don't understand what's being taught. You can ask questions about the material being presented but are expected to keep personal comments or suggestions to yourself.

To solve the many complex problems facing a school community, we need to draw on the insights, strengths, and expertise of all the members that make up that community. But how do we do that? This question pushes us past the individual problems of students and classrooms into the larger questions. Inquiry gives school communities a way of taking on challenges collaboratively, with the faith that doing things together with the aid of a systematic process will work better than trying to deal with them alone. After all, no *one* of us is as smart as *all* of us.

This process takes time, and lots of it. Good inquiry is hard and rewarding work. You won't solve complex behavior problems or daunting math challenges simply by sending a few teachers to one-day staff-development sessions in conflict resolution or math manipulatives. We've all seen that quick fixes and one-time injections rarely work. The Inquiry Process offers school communities a method for coming together to think, to look analytically at what's going on in the school, and then to find ways to address local challenges in a *lasting* manner. In using the Inquiry Process, a school community brings feelings, experiences, and hard data into a systematic process that yields results.

Some may still ask, "Why bother?" Why take this on when we're already bursting with classes to plan, papers to grade, meetings to attend, bills to pay, and homework to finish? Why should we take the time to look critically at what's wrong when we're doing the best we can right now? Well, the simple fact that you're reading this *Resource Guide* suggests that you want more for your children and yourselves than they're getting right now. You have a dream that goes beyond your present daily school experiences: you want real and lasting change—schools that work, educational success for your children, and eventual economic success for your entire community. Collaborative inquiry is the vehicle that will help take you where you want to go.

4.3. Stages of the Inquiry Process

Once you've set your priorities and created cadres to work on your school's key concerns, it would seem that your cadres should promptly begin to solve your school's problems, right? Not really. There are a few crucial steps to take before you can actually start picking out and implementing solutions. For example, suppose mathematics is a priority area for your school and you've formed a cadre to deal with math. Sitting down together and deciding to order a new math textbook series or computers or to implement cooperative learning *may* be an appropriate solution, but until you know

The Inquiry Process

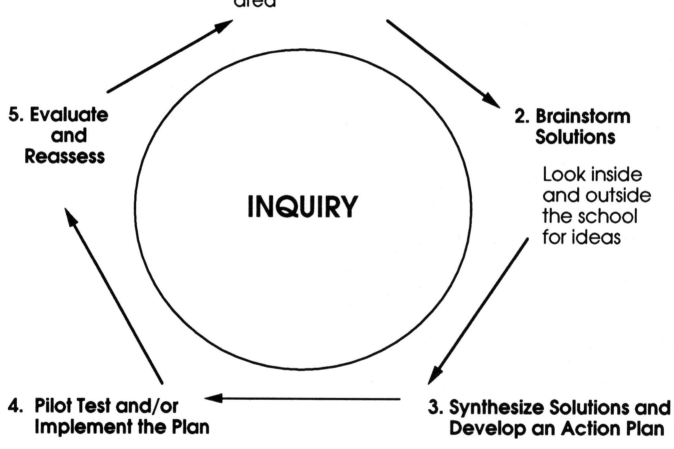

1. **Focus in on the Challenge Area**

   Explore the problem informally and hypothesize why challenge area exists

   Test the hypotheses

   Interpret the results of testing and develop a clear understanding of the challenge area

5. Evaluate and Reassess

2. Brainstorm Solutions

Look inside and outside the school for ideas

INQUIRY

4. Pilot Test and/or Implement the Plan

3. Synthesize Solutions and Develop an Action Plan

precisely what the underlying causes of the low math scores are, you won't be able to tailor the *best* solution to your *true* need. In order to solve your school's problems, you've got to know exactly why the problem exists. *The Inquiry Process is all about understanding why your challenge area exists. This entails discovering the underlying causes of your challenges before attempting to solve them so that when you do finally solve them, your solutions truly address your specific challenges.* Remember the car that wouldn't start? Finding out *why* had powerful implications for what path to take in solving the problem.

The figure on the previous page outlines the familiar steps of problem solving as they are implemented throughout the Inquiry Process in your cadres, in your steering committee, in your school-as-a-whole meetings, and throughout your accelerated school.

Accelerated School Staff Comments on the Inquiry Process

- "Inquiry gives us a definite path to solve our school's problems."

- "Inquiry allows us to look at long-term effects of things we do."

- "Reflection is important! . . . I like being able to look back at our original problem and goals even during other stages of the process."

- "Inquiry lets us know it's okay not to solve a problem in a day, let alone in a single meeting; it's okay to think and share together."

- "Inquiry empowers teachers!"

- "Inquiry builds trust among staff . . . because we can't be on every cadre, but every cadre is important to us. . . . Just knowing that my colleagues are following the Inquiry Process makes me feel good about what they end up coming up with."

- "Inquiry allows us to look at problems from a variety of angles, then try to fix them. We don't wait until test scores come out at the end of the school year to work on these problems, because our kids don't have any time to waste."

4.3.1. Stage 1: Focus in on the Challenge Area

The priority areas that you've identified for cadre inquiry merit careful and thorough examination. The Inquiry Process sets out a path for moving beyond quick-fix solutions—attempts to solve long-term problems in one-day staff-development modules, for example, or with simple hearsay ideas. In the first stage of inquiry, your cadre works to gain a clearer understanding of your challenge area and why it exists in your school community.

Throughout stage 1, you'll be continually refining your understanding of your challenge area by exploring the underlying causes of the challenge.

This initial stage of the Inquiry Process is the most important one, because the way your cadre understands your challenge will direct the way you think and the way you organize the rest of your cadre work. Your exploration and hypotheses should be broad enough to guide careful thought, analysis, and action in the direction your vision has indicated. To ensure this, your cadre should do the following:

- First, explore the challenge area informally and hypothesize why it exists.

- After developing a full set of hypotheses, test them to see if they hold water.

- Having tested your hypotheses, interpret your results to gain a clearer understanding of your challenge area and learn how to focus your search for solutions.

These three substages of stage 1 of the Inquiry Process are described in detail below.

1a: Explore the Challenge Area Informally and Hypothesize Why It Exists. Exploration and hypothesizing are steps that we sometimes overlook when we attempt to solve problems. We often approach a given problem with a solution in hand rather than first seeking a clearer understanding of the problem by looking at it from a variety of angles. Gaining a more complete understanding of the complex nature of your challenge area is an important step in working your way toward lasting change.

Your cadre begins by setting out the initial dimensions of the challenge area. Let's say that your challenge area is reading. Your first task is to flesh out the challenge beyond the simple word *reading*. Your setting-priorities data should help with this, because members of your school community shared some of their concerns when setting up the priority area. Instead of just focusing on the broad term *reading*, you might focus on two facts: your school's reading scores are below district average, and students reported, in the taking-stock surveys, that they don't like reading. Once your cadre has set out these initial dimensions of the challenge area, you explore the reasons why your students are scoring below the district average in reading and why they don't like reading.

You should explore the challenge from as many angles as possible and develop a comprehensive list of hypotheses that describe potential underlying reasons why your challenge area exists. The initial underlying causes on your list of hypotheses can come from your own cadre, but the list won't be complete until you've explored the challenge area informally with people who *aren't* in your cadre as well. Developing your own hypotheses, obtaining those of others, and synthesizing them into a common list of hypotheses are interrelated activities as you proceed toward a clearer understanding of a challenge area.

Beware of Solutions Dressed in Hypotheses' Clothes

In our excitement to solve our school's problems, we're likely to jump to what are really solutions instead of continuing to ask hard questions and hypothesizing about why the problems exist. Here are some examples of hypotheses people have put forth during stage 1 of the Inquiry Process that are actually solutions stated in hypotheses form:

I think our students score below district average in reading because:

- We should teach reading heterogeneously.

- We need a better reading series.

- We should involve children more actively in reading.

These statements raise valid issues, but they're lead-ins to very specific solutions (heterogeneous grouping, a new series, and active learning, respectively)—moreover, solutions that may not effectively address your problem area. Therefore, these statements need to be broadened into good, objective hypotheses, as illustrated here:

I think our students score below district average in reading because:

- Of the way we organize our reading.

- Our reading series is outdated and doesn't interest the students.

- We don't involve students actively in reading or build on their strengths.

Although these are similar to the first set of hypotheses, they're less loaded with solutions (and therefore more testable).

As you develop hypotheses, think about *why* your challenge area exists. For example, "Why do our students score below district average in reading?" Then to explore the challenge area more fully, you can also ask questions along the dimensions of *what, how,* and *context* (introduced in Chapter Two and developed in Chapters Seven, Eight, and Nine). These questions should help spark hypotheses as to some of the underlying causes of your challenge area. Consider these examples:

What

- Think about the materials of instruction being used.
  What materials do you use? Is there coordination across grade levels? Are the materials developmentally appropriate and challenging?

- What experiences or expertise do staff members have in these areas?
  Are any teachers specifically trained or experienced in teaching reading?

- How is teacher training conducted?
  What type of ongoing staff-development program do you have? Is it effective or not? Why?

- Look at test scores in this area in terms of the material being tested for.
  Look into the different concepts tested for reading. Look at the item analyses.

- How are decisions made about what's taught?
  Are teachers allowed to choose content areas or are those areas mandated from elsewhere? Are students given a role in choosing what they read?

How

- Think about the way that you deal with the challenge individually.
  Do you teach reading the way you were taught to read? Is that the best way?

- How does instruction address different learning styles?
  Do most teachers use traditional "book-learning" techniques, or do they regularly use a variety of teaching styles? How are you and your colleagues teaching reading? How effective are these strategies? What does the research say about reading?

- Look at test scores in this area in terms of the instructional techniques.
  Look into the different skills tested for reading. Look at the item analyses.

- Look at the situation from the students' perspective.
  How did your best readers learn to read? What are some of the reasons students give for liking or not liking to read?

Context

- Consider the students' home environment.
  Do the parents know how or like to read? Do they take time to read with their children? Do students have a place where they can read comfortably?

- Think about how you presently organize particular programs.
  Is reading always after lunch? Are the kids too tired to be engaged? What type of grouping do you use? Is it effective?

- Does the classroom and school environment stimulate reading?
  Are there books in every classroom? Do staff members model reading? Are there comfortable places to read?

To illustrate the process of developing hypotheses, let's envision, as in the previous examples, a cadre formed to deal with a school's low scores in reading. The nine members of that cadre were sitting around a cafeteria table asking themselves why reading presented a problem for students. As they brainstormed about why their students had low reading scores, one teacher exclaimed, "It's clear that our students can't read because they can't speak English." The group facilitator suggested that her hypothesis be expressed as "Children have difficulty reading because English is their second language." Another teacher commented that she thought even newly immigrated students could learn to read if the reading materials were less boring. "The basal readers are the pits," she stated; "I think reading is a problem because the curriculum materials we use are boring and have no relation to the students' real lives." The two students in the cadre nodded in agreement. Building on the last hypotheses, an instructional aide said, "I think reading is a challenge for our students because we have insufficient Spanish reading materials and the educational market hasn't caught up to where we are with our population." Finally, the principal suggested that the problem might be the time of day that reading was taught. "Perhaps reading is a problem because we always teach it in the late afternoon, when many of the children are too tired." The facilitator then summarized the four hypotheses:

> *Hypothesis 1:* Reading is a challenge *because our students are not native English speakers and therefore have difficulty learning to read English.*

> *Hypothesis 2:* Reading is a challenge *because the curriculum materials used in the school are boring and have no relation to our children's real experiences.*

> *Hypothesis 3:* Reading is a challenge *because we have insufficient Spanish reading materials and the educational market hasn't caught up to the needs of the school's population.*

> *Hypothesis 4:* Reading is a challenge *because we always teach it in the late afternoon when many of the children are too tired.*

As you develop a list of hypotheses in your own cadre, you also need to explore the challenge area beyond your cadre. As we noted earlier, this requires that you familiarize yourselves with all the details, complexities, and ambiguities of the challenge area. It also requires that you put aside your own theories for a moment and try to see your challenge area from the point of view of others. How do different people experience or perceive the challenge? While your cadre will have lots of different perspectives represented, a clearer picture of your challenge area requires that the views of those not represented (teachers, parents, support staff, administrators, and students) are understood and accounted for.

Some in your cadre may feel impatient, believing that you have a representative set of hypotheses without looking beyond your group. Indeed, most of us have been conditioned to think only briefly about problems and then, without being overly reflective, to draw conclusions or seek answers. We're not quite comfortable looking at ambiguous, complex situations for a long time and taking in everyone's point of view. We prefer to attempt to create order by categorizing problems and people and constructing explanations or solutions. This thinking habit can be very effective when we're taking a standardized multiple-choice or fill-in-the-blanks test. Unfortunately, it can limit our long-term effectiveness when we're dealing with complex problems in the real world, for it often means that we overlook important facts or details.

In exploring your challenge area informally beyond your cadre, you don't have to do any heavy-duty surveys. You simply want to pursue information that isn't readily available inside the cadre. For example, the cadre concerned with the challenge area of reading might think about exploring the challenge informally by talking with others in the school community and looking through materials. Perhaps some of the data your school community collected during the taking-stock process might shed some light onto your challenge area as well.

- *Who might you talk with?* Teachers of reading? Other teachers in the school? Parents? Students? Administrators? Community members? Resource people? Librarians?

- *What questions might you ask?* When do you read? How do you teach reading? Do you like to read? Why? Where do you like to read? What are your interests? Is reading important? What are your favorite books?

- *What materials might you look at?* Reading books? Other classroom materials? The school library?

Let's return to the fictitious Reading Cadre of the earlier scenario. Cadre members explored their challenge area beyond their own membership by talking informally with other teachers, support staff, parents, students, administrators, and the district office about reading. Each member talked with five different people before the next meeting, and they shared the task of observing reading lessons at each grade level. They found that many parents didn't know the importance of reading with their children at home, that many of the best readers had parents who encouraged leisure reading at home, and that most of the teachers taught reading in the traditional way—with three groups using the basal readers. After this further exploration, they developed two more hypotheses:

> *Hypothesis 5:* Reading is a challenge *because many of our parents don't reinforce reading in the home.*

> *Hypothesis 6:* Reading is a challenge *because the instructional strategies we use to teach reading are too conventional and narrow.*

For simplicity's sake, we're putting forth only six hypotheses in this example. In reality, accelerated schools cadre members usually develop from ten to thirty (or more) hypotheses in an effort to push themselves through all the appropriate doors and thereby develop a true understanding of their challenge area. Your hypotheses will serve you better if they address schoolwide challenges and perhaps have relevance for other schools as well. Solving a single student's or teacher's challenge in reading is important, but the Inquiry Process is about finding ways to solve schoolwide concerns.

With that said, it's also important to note that at times a challenge area will be so broad and complex that a cadre may have to cycle through the Inquiry Process several times before the challenge can be understood in its entirety. The example provided at the end of this chapter is a case in point. The cadre members came up with twenty-five excellent hypotheses about why family involvement was a challenge in their school, but they couldn't get enough

In exploring your challenge area informally, keep it simple. At this stage, each cadre member could talk to a few people between cadre meetings to get their perspective of the challenge. Save your more intensive surveying and interviewing for the testing-hypotheses stage.

family members involved to test all of their hypotheses fully. In a case like that, a cadre may consciously decide to move on through the Inquiry Process, addressing those hypotheses that were confirmed and coming back to other hypotheses in the near future. The important thing is to not discount a hypothesis that hasn't been adequately tested. Solving the more complex and difficult challenges in a community will take time. But with each cycle of inquiry, both your challenges and the solutions become clearer.

1b: Test Hypotheses to See If They Hold Water. After developing a full set of hypotheses about your cadre's challenge area, you should test the hypotheses to see which ones hold water—that is, appear to be accurate explanations for why your challenge area exists. You shouldn't expect to discover any single correct explanation. Unfortunately, a school's challenges are never neat or simple; accordingly, looking into the explanations for the challenges is never neat or simple.

Your informal exploration of the problem in stage 1a may have helped to confirm or disprove some hypotheses already. Now, however, you need to do more formal hypothesis testing. In testing hypotheses, you should attempt to gather data in a *systematic* way to confirm or disprove your hypotheses.

Formal testing doesn't always bear out a cadre's informal conclusions. In fact, some cadres have been extremely surprised about which hypotheses hold water. And because each school community is unique, each school will have unique results when cadres test their hypotheses. For these reasons, it's important to try your best to test all of your hypotheses. The more you know about the real causes of your challenge area, the better off you'll be later on, when you attempt to create solutions.

The reason for testing all your hypotheses is that if you only concentrate on several of them, your eventual solutions will be correspondingly narrow (and might not even address your actual situation). Remember, in hypothesizing, you're making *educated guesses* about a situation. Though putting all of your eggs in one basket may seem like the most efficient way to solve your problems, it will most likely be the least effective. Clearly, working systematically through the Inquiry Process represents a different way of doing business in a school, but accelerated schools have gotten some impressive outcomes as a result.

Avoid the trap of simply going with your gut feeling and moving on to brainstorm solutions based on the cadre's single pet hypothesis.

The important point here is to be systematic about testing *all* of your hypotheses. Notice, for example, how different the likely solutions are for each of our Reading Cadre's different hypotheses:

If You Simply Concentrate on:	Perhaps You'll End Up with:
Hypothesis 1: The students aren't native English speakers and therefore have difficulty learning to read English.	An ESL program
Hypothesis 2: The curriculum materials used in the school are boring and have no relation to our children's real experiences.	More relevant curricula
Hypothesis 3: The school has insufficient Spanish reading materials and the educational market hasn't caught up to the needs of the school's population.	New Spanish reading materials
Hypothesis 4: Reading is taught in the late afternoon, when many of the children are too tired.	Reading instruction in the mornings
Hypothesis 5: Many of the parents don't reinforce reading in the home.	A parent outreach program
Hypothesis 6: The instructional strategies we use to teach reading are too conventional and narrow.	New methods of teaching reading

But If You:	You'll Get:
test all six hypotheses.	important information that can guide your cadre's inquiry into improving reading. You'll be able to make sense of the ambiguities and complexities of your challenge area and begin the process of tailoring your solution to your school community's unique situation.

The above hypotheses are all apparently good; they make sense and address the priority area of reading. But while setting out a decent hypothesis may lead you to a decent solution, it may fail to truly address the complexity of your problem. For example, if you concentrate only on finding a solution for the lack-of-parent-involvement hypothesis and later find out that the parents were actually more involved than you thought, you will have (1) put a lot of effort into something you didn't need to, (2) overlooked the real problem, and (3) possibly offended the parents who were involved by insinuating that they weren't. Alternatively, the inadequate-materials hypothesis may be only a part of a larger and more complex problem. If so, buying a new series—while not detrimental—won't truly address your concerns.

> **Because exploring a challenge area informally and testing hypotheses formally are overlapping activities, some cadres get to this stage and feel that they've already tested their hypotheses. In some cases, this feeling will be a true representation of reality. In other cases, more formal testing will be necessary to confirm or disprove hypotheses. One strategy that cadres in this situation can use is to list each hypothesis, how it was tested, and the findings from the testing/ exploration onto chart paper. Many schools have found this strategy useful in visually assessing where they really are in the process.**

Cadres can use a variety of research methods to test hypotheses. Your cadre should think about how you want to test each of your hypotheses and then split up responsibility for testing. Among the strategies that cadres in accelerated schools have used to test hypotheses are these:

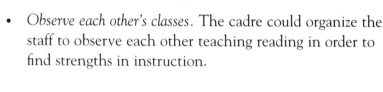

- *Observe each other's classes.* The cadre could organize the staff to observe each other teaching reading in order to find strengths in instruction.

- *Survey each other and/or other relevant groups.* The cadre could design a survey to measure parental involvement in their children's reading lessons at home, survey each other as to the instructional strategies used to teach reading, and survey publishers as to the availability of Spanish reading materials.

- *Interview each other and other relevant groups.* The cadre could conduct phone interviews with parents in their native language to see if and how they reinforce reading in the home, interview children about their likes and dislikes of reading instruction (and how they feel about the time of day reading is taught), and interview other staff members regarding reading.

- *Review test scores and achievement data.* The cadre should look beyond the summary scores to item analyses. Where do students score high? Do the scores change from year to year? From grade to grade? Where do they perform less well? How do the achievement levels of the various ethnic groups compare? How do these scores seem to relate to what's been taught? What do teachers think of student performance in reading? Are there other ways to assess performance?

- *Analyze curriculum materials.* The cadre could look critically at the reading materials used in the classrooms Do they meet the needs and interests of the student population? The cadre could also look into the availability of Spanish reading materials.

- *Discuss and meet.* Cadre members should regularly meet to discuss findings and build on each other's research.

Once you've tested your hypotheses through the methods above, you'll have a much clearer understanding of what your real challenge area is. You'll be ready to move beyond the thought that students have low reading scores, for example, to a much more focused understanding of the nature of the challenge at hand. Your new, honed challenge area will become a combination of the hypotheses that held water. Members of our fictitious Reading Cadre, for example, might have concluded (after all of their surveying and analysis) that the reading problem was due to a combination of several of the hypotheses to differing extents. Their explanations might have shown the following:

- *In relation to hypothesis 1:* Students who had recently immigrated did indeed have great difficulty reading. However, cadre research showed that these students had many verbal strengths in English that had been previously overlooked. The cadre decided to note these strengths and build them into their solution stage.

- *In relation to hypothesis 2:* While the basal readers were indeed boring and irrelevant to students' lives, the cadre learned that the district's

Wear bifocals when you test certain hypotheses.

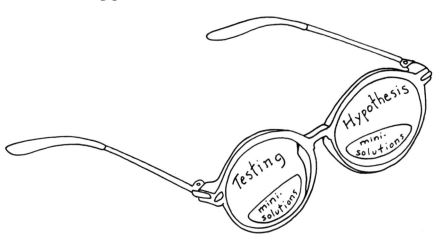

In testing your hypotheses, your cadre is looking to formally validate or disprove your compiled list of hypotheses. Many times the testing will take the form of surveys, interviews, and so on. Other times, the testing of a hypothesis will entail a mini-solution that you implement with an eye toward confirming or disproving a hypothesis. For example, if you're in a Family Involvement Cadre testing the hypothesis that many parents aren't involved with the school because they don't read or speak English (and all of the materials that the school sends home are in English), you could try translating a certain document that the school is sending home to see if the response from parents is better than usual—in other words, implement a one-time mini-solution to see if it makes a difference. We say that cadre members implementing such mini-solutions wear bifocals, because they split their perception: half goes toward the implementation of a solution and the other half goes toward analyzing the effect of that solution on their challenge area so that they can confirm or disprove a hypothesis. Once you've discovered whether or not the hypothesis holds water, you can proceed with the rest of the Inquiry Process and come up with a clear understanding of your challenge area so that you can search out the best long-term solutions. Take care not to get off track when you implement a mini-solution in the hypothesis-testing stage.

curriculum department had ordered a literature series that looked like a big improvement over the basals. The cadre would not be sure if the series would alleviate their curriculum worries until it actually arrived, but members felt encouraged by the brochures representing the series.

- *In relation to hypothesis 3:* While the school itself didn't have many books in Spanish, cadre members did find that educational publishers had made some impressive improvements in Spanish reading materials and that the district office had some of these materials on order.

- *In relation to hypothesis 4:* Not all teachers taught reading in the late afternoon. Moreover, the students in the classes where reading was taught in the late afternoon seemed to perform just as well as those who were taught in the morning. The student, teacher, and parent interview data on this topic eliminated this hypothesis.

- *In relation to hypothesis 5:* About one-third of the parents stated that they read with their children daily. The other two-thirds didn't read with their children but were interested in some training and information in this area.

- *In relation to hypothesis 6:* Teaching strategies in reading were fairly consistent and conventional, with some exciting exceptions. The consistencies were unsurprising: many teachers divided students into three groups by ability, used basal readers, and stuck close to the strategies in the teacher's manual. The exceptions were two teachers experimenting with teaching reading across subject areas through an interdisciplinary approach. The students in their classes were performing better than average.

1c: *Interpret the Results of Testing and Develop a Clear Understanding of the Challenge Area.* As we stated earlier, the explanations for your hypotheses won't necessarily fit into neat little compartments. You may uncover important information that significantly alters your understanding of your challenge area. For this reason, your cadre will need to reflect on the explanations and figure out how you want to organize your findings in preparation for looking for solutions. Which hypotheses turned out to hold water? Which hypotheses seemed promising but turned out to be inaccurate? Did your data suggest alternative hypotheses that you hadn't at first thought of? Of those hypotheses that turned out to be correct representations of your school's situation, how true were they? Were they representative in whole or only in part? Your cadre will need to take the results of your research and pull out what you believe to be the most important explanations for the challenge area. Remember, this first stage of the Inquiry Process is all about understanding your problem as completely as possible—getting a clear and detailed picture of your challenge area.

Keeping an Open Mind

Many important discoveries have come out of studies, experiments, and explorations that were originally intended to prove something completely different. Look closely at the data that refute your hypotheses and see if they might indicate something else that no one in your cadre had thought of. Your beliefs and hypotheses are ideas that will change, but your challenge area is very real, and it is what it is. Your hypotheses serve simply as guiding ideas for your exploration of what's real and why. At times the data may present a very clear picture of the situation that actually challenges the beliefs and assumptions of certain cadre members. Try to maintain an open mind. Remember, Christopher Columbus stubbornly held on to his belief that he'd found a new route to India until the day he died. And Alexander Graham Bell didn't originally set out to discover the telephone. *"When one door closes, another opens; but we often look so long and so regretfully upon the closed door that we do not see the one which has opened for us."*—Alexander Graham Bell

Once the cadre knows which hypotheses hold water, the members will have a much more accurate understanding of their challenge area. Low reading scores could involve thousands of "remedies," but by discovering *why* reading scores are low, our cadre members have brought the nature of their challenge area into clearer focus so that they can find the best solutions possible. Specifically, the cadre has discovered the following:

Our students score below district average in reading *because:*

- We use conventional strategies for teaching reading to students whose native language is not English. These strategies don't build on the verbal strengths of the children.

- Our materials aren't relevant to the children or compatible with the more interesting instructional strategies.

- Two-thirds of our students' parents are uninvolved in reading with their children.

This clear and focused understanding of the challenge area prepares the cadre for stage 2: brainstorm solutions. In searching for solutions, the cadre won't look at *everything* that has to do with reading: rather, they'll focus on the following:

- Finding better strategies for teaching reading to students whose native language isn't English—strategies that build on the verbal strengths of the children.

- Learning about better and more varied instructional strategies to use in tandem with the new literature series.

- Developing ways to involve the two-thirds of uninvolved parents in reading with their children.

Note that although the cadre has multiple areas to concentrate on, members have honed their initially broadly defined challenge area—children having lower-than-district-average reading scores—to one that's more focused.

We call the hypotheses that hold water the *focus areas*, meaning the areas toward which solution searching will be directed. (If only one hypothesis holds water, you'll have *a* focus area; if two or more hold water, you'll have focus areas on which to concentrate in searching for solutions.) There's almost always more than one hypothesis that holds water, however. Before you move on to developing solutions, make sure that your focus areas will lead your cadre in the direction of your school's vision.

Building a Knowledge Base

In addition to gaining a clear understanding of the challenge area, the Reading Cadre members have built up a real knowledge base on which they and other cadres can draw in the future. The cadre now knows the following:

- Which children have the most difficulty reading

- Which teaching strategies work and which don't

- That they need to expand their repertoire of strategies

- That there's a new (interdisciplinary) teaching strategy going on right in their school

- Which parents are uninvolved (and therefore whom to target)

- Which parents are involved (and therefore whose strengths they can build on)

- That they can test two promising new literature series already on order (one in English and one in Spanish) before looking for other materials

---

4.3.2. Stage 2: Brainstorm Solutions

After spending so much time discovering the underlying causes of your challenge area, you'll want to find the best solutions you can to address it. You'll get the "biggest bang for your buck" by finding the solutions that match your unique needs—a plan that fits your situation like a glove! For example, a whole language program used by your neighbor, who's a teacher across town, may sound interesting, but is it really the best option for your school? Does it address your particular students' needs? Is it really an effective program, or is it merely a well-publicized one? Have the students at your neighbor's school benefited from the program? In what ways? These kinds of questions should spring to mind whenever you hear about a prepackaged solution.

The two major steps in brainstorming solutions are to look inside the school for ideas and expertise and to look outside the school for programs, ideas, and expertise. These substeps are described more fully below.

2a: Look Inside the School for Ideas and Expertise. We suggest beginning your brainstorming stage by "looking inward." Ask yourselves what you could possibly do to address the focus areas determined at the end of stage 1 of inquiry. Perhaps your cadre should meet in a different environment, such as an area restaurant or someone's house, to help get your creative juices flowing. Remember, the most off-the-wall suggestions can spark really ingenious ideas from other cadre members.

In looking inward, you might begin by searching to see if anyone else in the school community is already doing things that could address your cadre's focus areas. You can begin this by simply talking with each other; perhaps you could have searching-for-solutions times at SAW meetings and in classes. Is anyone in your school presently using a particular instructional strategy that seems to be effective in addressing your cadre's needs? Are any other school staff doing things that address your focus areas? Do any of the parents have expertise in the focus areas? What do the students think would be a good idea? If one teacher, instructional aide, or parent is already doing something promising, can your cadre think of ways to expand his or her efforts schoolwide? Can you translate an individual's personal technique into a schoolwide organizational change? The accelerated schools process is an ambitious undertaking, but it doesn't mean you need to "throw the baby out with the bathwater." On the contrary, we suggest that you first look at your school's strengths in your challenge area and see if you can build on them.

2b: Look Outside the School for Programs, Ideas, and Expertise. Even if you find strengths that address your focus areas within the school community, it's useful to have several creative brainstorming sessions to look at resources outside the school as well. Remember, you're not trying to find a single answer. Rather, you're looking for good ideas that you can craft into a plan that's right for all the members of your school community.

After developing a list of possible outside resources through brainstorming, different cadre members need to follow up by researching the various resources. The type of follow-up you do will depend on the breadth of your group's brainstorming. When you explore these outside resources, you'll

undoubtedly come upon new potential solutions. For example, cadre members could

- Look through the educational literature.

- Invite speakers or consultants in to discuss potential programs.

- See if the district or state education office has any ideas or expertise in your focus areas.

- Call the appropriate community resources.

- Explore successful programs and alternative approaches in other schools.

- Talk with local community members.

In looking for solutions, keep the following advice in mind:

- *Build on your strengths.* The members of your school community will have many good ideas, from a strategy someone down the hall is using to the unique way one student dreams about learning. Your cadre's job is to find these ideas and tap into them for your plans.

- *Don't reinvent the wheel.* Educators all over the world are looking for better ways to do their jobs, and many have come upon good solutions. Look carefully at these ideas. You can visit other schools and other states, and you can look into the way other cultures organize their schools and learning environments. Even if you can't wander far afield, you can always go to a local university library and search through education books and periodicals. You'll find that your looking-outward efforts will snowball: one connection to one solution will probably lead to several new ideas. Just be sure to look through the lens of your cadre's focus areas.

- *Don't shy away from asking for assistance.* The school site is the place where change must occur. Yet if the school community members are the *only* ones working toward change, change will take longer to occur. District office administrators, state education agency staff, regional educational laboratories, universities, businesspeople, parents, and local social service agencies are all prime candidates for support. But you've got to ask for their help. A curriculum specialist from the district office could help a team of teachers design an interdisciplinary unit, for example, or researchers from a government laboratory could provide summer internships to science teachers to help them stay in close touch with real-world science problems. Those who ask, receive. If you never ask for it, you'll never get it.

- *Think big.* Think about solutions that will last. If your goal is to involve parents in their children's reading lessons and you send lots of notices home about a workshop, you may get a big turnout one night. But what about next month? Will they still be involved? And what about next year? Will the new parents get involved? Think in terms of making changes in the way your school does business; think in terms of solutions that will totally transform the way parents are involved in their children's education.

At the end of this stage, you'll have a number of viable solutions gathered and be ready to synthesize them.

4.3.3. Stage 3: Synthesize Solutions and Develop an Action Plan

In the previous stage, any idea that addressed your cadre's focus areas was worth follow-up and discussion. Now is the time to look critically at the resulting list of solutions. Just because your group likes a given solution doesn't mean you have to adopt it as you found it. You may want to mold it to fit your particular needs more precisely or combine ideas from different solutions. Think of yourselves as craftspeople interested in gaining ideas for alternative approaches.

3a: Synthesize Brainstormed Solutions. Your cadre should begin by sifting through all of your brainstormed solutions and seeing which ones best address your focus areas. You can use the following criteria to help evaluate and synthesize your solutions and decide which direction to go. For each proposed idea ask:

- *Will the implementation of this solution address our cadre's focus areas? Is this program going to meet the needs we determined in stage 1c? Will the solution address our clearly understood challenge area?*

- *Does this solution move us toward our vision?* If we implement this, *how* will it move us toward our vision?

- *What obstacles might arise if we try to implement this?* If district policy requires the school board to approve any changes in curriculum, how can we enlist board support?

- *Is everyone who's part of the challenge part of the solution?* Have we included the students, support staff, parents, district, and community in our brainstorming?

- *How might we modify this solution to fit the realities and interests of our students, their families, our classrooms, and our school?* This program is in English; can we have it translated into Spanish? We like the concept of the interdisciplinary units, but we prefer the topic of civil rights to health careers; can the district office help us adapt the unit, or should we design our own?

- *How might current school policies or classroom practices be refined, reorganized, or restructured to fit this proposal?* Do we simply need staff development, or do we need a totally new way of scheduling? Is extending the school day an option?

- *How might others (district representatives, school administrators, aides, parents, students, or university personnel) assist in designing and implementing this proposed program?* Ask for assistance!

- *What resources do we need to implement this program?* Do we need any training? Do we have the money to implement it now? If not, can we reorganize the budget for next year to accommodate the program or write a grant, have a fundraiser, or get money from the district?

- *Will the actions of the entire school community change, or just the actions of a few individuals? Will the change be sustained over the years?* The more thorough and broad the change, the more real and lasting it will be. Really *solving* this problem will allow you to move on to other concerns and further accelerate learning at your school.

Discussing the above criteria should help you see which ideas are most feasible and appropriate to your focus areas. While there may be barriers to

Hollibrook Elementary School in Houston has eliminated the words "We can't because . . ." from its vocabulary.

the implementation of your ideas, you will need to think of ways to overcome them whenever possible.

After working through these questions and communicating with your steering committee and the school as a whole, your cadre can begin weaving the best ideas into a proposed action plan.

3b: Develop an Action Plan. In developing your action plan, be sure to *delineate both the overall goals of the plan and the objectives supporting the goals.* Setting out goals and objectives is important for two reasons.

First, the vision that your school community created was not just a tool for setting priorities or the topic of a vision celebration day. It represents your dreams and your school's commonly agreed upon goals. How will you know when you reach your vision if you don't keep track of the benchmarks along the way? You should be able to relate the goals and objectives to each aspect of the school vision. For instance, if your vision includes statements such as, "We seek to create problem solvers; we seek to create students respectful of other cultures; we seek to create good citizens," think about how your plan's goals and objectives work toward improving problem solving, increasing respect of other cultures, and creating good citizens. Every action plan won't always relate to every single line of the vision, of course; however, every action plan should somehow address at least a *part* of the vision.

Second, once your plan obtains the approval of the school as a whole and you begin to pilot test the plan, your cadre will need to evaluate how well it works. But in order to evaluate whether a program works well, we need to see if the program *meets its stated goals and objectives.* Of course, setting out goals and objectives makes them easier to evaluate! It's all too easy to fall into the trap of moving into implementation without reflecting on what it is that you really want to implement. What we're talking about here is, of course, an assessment plan. It's best if you develop your questions for assessment before you actually implement the pilot program so that you can assess the plan during and after the pilot test. The questions should fall right out of your goals for the program.

Once you've decided on a direction to go, whether it be one single solution or a mix of solutions, you can begin developing the nuts and bolts of your action plan. Keep in mind the major components of the plan: *who* will do *what* by *when,* and *how?* Following is a chart that might help you organize and keep track of your plan. You can see that it includes an evaluation of the proposed pilot. The scale of your plan will depend on the needs of your school and the nature of solutions that become synthesized into the action plan. No matter what the scale of the plan, teachers, administrators, aides, parents, the district, the community, and students can all assist in implementing new programs.

TASK: *(List major title of task here.)*

Steps necessary for implementation:	By when:	By whom:
1. *(Break down the major task into individual steps—*		
2. *what needs to be done first, second, third, and so on.)*		
3.		
4.		
Etc.		
How will we monitor the program? *(This is for keeping track of program along the way.)*		
How will progress be evaluated? *(This is to see how successful the program was. Did it address your focus areas and goals?)*		

4.3.4. Stage 4: Pilot Test and/or Implement the Action Plan

After the steering committee and the school as a whole approve a cadre's proposed action plan, the steering committee and the cadre refine the plan, jointly set a clear timeline for completion, and allocate responsibility for implementing and assessing the program. Some pilot tests, such as assessing a new strategy for teaching reading in five classes over a three-month period, will be of a small scale. Other action plans, such as the establishment of a parent room on campus, will involve full-scale implementation.

Organization and clear outlining of responsibility are key. Specific people should be designated to coordinate the implementation and assessment of any pilot program. Although the next stage calls for a more formal evaluation, your cadre should begin to assess the program from its start and *record* the successes and challenges of the implementation process. Such records are essential. In the case of pilot testing, ongoing assessment of the pilot plan is important in determining whether to go to full implementation. As the cadre assesses a pilot test, members decide to fully implement it as it stands, modify it where necessary, or drop it and start over. In the case of full implementation, ongoing assessment is important in determining whether to continue with the implementation. It's critical that the cadre look thoroughly at the implemented program to see whether there are areas for improvement or refinement. Don't gloss over any difficulties; our mistakes sometimes provide the best opportunities to learn. If there were an easy "right" answer, we'd have solved all our challenges long ago!

4.3.5. Stage 5: Evaluate and Reassess

In this final critical stage of the inquiry cycle, cadre members pull together the assessment data gathered during the pilot test and/or implementation

Don't be discouraged if the results of your pilot test aren't perfect. This is all part of being innovative and entrepreneurial. Success involves taking risks—and even experiencing a few failures.

and evaluate the usefulness of the implemented action plan. Did it address the focus areas for which it was designed? Did it bring you closer to your vision? Did it meet the cadre's preestablished goals and objectives? Were the various components of the plan successfully implemented as planned?

Whether the action plan involved a pilot test or full implementation, evaluation and reflection are important. Based on the evaluation efforts, the cadre can decide to modify the pilot test, move to full implementation of the pilot efforts, continue full implementation efforts (depending on the nature of the plan), or disband the project.

Cadre members can use qualitative and quantitative evaluation tools to assess the strengths and weaknesses of the pilot projects. *Qualitative* assessments will seek out the opinions of all those affected by the project. How did parents, students, teachers, principals, and others feel about the project? What did they like about it? What did they dislike? Did they find it useful, interesting, or a nuisance? Why? How could the program be improved?

Quantitative evaluation efforts may look at changes in achievement, attendance, and so on. For example, if your cadre implemented an innovative reading program, did student reading improve? Did reading scores go up? Has writing improved? Did students begin to read more books on their own? How did improvements in language relate to achievement in mathematics? Did student attendance improve? Have teachers truly adopted more interesting and exciting methods of teaching?

If the pilot worked, the school community may decide to move to full implementation of the plan. If it worked but had some kinks, the school community can try to work out why the problems occurred and modify the pilot test accordingly before fully implementing it. *If the plan involved full implementation of a project and successfully addressed the focus areas*, it can operate with just routine assessment, and cadre members can start talking with the rest of the school community about other priorities they want to address.

If the plan did not address the focus areas or meet the stated goals and objectives, the cadre should try to figure out why. Don't be discouraged if the results aren't perfect. This is all part of being innovative and entrepreneurial. Success involves taking risks—and even experiencing a few failures. Cadre members should look back to their other solutions and look outward for some additional ones that will better match the school's needs. Most important, they can use failure as an opportunity to learn more about the nature of their challenge and the process of inquiry itself.

4.4. Inquiry Process Reflection Questions

As you go through the complex Inquiry Process, the following questions may help keep you on course.

Stage 1: Focus in on the Challenge Area

1a: Explore the challenge area informally and hypothesize why it exists. What was the cadre's initial understanding of its challenge area? How did the cadre explore its challenge area informally? How did cadre members make use of the taking-stock data? How did they explore the challenge area outside of the cadre? With whom did they talk? What questions did they ask? Did they invest adequately in understanding the challenge area and hypothesizing why it exists? What were the cadre's hypotheses? Were there at least fifteen hypotheses? Did the cadre report its research to the steering committee and the SAW and obtain their input?

1b: Test hypotheses to see if they hold water. How did the cadre look for evidence to see which hypotheses held water? Did cadre members adequately test each hypothesis? How did they test each? With whom did they talk? What did they do (surveys, interviews, and so on)? Which hypotheses held water? Were the hypotheses that held water relevant to the cadre's initial understanding of the challenge area? Did the cadre report its research to the steering committee and the SAW and obtain their input?

1c: Interpret the results of testing and develop a clear understanding of the challenge area. How did cadre members interpret their findings? Did they look at all the evidence gathered? How did they communicate with the steering committee and the SAW about their findings? What is their clearest understanding of the challenge area—the focus areas for which they plan to brainstorm solutions? Did the cadre's final understanding of the challenge area affirm or redefine their initial understanding of the challenge?

Stage 2: Brainstorm Solutions

How did cadre members search for solutions to address the focus areas—that is, the hypotheses that they found to hold water? Were all members of the school community included in compiling ideas? Did cadre members incorporate any solutions that surfaced in stage 1? Did they look both inside and outside the school for potential solutions? How did they obtain input from the school community? How did they look outside the school for possible solutions? How did they communicate their brainstormed ideas to the entire school community, including students and parents?

Stage 3: Synthesize Solutions and Develop an Action Plan

How did cadre members synthesize their brainstormed solutions before pilot testing? Did they ask themselves what the consequences of implementing each solution should be? Did they ensure that the *consequences* of the various solutions would address their final understanding of their challenge area (focus areas) and lead toward the vision? If the recommended plan is implemented, will the actions of the entire school change, or just the actions of a single teacher? Will the plan lead to the vision? Will the resulting change be sustained over the years? Were the three major dimensions—*what* (curriculum), *how* (instructional strategies), and *context* (school organization)—considered during this stage? Is the plan feasible? What obstacles might arise if the plan is implemented? What resources will be needed to implement it? Did the cadre modify the solutions to fit the realities of the students, classrooms, and school? Did the cadre attempt to refine, reorganize, or restructure current school policies or classroom prac-tices to fit its proposal? Does the plan actively involve all members of the school community? Are all people who are part of the challenge (teachers, support staff, parents, students, the district office, school administrators, and the community) part of the action plan as well? Did the cadre obtain the approval of the steering committee and the SAW? What goals and objec-tives were set out for the action plan? Did the cadre carefully plan imple-mentation and assessment strategies before pilot testing the action plan? Are all the elements of the pilot plan present (*who* will do *what* by *when*, and *how*, as well as details about how the plan will be evaluated)?

Stage 4: Pilot Test and/or Implement the Action Plan

How was the action plan approved? Were the steering committee and the SAW appropriately involved? If the cadre proposed a pilot action plan, did the school pilot test the plan thoroughly before recommending schoolwide implementation? If the cadre proposed a full implementation plan, how was it implemented? How was it determined to go with a pilot test? full imple-mentation? Did the action plan specify who was responsible for doing what, and by when? Were all members of the school community (teachers, support staff, administrators, parents, students) involved in implementation? In pilot testing and/or implementing the action plan, did the cadre, the principal, the steering committee, the SAW, and central office personnel work together productively? Was a time set for evaluating the pilot plan? If that time has come, has the cadre taken steps to evaluate the action plan? Who was involved in its evaluation? Did all the people involved in the plan participate in its evaluation? What were the actual evaluation plans? What checkpoints were built into the implementation process to assess progress toward the intended goal? Did the cadre routinely report its progress to the steering committee and the SAW and obtain their continued input?

Stage 5: Evaluate and Reassess

Is the cadre formally and informally evaluating the success of its action plan? How? Did the activities proposed in the action plan and then implemented directly address the problem as finally defined in stage 1? Did the action plan help move the school toward its vision? How did the action plan build on the strengths of all members of the school community? Were all members of the school community involved in implementation? Did everyone take responsiblity for his or her role? How were the areas of curriculum, instructional strategies, and school organization addressed? Did the cadre report its research to the steering committee and the SAW and obtain their input?

4.5. Case Study: A Middle School's Family Involvement Cadre

We've described the Inquiry Process in prose. Now let's look at a real-life example of the Inquiry Process in action as a middle school addresses its concerns about family involvement. We've included case studies of other cadres' work in other chapters of this *Resource Guide*. In Chapter Seven, for example, you'll find an elementary school's inquiry into the area of problem solving in the curriculum. In Chapter Eight, you'll find an example of a middle school's Instruction Cadre's Inquiry Process. In Chapter Ten, you'll find two examples—one illustrating how an elementary school approached its challenge area of family involvement and another dealing with an elementary school and community involvement. As you read these cases, you'll notice that there's no "textbook" or "model" case of inquiry. The process may seem slow at times, and fraught with obstacles, but the more you utilize it, the better you'll become at it and the more lasting will be your school's changes.

Stage 1: Focus in on the Challenge Area

1a: Explore the Challenge Area Informally and Hypothesize Why It Exists. The cadre began in February 1990 as the Parent and Community Cadre, but by the end of the first meeting, the staff, parent, and student members decided to focus on parental support of students (a role sometimes played by aunts, uncles, grandparents, and so on) and therefore changed their name to the Family Involvement Cadre. The cadre set out the initial dimensions of its challenge area  from the information generated during setting priorities. Parents weren't involved in school, as evidenced by their low turnout at parent events and the low response rates to notes sent home from school and on the taking-stock parent survey. Cadre members tried to define what ideal family involvement would mean to them and to the rest of their community. Over the course of a few meetings, they agreed that their goal for family involvement would be *positive and active support for students both at school and in the home*. During the meetings that the cadre spent defining *family involvement*, the cadre also engaged in an exploration of the challenge area and hypothesized about its underlying causes. Teacher, parent, student, support staff, and administrative cadre members each offered a unique perspective on why they thought family involvement was a challenge for their school. The student members spoke honestly about their feelings about having their parents more involved in their education. These feelings varied from pride to embarrassment.

In order to gain the fullest perspective possible, the cadre also explored the problem with people not on the cadre. Between cadre meetings, each member informally asked at least five parents, teachers, support staff, administrators, and/or students to discuss the issues surrounding family involvement. One parent on the cadre contacted fifteen Spanish-speaking parents by phone to explore the problem. The more the cadre members talked to parents, the broader their perspective became. This informal exploration helped the cadre develop representative hypotheses. In fact, one hypothesis—that parents feel like second-class citizens at school—originated in this informal exploration outside the cadre. (*As you can see, problem exploration, problem definition, and hypothesis generation are interrelated.*)

During stage 1 of inquiry, cadre members developed a list of twenty-five hypotheses that they wanted to test:

- Some parents have negative feelings toward the district because their children were denied access to their first choice schools based on their race once predetermined quotas were filled.

- Working hours of parents often conflict with school activities.

- Family problems, such as parents in jail or abusive behavior, preoccupy some families.

- Some children live in foster homes.

- Many parents don't trust the school or the teachers.

- Some parents don't speak English and are afraid to try to communicate.

- Parents who didn't receive much formal education may look on the school as a "holy" place. If they feel embarrassed and out of place, they may be afraid to come through the doors.

- Most parents don't feel equal at the school; they feel that they're not as important to their child's education as the teacher is.

- The feeling of a close, tight-knit community is lacking, perhaps due to desegration efforts and busing.

- Most school communication with parents is negative.

- Parents may be "burned out" by the time their children reach middle school. In elementary school, they deal with only one teacher, whereas in middle school, they must deal with several.

- Parents are rarely invited to school, and they don't feel welcome.

- Some students don't want their parents to be involved.

- Parents often don't like the way their own children treat them at school.

- Students often don't like the way their parents treat them at school.

- Many families are run by a single parent.

- Many kids don't have fathers at home.

- Parents and students may fear retribution or revenge: they may be afraid that if parents complain, the teachers or the school will take it out on them.

- There's a lack of understanding among parents that they can be involved at home by providing adequate time and space for a child to do homework (and so on).

- Parents generally don't have anything substantial to do when they come to school; they don't know what to do.

- Many parents don't know how to deal with adolescents, and they need help.

- Teachers are often reticent to talk to parents, perhaps because of a bad experience or lack of success when contacting parents.

- Parents are sometimes treated unprofessionally at schools. Appointments aren't kept or are riddled with interruptions.

- Perhaps the school's expectations of communication are unrealistic.

- Some parents refuse to come to school and give no reason; they won't even discuss it.

1b: Test Hypotheses to See If They Hold Water. Within a few weeks, cadre members were ready to more formally test their hypotheses. They were eager to gain a more accurate understanding of which of the twenty-five hypotheses helped to explain why families in their community are not more actively involved in their children's education both at school and in the home. After some random attempts at testing such a wide array of hypotheses, cadre members decided to group them according to the following categories: negative parental attitudes toward school, student attitudes, restrictions on parent involvement, and problems residing in the school. In order to test these sets of hypotheses, they decided to gather a representative group of diverse parents for a discussion; such a discussion, they felt, could give them a sense of which hypotheses were accurate explanations of their challenge area. Then they could search for appropriate solutions.

The cadre decided to use the school's upcoming evening open house to solicit names of parents who would be interested in attending a focus-group dessert meeting to discuss issues surrounding the challenge of family involvement. Since the open house was an already scheduled event, the cadre asked the steering committee for permission to help host it.

In cohosting the event, cadre members wanted to accomplish three things. First, they wanted to introduce themselves, as it were, before soliciting volunteers for a focus group of parents. To obtain volunteers, the cadre distributed a three-item survey to parents as they arrived at the open house. The names of parents who turned in the survey were entered for a door prize. The survey said this:

I would like to help reach our vision at our school.

☐ I want to help our school understand the area of family involvement.

☐ I want to serve on a committee with teachers and students to help achieve the vision.

☐ I want to be involved, but I don't know how.

The second reason cadre members wanted to help host the event was so that they could do something good and concrete with families while they were still working to understand their larger underlying challenges. Toward this end, they decorated the cafeteria with felt banners from countries around the world, placed colorful placards with excerpts from the school vision on each of the tables, incorporated student and parent speeches in many languages about accelerated schools as part of the program, offered name-tags, and took family portraits in the library.

Third, the cadre wanted to ensure that the parents (and especially the parents of incoming sixth graders) understood what the Accelerated Schools Project was all about.

Here we see cadre members taking responsibility for improving things while gaining important insights into their long-term challenge area (remember the discussions of little wheels and bifocals!). They had enough of a sense of their challenge area to know that they didn't have to wait until the end of the Inquiry Process to make small changes, such as speaking to parents in their native languages, decorating the cafeteria with poignant quotes from the vision, and taking family portraits of the many members of their school community who didn't own cameras!

The cadre followed up immediately on the 100 parent survey responses with a letter (translated as necessary) inviting them to a focus-group dessert meeting. Follow-up phone calls were planned, but time was short and few were made, unfortunately. The cadre meeting before the focus-group meeting was devoted primarily to determining how to structure the focus-group meeting and dividing up roles and responsibilities. The primary goal of the evening meeting was to test cadre hypotheses by involving parents in small-group discussions about factors that impede family involvement, but cadre members also wanted to take the opportunity to bring parents into the entire accelerated schools process.

Out of the 100 parents who returned surveys, only ten attended the meeting—a fact that did not erode the enthusiasm of the cadre members and administrators present. The student cadre members greeted the parents individually and showed them to the dessert table. Various cadre members then took turns describing the accelerated schools philosophy and process, sharing a slide show from the vision celebration, and discussing the various opportunities for participation on cadres.

The majority of the evening, however, was spent in small-group discussion centered around understanding the obstacles to supporting students both in the school and at home and generating ideas about how to overcome those obstacles. At the end of the meeting, the small groups reported back to the group at large. In addition to learning more about which hypotheses held water, cadre members also learned about some possible solutions that they could eventually pursue. Several parents volunteered to start a family room and serve as "hooks" for involving other parents, for example. This idea caught on, and all ten parents began excitedly sketching out how they'd like the family room to work and when they could use it.

Although the cadre had hoped for a bigger turnout, members felt that the meeting was a success: they had identified a diverse core of committed parents who represented all ethnic groups at the school and who were anxious to help bring in their peers. Because the turnout was lower than expected, the cadre also conducted phone interviews with parents to further test their hypotheses.

Because of low parental involvement in the formal hypothesis-testing process, the cadre could not conclude that some of the unconfirmed hypotheses were necessarily false. After all, the parents who didn't trust the school or feel comfortable answering questions probably weren't the ones who attended the open house or responded to questions over the phone. In order to understand why these parents weren't participating, the cadre would perhaps have to return to stage 1 of the Inquiry Process in the future. At the same time, however, this initial connection with interested parents could lead to increased involvement from which the cadre could expand and build outward.

1c: Interpret the Results of Testing and Develop a Clear Understanding of the Challenge Area. After the focus-group meeting, cadre members divided the ideas and suggestions into these categories: communication, public relations, obstacles to participation, and need for specific information. The cadre compared the ideas and suggestions of the parents to the hypotheses generated by the cadre and were pleased that these parents appeared to confirm some of their hypotheses. This would guide the cadre in searching for solutions. As they approached the end of the 1990–91 school year, the Family Involvement Cadre had clear focus areas on which to concentrate in the coming school year.

In the fall of 1991, one of the first things that members of the cadre did was to revisit the May focus-group meeting and study the findings so that they could reestablish which hypotheses held water and begin brainstorming solutions to address their focus areas. Out of the original list of twenty-five hypotheses, the following three hypotheses were confirmed by the parents: parents don't always know where to take their concerns; communication is scarce and many times negative; some parents are reluctant to criticize the school when they feel that something is wrong or needs improving (and related to that, some parents feel like second-class citizens when they come to school).

This last confirmed hypothesis is especially noteworthy in that it forced the school community to take responsibility for the problem. This taking of responsibility is relatively unique. Accelerated schools that haven't included parents on their cadres have tended to focus their hypotheses on the shortcomings and lack of responsibility of parents. Having parents on the cadre is crucial in helping cadre members come up with a more well-rounded set of hypotheses.

Stage 2: Brainstorm Solutions

Focusing on these confirmed hypotheses, the cadre worked on generating ways to better communicate with parents and make them feel more welcome. In their search, they looked both inside and outside the school. The cadre had been saving a list of solutions that they'd come up with during stage 1 of the Inquiry Process, including ideas from other schools and the research literature and successful strategies that were being used at their own school—strategies that had to do with making parents feel welcome and building on strengths of the students, staff, and parents. Cadre members also returned to the ideas suggested by the parents at the focus-group dessert meeting.

Stage 3: Synthesize Solutions and Develop an Action Plan

3a: Synthesize Brainstormed Solutions. After considering their focus areas and all of the ideas and information gathered the previous spring and early in the fall, the group decided to move forward on plans for a family room and a family newsletter. Based on the confirmed hypothesis that parents often feel "out of place" and like "second-class citizens" when they visit the school, the family room was conceived as a comfortable space in which parents could relax, consult with other parents or teachers, see their children's work displayed, find out about volunteer opportunities within the school, use the telephone, read, work on a project, or do just about anything. Cadre members were anxious to call the excited parents who had promised to help create and run the family room the previous spring.

The second solution that emerged from their search was to reach out to parents and families through the establishment of a weekly family newsletter—one that would go home with students and that would give lots of positive information in different languages to parents on a regular basis.

3b: Develop an Action Plan. Planning for the family room was the primary activity of the cadre throughout the fall of 1991. The group's first task was to present the idea to the steering committee and to request the use of one of the spare rooms in the school. The steering committee was in favor of the proposal but couldn't automatically give a room to the cadre because many other groups—for example, the humanities department—were also in need of more space. It was decided that the school as a whole should make the decision, and at their next meeting, the SAW did approve turning a spare classroom in a prime location into the family room.

This unanimous SAW approval illustrates a growing unity of purpose in the school: many groups gave up their requests to use the room because they felt that establishing the family room would help them move toward their shared vision.

The cadre turned then to planning the details of setting up the room, stocking it with various supplies and refreshments, staffing it, and getting the word out to parents in the community that it was available. From the earliest discussion of these issues, cadre members felt that they must include parents in these decisions. Cadre members realized that they needed to recruit new parent collaborators who could contribute their ideas about the purpose of the family room before they could tackle painting walls and decorating the room. Consequently, a subcommittee of two teachers and one support staff member was formed to hold a meeting with parents and solicit their input. Unfortunately, the cadre had still not come up with an effective means of contacting parents: letters were sent home about the meeting, but only one parent showed up. In late October, however, the group decided to set a deadline for setting up the room to coincide with the school's holiday dance on December 13; they also decided to set up the room with or without parent input (but to continue to solicit this input and to be receptive to parent ideas at all times). Various subcommittees were formed: the opening-night committee, the room-setup committee, the painting committee, and so on.

Because so much time had elapsed between May 1991, when the ten parents conceived of the family room, and November 1991, when the family room began to be a reality, the cadre had trouble regaining the momentum from the parents who had volunteered to help. Summer vacation was an interrupting factor that they couldn't control, but it definitely contributed to a loss of momentum by those parents who felt ownership of the idea of a family room.

The process of planning and setup was handled efficiently and cheerfully by all cadre members (and even a few people from other cadres):

- Some members came in on a Saturday to paint the room and stayed after school hours to do the second coat.

- One cadre member telephoned General Electric, the school's corporate sponsor, and got the company to donate a great deal of furniture.

- The group decided to create a flier describing the room and stating its hours, but at first no one would volunteer to write it up. Finally an aide in one of the special education classrooms said that she'd take a crack at it, although she initially felt insecure about her ability to write clearly. Two other cadre members volunteered to help her, and all three stayed after school one day to draft the flier.

- Cadre members felt strongly that there should be a school representative in the room at all times and arranged for it to occur.

- An aide made a logbook to keep track of visitors.

They were ready for opening night! Despite their disappointment at low parent involvement thus far—which they hoped to counter by talking with parents informally when they visited—they were excited.

The cadre was "between a rock and a hard place." Cadre members desperately needed parent participation to flesh out the purpose and plans for the family room, and they were frustrated at their inability to recruit parents' input. However, the entire cadre was formed to address the challenge of family involvement! But what sometimes occurs is a ripple effect: a few parents' involvement leads to the involvement of others. The cadre shouldn't abandon hope!

The second action plan that the cadre developed during the fall of 1991 outlined the creation of a weekly family newsletter. In an effort to address its focus areas, the cadre planned that the newsletter would contain positive information about upcoming events at the school, recognition of students and parents for outstanding achievements, calls for volunteers in teachers' classrooms or on special projects, advertising for the family room, highlights of steering committee minutes, and other information that would be useful and interesting for parents. The cadre was very sensitive to the diversity present in the student body and made a commitment to have the newsletter translated into several languages each week; students could help with this task. While cadre members were very excited about this idea, they were aware that other teachers might think of a newsletter as more work for them and thus not support the concept. When the cadre brought the idea before the school as a whole, they were surprised at the enthusiasm with which the proposal was accepted. Teachers, other staff, and students were eager to communicate more with parents, and the newsletter was seen as a handy vehicle for that communication. The cadre divided up responsibility for producing the newsletter: one cadre member would serve as the editor, another would handle the layout and production, and the balance would serve as reporters and help out in other ways as needed.

Stage 4: Pilot Test and/or Implement the Action Plan

Family Room: Implementation. The family room looked wonderfully inviting on its opening night. Candles and colored lights led the way to the room, and the smell of fresh coffee and homemade cookies lured people in. One corner of the room held a couch, an end table, and a chair and formed a semi-separate sitting area, while the adjacent corner housed a desk, filing and storage cabinets, and a telephone. The middle of the room was dominated by a new table (donated by GE) that was covered with snacks and goodies, and by the door was a long table piled high with accelerated schools information and the new welcoming fliers. Each parent was asked to sign the room's guestbook, which one of the aides had made by hand. Soft music from a teacher's tape player filled the room.

Despite wonderful preparations, only a handful of parents visited the family room for the grand opening. Much to the cadre's disappointment *none* of the parents had received invitations! Cadre members found out later that there had been a problem with the mail. Cadre members realized that they needed to plan for sufficient lead time to allow for problems beyond their control. Those parents who did come, however (having heard of the opening through their children), were extremely pleased with the room and stayed for more than an hour, on average, chatting with the various cadre members and sharing their views.

After opening night, the cadre began assessing how it could make better use of the parent room. Much of the evaluation was formative in nature and fed directly back into implementation. Subsequent cadre meetings focused on how to spread the word about the family room and draw more parents. Cadre members held meetings with groups of parents to further understand the nature of their challenge and the reasons behind the family room's initial low turnout. They found that parents are very rational: they don't want to leave their homes or work to sit in a relatively bare room. They requested that the room be plastered with information—notices of volunteer activities, minutes from the cadres, the steering committee, and the SAW, and student work. In short, they wanted action! Staff on other cadres reached out to help as well. The Culture Cadre, for example, scheduled a meeting for parents on gang awareness in the family room, and one P.E. teacher suggested opening the room during the two nights a week that basketball games are held at the school (an idea that was met with strong approval). Cadre members are aware that the grand opening of the family room on December 13 was just the beginning of the process of involving more parents in the school. They're committed to understanding their challenge through the process of inquiry and to constantly reassessing their progress.

Family Newsletter: Pilot Test. The family newsletter was designed as a pilot test to run for the last few months of the 1991–92 school year. These initial issues ran smoothly and received wonderful reviews. Many of the staff eagerly contributed descriptions of creative classroom learning experiences, the principal included a note in each issue, student writing was highlighted, students were recognized for positive things, upcoming events were advertised, and parents were notified of important upcoming meetings and school community decisions.

The pilot newsletters succeeded at getting more parents involved at school, both on the cadres and on the steering committee. The newsletter also seemed to serve a bonus role of highlighting the wonderful accelerated instruction occurring in the school.

Stage 5: Evaluate and Reassess

Family Room. Because of the many challenges cadre members faced in implementing the family room, they still feel that it's too early to conduct a formal evaluation. In the meantime, they're using the Inquiry Process to formulate strategies to recruit as many parents as possible—not only to use the parent room but also to help the cadre assess the purpose of the room and revise its plans accordingly.

Family Newsletter. The cadre decided to go from the initial pilot test to full-scale implementation of the parent newsletter in 1992–93. This decision was based on informal comments about the publication from staff and on a parent survey on readership and interest that was both sent home and conducted at an open house. The cadre planned to mail the first issue to every student's home address so that all parents would be sure to receive it and be informed at the start of the school year that the family newsletter would come home every Thursday.

Here we see inquiry as a cyclic and interactive process rather than a linear one. Continual hypothesizing and retesting are balanced with taking action and reflecting on it. Sometimes the very nature of a given challenge prevents cadre members from understanding it completely at first. In the case described here, for example, the challenge of family involvement may bring out very different issues for different people. Thus the challenge as it relates to certain families may be understood before other aspects of the challenge. As the families who are first reached become involved, they provide an expanded base from which the cadre can move outward. The process of solving complex problems takes time. That's why top-down solutions don't work. Instead, communities must engage in careful inquiry and solve their problems for themselves.

4.6. Solving Other Problems— In Groups and on Our Own

In this chapter, we've described a systematic process for addressing your school's challenges. Although our discussion has been limited to how cadres use the Inquiry Process, that tool isn't reserved for cadres. In an accelerated school, the Inquiry Process soon becomes a habit: grade-level meetings, department meetings, office meetings, student council meetings, and parent conferences all make use of it. Once accelerated school communities realize the power of systematic problem solving and decision making, they begin to use it in all of their groups.

Individual teachers also use the Inquiry Process in making decisions about what to do in certain classroom situations. In addition they model the process to their students and introduce it in their teaching (see Chapters Seven through Nine—particularly Chapter Seven, "The *What* of Powerful Learning").

Even though collaborative inquiry takes time, many accelerated schools have found that it helps them with the sudden crises that crop up from time to time. Let's take budget cuts, for example. They're important challenges, but they aren't necessarily problems of the sort for which you'd create long-term cadres. If issues or crises involve the entire school community (as budget cuts do), then it's appropriate for everyone in the community to be involved in addressing them. The staff can work on these problems in small groups, using the same systematic, methodical approach used on bigger challenges—in other words, following the basic steps of the Inquiry Process. The following is an example of how Burnett Academy used inquiry and newly formed governance structures to deal with districtwide budget cuts:

> **At the end of its first year as an accelerated middle school, Burnett Academy was told by the school district that its budget was being cut considerably, it would be losing a number of teachers and support staff, and its student population was projected to increase. Initially, the school was devastated. Then the steering committee decided to bring the problem to a school-as-a-whole meeting. The committee presented the facts and then asked each cadre to discuss the problem,**

using an abbreviated form of the Inquiry Process to see what solutions they could generate.

The discussions at the cadre level ran from angry to sad at the beginning. But once people started defining their challenge and brainstorming solutions, the tenor changed. As each group reported back to the school as a whole, excitement mounted. Several workable suggestions were finalized, and a plan of action was developed. Staff took leadership positions in the district and in the state, defending their work as an accelerated school.

One of the things that the school community did, through the Family Cadre, was to attempt to save the school's staff and resources by participating at a district board of education meeting. When the meeting began at 6:00 P.M., Burnett staff and students filled two whole rows of seats. As the meeting went on, the students gained the confidence to let the board know how they felt by speaking out publicly. They moved into the corridor to work in groups to jointly write and edit speeches to the board proclaiming what they felt about their accelerated schools experience, their music program, and their sports program. At 10:45 P.M., they were finally recognized and allowed to speak. Their speeches were eloquent, well delivered, and well organized. Although tired, the board members perked up quite a bit when these students from the "bottom-of-the-barrel" middle school delivered a stunning trilogy of speeches.

Although budget cuts were still implemented, the district had a clearer understanding of Burnett's needs, and the school community felt a greater sense of unity in facing some of these changes. As a result of Burnett's willingness to speak out and challenge the district on its plans, the school was the talk of the town.

Burnett Academy, San Jose, California

The Inquiry Process may sound much harder than the quick-fix process of seeing a problem and coming up with a quick solution. But using a critical, inclusive process gives you a solid basis for your actions and gives everyone involved a clear understanding of why a course of action is chosen. If all problems are approached in this manner, eventually you'll find a school in which all decisions seem to stem from each other and all parts seem to work as a harmonious whole.

Refer to the Appendix for an Inquiry Process note-keeping device—it will help you at your cadre meetings.

Inquiry Tips

- Inquiry isn't an add-on—something that you think about only when your cadre meets. Rather, it provides a framework for all change. Inquiry is a new habit to learn.

- Inquiry moves slowly. It takes a while to get to solutions, but the solutions that result will make sense and the changes that they engender will last.

- Make sure to bring new staff members up to speed on the process, or they'll feel lost and end up getting the cadre off track. Plan a new-staff orientation to the Inquiry Process and delegate specific roles to new cadre members.

- Inquiry can be frustrating during the nonconcrete stages. Have patience and trust; relax and enjoy the reflection and sharing. "Doing" is much more productive when it's preceded by careful thinking!

CHAPTER 5

Group Dynamics and Meeting Management

Turning an ordinary school into an accelerated school isn't an easy task. It requires that large numbers of individuals begin to work together collaboratively, support one another, and think creatively. It's through this process that ordinary institutions are transformed into caring and supportive educational communities where *all* children's learning can be accelerated.

This transformative journey is a long and challenging one. Along the way, numerous problems and obstacles may arise—issues that an emerging community will have to explore and deal with in order to progress and develop. In this chapter, we'll examine a few of the more common group dynamics issues that accelerating schools often encounter. Although we can't offer any simple solutions, we'll suggest some ways that you might approach them. We'll also discuss successful meeting management approaches, formal group roles, decision-making structures, and procedures with which you can address these issues before they even arise.

5.1. Interpersonal Relationships

5.1.1. Focusing on the Values, Strengths, and Qualities of *All* Individuals

Successful collaborative activity in an accelerated school requires that we bring out the best in ourselves and each other. As we begin to internalize the three basic accelerated principles (unity of purpose, empowerment coupled with responsibility, and building on strengths), certain core human values— values such as trust, respect, caring and equity—start to shape the way that we think about and act toward each other. These values can create a supportive social environment in which the unique strengths and qualities of each individual are valued and recognized and in which people feel safe enough to trust each other, take risks, and be open.

The process of translating principles and values into beliefs and actions, though difficult at times, is essential. For it's the transformation of thinking and action that helps to make children's accelerated learning possible. Because these values can come alive only when we allow them to guide our everyday person-to-person interactions, it becomes the responsibility of each individual to prioritize and implement them. Not everyone will be able to do this immediately or easily. Individuals and schools have unique situations and histories. Feelings of mistrust, disrespect, and inequity are often based on *real* situations existing in the present or *specific* experiences that happened in the past. Thus, developing an enthusiastic, trusting, and caring community environment takes time.

Fortunately, in the changing culture of an accelerating school, positive, self-initiated changes in thinking and action by a few *can* effect the gradual transformation of the entire community. This is where the principle of building on strengths becomes key. As individuals begin to experiment, take risks, and share their findings, they encourage and guide the development of the larger emerging community. By valuing each other and *sharing* their experiences, both adults and children become models and motivators for each other, creating a supportive social environment that nurtures and sustains powerful learning.

5.1.2. Shared Responsibility: Working Together in Groups

It takes time to develop the informal attitudes and the formal group structures that enable a thriving democratic community to emerge within a school. During this time, there are certain group dynamics issues that must often be addressed by a developing community.

A Safe and Secure Environment. Within an accelerated school, ensuring each community member's active participation requires that individuals feel comfortable voicing their opinions, disagreeing with others, and being honest about their feelings and personal difficulties. Failure to address these issues can greatly inhibit a group or community's interaction. People trust each other when they feel safe and secure in their surroundings. One by one, individuals begin to build a safe and secure environment in which each person's contribution is respected and valued. Trust is the foundation.

> **One of the cadres at Burnett Academy had a large number of support staff as members. When the group first got together, the aides, office personnel, and yard supervisors always deferred to the "real teachers." As the meetings continued, the facilitator became increasingly aware of this pattern. She started directly asking the support staff for their input, validating their contributions. She asked them to take various roles during the meeting, offering help and support along the way. By doing so, she modeled positive behaviors for the entire group, and a more trusting environment emerged. The feeling shifted as the support staff began to feel valued and empowered by fellow members of their cadre. Before long they were as active and confident as the teachers and saw themselves as vital members of the school community, contributing toward the school's vision.**
> Burnett Academy, San Jose, California

Communication. Open and honest communication is a crucial factor in creating a truly accelerated school. Community members need to share what's on their minds—not let things fester—as well as understand and validate each individual's situation, perspectives, and feelings. Within the accelerated school, communication is certainly key to the functioning of the governance structures, yet it also extends to the everyday interactions of all members of the school community.

> **At the end of the second year of the accelerated schools process at Burnett Academy, a teacher commented on how liberating it was for her when she realized that she could express her concerns and her insecurity about handling some of the challenges relating to her students and get positive support and feedback from her colleagues (instead of the negative feedback she would have experienced in the past). She said that her experience opened the door for other teachers to relay their difficulties and start sharing solutions, ideas, and dreams.**
> Burnett Academy, San Jose, California

Commitment and Responsibility. When people have committed themselves to a group task, that group depends upon their full participation to
accomplish its goals. Such commitments can vary from individual to individual and over time. It therefore becomes important that levels of commitment not be taken for granted and that this issue be discussed respectfully
and addressed directly.

> **A strong sense of group commitment and responsibility was evidenced
> in the way members of the Rancho Milpitas Middle School arranged
> and rearranged their meeting times. As often happens, extra meetings
> and curricular responsibilities were scheduled before and after school.
> When the steering committee was set up, its meetings were initially
> scheduled for Tuesday mornings from 7:00 A.M. to 8:15 A.M. This
> happened to coincide with the special "A" period that the school
> offered. One of the cadre facilitators taught during that period and was
> thus unable to attend the meetings. The group discussed the possibility
> of changing the meetings to the afternoon, but that conflicted with the
> sports program, which two other staff members were committed to.
> As a compromise, the steering committee decided to meet every
> other Tuesday from 7:30 A.M. to 8:15 A.M. and every other Monday from
> 2:30 P.M. to 4:00 P.M. The revised meeting schedule allowed all mem-
> bers to keep both their initial responsibilities and their commitment
> to actively participate on the steering committee.**
> Rancho Milpitas Middle School, Milpitas, California

Collaboration and Sharing. Most of us learned to cooperate and share well
before we finished kindergarten! Yet collaborative behavior wasn't often
considered a priority or rewarded as we moved upward through the traditional education system. Independence and comparisons of individual work
are still emphasized in most schools, for both students and teachers. But
independent accomplishments *alone* won't help to create an accelerated
school. Rather, it's by *sharing* our gifts, talents, and insights with each other
that the gifts and talents of *all* individuals can be identified, nurtured, and
developed. This doesn't mean that successful individual performances
shouldn't be rewarded. But it does mean that consideration should be given
to constructing social environments (in cadre meetings, classrooms, and
anywhere else that people come together) that value collaboration and
sharing at *least* as much as individual accomplishment.

> **As a result of a Curriculum Cadre proposal that was approved by the
> SAW, the language arts and social science teachers at Burnett Acad-
> emy integrated their efforts and formed a humanities curriculum. The
> humanities books that were on order hadn't yet come in, so the
> teachers really had to share their individual talents as they created a
> joint curriculum for the students to pilot test in the fall. The
> curriculum couldn't have come together without the combined efforts,
> creativity, and determination of everyone present.**
> Burnett Academy, San Jose, California

Reflection. Often we get so busy transforming our school that we forget to stop and reflect on where we've been and where we are. Our vision is so alive that we're continually thinking about where we want to be. Yet individual reflection is always a value, whether it's the principal taking time to reflect on how he or she has changed in relating to the rest of the staff or the yard-duty supervisor reflecting on how he or she is handling the stress of a rainy-day schedule. Group reflection is also important for an accelerated school. It can provide tremendous opportunities for a school to examine itself during the journey toward acceleration. While it should occur as an ongoing activity, it should also occur at set times.

At the end of the first year of acceleration at Rancho Milpitas Middle School, the staff, through the steering committee and the school as a whole, decided to have a day of reflection. A volunteer group of staff members, composed of two regular classroom teachers, one special education teacher, one secretary, the library aide, and the principal, got together to talk about how the day would look. The principal checked the calendar and found that it wouldn't be possible to take a full day, but there was a district staff day on which they could have an *afternoon* of reflection. The group decided to ask each cadre and the steering committee to prepare a presentation for the school as a whole of their successes and challenges during the first year of acceleration—using the Inquiry Process as their guide. They also decided to have time for each individual member to share the successes and challenges they'd experienced that year. The afternoon, a great success, ended with identification of the challenges that the school would address as it started its second year.

Rancho Milpitas Middle School, Milpitas, California

All of the values described in Chapter Two, "What Are Accelerated Schools?" will help school community members strengthen their relationships with others and pursue their focus on providing powerful learning experiences for all students.

5.2. Formal Structures, Techniques, and Strategies*

Most of our school decision making in the past has taken place at the administrative level—in the principal's office or the district office. As we incorporate the three accelerated schools principles, we begin working more and more with others—usually in formal situations such as committees or cadres. In an accelerated school, participants use the Inquiry Process—the systematic approach (described in Chapter Four) designed to guide creative and collaborative problem solving and decision making. Although the

---

*Much of this section is drawn from *Teaming with Excellence: Skills for Collaboration* (LeTendre, Funderberg, & Wippern, 1989).

Inquiry Process may seem straightforward and logical on paper, it's often very challenging to follow in a real-life group setting.

Not only are the interpersonal relationships mentioned earlier important; so are the more formal relationships that take place during meetings. We've all attended meetings at which the behavior of one or two people influenced the whole group in a positive or negative way. How often have you been at a meeting at which someone is totally off the topic? Have you ever felt that a meeting participant was paying more attention to correcting papers than to you? Have you been frustrated by someone who always offers a reason that something won't work? What about people who agree with everything during the meeting—but wait until they get to the parking lot! Or people who always come late and need to be caught up to the rest?

In actuality, we've all exhibited these behaviors at one time or another. And all of these behaviors (and many others!) certainly detract from and inhibit a successful meeting. In the following section, we'll look at what contributes to good meetings. The formal roles, strategies, and procedures described can provide a guide for group interactions—one that supports the sharing of power and responsibility, the beginning of honest and open communication, and the development of positive interpersonal relationships.

Key to the success of any group working together is the ability of all members to *share* their concerns, *own* the concerns or problems, and work with others to *solve* those problems. We refer to this as the *S-O-S* strategy (share-own-solve).

Indeed, no *one* person is responsible for making the meeting work; we're *all* responsible. The following meeting management strategies should help your school community have effective meetings, use the Inquiry Process, and move along toward your vision!

5.2.1. Roles and Responsibilities

The three principles of the accelerated schools process (unity of purpose, empowerment coupled with responsibility, and building on strengths), imply that everyone participates in the leadership and decision making in an accelerated school.

This emphasis on participation has numerous implications for interactions at the small-group level. Student project groups, whole-school meetings, and cadres each provide a specific social context in which these principles can be put into action. The emphasis on participation also implies that everyone helps set goals and agendas for meetings and that each individual takes responsibility for following through on particular tasks. Members are encouraged to think deeply and critically and to assess the progress of the group. Natural gifts of enthusiasm, energy, and a sense of humor are essential at all times.

We've found that important challenges are best tackled when individuals take responsibility for specific roles in the group. As you know, this isn't a new idea! However, along with the more traditional roles, we offer some new ones that you may wish to consider to ensure that "the meeting"—your vehicle for creative and collaborative inquiry—runs smoothly.

Most of these roles can be rotated several times during the course of the year; many can change from meeting to meeting. And realize that these descriptions aren't carved in stone. You can share roles, blend roles, change role names, and construct new roles. Be flexible! Regardless of the roles people fill, *everyone* is responsible for keeping the meeting productive, on task, and running smoothly.

Some specific roles that we've found to be helpful are described here:

- *Facilitator.* Every group needs to have someone to help prepare the agenda, guide discussions, move the group forward, and make sure that someone takes responsibility for each task. This person, the facilitator, also takes responsibility for making sure that all concerns and opinions are voiced, that topics are discussed thoroughly, and that "bird-walkers" (those who love to wander out on a limb) are brought home. Good facilitators are able to "read" people and sense the unspoken messages that they often convey through their facial expressions, emotions, and behavior. In addition, through words and actions, the facilitator helps to establish a safe environment for all members to participate. Whoever you choose as a facilitator should be committed to the accelerated schools process and the Inquiry Process, should have time to devote to the task, and should have the support of other staff members. Because the facilitator attends the steering committee meetings, we suggest not rotating this role any more often than twice a year. Remember, although the facilitator role exists, *everyone* is responsible for contributing to the productivity of the meeting and making sure that everyone participates.

- *Recorder.* The recorder, who keeps the "memory" of the group, takes minutes of the meetings and makes sure that they're received by all cadre and steering committee members. The recorder also posts the agendas and minutes in a public place and keeps a record of them in a cadre notebook.

- *Timekeeper.* The timekeeper sees that each meeting starts and ends on time. If the agenda has been developed with specific times for various items, the timekeeper keeps the group on schedule.

- *Gatekeeper.* The gatekeeper helps the facilitator keep the group on task, making sure that no one wanders off the topic. If the gatekeeper recognizes any "bird-walking," it's his or her responsibility to draw the group back to the topic. (But remember, *everyone* has the responsibility of helping keep the group on track.)

- *Visionary.* Once the school has established its vision, it's often helpful to have someone take responsibility to see that the group's work leads to the vision. Because everyone in the school community helped to create the vision and is trying to bring it to life, this role really belongs to the entire group and can be rotated very easily.

- *Inquirer.* As the group addresses its challenge area, it often helps to have at least one person responsible for guiding the group in its use of the Inquiry Process. Is the group starting with the solution or with the problem? Have all hypotheses been adequately tested? Because everyone should know the Inquiry Process, this role can also be easily rotated. When everyone has mastered the Inquiry Process, everyone is an inquirer.

- *Resource person(s).* Resource people are responsible for bringing the necessary information and materials to a meeting. Usually everyone in the group is an unofficial resource person to some extent: each person is responsible for being prepared for the meeting and contributing to the discussion and decisions. Specific people, however, may be asked to do research or follow up on certain aspects of the discussion; others may have experiences or expertise in certain areas that would be beneficial to the whole group.

- *Closure person.* At the end of the meeting, the closure person summarizes the important discussions and decisions of the meeting (such as *who* will do *what* by *when*, and *how*). This provides an opportunity for clarification, evaluation, and verification of what happened at the meeting and how the meeting went. Closure also sets the direction for the next meeting, helps the group establish the next meeting's agenda, and assists the recorder with the task of minute taking.

- *External communicator.* It's the external communicator who alerts parents, district representatives, community members, students, and other members of the school community to the next meeting or activity—even if some of these people were at the previous meeting. Cadres have found that this extra "human" touch greatly enhances continued participation, especially of individuals who might not be in the school staff's information loop.

- *Reporter.* When the cadre (or other committee) needs to report to a large group verbally, the reporter takes the job. This role isn't always needed.

- *Refreshment person(s).* This very unofficial (and highly rotatable) role certainly adds to the positive and friendly atmosphere of any meeting!

If necessary (due to absences, for example), the roles can be adjusted at the beginning of the meeting. At the end of each meeting, new roles can be volunteered or assigned for the next meeting. Alternatively, the cadre can create a monthly or yearly matrix of the meeting dates and roles, and members can volunteer for the roles they want.

Remember, don't become rigid about these suggested roles! The needs at your school might suggest different ones. A cadre in one accelerated school set up enough roles so that each individual had a specific responsibility, yet in groups that are small (or are established for a one-time project), a facilitator, recorder, reporter, and closure person are often sufficient. It's also helpful to revisit the roles periodically because, over time, group members can get caught up in the process and forget their responsibilities. The key is to provide a structure or system that will assist your group in tackling the tasks it feels are necessary to enable all students to experience success.

During the middle of its second year as an accelerated school, Burnett Academy realized that it needed to take another look at how committees and cadres were operating. One teacher suggested to the steering committee that the school revisit the roles and encourage everyone to again take individual responsibility for the collective good. The steering committee facilitator and facilitators of the cadres met and went over the various roles as presented at their original training session. They made some adaptations that were specific to their school. The cadre leaders then went back to their cadres rejuvenated and passed on the excitement to the other cadre members.

Burnett Academy, San Jose, California

5.2.2. Meeting Standards

Whenever two or more people come together for a specific purpose, certain modes of behavior naturally take place. You know the unwritten rules of your school. Do the meetings usually start on time? Do they usually end on time? Who sits where? Is there a written record of all meetings?

Everything works well when everyone follows these unwritten rules. But what happens if your meetings are supposed to start on time and someone always comes late? In every organization, there are probably some unwritten rules that aren't conducive to productive meetings. If you haven't agreed on shared meeting standards, it's hard to hold others accountable and be effective.

For individuals coming together to work as equals for the first time, collaboratively setting meeting standards is often an essential process. It allows a group to construct a series of agreed upon expectations that guide subsequent discussions and interpersonal relationships and enable each person to feel a sense of ownership of and commitment to the expectations that guide the workings of the group. An example of such "home-grown" standards are these constructed by the school community at Rancho Milpitas School in Milpitas, California.

Rancho Milpitas Meeting Standards

- **Start and end on time.**
- **Form attendance rules.**
- **Form an agenda.**
- **Determine and rotate the roles (except facilitator).**
- **Have desirable and flexible meeting times.**
- **Stay on the agenda.**
- **Make the meetings worthwhile.**
- **Allow no side-talking.**
- **Follow up.**
- **Be brief and directive.**
- **Allow no put downs.**
- **Include everyone in the decision-making process.**
- **Provide a way for everyone to contribute.**

An interesting sideline on Rancho's meeting standards: **After the meeting standards were developed during one of the early training sessions, they were filed away. Once the school community began to address some real issues, people realized that they weren't consistent in their approaches. One of the teachers pulled out the standards and went**

over them with the entire staff. Immediately, the office personnel typed up and enlarged the standards and laminated a set for every cadre and department and the steering committee. With the standards available for everyone to see—and to follow—the meetings again became more effective and efficient.

Rancho Milpitas Middle School, Milpitas, California

Decisions Through Voting and Consensus Building

Accelerated schools make decisions by voting or by reaching consensus. Even when they vote, however, they're in a consensus-building mode; in most schools, approval of a decision requires a 90 or 100 percent vote! With either consensus or voting, "winning" thus becomes a group goal rather than an individual one. Achieving consensus is harder work than conventional voting, but the time and energy spent getting to substantial agreement can lead to better decisions and more successful implementation of the decisions, because everyone's strengths, ideas, and perceptions have been included.

In reaching consensus, the members of the group come to an agreement that all can endorse or at least live with. Complete unanimity isn't the goal; in fact, it's rarely achieved. But all members should feel comfortable with the group decision even if a few don't fully agree with it. We'll all have times when decisions go our way and other times when they don't.

Differences of opinion are natural and expected when a school community engages in collaborative work. These disagreements can even enhance the group's final decision: with a wide range of information and opinions, there's a greater chance that the group will come up with the best solutions.

Using the accelerated schools process greatly enhances the likelihood of reaching consensus for the following reasons:

- Everyone contributed to and is working toward a common vision, so people aren't working at cross-purposes. Sometimes simply referring to the vision during a disagreement can help clear things up.

- Using the Inquiry Process and communicating with each other regularly eliminates "surprise" proposals that seem to have no basis. By keeping the entire school community in touch with what each cadre is doing, we *build* consensus over time.

If you're having trouble reaching consensus and all else fails, remember the following:

- Present your ideas and listen to the other members' reactions, considering them carefully. Avoid arguing for your own position.

- Look for the most acceptable alternative for *all* parties.

- Learn to be comfortable with some level of conflict. Don't change your mind simply to avoid conflict and reach agreement and harmony. Harmonizing can be helpful in the short term but causes problems in the long term.

- Avoid conflict-reducing techniques such as voting, averaging, flipping a coin, or bargaining.

Consensus isn't a democracy of opinion in which a simple majority vote equals the final decision. It's a process in which the outcome emerges as people listen, discuss, reflect, and respond to each other. In order to define consensus in your accelerated school community, you can have small groups set out their definitions and then have the large group come to agree on your school's working definition of consensus!

5.2.3. Meeting Management

Most major community decisions in accelerated schools are made at meetings. Thus meetings really *matter*. Unlike the traditional faculty meeting, at which we might be asked to listen to a list of announcements from the principal or decide when in May students should be allowed to wear shorts, at accelerated school meetings, important decisions are made that systematically incorporate everyone's ideas.

But effective meetings don't just happen; they're orchestrated at these four stages: (1) planning the meeting, (2) starting the meeting, (3) managing the meeting, and (4) closing the meeting. Each of these stages has its own set of tasks and key players, though each member of the school community is an important player in one way or another throughout the entire process.

The following outline of these stages can help you structure meetings early on, though you may want to expand this framework with time:

Planning the Meeting. Deciding on the logistics of the meeting is the first step. Where and when will it be held? What materials are needed for the meeting? Who should attend? And, most important, what's the agenda? The agenda sets the framework for the meeting; it describes what's to happen (and when), who's to take care of each item, and how much time will be devoted to each item.

An agenda outline is usually constructed at the end of the previous meeting so that all group members can provide input. This outline is then completed in sufficient time by the facilitator (or whoever is designated) to be posted, as well as distributed to each member of the committee or cadre, prior to the meeting. This way everyone can be prepared to discuss the issues presented.

As with any flexible instrument, the agenda should be looked at again at the beginning of the meeting to see if any changes are needed. The sample agenda below is a compilation of the most effective agenda formats from several schools:

Agenda Title

Date: Time: Place:

Members:

Materials needed:

Roles for this meeting:

- Facilitator—
- Recorder—
- Timekeeper—
- External communicator—
- Closure person—

- Gatekeeper—
- Inquirer—
- Visionary—
- Refreshments person—

	What	How/Who	Time
1.	Approve minutes.	Facilitator	2 minutes
2.	Adjust & approve agenda.	Facilitator	5 minutes
3.	Hear report from steering committee.	Facilitator	5 minutes
4.	Review old business.	As appropriate	?
	a. Item	As appropriate	?
	b. Item	As appropriate	?
	c. Item	As appropriate	?
5.	Introduce new business.	As submitted	?
	a. Item	As appropriate	?
	b. Item	As appropriate	?
	c. Item	As appropriate	?
6.	Have closure.	Closure person	5 minutes
	a. Review the meeting contents and decisions.		
	b. Review the responsibilities/tasks for the next meeting. (*Who* will do *what* by *when*, & *how*?)		
	c. Review the meeting dynamics and process.		
7.	Prepare for the next meeting.	Facilitator & all	5 minutes
	a. Assign roles for next meeting.		
	b. Set next meeting time, date, place.		
	c. Plan next agenda.		

Starting the Meeting. Getting the meeting started is usually the shared responsibility of all group members in accordance with the standard meeting procedures established by the group. Some suggestions:

- Start on time.

- Post the school vision, meeting standards, and a diagram of the Inquiry Process.

- Approve (or revise) and post the agenda before getting into the actual meeting.

- Review the roles and meeting standards.

- Go over the minutes from the previous meeting to set the context for the current meeting.

Managing the Meeting. The task of managing the meeting belongs primarily to the facilitator, the gatekeeper, and the timekeeper. However, *everyone* in the group is responsible for keeping the meeting going. Because the agenda is prepared and seen ahead of time by all the members (and amended if necessary), members can more easily address meeting topics.

When moving from one point to another, the group needs to make sure that all issues relating to the previous point have been addressed. This may mean acknowledging that there are issues that can't be immediately resolved and setting up a structure for dealing with them in another manner or at another time.

Another responsibility of the facilitator (along with everyone else in the group) is to involve all members in the discussion. How can everyone be involved? When should you use consensus? These are broad issues that facilitators might explore and discuss with their cadres, in formal training sessions, or with other facilitators. A few tips:

- Ask questions for clarification and understanding.

- Listen actively.

- Provide wait time for assimilation of ideas.

- Be in touch with the whole person: feelings, words, and actions.

Closing the Meeting. The closure person assumes primary responsibility for closing the meeting. He or she gives a summary of what happened, what was decided, and what needs to be done. In addition, the closure person can help members reflect upon their group dynamics. Did group members follow their agreed upon standards? Did they stick to the agenda? Did everyone take responsibility for ensuring the productivity of the group? What needs to be done differently next time?

The group then sets the agenda, time, and place of the next meeting and establishes who will take which roles before the meeting closes.

5.2.4. Taking Minutes

Printed minutes allow all school members access to information about what other groups are doing, serve as a group memory device, and provide a reminder of agreed upon tasks. In order to keep the entire school community informed, accelerated schools set aside a place to post all groups' minutes and agendas. We offer you the following suggestions on taking minutes. Try them out (along with your own innovations), remember what works best for you, your school, and its needs, and then develop your own guidelines. Although a standard, agreed upon format is helpful, the important thing is to *take* and *keep* your minutes in an orderly fashion.

- Include the name of the cadre or committee, the date and location of the meeting, the facilitator, the recorder, and members of the committee with every report. This standard format allows the recorder to merely change the variable information and put an asterisk next to (or underline) the name of the members present at the particular meeting.

- Be careful that your minutes are rich descriptions rather than sketchy outlines. For example, have the recorder provide an account of the general discussion leading to decisions as well as the decisions themselves. As a rule of thumb, record enough that ideas can be understood later, using speakers' names and words when possible (although the minutes aren't meant to be a verbatim report).

- Summarize the decisions at the end of minutes. A helpful format for the summary is *who* will have done *what* by *when*, and *how*. The recorder should note actions to be taken or tasks to be accomplished between the present meeting and the next. The final item includes the time, date, location, roles, and agenda items for the next meeting.

- Develop a schoolwide format to be used by all committees. This has proven very helpful in keeping the whole school community informed.

Guidelines for Cadre Minutes

Cadre Name
Date of meeting

- Facilitator—
- Recorder—
- Timekeeper—
- External communicator—
- Closure person—

- Gatekeeper—
- Inquirer—
- Visionary—
- Refreshments person—

Members present:

Members absent:

1. Call to order, adoption of agenda, and approval of minutes:
2. Reports:
3. Business items:
   Record the discussion and decisions made; underline or highlight each topic for easy reference; include names where appropriate.
4. Decisions:
   Summarize decisions, including who's responsible for what action and by what date.
5. Assignments:
   Between now and the next meeting, who will do what by when, and how? List tasks to be completed, persons responsible, and due dates.
6. Next meeting:
   Record time, date, location, roles, and agenda items.

5.2.5. Capturing Time

Finding time, or making time, is a major challenge in everyday modern life, and it's one of the biggest challenges in any school day. As you've no doubt already concluded, transforming a school into an accelerated school takes lot of time—time to reflect, to plan, to discuss, to decide, and to do. Unfortunately, we don't have a magic formula for *making* time, but we can suggest a few ways to *find* time—time to meet with your cadre, time to meet in your steering committee or as a whole school, time to think, plan, and work creatively, and time to work with others.

Finding and Choosing Meeting Times. Lay out all the time that you presently use for meetings of any type. Examine each segment to see how the time is used. Is there some way to rearrange the time you already have to use it more effectively and efficiently? Can some things be combined in order to create more time? Assess each time commitment in terms of how well it leads to your vision for the children. If you can't link a time commitment to your vision, maybe the commitment should be released.

We can't manufacture time, but we can "capture" it in the ways suggested below. You can probably add to the list from your own experience. Each school has its own unique situation with regard to capturing time, but the following ways that some accelerated schools have handled their time will work in many other schools as well.

- **"Bank" instructional minutes to provide for early release days.** Some schools have been able to work out additional time by extending the school day in order to have early release time on a regular basis.

> **Staff and administrators of one school in Missouri wanted to extend the school day by five minutes so that they could "bank" instructional time and later have an early dismissal day. No school in the district—indeed, in the surrounding districts—had ever done such a thing. In fact, it was falsely rumored that such schedules were against state law. After presenting their case to the super-intendent and the school board, faculty members secured permission to extend the school day. Now the practice of adding minutes to the school day to "bank" instructional time is an accepted practice.**
>
> Missouri Accelerated Schools Network

- **Meet before or after school.** Capturing time may mean meeting before or after school, if by doing so you can still include the majority of people in the group. Some schools schedule meetings at night to allow for more parental input.

- **Use grant money.** One slant on meeting before or after school is to use grant money to pay teachers stipends for staying beyond the contracted day, for extra days before school starts in the fall, or for weekends or other days. Grant money can also be used to pay for substitutes during the school day so that groups of teachers can meet.

> **Several of our school staff members have written proposals to receive grant funding that will support their school-site decision making. They recently received a $5,000 grant to bring in a consultant to conduct a workshop on the two days before the fall semester begins. And rather than receiving a per diem sum for their attending this workshop, the teachers decided to use this part of their grant money to buy themselves substitute time that they'll use for further planning time during the year.**
>
> John Baker, Principal, Hoover Elementary School, Redwood City, California

- **Use regular meeting times differently.** Sometimes you can use regular faculty meeting times for school-as-a-whole meetings or for planning among staff members. Making more effective and efficient use of the time that you have for regular meetings not only aids in moving toward your school's vision; it also makes your members feel better about their contributions to the school. District in-service days can often be used for accelerated school meetings as well: by communicating with the district, many accelerated schools have been able to arrange to use their district staff-development days for accelerated school training and cadre meetings.

- *Utilize substitute time creatively.* Some schools have arranged to have substitutes (paid or volunteer—even the principal!) take a class for a teacher to enable that teacher to meet with others who have a prep period.

> **The former principal of Daniel Webster Elementary School regularly gathered the students from several rooms for an aerobics activity so that teachers could meet in their cadres.**
>
> Daniel Webster Elementary School, San Francisco, California

> **Hoover Elementary School had four cadres with full representation of all staff and some parents. The school scheduled one of its two cadre meetings per month on two days:**
>
> **Second Wednesday:** A.M.—Parent Involvement
> P.M.—Self-Esteem
> **Fourth Wednesday:** A.M.—Language Arts
> P.M.—Organization

> **Four substitutes were used to cover the classes of teachers on these occasions.**
>
> Hoover Elementary School, Redwood City, California

Teachers and parents, often wary of depending too much on substitutes, are much more comfortable with people whom they know and have worked with before. "Permanent" substitutes can often be obtained through local volunteer groups or from a nearby university. One school district even assigned a number of teachers as permanent substitutes in schools that were going through restructuring.

- *Enlist district help.* Because you're embarking on an exciting new venture that helps to accelerate *all* students, your district may offer special release time for planning, as mentioned above. In addition, the district may assist you in extending the teacher contract so that you can get paid for your extra meeting times. It doesn't hurt to ask!

- *Sponsor special-event days.* Time can be captured for the staff to meet during the normal school day without interrupting the learning of the students. Some schools have done this by organizing special-event days and hiring substitutes to help supervise the activities.

An accelerated school in Missouri used about $500 of grant money to buy substitutes for an afternoon to supervise each teacher's class. The principal and staff arranged for eight special speakers to come to the school that afternoon. A former student who went on to success in the army, the local television weathercaster, and a storyteller were among the special speakers who gave of their time free of charge. The students rotated from speaker to speaker. This arrangement allowed the staff to meet for three hours during the school day and provided enriched learning for the students.

Missouri Accelerated Schools Network

- *Reschedule the school day.* Free periods or prep periods can often be adjusted to help teachers working with other school staff on cadres. As long as teachers aren't forced to give up these periods—or asked to do so on a regular basis—many appreciate this time to meet and work together. At the elementary school level, time can often be captured by creatively scheduling music, art, physical education, and recess.

- *Hold meetings over lunch.* Occasionally a group will work over lunch in order to capture thirty or so minutes to complete a task, launch a project, or gather ideas from a larger group of people.

- *Rearrange parent conference time.* Most elementary schools set aside time twice a year to hold parent conferences; middle schools generally do so at least once. Creative use of these conference days can be an additional way to capture time for meetings.

Teachers are sometimes using their conferences for grade-level and individual planning. . . . In November, at our first break, we've scheduled five days in a row for conferences. On these days, the children are let out at 1:30 P.M. What some teachers have chosen to do is to schedule back-to-back parent conferences for three days, from 1:30 P.M. till the early evening. In this way, they finish all their parent conferences in three days, leaving them with a two-day block without any conferences, which they use for group or individual planning.

John Baker, Principal, Hoover Elementary School, Redwood City, California

Whatever the case, as you choose your meeting times, be sure to keep in mind your mental, physical, and emotional state—and the state of the others in your school community. Some people work better in the morning, some in the afternoon, and some at night. Maybe that means you need to rotate your meeting times. Similarly, you may have to rotate your times to accommodate the other obligations of group members—yard duty, office duties, parents' work schedules, and so on. And certain days of the week may prove better than others.

Managing Time Between Meetings. One of the best ways to ensure an effective, efficient meeting is to see that everyone is prepared for the meeting. Then, as part of closure, review who has what tasks to accomplish before the next meeting. If you have a task, remember that the rest of the group is counting on your input.

What's to Come

The next four chapters of this guide deal with powerful learning in accelerated schools. We hope that by utilizing the strategies suggested in this chapter, your school community will be able to come together and collaborate on providing exciting and powerful learning experiences for all members of the school community.

CHAPTER 6

Creating Powerful Learning Experiences

As you can see, the elementary students in the preceding drawing are all quite engaged in their project: recreating different societies. One group is building an irrigation system for crops in a European agrarian culture; another is constructing pyramids in an early Egyptian culture; a third is organizing a hunting expedition in a traditional tribal community; and a fourth is working out a computer simulation for a modern industrial-based society. The class chose which cultures they wanted to study before breaking into groups. Once a week, the students change "stations" so that each child has an opportunity to experience every society. Together they read, write, build, negotiate, present, analyze, and compute. (And sing, dance, paint, hunt, gather, plant, and fish!) Spelling, reading, writing, speaking, mathematics, science, social studies, art, drama, and music are all covered in an interdisciplinary manner. At the end of the unit, the students will compare, contrast, and celebrate the different technological innovations, spiritual beliefs, art forms, economic systems, social customs, and governance structures of each culture. Then they'll present their findings in a schoolwide publication.

The drawing illustrates a *classroom*-based powerful learning experience. Many different examples of such experiences will be presented throughout the next four chapters, giving us the opportunity to explore some of the ways that powerful learning can occur. Our examples come directly from the discoveries and creative innovations of accelerated school communities. Like the various cultural systems described above, powerful classroom-based learning environments can take countless different forms.

In fact, classrooms are really only one of the many arenas in which powerful learning occurs. In school, everything that happens—from the initiation of a new tardy policy to the implementation of playground rules—teaches something important to children. And at home, children learn many things from their parents and other family members—their first and foremost teachers. Finally, children learn all sorts of lessons from their peers and members of their local community. As a traditional African proverb puts it, "It takes an entire village to raise a child."

As teachers, support staff, and principals in accelerated schools, we may at first be primarily interested in creating powerful learning experiences at the school site. Yet the long-term success of these efforts requires that we also create partnerships with parents and the local community so that we can provide children with positive learning environments *everywhere*. The learning in one environment can complement and build on the learning in each of the others. That's why in an accelerated school, the staff, parents, students, and community work together to create powerful learning opportunities in a child's home, school, and after-school life.

How such learning develops and occurs will vary from school to school. Each community faces a particular set of challenges and possesses a unique mix of resources and strengths. That's why the Accelerated Schools Project isn't prescriptive: it doesn't set forth a *formula* for creating powerful learning experiences. The knowledge base is already out there; as educators and parents, you understand what makes learning powerful. In addition, there are many strong curricular and instructional innovations in the education literature and in districts and in states that you can tap into. What we offer is a **philosophy**, a way of thinking about children and learning, and a **process**, a way to make lasting and effective changes in a school. You'll recognize some of the information in the next few pages from Chapter Two, "What Are Accelerated Schools?"

6.1. Philosophy

First, we believe that the education we now provide for so-called gifted children is what actually works best for *all* children. Keeping this in mind, we try to create learning situations that build on what we know about how children's talents and gifts are nurtured, challenged, and developed. As the drawing on the first page of this chapter suggests, our philosophy encourages us to create situations in which each student has an interest in learning, sees a meaning in the lesson, perceives connections between each school activity and his or her real life, is able to learn actively, and learns in ways that build on his or her own strengths.

Accelerated school communities work together to create powerful learning experiences in which *each* child is treated as gifted. Complex activities are stressed, content is relevant, and children actively discover the curriculum objectives in a safe and caring environment rather than passively going through textbooks and filling out worksheets. With time, opportunities for powerful learning can extend far beyond the classroom into every aspect of the school, home, and community. By thinking about our own powerful learning experiences (and what made them so powerful), we can come up with ideas and themes to guide us in constructing environments that accelerate learning.

The second part of our philosophy is that we see every learning experience as having three interrelated dimensions. The first dimension is *what* is learned. This includes specific content or curricular knowledge, as well as beliefs about one's personal abilities and relationship to the world. The second dimension is *how* the content is learned—through various learning opportunities and forms of instruction, for example. The third dimension is the *context* in which one galvanizes all available learning resources in order to provide a setting for the *what* and *how*. *Context* includes time and resources, flexibility of the schedule, deployment of staffing, physical and social environment, and funding.

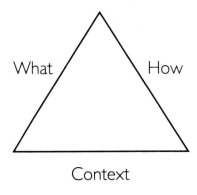

Learning experiences that are *powerful* are more easily orchestrated when we make use of our knowledge of **what** children like, need, and want to learn; **how** they best learn; and what types of **contexts** best support and promote this learning. Our philosophy views these three dimensions as *totally and necessarily integrated*. A change in what students learn almost always necessitates a change in both how they learn and the context that supports that learning, and vice versa. For example, it's difficult to make your lessons more interdisciplinary if you continue to use rigidly defined subject-area textbooks, forty-five-minute blocks of time, and a predominantly teacher-centered instructional strategy. Interdisciplinary content lends itself to more active instructional strategies and a more flexible use of time. Similarly, if you want to use more cooperative grouping in your class or school, you might have to move from whole-class instruction using textbooks and worksheets to activities that provide students with opportunities to actively discover concepts through interaction with a variety of resources. This would probably also necessitate longer blocks of time.

As we stated in Chapter Two, we believe that the traditional piecemeal approach of adopting isolated changes in what we teach, how we teach, or the context of our teaching doesn't lead to unified and lasting change for two reasons: (1) the three dimensions of learning (*what*, *how*, and *context*) must be integrally linked, and (2) most isolated changes traditionally result from either top-down mandates or from a small group within a school rather than from careful and systematic analysis of a school's strengths and challenges by the entire community.

Therefore, the first step that a school community can take toward creating long-lasting change in students' various learning environments is to recognize powerful learning and its integrated nature. With this philosophy in mind, the school community can delve into the active process of creating powerful learning experiences in the school, home, and community.

"Variety is the spice of life." Sometimes we who are in education forget to add this important element in our classroom. Accelerated schools opened the door for our school to put new *fun* ideas in our classrooms and the school as a whole. Throw out all those ruts you feel have "appeared" in your path. Put your students in groups and let them learn to help each other cooperatively and enjoy learning! Apply this from your classroom to the school as a whole, and you have a faculty and staff working *together* toward a common goal—excellence in education. Change is the key! Be open to new ideas; modify them if necessary to make them work! "Buddy up" with another teacher to get new methods and ideas to use in your classroom. The Accelerated Schools Project opened a new world to our faculty, staff, and students.

Julia Bell, Teacher, Shady Grove Elementary, Monroe, Louisiana

6.2. Process: The Big Wheels and Little Wheels of Creating Accelerated School Change

How does your school go about making powerful educational innovations? You've already taken the first step: your school community has demonstrated a willingness and commitment to be creative, reflective, and courageous in deciding to become an accelerated school. Once this risk-taking attitude is in place, there are two key processes by which accelerated school communities transform students' learning experiences. We refer to these two processes as "big wheels" and "little wheels."

As we noted in Chapter Two, the term "big wheels" refers to the formal processes of accelerated schools (taking stock, forging a vision, setting priorities, forming governance structures, and using the Inquiry Process). These big wheels bring about long-term institutional changes through the careful and collaborative efforts of the whole school community (as described in Chapters Three and Four). In the chapters that follow, we provide several detailed examples of how cadres have used the Inquiry Process to help accelerate students' learning. In order to create powerful and long-lasting improvements, an accelerated school *must* use these systematic and collaborative big-wheel processes.

On the other hand, many of us are ready to change *now*! The "little wheels" of the accelerated schools process are the innovations that you can begin to make *today*! Whether you want to design a thematic unit based on your favorite hobby or have the students take a bolder role in choosing the topics they want to study, an accelerated school community creates an environment in which *we're free to do so*—on our own or with others.

The little wheels represent the ideas and innovations that individuals in the school bring to life, beyond their work in their cadres. By assessing what made some of our *own* learning experiences powerful, we can come up with a long list of essential elements and work to incorporate them in the classroom. Our own powerful learning experiences rarely encompass worksheets or end-of-the-chapter questions; rather, they're experiential, hands-on, interactive, responsive, and so on. We've found that when adults in the school community go through the process of transforming their school into an accelerated school and reflect on the three principles of unity of purpose, empowerment coupled with responsibility, and building on strengths, they begin to experiment with new types of ideas and strategies in the classroom, on the playground, in the office, and at home.

Through the big-wheel and little-wheel innovations, changes in accelerated schools happen simultaneously in many places, at different speeds, and at different levels.

6.3. Foundations of Powerful Learning

Whether we're involved in big- or little-wheel activities, there are certain foundations that can help guide the development of powerful learning experiences in accelerated schools. These foundations can serve as criteria as you design your own powerful learning experiences — whether with your cadre, in teams, or on your own:

- The three principles of the Accelerated Schools Project

- The values of accelerated schools

- Your school's vision

6.3.1. The Three Principles of Accelerated Schools

The principles of acceleration—*unity of purpose, empowerment coupled with responsibility,* and *building on strengths*—provide the framework for the accelerated schools philosophy and offer general guidelines for the development and orchestration of powerful learning experiences. Your school's evolving *unity of purpose* will be reflected in the way staff, students, and their families work together in order to provide powerful learning environments and experiences for all students and in the way different grade levels articulate their objectives with each other so that all students have equal opportunities to participate in all school activities and equal access to the same quality educational experiences.

As educators, you can *empower* your students by encouraging them to take *responsibility* for their own learning. You can provide learning opportunities that allow your students to produce their own knowledge and to apply already existing knowledge to issues and problems that are meaningful to them. Taking responsibility for a school environment that's conducive to learning and that builds on the strengths of your students is also empowering to you and all other members of your school community. As you model for your students the attitudes and strategies of creative thinkers and life-long learners, you help empower them to take personal responsibility for the future course of their lives.

Every single person in your school community has *strengths* that you can *build on* to create powerful learning environments. These strengths might lie in experiences, skills, cultural backgrounds, interests, aptitudes, or human needs. Let's begin by looking at the strengths of teachers.

Teachers have talents and interests that influence their teaching and their choice of materials, and these interests should be allowed to flourish. If, for example, a teacher at your school is interested in snakes and keeps them as pets, she could become your resource for a schoolwide experiential learning unit on snakes. You might study their habits and their habitat, write stories and read legends about them, study their bodies and their reproductive systems, observe them and touch them, write poetry about them and compose songs, put together a slide show or create a computer learning program on HyperCard. In many ways, teachers' personal experiences can create powerful learning experiences in the classroom.

- **Joan Moss, a teacher at Daniel Webster Elementary School in San Francisco, developed an interdisciplinary unit on the culture of the Lakota Sioux. She had prepared a unit on the Sioux while in education courses at San Francisco State University and decided to make Sioux culture the core of all her lessons for the year. Her mentor teacher, who's Native American, came to visit the class to help prepare students for a field trip to a real powwow. Her students' work, and that of two other classes in the school, culminated in the organization and presentation of a full-fledged Native American museum for the rest of the school to visit.**
  Daniel Webster Elementary School, San Francisco, California

- **Mima Parsons, a teacher at Hoover Elementary School in Redwood City, California, who spent a sabbatical year in China, starts each school day with t'ai chi, in order to help her students concentrate and tune in to learning. She also developed an interdisciplinary unit around the theme of the Chinese New Year.**
  Hoover Elementary School, Redwood City, California

There are other staff in your school whose talents could make a difference in the learning of your students too. The administrators, aides, secretaries, custodians, librarians, bus drivers, and food servers are all people who love children and are willing to share their wealth of experience and their special talents.

- **Oscar Chinas, the custodian at Hoover Elementary School in Redwood City, California, designed and sketched the school mascot. His artistic talent has made him a role model for some of the students, and he's become a resource for teachers planning art projects. Oscar is also the plant doctor and summer plant-sitter for all classroom plants in the school. His green thumb makes him a perfect resource for lessons about plant development and our responsibilities as owners of houseplants.**

- **Willie Santamaria, former principal at Daniel Webster Elementary School in San Francisco, California, taught a daily aerobics class to all her students in order to free teachers up to meet. She asked one of her fifth grade students—a girl who had grown more than anyone else in the class and felt very uncomfortable with her new body—to be her instructional aide. The student's success as an aerobics teacher changed her attitude and that of her fellow students and improved her classroom performance.**

- **Hope Marquez, a campus assistant at Burnett Academy in San Jose, California, was named an honorary English teacher at a school-as-a-whole meeting. Although she isn't certificated and doesn't teach a formal class, Hope works every day to build the language skills of the children. Whether teaching a new vocabulary word to a Spanish-speaking student or correcting the grammar of a student who already speaks English, Hope takes her work beyond student supervision, and the school community has recognized her for it.**

Your students and their families are also amazing resources for making learning rich and exciting. All your students have strengths that you might not be aware of. Some of them are involved in after-school programs (soccer, gymnastics, theater), some work in the afternoons helping their parents around the house and taking care of siblings, some have extraordinary skills as model builders, carpenters, pianists, and even computer programmers. The key is to create opportunities for identifying these strengths and building on them.

All communities have unique traditions, histories, and strengths. Community members have pride in their achievements, and they have hopes and dreams for their children. Providing opportunities for parents, students, and other community members to work on projects or learn together can forge powerful bonds between culture, community, and education. New expectations and perceptions for learning may emerge.

- **J. Will Jones Elementary School, in Houston, Texas, has opened its doors to the community, establishing a tutoring program that has** the support of almost fifty volunteer tutors from the Chevron Corporation, many of whom work in bilingual classrooms. The first graders wrote a song for Mr. Feldman, their Chevron tutor, that expressed the many activities that had taken place during their year with him: the song touched on estimating his weight before and after his diet, writing letters to his family members, and reading a city map of the locations where the Feldmans work.

- Jesse Tello, a parent at Daniel Webster Elementary School in San Francisco, accompanies his children to school every day, and he doesn't go home until after they do! Jesse has become part of the school's spirit. For four years now, he's helped in the office, organized parent meetings, worked in the classroom, and helped make the neighborhood safe again.

- An elderly retired man who lives down the street from Hollibrook Elementary School taught a minicourse in fly-fishing to some of the students. He decided it was something they should know, so he came to the school with an inflatable swimming pool and sat out back with a whole group of students. They learned all about different insects, how to make the flies, and how to operate rods and reels. The children loved it. And that man has gone back out into the neighborhood as a tremendous advocate and supporter of the school. You can just see the potential for the whole school community!

....

As a group, take a close look at one unit in a textbook and do the following:

Exercise

- Analyze how much it promotes the three principles of accelerated schools.

- Explore how you might design learning activities for this unit that guarantee that all students have equal access to the information and the concepts to be learned, have equal opportunity to participate in the activities, and have successful learning experiences that build on their strengths.

- Develop some of the alternative learning activities you explored and try them out with your students. Compare results with your fellow teachers.

....

6.3.2. The Shared Values of Your School Community

In Chapter Two, we discussed a set of values, beliefs, and attitudes that underlie the principles and processes of acceleration and create the culture for accelerated school change. These values come to life when we consciously utilize them as we construct powerful learning opportunities for our students. In the following section, we describe the implications many of these values have for creating powerful learning.

Equity. The value of equity suggests that all students have access to high-quality learning experiences. All children have incredible untapped potential for developing their talents and abilities. Children are by nature prodigious learners. Unfortunately, most educational curricula and instructional strategies that acknowledge these facts are reserved for the "top" level of students. Children who are labeled "slow learners" typically have much more mundane school experiences. In fact, when students are labeled "slow learners" or "troublemakers," these labels may be the main lessons those students learn at school. Research in fields such as sociology and psychology now indicates that when we categorize children and offer them different levels of education, we actually help *create* the differences. Accelerated schools embrace the value of equity by ensuring that all children have access to exciting, quality learning experiences.

> At the beginning of September, we got a call from a Shakespeare acting troupe offering to perform at our school in late October. Of course, we said yes right away, and only afterward did we realize, "Oh, I guess we have to teach the kids some Shakespeare!" The eighth grade English department had a meeting to discuss which classes would get the material, you know, would it be only the GATE [gifted and talented] kids, or some other subset of students? We had only just started the accelerated schools process—we hadn't even finished taking stock—but everyone at that meeting felt strongly that we had to teach Shakespeare to every child. We had a heck of a time finding enough books, but every eighth grader in that school, including special ed and ESL students, read *A Midsummer Night's Dream*. The accelerated schools philosophy is extremely powerful. When you begin to internalize it, the way you do things can change quickly and dramatically.
>
> Carol Weiss, ESL Teacher, Rancho Milpitas Middle School, Milpitas, California

Participation. The value of participation suggests that learning is interactive and relevant to the lives of the students. Learning opportunities encourage active participation when they are structured in such a way that students are interested in and responsible for constructing knowledge or for making use of resources outside the classroom in order to facilitate the learning of everyone. Students can help in selecting and developing lessons, in making decisions about how much time to spend on them, what content to focus on, which tasks to perform, and which materials to use. If you create learning experiences that address students' personal interests and concerns, you may help them become experts in those areas that are most important to them. When given the opportunity to actively participate, students learn that their personal and cultural experiences, thoughts, talents, and interests are valued and can contribute to the learning of the community as a whole.

> The culminating activity for a unit that I did on animals with my fourth graders was to create a museum for the rest of the school to visit. I had a pretty good idea of how the exhibits would be structured, and I just

told the children what they'd be doing. Then the most dynamic thing happened; two boys came up with the idea, all on their own, to make a "zoo key" and a "zoo box." They wanted to tape-record themselves giving information about each exhibit, just like in a regular museum, and the tape recorder would be hidden in a decorated box. When you put the zoo key in the zoo box, the tape started. It was such a great idea. At first, though, I thought it was crazy—way too complicated. I didn't think they could pull it off, so I told them no, we weren't going to do it. But they kept hounding me, and finally I just said, "Okay, we'll get some tape recorders." I just let them go with it. They became leaders; they led me. They were the ones who were taking responsibility, and therefore they were much more excited about it. They were incredibly motivated to learn about the exhibit that they'd be tending. They saw themselves as teachers. They took it really seriously, because it was theirs; they took pride in it. My attitude was, "I don't know how this is going to work out, but I trust you guys; I'll give you the responsibility." I was taking a lot of risks, and I was holding my breath all the time. But I'll do it again next year, because the payoff was so fantastic. The kids learned so much.

Amy L. Meyer, Hoover Elementary School, Redwood City, California

Communication and Collaboration. *The value of communication and collaboration suggests learning experiences that allow for student interaction and cooperation.* Because learning is an *active* process of figuring things out and constructing meaning, it can be promoted through structured social interactions. Learning opportunities that encourage students to cooperate and communicate with each other draw on what students know and allow them to share that knowledge with one another. As students grow comfortable with this, they begin to view all members of their environment as potential resources for powerful learning. (With younger children, this may actually be a natural way of viewing the world.) And not only the children benefit: for those who serve as resources and supporters of learning, the experience can help to enhance their sense of personal competence, self-worth, and self-esteem.

I have a kindergarten class that comes into our class, and we go into their class. The teacher will come drop off half of her class into mine and take half of mine with her. We'll bring in books to read with them; each student has a buddy, and they read together. The kindergarten teacher takes the other group to the computer lab, where they pair up with their buddies. Her kids are able to do things on the computer, with my students' help, that they normally wouldn't be able to follow so well. For example, my fourth grade students can help them with a computer program that involves a lot of reading.

Back in my room, we're reading books, and then we do an art activity together. One time we made little books. The older kids would do the lettering, and then the kindergarteners would trace it. My kids would cut out pictures, and the little kids would paste them in. There was a lot of spontaneous cooperation. The older kids absolutely loved having such a captive audience, and it was great one-on-one attention for all of them. It was very satisfying for them to know that something they created was challenging and fun for someone else.

Amy L. Meyer, Hoover Elementary School, Redwood City, California

Reflection. The value of reflection suggests learning experiences that promote critical thinking and holistic understanding. When we emphasize reflection rather than the rote memorization of facts, students begin to understand how phenomena in the world are connected and interrelated. At the same time, as they learn to apply concepts and to analyze the world that surrounds them, they become more able to make critical judgments and decisions. Intuitive reasoning, analytic reasoning, lateral thinking, visual thinking, and problem solving are all intellectual skills that promote reflection and make learning exciting—not only for the students but for the teacher as well. They also provide children with the cognitive skills needed to successfully meet the challenges of their lives.

At the end of our first year as an accelerated school, I assigned a reflection writing assignment to the eighth grade students. Many of them had been at Burnett for three years, and I was interested in their opinions of the school and how it had changed. I especially wondered if they thought that being an accelerated school had made an impact on life at Burnett. I really didn't know how the kids would react to this assignment. I prepared a list of questions such as, "What's special about our school, or what sets it apart from others?" and "On a scale from 1 to 5, how would you rate Burnett?" as well as more personal questions such as, "Do you feel there's much prejudice at this school?" and "What are your goals after graduation from high school?" I told the students that they could keep their comments anonymous (that's the only way I thought I'd get any responses), but most of the kids really insisted on putting their names on their papers! They were so personally invested in the assignment! I think for a lot of them it was the first time that they'd ever been asked formally for their input into the school. I could see that they felt empowered and proud of themselves. They also felt proud of our school.

Overall, the comments were very positive. One wrote, "Accelerated schools has made our school a harder challenge to face. Instead of the basics, we're taking algebra. When we're in high school, we'll know more." Another wrote, "Teachers focus on the good things about you. If you're a hoodlum, they don't say, 'Oh, you're a hoodlum, you can't learn.' They call on everyone and it makes them feel good. They treat us all equal." This year I repeated the assignment, but I expected to get more mixed results. You see, we had a shooting this year only a few yards away from our campus, and I thought students might write about how they don't feel safe here. I was really surprised—not a single student even mentioned the shooting! Their comments were even more positive than last year!

Kris Estrada, Teacher, Burnett Academy, San Jose, California

Experimentation and Discovery. The value of experimentation and discovery encourages the use of novel approaches to learn about the world. As students move beyond the simple assimilation of information, they become partners in the discovery of possibilities. The world isn't taken as an unchanging collection of facts but as an ever-evolving process in which facts acquire new meanings when we change our frame of reference. Involving students in hands-on and real-life discovery exercises helps them understand the world and be better able to deal with it. Many teachers have found that the Inquiry Process they use in their cadres provides a strong model for teaching their students to learn how to learn.

Henry Suder School has an exciting program that takes students beyond their immediate environment into a world that they could only imagine before. Project Africa consists of an annual trip by sixth and seventh grade students to three African nations, in order that students may discover their cultural roots as reflected in language, art, music, and religion. In preparation for this experience, students contact African pen pals, study French to facilitate communication, attend cultural awareness classes, keep journals during and after the trip, and appear at community functions. The fine arts are integrated into the curriculum through grants from the Illinois Arts Council and the artists in residence program.

Henry Suder School, Chicago, Illinois, Illinois Network of Accelerated Schools

Risk Taking. The value of risk taking suggests that we provide opportunities to take risks in a safe environment. Risk taking means that we adults open ourselves up to learning along with our students. Accelerated school community members become innovators in their classrooms, schools, and communities, increasingly unafraid to go beyond the limits of what has previously been thought of as possible. In order to create fantastic learning experiences, we need to analyze and discuss openly what works well for us and what doesn't. However, only in an environment of trust, respect, and caring for each other will we really feel free to take risks. As we encourage our children to take risks in the pursuit of knowledge, we support them in their efforts and assure them that their learning *processes* are as much valued as the final outcomes. Accordingly, the accelerated school context supports staff, parent, and student exploration, discovery, and honesty. This context can help to build trust among staff, students, and parents; and it allows us to all become partners in discovery, to interact freely and respect each other, and to analyze our world critically and honestly—together.

In terms of teachers' risk taking:

> **I've always started the year off by going over my classroom rules and having my students write about what they did over the summer. That way I can set the tone for the classroom and get a sense of my students' writing skills. This year I feel like trying something totally new; in fact, these ideas came to me in a dream! My feeling now is that, hey, if I don't let it hang out, how the heck can I expect my students to?**
>
> Connie Posner, Teacher, Burnett Academy, San Jose, California

In terms of students' risk taking:

> **In my class, there's no wrong answer. Sometimes someone may give a totally off-the-wall answer, and the kids learn that while you might giggle a little bit, we can always find a validation for what anybody says. The kids are really nice to each other once they internalize this idea. They're not threatened by each other, and they start to support one another. This type of learning and cooperation among children opens up doors to every single one of them. They all discover that they have value and worth.**
>
> Jackie Dolan, Daniel Webster Elementary School, San Francisco, California

School as the Center of Expertise. *The value of school as the center of expertise suggests that everyone in the school community is an expert at developing powerful learning experiences for children.* You are the experts when it comes to recognizing successful teaching and knowing what the strengths and the needs are in your school. Therefore, educational decisions should begin at the school level. The entire accelerated schools philosophy and process is specifically designed to unleash the talent in the school community in order to create the most powerful learning experiences for all children. As you continue through Chapters Seven, Eight, and Nine, you'll see more examples of how accelerated school communities have used their own expertise to accelerate children's learning all across the country!

6.3.3. Your School's Vision

Your vision statement encapsulates the philosophy of your school community concerning education and the preparation you want to give your students. Fully realizing your vision will take lots of time. It will take small, step-by-step changes by the cadres, the steering committee, and your entire school community that gradually—but systematically—move you toward your shared dreams. However, the entire school community can begin to discover how to bring the values and goals stated in your vision to life by thinking through what the vision means for you, your classes, your offices, the school grounds. For example, what might the following excerpt from Burnett Academy's vision statement imply for the way learning occurs in that school? *"All students connect the past, the present, and the future by applying their academic knowledge to the world around them and learning through experience"* (vision statement 1991).

> **One Burnett teacher, Connie Posner, brought this piece of the vision to life in her humanities classroom during a unit on the American Revolution. One morning she announced to her eighth grade class that they'd have to pay $.10 for each handout she gave them, including quizzes. The students were furious. Some shouted, "I won't pay for your handouts. I don't care what you say"; "I'm going to call our lawyer"; "Let's petition the school board." Others complained, "How can you do this when so many people are out of work and we don't have even enough money for lunch?" What the students were experiencing firsthand, of course, was the outrage and rebellion that must have been felt by the Colonists as the British levied tax after tax on them. That one class taught the students more about Colonial unrest than days of lectures could have. Ms. Posner commented after the class, "I can't remember the last time *every* student in class was totally involved in a lesson."**
>
> Burnett Academy, San Jose, California

Through powerful experiential learning and debriefing, Ms. Posner's students have definitely connected past events to *their* lives. They'll carry this knowledge, gained through an active simulation, with them into the world and apply it to many situations that they find themselves in.

When you start to discuss (in your cadre meetings or informally among staff members) how you can translate your vision statement into reality, you may find that people interpret the vision in many different ways. As you explore and discuss your different personal interpretations, you should be able to negotiate commonly accepted interpretations for all and come to decisions that bring these interpretations to life. Nevertheless, it will take lengthy discussions among teachers and the other members of the school community before you'll be able to articulate what your students should know when they leave school, what skills they should be able to master, and what values they should espouse to be able to live up to the vision that you've developed collectively.

You may find that your vision sparks discussions on many unforeseen and difficult issues. Here we offer you a few examples:

- *Your vision may challenge some of the requirements of the state framework or the central office, or it might challenge your* perceptions *of what those requirements are.* Your school's vision, along with the state framework for the different disciplines, can inform your decision with respect to the goals that you develop for each grade level and each subject area. In some cases, your vision may challenge a state or district mandate.

If that happens, you can discuss disagreements with the district office or state education office and jointly find ways to work around your differences. Schools can apply for waivers from certain mandates, for example. You must do whatever you need to do in order to create powerful learning experiences for your students.

> **It's okay to take chances. We learned that when we first began the accelerated schools process. The principal allowed the teachers to rewrite the curriculum; we decided to create a humanities core, combining language arts and social studies. A lot of people thought it wasn't really going to happen, because we were breaking district policy. Well, we'd go to district meetings and all the administrators would look at our principal and say, "You changed what? You did what?" He got beat up all year because of it. But we made the decision as a group, allowed it to happen, and we're going to have a better curriculum because of it. When we talked to the superintendent about the change, he paused for a while (it seemed like a *long* while to us!) and then he said, "Good. Let's see how it turns out."**
>
> Frank Howseman-Cabral, Vice-Principal, Burnett Academy, San Jose, California

- *In reaching for your vision, test-score improvements will become a by-product rather than a final goal.* Instead of "working toward the test," accelerated school communities work toward their vision. Even so, many accelerated schools have experienced dramatic improvements in standardized test scores after just two or three years of the accelerated schools process. People in these schools will tell you, however, that improving test scores was the last thing on their minds as they worked collaboratively to build on their school's strengths and address their challenges. Most of what they changed is never measured formally by the district or state: high expectations for all children; new staff-developed curricula that focus on the lives of children; active, hands-on instructional strategies; a governance structure that includes the input and responsibilities of parents, teachers, support staff, faculty, students, and community members. When these aspects of any school change, however, the students are the real beneficiaries, and test scores can't help but go up!

> **As described at the end of Chapter Two, the efforts and hard work of the entire school community at Hollibrook yielded enormous dividends in just two and a half years. Test scores on standardized tests soared. In 1988 fifth graders at Hollibrook had composite scores at the 4.8 level on the SRA standardized tests used in Texas. In reading and language arts, they scored at the 3.7 level. In early spring of 1991, fifth graders had composite scores at the 5.8 grade level, and reading and language arts scores had risen to 5.2 and 5.6**

respectively—a gain of almost two grade levels in just two and a half years. Even more remarkable, students were scoring a year above grade level (6.6) in mathematics.

Hollibrook Elementary School, Houston, Texas

- *Your own ambitious vision may lead you to develop a comprehensive set of enrichment activities that aren't now present at your school.* When students are encouraged to express their individual needs and to develop some of their talents that are traditionally not considered relevant to school learning, your traditional curriculum and instructional strategies may be too limited to accommodate your students' aspirations. As you bring your vision to life, you'll begin to create a variety of activities through which students can express their artistic accomplishments, their intellectual curiosity, their desire to communicate and to become friends with students from other cultures, and their desire to make this planet a better world for everyone.

> In preparation for their annual multicultural May Dance Festival at Sanchez Elementary School in the Mission District of San Francisco, students, parents, teachers, support staff, and many members of the community spent countless hours practicing dances from their home countries, designing colorful costumes, and decorating the schoolyard with May flowers, banners, flags, and posters. In their 1992 program, the children performed dances from the United States, Mexico, Peru, Brazil, El Salvador, Haiti, Cuba, Israel, and Europe. While the students practiced their dances, they learned about the history and geography of the countries and about the traditions of the people. In the coffee-picking dance from El Salvador, the children danced the hard life of the Indian coffee-pickers; and in the Aztec dance, they celebrated the glory of pre-Columbian Mexico. They learned how African traditions are expressed in Brazil and Haiti, and they brought their European heritage to life in the ancient maypole dance. Dancing in front of their peers and families and the people from the neighborhood (who'd been invited through flyers and banners), the students embodied the joy of life and the creative energy that emerges when different cultures come together to celebrate the human spirit.

Sanchez Elementary School, San Francisco, California

What's to Come

In the next three chapters, we discuss powerful learning through descriptions of the dimensions of *what*, *how*, and *context*. While we've separated these three dimensions into chapters for discussion purposes, you'll find that because the dimensions are so integrated, the chapters themselves are interrelated and draw heavily on each other. You'll also see rich examples of powerful learning from accelerated schools across the entire country. We hope to inspire you with these examples to use both big wheels and little wheels to create educational innovations that suit your own school.

We recommend that major changes be approached carefully, through the Inquiry Process. Whether you're in a cadre, grade-level team, department, or working individually, the Inquiry Process serves as a guide for understanding your challenges and approaching them creatively yet systematically. This ensures that dramatic changes are in alignment with your school's vision and that the unique strengths and needs of your learning community are taken into account.

CHAPTER 7

The *What* of Powerful Learning

Developing Meaningful Curricula

What we want our students to learn is typically described as the content of our lessons—the curriculum. Research and our own common sense tell us that we learn best when the content of the learning situation is relevant to our own lives, when connections are made among subject areas, and when the learning situations build on our strengths and experiences, including our cultural backgrounds.

All students enter school with a wealth of knowledge, strengths, and experiences. They know how to speak and listen; they interpret body language and social situations; they reason and rationalize; they create meaning from facts and bits of evidence accessible to them. Children also have an acute sense of who they are and who they want to become. Learning that coincides with their interests, hopes, and dreams comes easily to them.

For *all* children to become truly interested in and committed to learning, what happens in the classroom should be integrated with the children's present identities and with the futures they imagine for themselves. They have to "see themselves" in what takes place in the classroom. Think of the sorts of activities in which children voluntarily invest great concentration and commitment: some boys and girls spend countless hours practicing basketball, learning ballet, debating, or playing the trumpet, for example. These challenging skills are perfected through the students' self-motivated hard work, concentration, and commitment. Children are willing to make this serious investment of themselves because the activity in which they're engaged is tied intimately to their sense of who they are and who they're becoming: I'm an athlete; I'm a dancer; I'm an orator; I'm a musician.

Students' lives are the centerpiece of curricula in accelerated schools, and content areas span the terrain that we all encounter in daily life. Every day we find ourselves in all sorts of situations related to a variety of "subjects."

For example, on a walk around the neighborhood, your students might see a mural depicting civil rights heroes, hear a sidewalk musician playing the saxophone, taste delicacies from a street vendor, negotiate the price of an item with a shopkeeper in English and possibly another language, and pass the local recycling center. In reality, we experience situations that involve a combination of music, arts, literature, human relations, mathematics, food, and technologies together—not in separate doses! Accelerated schools build on the varied and rich experiences of students and make them the focus of an integrated curriculum. In the examples throughout this chapter, you'll see accelerated schools teachers embracing children's life experiences as they decide on the *what* of the powerful learning situations that they create in their classrooms.

This year I trained my classroom as a newspaper staff. I was a college newspaper editor, and I learned more during my years with the school newspaper than I ever did in a lecture hall. My dream was to produce a school newspaper in an elementary school. We've structured ourselves like a regular newspaper, with editorial meetings, a photography crew, and news departments ranging from op-ed to business. Students cover news as it affects 99th Street School, but that includes learning more about their lives outside of 99th Street School. For instance, one of our news articles covered the unveiling ceremony of a community library. While it's not our school's library, many of our students will be using it. The 99th Street reporter was jockeying for position with channels 4, 7, and 11 to talk with the councilwoman who spearheaded the effort. Another story featured the swarms of black flies that were invading our neighborhoods and biting everyone, including students. Student reporters had to call the L.A. County Health and Human Services Department and interview people who worked there. They had to prepare questions ahead of time and know exactly what they were talking about. Through these interviews, and their whole experience working on the paper, the kids were able to relate to *real* people in the *real* world. It's given them a feeling that their actions count and that they're professionals.

Anthony Jackson, Teacher, 99th Street School, Los Angeles, California

7.1. Big Wheels and Little Wheels of the *What*

How does your school go about deciding what will be taught? In Chapter Six, "Creating Powerful Learning Experiences," you read about the big wheels and little wheels of change in an accelerated school. Both processes can help you focus on the *what* of powerful learning situations, and both can lead to extraordinary change in your current curriculum. While the little wheels are turning out stimulating learning experiences, the big wheels are turning as well—perhaps more slowly, but ever so surely and productively. Two examples of innovations in the *what* follow: a little-wheel example from a school in Texas and a big-wheel example of a cadre's inquiry into the curricular area of problem solving.

7.1.1. Little Wheel: "When in Texas, Do As the Romans Do"

What follows is a concrete example of an innovative *what* put together by Suzanne Still, principal-turned-teacher, at an accelerated school. Still taught this class at the same time that she was a full-time principal. In accelerated schools, all staff become important teachers of all of the children; hard and fast roles and boundaries between jobs become more flexible, encouraging everyone to get involved in powerful learning! Within the vignette, we highlight the ways in which this experience illustrates the foundations of powerful learning presented in the last section, with a special focus on the *what*. We hope that this passage sparks some little wheels in your community!

> **I received an invitation in the mail to see a preview of the "Last Days of Pompeii" exhibit at the Houston Museum of Fine Arts. I've always loved Roman history, so there I was walking around the museum, and I could hardly get up to the different cases for stepping on five- and six-year-olds. All the yuppies were there, and they'd brought their kids. I thought to myself, "Suzanne, the Hollibrook kids have got to get to Pompeii." Well, what happened was that I transformed from an old-timey traditional teacher to a great new-fangled teacher.**

Seizing the moment. Suzanne Still picks a theme, based on the current availability of a potentially powerful educational resource in the local community and the recognition that the school's children are "at risk" of missing an opportunity to utilize this resource.

> **The first thing I did was forget about the word *unit*. A unit means that there's only so much information, only so much time. Why couldn't you study Roman history all year long and plug all of your requirements**

into that curriculum? Why not? Where is it written that you can't do that? I taught this course on Roman history to all grade levels. I had first and second graders and fourth and fifth graders gather in my office.

Taking a risk. The shift in values occurs. The children's natural learning needs are being put first, while the relevance and importance of traditional curricular guidelines are being critically reassessed.

I started planning my course using guidelines for writing interdisciplinary curricula that I found in our library. Okay, we're studying Pompeii. Well, we need to know a little bit about the history of Pompeii. We had only one book about Roman history in our school library. It was a start, and reading that with them got us into the realm of language arts. Then I found one story called "Pompeii's Tragic End" in a reader, and I started building vocabulary lists around that.

Planning without a textbook. Still seeks additional information and guidance on how to proceed and connects the resources she discovers to the chosen theme.

Now when you start studying about Pompeii, you have to start learning about the caste system, because that's the way it was there. You were born into a certain social station. We could talk about whether that kind of thing went on today. Science? Well, you have to know a little bit about volcanoes to learn about Pompeii; and going to Rome, you have to know about Roman numerals, so that's math.

Making it interdisciplinary. With creative brainstorming, she begins to connect the different subject areas—math, science, art, history, and so on—to the core theme.

I'd planned all kinds of activities and lessons around these things. Then, about eleven o'clock the night before the first class, I realized that I'd left out one of the most important ingredients. Children learn by doing, and I didn't have anything experiential for them to do. The rest of the night I spent tearing apart flower arrangements in my house so that they could have eucalyptus leaves to wear in their hair and tearing sheets off of beds to make togas. I made things that would turn my office into a Roman classroom. That just barely scratches the surface of what we did in the class, though.

Adding that experiential umph. She realizes that the material hasn't yet been personalized in a way that will create a powerful learning experience for the children. Her caring, enthusiasm, and dedication are evident in that extra ounce of effort that she devotes to making the next day's experience special.

When they came in the first day, we brainstormed about different words that you could use to describe people: large, tall, young, pretty, smart. Some of them learned what a thesaurus was that day. Then we started picking words that would describe ourselves, and we learned about how Romans named themselves, and how they didn't have last names, and why. We all made nametags giving ourselves Roman names. I was Suzanne the Elder. One little girl was Rosie the Quiet.

Grounding the curriculum in the here and now. She literally "wraps the theme around her children" so that they become the center of the curriculum. When a thesaurus is needed, they don't receive a *lesson* on its purpose; rather, its use is modeled, and the children participate in this meaningful usage.

From there we learned how to greet each other. We would say, "Hail, Juan the Reader," and "Hail, so and so." We would talk about things like where we get the expression "hail a taxi." One little boy came to me and said that he'd seen a movie on television about Hitler and that Hitler had hailed people like the Romans had. That led him off into an independent research project about World War II that carried over into his fourth grade class. What was happening was that these kids were learning to love learning. It was incredible how it took off.

Allowing things to snowball. The children's learning experience doesn't follow a linear path; rather, the children explore topics that arise naturally from the theme. Questions and observations made by individual children become catalysts for further independent study. It's clear to the teacher that the children's learning is accelerating.

We did map studies of the area and made books of the geography and topography of the city. We found out that they had fast food in Rome. I never knew that before! They had a contraption like a big stone table that held a reservoir of water that could be heated to keep food hot. People could just walk up with a plate. We went straight from learning that to our school cafeteria, and we took apart the steam tables to figure out how they worked. The kids were starting to realize that lots of things around us have their origins in Rome.

Transforming the mundane into the interesting through hands-on study. Studies lead to surprising discoveries. These are not only talked about but compared and contrasted experientially through active exploration of an item in the "real world." Children develop a new level of awareness about the origins and meaning of things all around them.

We studied why the people [in Pompeii] really died. It wasn't the lava; they were dead before that got to them. We had to learn the word *suffocate*, and we studied the respiratory system and how people can suffocate. We learned about volcanic ash, and we studied Mt. Saint Helens. One child brought in a pumice stone that he'd found at home; his mother used it on her feet. It seemed so light that the children wondered how it could hurt if it fell on you. So we started talking about the laws of physics, and we went outside and started playing catch with pumice and chunks of volcanic rock. The kids found out that the farther away the person throwing the stone was, the more it hurt your hand when you caught it.

Discovering hands-on, hands-hurtin' science. Explorations lead into many different areas of the physical sciences, where an integrated and experiential knowledge of biology, geology, and physics is required in order to develop adequate understanding. When puzzles can't be solved easily, the children actively engage in scientific research, experimentation, hypothesis generation, and testing.

As other teachers in the school heard about what we were doing, they'd come and say, "Hey, I have this piece of volcanic rock in my room; do you want to use it?" You bet. Pretty soon I didn't have enough boxes to hold all of the materials I'd collected, and my office was constantly full of children building volcanoes on one side of the room or playing a dice game that Roman soldiers used to play, doing some pretty complex math with Roman numerals. We looked at books to learn how to drape our togas, and we learned about all the different kinds of materials togas were made from. Everyone made his or her own wreath of leaves, and we wore them on our big field trip to the Museum of Fine Arts.

Merging the past with the present. The entire project takes on a creative life of its own. What would seem like chaos to many is nurtured and then given focus as the class prepares for a final event—a big field trip that will tie everything together academically and bring a new level of meaning to all the "fun" learning activities that the children had engaged in.

We even ended up doing some time and rate problems. The health fitness teachers were working with me and the kids on these questions: If a human being walks this fast, and lava flows this fast, how early would you have to leave Pompeii to get out safely? And can you sustain a walk that fast that long? We ended up finding out that we'd have to be able to predict that it was going to erupt in order to leave in time.

Encouraging learning, learning everywhere! Every possible experience becomes an opportunity for applying knowledge and solving problems. Teachers serve as collaborators, resources, and co-investigators.

We never limited ourselves. Whatever question came up, we answered it, and that took us into every conceivable curriculum discipline. We even learned recipes and talked about the kinds of food they ate, and whether that kind of food exists now. **We learned the words** *feast* **and** *banquet.*

Imposing no limits, no boundaries to learning. The children are empowered and accepted as co-explorers and discoverers. Their natural questioning and curiosity often define what actual content is covered (and in what order). Yet in the end, nothing is left out.

After our field trip to the museum at the end of the course, we walked down the street to a little park and had a Roman feast. We were all reclined on pillows in our togas, eating grapes and bread and cheese. So there we are out in the park and one of the students says, "Look across the street! That building has Doric columns. That's from Roman architecture!" Another boy lifted his box of grape juice and said, "Mrs. Still, we need a toast." He explained what a toast was to the rest of the group, because some of them didn't know, and then he toasted, "To Rome!" Everyone toasted, and then one boy said, "You know, Mrs. Still, this is the way school should be every single day." And another girl said, "You know what? No one would ever be absent."

Suzanne Still, Former Principal, Hollibrook Elementary School, Houston, Texas

Savoring the fruits of acceleration. A sense of completion and accomplishment permeates the atmosphere as the experience is brought to an end. Discovering new things with others has become its own reward, creating an educational experience that neither teacher nor students will ever forget.

We hope that you enjoyed reading about this adventure! When a school begins to accelerate, learning experiences seem to take on an almost magical quality. A community of learners becomes so engrossed in their journey that the process of the journey becomes valued as much as any final "product." Though the overall curriculum of the school as a whole will change more slowly, this little wheel has already accelerated these children's learning into a new realm of experience and education. The vision isn't always something far off in the future: it's an *experience* brought to life more and more every day in an accelerated school community.

7.1.2. Big Wheel: Using the Inquiry Process for Decisions About the *What*—A Case Study

As you get into your cadres and begin to work with the other members of your school community to address your school's curricular challenges using the Inquiry Process, you may wonder where on earth to begin. As you remember, the Inquiry Process offers a systematic method for addressing the complex challenge areas of your school in a collaborative way. Inquiring into what your students are learning and should learn is among the greatest challenges that a school community can face.

In addressing your school's challenges through an exploration of the *what* of powerful learning situations, your cadres should take care to understand your school's challenges and find solutions that truly *address* these challenges. There are so many good ideas in the field of education that it's tempting to adopt a specific program without making sure that it actually meets the needs of your school. Relish your many strengths (including your resourcefulness!) and use them to understand and address your particular challenges.

We turn now to a detailed description of the Inquiry Process in action as it occurred within a cadre assigned to tackle the challenge of students' problem-solving skills during Hoover Elementary School's first year as an accelerated school. You'll see how teachers at Hoover were able to shape a specific program to meet their needs only after they'd spent considerable time understanding why the challenge they faced existed at their school.

Stage 1: Focus in on the Challenge Area. The first task facing members of the Problem-Solving Cadre was to transform their broad challenge into a clearly understood focus area that could direct the group's efforts throughout the Inquiry Process. In many ways, the members of this cadre were like Wilbur and Orville Wright. The Wright brothers needed to move beyond the mere vision of an aircraft driven by a machine. They needed to consider a specific problem—how to develop adequate lift—that would focus their experimental efforts. Similarly, cadre members set out to lessen the gap between their present situation and their vision in the priority challenge area of problem solving.

1a: Explore the challenge area informally and hypothesize why it exists. Initial discussions revealed that group members were particularly concerned with higher-order skills in the area of mathematics, which are commonly associated with problem-solving abilities. Students in the upper grades frequently experienced difficulty with word problems or other problem-solving exercises in math. Standardized tests showed that Hoover's students had increasing difficulty with these types of questions as they rose through the grade levels, even though they scored relatively high on tests of math computation.

These initial discussions, which occurred during biweekly meetings and interviews with other members of the school community over eight or ten weeks, crystallized the cadre's sense of the problem. The cadre developed the following question: Why does the discrepancy between math computation scores and math application scores grow between second and sixth grades?

Members of the Problem-Solving Cadre offered a wide range of hypotheses for the students' difficulties with problem-solving exercises in math. Some hypotheses focused on the teachers: perhaps the teachers at the lower grades placed a greater emphasis on this area or were more highly trained in math instruction, for example. The cadre also considered the possibility that the difficulties with problem-solving exercises were somehow related to the students' background: could it be, they wondered, that the school's many native Spanish speakers were having trouble reading word problems? At this point, they weren't trying to answer the question; they were just proposing hypotheses.

1b: Test hypotheses to see if they hold water. After developing an extensive list of hypotheses, cadre members then discussed how they might examine existing school practices to shed light on these possible explanations. They used a variety of data-gathering techniques during this phase of the inquiry. Teachers from the cadre observed one another during mathematics instruction, then observed other teachers in the school. They also developed an interview form for questioning their colleagues about math curriculum and instruction. Interview items touched on common challenges that teachers face, such as use of manipulatives and evaluations of textbook quality. In addition, the cadre conducted a survey of mathematics-related resources (manipulatives, games, computer programs, textbooks, curricula) available in the school.

1c: Interpret the results of testing and develop a clear understanding of the challenge area. The Problem-Solving Cadre noted a marked difference between the instructional approaches used for the primary grades and those used for the upper grades. In the primary grades, math instruction tended to be more child-centered, featuring hands-on exercises in small groups. Teachers made extensive use of manipulatives and math games in these lessons. In the upper grades, on the other hand, teachers tended to use the math textbook for whole-group instruction. The cadre also observed that students in the upper grades often saw little connection between the real-world math problems that they encountered at home and the word problems included in the math textbooks. Many students who were able to use their own methods to figure out the math that they needed at the local store or in their after-school games were lost when they were asked to use the formulas taught in school.

After the cadre identified these patterns, the facilitator asked members to consider the relationship between these patterns and commonly held assumptions about the school and the students' homes. This discussion revealed teachers' assumptions about child development as well as perceptions of pressures to keep up with the standardized curriculum. Cadre members observed that these assumptions were buttressed by the system: primary teachers were given manipulatives and received training in hands-on instruction, while upper-grade teachers were issued textbooks and expected to prepare students for the curriculum in the next grade. Cadre members also concluded that the students' inability to connect math in school and in the real world pointed to a general dissonance between school and home life and questioned why alternative approaches to problem solving promoted in the home weren't accorded more respect in the school.

Because members of the Problem-Solving Cadre now had a clearer understanding of what was once a broadly defined challenge area, they had a direction—a set of focus areas—in which to concentrate their search for solutions. Their focus areas were (1) to look for ways in which families and the school could develop more child-centered approaches to mathematics instruction for the upper grades and (2) to look for ways in which the school could better integrate school math with the real-world math of the students' home lives.

This cadre shared its report with the rest of the cadres at a schoolwide staff-development day. The school as a whole provided feedback to each cadre's work, suggesting new ideas that were integrated into the reports.

Stage 2: Brainstorm Solutions. During this second stage, cadre members read a series of articles on the use of hands-on learning in elementary mathematics. Many of the articles described specific instructional programs and manipulative packages. The cadre focused on reading them for general understanding rather than in search of hard and fast rules for practice.

After reading these articles, cadre members discussed the relative merits of different instructional approaches. They commented on the relationship between specific approaches and underlying beliefs about schooling. In addition, cadre members discussed the challenges of transforming present attitudes and practices.

To learn more about ways to address the dissonance between the home and the school, the cadre invited a speaker from *Family Math*, a program developed by researchers at the Lawrence Hall of Science (University of California, Berkeley) to involve parents in their children's mathematics education through fun puzzles and games. Cadre members found many features of the program consonant with ideas that they'd been independently developing. Nevertheless, rather than looking at Family Math as a finished product ready to import in its entirety into the school, cadre members asked how the program might be adapted to the particular needs of their school.

At the conclusion of this stage, the cadre developed a second report for the schoolwide audience. This report contained conclusions from the literature, strengths and weaknesses of individual programs, and lessons that the literature and programs held for the needs of the school.

Stage 3: Synthesize Solutions and Develop an Action Plan. The Problem-Solving Cadre considered proposals ranging from creating a schoolwide "problem of the week" to developing a homework hotline for students. To address the gap between the students' perceptions of school math and real-world math, some cadre members suggested adapting the Family Math program to the needs of Hoover. Cadre members believed that they could create a similar program featuring games using cards or dice; these games would call upon the students to use problem-solving strategies and arithmetic functions taught in the classroom. One cadre member, a teacher, suggested that a Family Math class serve students from all grades and meet weekly throughout the year. Some cadre members liked that idea; others objected to the dimensions of the plan, arguing that, as a pilot test, the program should be both shorter and limited to the younger students. While the entire cadre agreed to a shorter pilot class—one that would run for seven weeks—members decided to include students from the upper grades, who were the original focus of the challenge area.

Once the cadre decided to pilot test a class for students of all ages, it turned to developing a plan of who would do what by when, and how. The cadre sought out the school's resource teacher, who agreed to help coordinate the class from week to week. With her support in hand, the cadre then asked faculty members if they'd pledge to teach one class each. To finalize the proposal, the cadre estimated the minimal material costs that the program would entail. Cadre members also decided to weave math-problem-of-the-week exercises into the proposal because—as they learned from a steering committee meeting—that would dovetail nicely with the Self-Esteem/School Spirit Cadre's work. The draft proposal met with a favorable response from the rest of the school community. At the request of several teachers from other cadres, it was amended to ensure that the teachers of the family classes be fluent in English and Spanish, the native language of many of the parents.

Stage 4: Pilot Test and/or Implement the Action Plan. The cadre implemented the program for seven weeks on a pilot basis. Several teachers went through special training at a nearby college and ran the program on a series of Saturday evenings.

> **The first night we got twenty families, and it was a lot of work setting it up. The parents loved it! We'd scheduled the session from seven o'clock to eight, but we went until nine; they didn't want to stop. They kept coming back too, and they always brought their kids. We had casino night, when we used dice and estimating and card games to show parents how you can really get into some concepts with your kids at home. Then we had computing night, when we took them over to the computer lab and just let them go with all kinds of math programs that**

we'd plugged into the computer. We had puzzle night, and everyone worked on puzzles all evening. We always connected what we did with what they could do at home, and we always gave out the same materials we used. Of course, we couldn't give out comptuers, but we certainly gave out cards and dice and puzzles. We even got little $7 calculators from Radio Shack, and each family got one.

A lot of us brought our own kids, and we sat right down at the tables with the families and did the activities with our own children. I remember at my table, my son and I were teaching this family to play kings in the corner, which is a great card game. The father came back a couple of weeks later and told me, "We've had more fun with that kings-in-the-corner game!" Things like that made me think that these nights went way beyond math. Families were spending some time together.

Barbara Ruel, Resource Teacher, Hoover Elementary School, Redwood City, California

During the pilot test, teachers, parents, and students informally assessed the success of the program. As you can tell from Ruel's comments, the Family Math pilot test served multiple purposes: it seemed to provide real-life problem-solving experiences as well as to connect parents and children in areas aside from math.

Stage 5: Evaluate and Reassess. Based on the positive response of parents, students, and staff to the pilot test, members of the Problem-Solving Cadre suggested that the school should consider tying the games students played and the types of experiences they had in the pilot phases into their regular math instruction. All of the upper-grade teachers received hands-on math materials and training so that more real-life problem solving could occur in the classroom.

The next year, the cadre compared the math achievement of students who'd participated in Family Math with that of those who had not. *In every case, students who had participated in Family Math improved by at least one grade level, whereas those who had not participated did not improve.*

After evaluating the results of the process thus far, participants also looked forward and considered new directions for their inquiry. The Problem-Solving Cadre became the Mathematics Cadre and continued to work on improving student performance in mathematics and problem solving throughout the school.

The example of Hoover's cadre illustrates how, in accelerated schools, a small change leads to a larger change, which leads to the vision. All participants take incremental steps toward that goal. In this example, a small change (a seven-week Family Math program) turned into a larger change (manipulatives and real-life problem solving in the regular classrooms), which will—with fine-tuning and care—turn into partial realization of the vision for Hoover Elementary School. Part of their vision statement says, "Our students will acquire the problem-solving and critical-thinking skills which will enable them to participate successfully as citizens and workers in the twenty-first century."

The story of Hoover's Problem-Solving Cadre also clearly illustrates the intertwined nature of the *what*, *how*, and *context* of powerful learning situations. To solve their curricular challenge, cadre members had to examine *what* was being taught, *how* it was being taught, and the *context* in which it was taught. They observed each other's instructional strategies to get an idea of how the strategies interacted with subject matter to produce powerful learning. They assessed and inventoried all of the math teaching materials at their school to get a sense of how they were presently organized to teach math at each grade level and contemplated how they might like to reorganize. The Family Math program was an organizational and instructional feat that went far beyond the realm of the *what*. As you work together in your cadres, you too will find that challenges first labeled as curricular, instructional, or organizational necessarily involve all three dimensions.

7.2. Creating the *What* in Accelerated Schools

The traditional approach to curriculum development separates disciplines, such as art, math, social studies, and music, into distinct subject areas with very little overlap. Whether they have a different teacher for each subject or know that at eleven-thirty they should get out their science books, students learn through this approach that the world is composed of separate compartments of knowledge instead of existing as a unified, integrated whole. Unfortunately, this approach fails to appreciate the importance of math to music and science or the relationship between literature and history. When content is presented in this compartmentalized fashion, students aren't encouraged to make the connections between disciplines that we call higher-order thinking and creativity.

Imagine how disjointed and discordant an orchestra would sound if each musician played her part consecutively instead of in harmony with all of the others! Symphonies, like knowledge of the world we live in, were meant to be understood and experienced as a whole, with each individual instrument contributing to the total sound.

Even so, symphonies and orchestras would not be complete without solos and soloists to highlight the special strengths and contributions of each type of instrument. Similarly, in teaching and learning, disciplines can "solo" as a unique interpretation of a particular theme or topic. Total understanding, however, comes when the "solo" is perfectly integrated with its context—the world of knowledge that we all experience each day.

Throughout the rest of this chapter let's listen to the "music" that accelerated school communities have created, paying particular attention to the balance between integrating and highlighting subject areas. We'll explore how the various disciplines, such as math, art, social studies, science, home economics, language arts, and physical education, complement each other to promote powerful learning for all children.

Research on Curricular Integration

Scientists and educators are now beginning to understand that the separation of disciplines has important implications for learning, especially when no efforts are made at integration. The strict division of learning content into subjects such as science, social studies, language arts, and reading makes it hard for children to find meaning in and see the

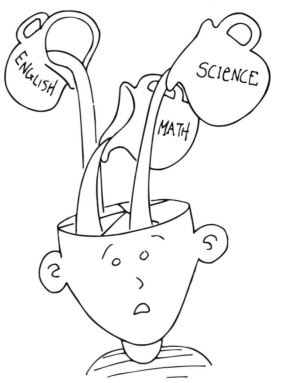

relevance of what they're taught in school. Research has shown that when students can't see how isolated facts and individual bits of knowledge fit into the "big picture," they have little use for those knowledge-bits and discard them after they've taken the required test. Integrated curriculum units attempt to bring these discrete knowledge-bits together into a cohesive whole.

The many ways to integrate curricula range from discipline-based to interdisciplinary units or courses and from the concentration on a limited number of subjects at a time to a curriculum devoted to solving actual problems in the social environment of the students. Of these, there's certainly no *one best* approach. Your decision on how to integrate whatyou teach will depend on your school's vision and the accelerated principles and values.

The current demand for integrated curricula in many state frameworks and at the district level has promoted the development of many exciting curricula that are now commercially available (Jacobs, 1989).

7.2.1. Expression Through Language

We use language in many different forms to express ourselves: writing, reading, speaking, and listening. Traditionally, we've thought of teaching students to communicate as the discipline of language arts, with a heavy focus on getting them to master the "basics" of grammar before they can move on to more complex and intrinsically enjoyable reading and writing instruction. However, this isn't how we human beings learn a language! Language is a means of communication and expression, and we learn to use it in the context of our social experiences. Our parents never sat down with us to explain the use of past participles; rather, they modeled language use in every interaction they had with us. They used language to teach us many things other than "language arts," from how to tie our shoes to how to make a waffle. In our daily lives, language has always occurred "across the curriculum!"

Teachers in the examples that follow have found that what works for so-called gifted and talented students in the area of language development works just as well with students in at-risk situations. All children respond best to reading and writing instruction that focuses on comprehension and the search for meaning in their lives. Often the best way to create powerful language learning for children is to contextualize language in the search for knowledge in social studies, science, math, and other areas.

In the following vignette, Henry M. Levin, the founder of the Accelerated Schools Project, got to see reading, writing, speaking, acting, and listening all taking place at once in an accelerated classroom. He even got to do some "acting" himself!

> **One class at Daniel Webster had organized its curriculum around the theme of bears. Students had a bear parade and brought bears from home to decorate the classroom. (The teacher arranged for an agency to donate bears for those students who didn't have one at home.) The**

children named the bears and wrote about them. They read literature about bears, and they worked with bears in science, social studies, and every other subject. They used the fact that bears gain weight to learn math, and they even discussed a bear's diet after hibernation. When Levin was visiting their classroom, the children told him all about the bears. Levin asked if they knew that bears sleep all winter. "Of course we do!" they shouted. "That's called hibernation!" Levin pursued the subject, asking whether bears sleep so much because they're tired. "No," the children replied. "Their metabolism is low." "What's *metabolism?*" Levin asked. One of the children got up and demonstrated, by drooping around the room, what happens to someone whose metabolism is low. Levin tried it and all the children laughed, because he had far too much energy in his walk to be hibernating!

Daniel Webster Elementary School, San Francisco, California

The "bear" facts. In this interdisciplinary classroom, language is an everyday, every minute affair. Providing a theme around which students can contextualize the abstract knowledge that they're learning is a good way to build vocabulary, writing, and reading skills way beyond what's traditionally expected of students in the early grades. These students could rival many a college professor in their knowledge about bears.

At the middle school level, curriculum integration often requires changes in the school schedule and subject-matter focus for teachers. For example, members of Burnett Academy's school community have taken a schoolwide step toward curricular integration by creating a humanities core. Using the Inquiry Process, Burnett's Curriculum Cadre recommended to the school as a whole that Burnett combine social studies and language arts. In the following vignette, Kris Estrada, the head of the new humanities department at Burnett, describes how well these two disciplines fit together and how enthusiastically students respond when they're able to see the relevance of academic topics to their own lives.

I always try to develop challenging curricula that the students will find interesting. In my humanities classes, I was teaching about the Great Wall of China and Chinese history. Instead of just lecturing to them about specific facts, we had really in-depth discussions about issues in Chinese history and culture that I knew they'd be interested in. For example, we talked about the roles of men and women, foot-binding, how the concepts of love and marriage were very different in Chinese culture, and what the proper rules of etiquette and conduct were between generations. Of course, we also talked about how the Chinese invented gunpowder and noodles. We discussed Buddhism and the Chinese calendar.

Using cultural history to draw students in. By discussing issues informally rather than lecturing about historical facts, Estrada is able to connect with her students' own life experiences. Clearly, as interesting as great architecture, wars, and politics can be, it's the everyday experiences of people in Chinese society that interest the students initially.

There were several Chinese American students in my classes, and some of them brought in coins and other artifacts from China. They were very proud to share these things with the other students, and it was a great connection between what we were learning about and the real-world experiences of these students. All of the students got really involved, though. When we were talking about the yin and yang symbol, one boy said, "Hey, I've seen that on surfboards!" Another one had seen it on a T-shirt. They were really motivated to find out more.

Connecting history to the present. For the Chinese American children, this is an opportunity to share their culture with their school community. Their cultural background and heritage are becoming something real for the other students—respected as something interesting, something important—and they feel proud. Every student in the class is encouraged to think about how Chinese culture has influenced our common world.

After we'd discussed these issues and the students had a good understanding and appreciation of the culture, I had them do a writing assignment over a period of several days. My classroom is the writing lab, and each student works on a word processor. They had to do two things. First, I gave them a copy of a letter from a father to his firstborn son congratulating him on finishing school. They were to write a letter of response, making sure that they addressed their elder in the proper, respectful manner. Then each one had to keep a diary as if he or she were a young girl who'd just been informed that tomorrow she'd be married to a man she'd never seen before.

Encouraging the imaginative application of knowledge. Now the children are being given an opportunity to use, in a more formal manner, the cultural knowledge that they've gained. Estrada has structured the writing assignment so that it has both strict constraints and broad creative freedom. In order to complete the task, students have to use and develop additional skills not connected directly to the topic—typing skills, computer skills, spelling, art, and writing skills. When combined, these curricular elements make the writing task more challenging, but also more interesting.

I've used this technique across many topic areas. We did a unit called "Hear Me Speak," about the Native Americans. We talked about their attitudes toward worship and the natural environment. Inevitably, we

talked about the Indians' relationship with white people, and how destructive it was. I had them read a testimony written by a frontier soldier who'd been ordered to kill a friendly tribe. It was an incredibly moving piece: this man didn't want to do it; he was being forced to. Then I told the students to imagine that they were living on a reservation and a white man had come to visit. They had to write what they'd say to him.

We did the same thing while we were studying the Constitution. Each of the students had to play the role of a Colonial person and write a letter to the editor of a Philadelphia newspaper regarding ratification of the Constitution. Some of them chose to be free blacks; others were loyalist merchants; yet others were wives of revolutionaries. Their writings were very moving. The students in my classes come from many different cultures themselves—Mexican American, Asian American, African American, and Portuguese American, to name a few—and it was powerful for them to put themselves in someone else's shoes. It encouraged them to appreciate and understand their own culture more, as well as others'.

Kris Estrada, Teacher, Burnett Academy, San Jose, California

"First walk a mile in his shoes." Here we see that the learning goals of Estrada's lessons go light years beyond "remedial" social studies and literature curricula. While the students do develop writing skills and a basic knowledge of other cultures, these aren't the sole focus of their activities. Rather, what makes the learning powerful is that students are able to take the perspective of people in other cultures and thereby understand why they value certain things and think the way they do. This type of understanding gives the children greater insight into themselves and is essential in a multicultural society such as ours.

In the previous example, we saw how a teacher prepared her students for a writing assignment by first discussing the topic in a way that made it relevant to them. This technique enabled the students to develop the knowledge that they would need to complete their writing task. In the example that follows, we see how another teacher takes a different approach when she teaches literature:

In language arts, it's a matter of reorganizing the way you teach literature. The traditional way is to prepare the kids for a story or a book for days before you actually start reading it. First there's vocabulary and spelling from the story; then you have to write sentences with those words, etc. That approach wastes time, though. I always dive right into the literature and worry about the rest later. We'll read the whole thing, let the child experience the piece as a whole. You don't break things up. Then, when everyone's been exposed

to the whole, you take care of the individual needs of your students. This student needs help here; that student needs help there. But everyone's working from the same starting point.

Amy L. Meyer, Teacher, Hoover Elementary School, Redwood City, California

Jumping right into learning! There are many different ways to organize and approach a curriculum. If a story or book is interesting and relevant, too much preparation may dilute the learning experience for students. Yet there's no right or wrong way to do things. The key is to know your students and your curriculum and then organize instruction so that they come together in a way that's relevant and interesting.

Some of the most important skills that our students can develop in writing, reading, and speaking relate to problem solving and reflective thinking. When a child learns how to think deeply and analyze problems, her approach to life's challenges often improves dramatically. Many programs that teach such skills exist, each with a different emphasis and approach. One elementary school teacher found a simple yet powerful tool in this basic approach from the Project Read program:

One strategy that I have to teach kids to read through writing is called "problem, response, action, and outcome." It's a strategy for having children analyze a story or chapter or excerpt, but you can use it to teach them writing. It's a beautiful skeleton frame for beginning story writing. So first you read a story to the children; they listen, and then you talk about it. What was the problem that the character faced in the story? and so on. I use a television analogy to explain it to the kids. When you watch television, there's a segment of a show, then a commercial, then another segment, and so on. Everything between the commercials is called an *episode*; it advances the plot one step. Every episode has a *problem*. What are the characters facing? What are they trying to accomplish? Then we talk about the *response*. What does the character feel about the problem? What was the first thing he or she felt after this problem occurred? The *action* is what they did about those feelings. We talk about the next step that the character takes to begin to solve the problem. The *outcome* is what happened after this action was taken. If the outcome doesn't solve the problem, it leads to another episode, and you start the process all over again.

Keeping it relevant, simple, and powerful. This way of analyzing a story is as powerful as it is simple. It enables these fourth graders to put themselves in a story character's shoes and understand the situation that he or she is facing. Jackie Dolan links learning reading and writing to the development of analytic and reflective thinking skills so that her students are actually gaining two sets of skills at once. She also makes the lesson more inviting to her students by having them utilize something that they interact with everyday: television. The lesson will continue to come alive as students begin to watch television critically. As we see below, Dolan recognizes the potential in this approach and uses it to help the children explore and make sense of a variety of human experiences.

Every time I get a new class—I don't care what grade level they are—they need to learn this process. You can use it for expository writing; you can use it for science; you can use it when you're doing any kind of investigating or experimentation. What's the problem we have? What's our response? What's our action? What's the outcome? We used this process to study the Alaskan oil spill. It's a technique you can use clear across the curriculum, in any subject. Once children learn the process, you see a big change in the way they write, the way they think, the way they talk. There's a higher level of thinking going on. The logic is there. Most kids start to think before they speak once they go through this several times. They internalize the process and the subprocess of thinking, and that's one of the prerequisites to developing higher-level thinking skills.

Jackie Dolan, Teacher, Daniel Webster Elementary School, San Francisco, California

Building on our strengths. This is only one example of how teachers in accelerated schools have made use of powerful learning approaches and programs created by other educators. In fact, people often find that their past training comes alive in a new way as they're encouraged to take risks, be innovative, and apply the values and principles of accelerated schools to their teaching techniques. Of further note in this example is how Dolan takes an instructional technique (a *how*) and transforms it into an element of the content of powerful learning (a *what*).

7.2.2. Exploring Scientific and Quantitative Understanding

Much of our modern global culture relies on advances in mathematics, science, and technology. While this reality puts pressure on educators to teach these topics thoroughly, it also means that there are many real-world resources available that we can use to create powerful learning situations. Math can be a dynamic, problem-solving tool when students are presented with real-life problems that they can master with mathematical concepts. There's a science lesson—far from boring—waiting to be discovered in anything that a child might find interesting or "cool": the technology of an electric guitar, a computer, or a video game; the chemistry behind cooking, photography development, or fabric dyes; the physics that explains why a curve ball curves—or whatever else might fascinate our students. We believe that all children are capable of enjoying and mastering math and science. What they need is a curriculum that builds on their strengths and captures their interest. There are also many different ways to build a student-centered math and science curriculum: doing experiments, writing stories, reading books, watching movies, and even setting up dramatic situations.

As the following example shows, exploration of the world from the perspective of science can lead to amazingly powerful learning in mathematics, social studies, and even reading. And you don't have to be an expert in science to help your children learn about it! In fact, you can become a co-explorer, learning with them about the role of science in the world that surrounds us.

We did a space unit with the first and third grades together. It came about initially because my kids wanted to start studying space; they were showing a great deal of interest in space books and other materials. Betty's aide also had to write a unit as part of her requirements, so the three of us got together to put something together. I'd never taught anything on space before, so sometimes it felt like we were making it up as we went along. We went to the public library and got as many books as we could find on space, and we started planning activities that our classes could do together. All of this began happening around Thanksgiving, so we decided to have a feast: the bilingual first grade and my class were astronauts visiting the planet of the third graders, who were aliens. We also set up an astronaut training center with the different types of physical activities that you have to go through to become an astronaut. The P.E. department helped us with that. We made a little card for each child, and as the kids passed through each activity station, they got their card stamped.

Teachers "boldly going" where they haven't been before. Here's a nice example of educators creatively building on the strengths of their situation. They begin their unit based on a natural interest that they see in their students—never mind that it isn't a subject in their current repertoire. When Thanksgiving arrives, they don't suspend their studies; rather, they find a way to connect them to the theme of the holiday. They then continue to expand on this new role-playing idea by coordinating physical "training" activities with the P.E. department!

The very last day of the unit, we took all the kids to the planetarium for a show on the solar system. It was an incredible field trip! The students were so excited as the different planets flashed across the screen, because they *knew* the name of each one, and they *knew* all sorts of information about them. It was wonderful to plan a field trip to be the culminating activity to a unit that we wrote ourselves, instead of the district or the grade level announcing, "Students will go see this; now teach something to prepare them for it." The field trip was part and parcel of our curriculum, not just something extra.

Integrating field activities meaningfully. What we see here is that as a subject becomes more relevant to children, all the activities connected to it become more meaningful. A field trip that connects to the topic that both students and teachers want to study has a powerful impact, and such experiences become an integral part of the curriculum instead of just an extra.

Then we went to see the movie *The Blue Planet*, and the kids were really inspired by that. The fifth graders had also gone to see that film. All of the students were very concerned. Now that they understood how fragile our world is, they wanted to know how to protect it. So we decided to follow up with a mini-unit on ecology. There were so many wonderful activities we came up with; we created an oil spill in the classroom by pouring some crude oil into a bowl of water. The kids broke up into groups, and each group had a collection of materials—a cotton ball, a string, and a spoon—and they had to figure out how to clean up the crude oil. The oil smelled very bad, and the kids got the feeling that this stuff was really nasty. They could tell immediately that it had a very different consistency than the cooking oil their parents might use at home.

Going with the momentum of powerful learning. These students have become scientists. Information about our physical world leads to natural questions about conservation and the environment. There's no stopping their drive to find answers to their concerns. Once powerful learning has begun, teachers are challenged to design activities that will meet children's intrinsic desire to understand things and make a difference in the world.

Another activity was having the children keep track of their trash for a week. Each child walked around the school all day with a little bag, putting all of his or her trash in it. We kept track of everyone's trash: we sorted it, graphed it, weighed it. A lot of math came in at that point; we started figuring, "If one child produces this much trash, and there are so many kids in the school, how much trash does Hollibrook generate?" That led us into talking about recycling, and we made recycled paper. I gave groups of children a basin full of water and lots of toilet paper or facial tissue and had them shred it into fine pieces. Then you press the wet, shredded fibers between two screens and push it down so it's really flat. When it dries, it becomes a new sheet of paper. It really worked, and the kids were so proud.

We also buried ten different types of trash out in the courtyard; we call it our "trash garden." Tomorrow we'll be digging up one row of items to see if any of them have decomposed at all. That'll give the kids an understanding of what happens to all the waste that they produce; they'll see that if they could produce less, it really would benefit the environment. We also did an experiment in which we put a coffee filter on the exhaust pipe of a car to see the pollution that comes from that.

Making classroom walls disappear so that learning is everywhere. No doubt about it: once learning accelerates, teachers are challenged as never before! Math is taught with relevant applications and references to real phenomena instead of abstract problems that have nothing to do with the students' lives. Science revolves around real-life experiments in which children propose hypotheses, perform experiments, and check the results. Students' hands-on exploration of scientific concepts is the way that science education applies the spirit of inquiry central to accelerated schools! Constructing lessons that really engage students often requires an interactive curriculum that extends far beyond the bounds of textbooks, ditto sheets, and the classroom. It demands risk taking, flexibility, and creativity of teachers. When students become responsible for their own learning, teachers often begin to take on a variety of new roles. In this example, we see teachers becoming the lead scouts on a discovery expedition. In order to keep the momentum going, they must locate suitable learning terrains, guiding the party to those resources and experiences that are rich with potential for powerful learning.

Throughout the space unit and the ecology unit, we found tons of relevant children's literature. In my class, we read everything from myths, to American Indian tales, to modern stories about how the planets came to be named what they are, to what might exist on different planets. Some kids began reading science fiction on their own. Once you start looking, you find that there's an inexhaustible supply of books out there. It takes time to go to the library and find good ones, but it's really worth it. We also scour the children's bookstores. None of us is reimbursed for the books we buy, but we don't really mind. The books become ours, and we can use them again and again. We're all collectors of children's literature. We even try to give each other children's books on birthdays and at Christmastime. Having lots of books about subjects the kids are interested in around the classroom

makes a difference in the amount they read (and even in when they learn to read). In my first grade class, many of the kids aren't reading yet, but when we did the space unit, they were so motivated to learn and so excited about the subject that I'd find them in corners of the room, trying so hard to teach themselves to read!

Valerie Johnson, Marla Brower, and Betty Mundinger, Teachers, Hollibrook Elementary School, Houston, Texas

Launching a lifetime of learning. Once children develop a love of learning, there's no turning back. Their interests begin to carry them over the boundaries of class assignments and separate disciplines. Learning becomes a challenge that's both treasured and chosen, and students begin to understand the utility of knowing "the basics."

Many of the skills and understandings central to math and science are grounded in the scientific method—an inquiry cycle that involves concept formation, hypothesizing, and validating or refuting your hypothesis through observation or experimentation. Usually the results of observation or experimentation suggest further hypotheses; and so the inquiry cycle continues, with knowledge building on knowledge. *This should sound very familiar to the Inquiry Process employed at your last cadre meeting!*

As the school community internalizes the Inquiry Process, it will undoubtedly become a useful tool for scientific inquiry in all different subject areas (and even outside the classroom). The next example illustrates how a Burnett administrator used the Inquiry Process in her work with students, teaching them to approach any problem scientifically:

After the Oakland firestorm last year, the CJSF [California Junior Scholastic Foundation] kids wanted to do something to help the fire victims. Their idea was to collect blankets and clothes from students and send them to Oakland. I was about to go with that and start organizing a clothing drive, but then it occurred to me: Is that what the fire victims really need? The Inquiry Process kind of went off in the back of my head, and I realized that we should follow a problem-solving process instead of just jumping to a solution. So I asked the kids, "How do you know that's what they need in Oakland?" Well, they didn't know. They'd just assumed. The next step was to figure out how to find out what they did need. One student called the Oakland Red Cross, and sure enough, blankets and clothes weren't needed half as much as food. The students were delighted with this information, and they went happily about collecting food for the fire victims. They had a real lesson in not jumping to conclusions, and they felt more committed to the effort.

Fran Laplante, Vice-Principal, Burnett Academy, San Jose, California

7.2.3. Social, Historical, and Cultural Studies

Just as technological innovations are driven largely by the disciplines of math and science, equally vital social processes, such as peace negotiations, disarmament talks, and legislation for social justice, are driven by our understanding of the histories and cultures of our own and different parts of the world. We participate in the social world constantly: it's one of the first aspects of our world that we come into contact with, and it remains a central—if not the most central—aspect of our lives. Students and teachers in accelerated schools understand that—especially in a multiethnic society such as ours, with a variety of histories and cultures—it's vital to explore our social environments with the same rigor we apply to reading, writing, and arithmetic. In fact, social studies is an *excellent* forum through which to learn all of those other skills!

Producing a powerful curriculum unit often requires high levels of collaboration, creativity, and experimentation. In this next example, we see how an entire school successfully organized its studies around a common theme—our world. Though the challenges were great, the curriculum sparked powerful learning and served to heighten everyone's sense of the school—and the world—as a unified community.

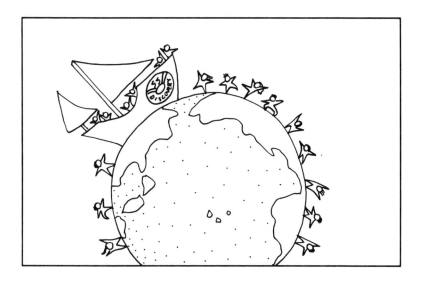

The entire school participated in a unit we called "Around the World" last year. We wanted to do something that would bring the whole school together to celebrate all the different cultures that are represented here. Several teachers started brainstorming, and finally they came up with the idea that each grade level would take a continent: pre-K had Antarctica, kindergarten had Australia. We wanted to make sure that everyone could be involved. Classes within grade levels would take particular countries to work on, and everyone's responsibility was to find out as much as they could about their area. All subjects were taught around a class's country or continent. We still taught language arts, but focusing on content about their countries. Their vocabulary and spelling lists would all be words from or about the country. We

even tried to write word problems in math that would be relevant. **We also did all kinds of enrichment activities with them. By the time the unit was finished, all the children had cooked their country's food, had made native costumes by hand, had learned a little bit of their country's language, and were completely immersed in their country's culture.**

Designing an organizational, educational, and creative feat! From the start, we see the importance of the principles of accelerated schools: developing a unity of purpose, sharing responsibilities, and building on strengths. By putting these principles into action, teachers at Hollibrook lay a foundation for community learning. They work together all over the school to create powerful learning for all of their students. But as we shall see, this is only the beginning. As they build on the strengths and creativity of the entire community, things really start to take off.

When we first sat down to plan the unit, we thought maybe we'd do it for a week or so. Well, by the fourth week we were still going strong. This school looked like a different place. All the classes created displays to hang outside their classrooms, illustrating facts about their country or the culture of the people who live there. The office staff wanted to get involved, so they made passports for every child in the whole school. Then each student could walk from room to room and get his or her passport stamped. The following week we began to study about passports: Why do you need one when you travel? Who gives them out? Where can you get one? Do all countries have them?

Revolutionizing learning. As learning cuts across the traditional boundaries of age, grade, and position, some virtually unheard of things begin to happen. Having the support staff play a major role in children's learning? Empowering children to present knowledge to students in other grades? It seems that in accelerated schools, almost anything is possible!

We were all so engrossed in this unit, but it didn't happen all at once. At first a lot of us said, "Oh, just another thing to do." But by the end, we recognized how important it was because *the kids really learned*! They learned that they're not so different from the rest of the world, and that they're not so different from each other. They learned from each other, and that's what really brought the whole school together. For a culminating activity, we held dance performances. The class that was doing Brazil held a street dance, sort of a Mardi Gras type of celebration, complete with costumes and music. It was wonderful.

Maria Eugenia Fernandez, Teacher, Hollibrook Elementary School, Houston, Texas

Collaborating: the hard work is worth it! Sharing a common experience with a large group of people is part of what makes sporting events, plays, and concerts so enjoyable. Here we see how a common curriculum can bring a community—even one that may never have been unified before—together in a productive and educational way for everyone. The fundamental message of social studies, that "learning from each other is what really brings people together," is lived and breathed through this experience.

Powerful learning about others' cultures and experiences can take the form of short-term experiences, as in the above example, or it can be the foundation for an entire year of study. Joan Moss, an elementary teacher in San Francisco, California, helped her students explore the world of a Native American tribe in all of its richness and complexity.

My curriculum for the 1990–91 school year was the culture of the Sioux, because that's what I know. I have very strong ties to Sioux culture, and it's very important to me. In fact, I'd prepared a unit on the Sioux when I was in education courses at San Francisco State University, where I also minored in American Indian Studies. I had the curriculum (drawn from the United Tribes of North Dakota Development Corporation and the teachings of Dr. Bernard Hoehner) and was waiting for the opportunity to use it in its entirety, rather than in bits and pieces, so that it could be most meaningful to the children. Camilla Schneider, another teacher at my school, and I went to visit Yolanda Woo, a teacher who runs the art department at Horace Mann Middle School. She'd created an Indian museum with her art students. We said to ourselves, "Hey, we could do something like that with our kids!" So we wrote two grants to fund it, and we got them both. Three of us participated in planning the curriculum—each of us emphasizing a different cultural area—and eventually setting up the museum at our school. We loaned whatever materials we had to one another.

Empowering oneself to teach what's personally important. Building on her own strengths, Moss empowers herself through collaboration with her colleagues and takes responsibility for funding and carrying out a wonderful learning experience for children.

I began the unit in early October, and I first had the students write down everything they thought they already knew about Indians, so that they could compare that information to a list at the end of the unit. They could see how much they'd learned when we completed the unit. The first thing we talked about in my third grade was how Indian children receive their names: through something seen in nature, through an object important to the family, a special event, a brave deed of a warrior, etc. Each student worked with a partner, and they talked

203

to each other about themselves. Then each person would look at the information they had collected about their partner and give that person an Indian name based on something personal. It was amazing to watch the bond that formed between the partners; they'd made a connection that was theirs alone.

Connecting students to the subject matter and to each other. Moss takes an active interest in the students' existing knowledge and builds on it; she also plans to use it later in her assessment. She takes her specific students into account as she plans her curriculum and instructional approach. Additionally, she knows that students are naturally interested in communicating and interacting with each other, and she takes advantage of their sociability. She turns what many children might think of as just "talking to your friends" into a meaningful, reflective exercise. The students are asked to really ponder what it is that makes themselves and their friends special and then explore their creativity by coming up with a name for it. It's not likely that the children will forget the symbolic importance of naming.

Then we made a name shield out of papier mâché. They made an armature, and it didn't come out exactly round; it came out in all different kinds of shapes, which made it really neat. Everyone illustrated his or her own name with construction paper and pasted the cutouts on the shield. Then they put a glaze on the shield, which really cemented everything, giving the shield a special look. The illustrations were fabulous. The person who'd named him or her wrote a paragraph explaining the choice of the particular name. The artwork was incredibly beautiful. One girl's name was Sunshine Girl, and she drew a fringed Sioux dress and then a sun for the head. It was just wonderful. After we'd finished the shield, the children were each invited to show their artwork and explain why they'd chosen that particular symbol for themselves and what their name meant to them. Their homework was to go home and find out how they got their name and to write that information up. There were some really interesting things that came out. One girl was named April because she was born in April. One boy was named Travis because the family had passed Travis Air Force Base, and his mother liked the name. One girl was named after Vanessa Williams. It was very interesting for them.

Celebrating the students. Moss creates the opportunity for students to learn facts about the Sioux by connecting those facts to the students' personal lives and experiences. Students celebrate and express themselves through writing, art, and presentations to the whole class, all the while internalizing aspects of Sioux culture. Parents are even brought into the experience through a creative homework assignment. The students are the stars!

We did writing throughout the curriculum, but the best writing that came about was when my professor from State, Dr. Hoehner, who's an American Indian, came to class and taught music and dance, preparing us to take our field trip to the Stanford University Powwow. This was an important culminating event. He also blessed the museum for us. Afterward, the children wrote letters to him thanking him and telling him one thing that they'd learned. They were fabulous, incredible letters. Their sentence structure showed tremendous growth from previous assignments. They were writing in complete sentences, and they really knew their information. The letter that impressed me the most was from a girl who wrote, "And I just want you to know that I took the music and the dance and all of this very seriously." That told me that these lessons meant something to her. I was very, very impressed.

Encouraging reverence and respect for other cultures and for the learning experience. By bringing in a member of the local community who represents Native American culture, Moss demonstrates yet another connection between what the students are studying and the real world. Because the lesson is so personalized and relevant, the students take it "very seriously." Their respect for their visitor and the information he shared shows itself as an improvement in their writing skills. When writing is contextualized and has a goal—communicating real gratitude—the children push themselves to new heights.

We took a great field trip together, all three classes, to two different Indian museums in the same day. That was wonderful, because at both places they could go sit inside shelters or they could do hands-on experiences, like pounding acorns and playing games. We also went to the Indian Walk at the San Francisco Arboretum. This trip was a revelation for the kids, because they could see and touch and experiment with common, everyday plants that were significant to the Indians. Something common that you might find in your house, like an iris—well, many years ago, the stalks were used to make thread. We also took a culminating field trip to the Stanford University Powwow. It wasn't just for fun; it was really a learning experience for them. They had a great deal of information about the different rituals and the significance or the symbolism of different things, so it was a very personal experience for them. These kinds of trips are what make learning come alive.

Learning outside the school. The school's backyard, the San Francisco Bay Area, becomes relevant to the learning process. Field trips are a mix of guided museum experiences, special opportunities such as the powwow, and walks through places that the children may have been before but now will understand in a different way.

The name shield that we'd made became a display in our Indian museum. Another display consisted of things in nature that were round, because the circle is a very sacred symbol to the Indians. We built a large tipi from scraps of material. We talked about the buffalo and all that was involved in preparing the hide for tipi covers. After learning how to use a needle and thread, the children did several sewing activities. They sewed the tipi cover by hand and made medicine bags and necklaces from real glass beads. This activity involved patterning skills as well, since several colors of beads were available.

We also did a great deal of writing about the Sioux, much of it on the computer. They learned a lot about word processing! Several of my students aren't English-language-proficient, so I used the webbing method from Project Read. Students were able to take small chunks of information and turn that into complete sentences and paragraphs. I also wanted them to learn how to find information, so we learned about doing research in the library.

Contributing to the common goal. As the learning experience continues, the students begin to focus their energies on creating a museum for their school. They synthesize what they've learned, and in this context, Moss introduces some useful tools, from simple ones (such as needle and thread) to complex ones (such as computers, library research, and instructional innovations). The students have a goal in mind as they learn these complex skills; therefore, the skills come faster and more effectively.

When the museum was complete, we trained the students to be docents and show the other classes around the various exhibits. The students really enjoyed this aspect of it: they got to teach other kids what they'd created and learned. It worked so well; the kids really knew what they were talking about! We plan to put the museum up again next September, and my limited-English-speaking students will be the docents. That will give them an opportunity to work on their speaking skills.

Joan Moss, Teacher, Daniel Webster Elementary School, San Francisco, California

Making students into teachers. All teachers know that concepts are truly internalized when you're able to explain them to another person. Moss and her colleagues build on the newly developed strengths of these students as they help them to develop other strengths, such as public speaking, mastery of English, and a sense of pride about sharing their knowledge and experiences with others.

7.2.4. The Experiential Disciplines: Music, Arts, Home Economics, Industrial Arts, Physical Education, and Other Electives

Teachers of art, band, home economics, shop, and physical education use many of the principles of powerful learning in their classrooms every day. These classrooms are usually characterized by a high degree of hands-on activity and experiential learning, with the teacher serving a facilitating, not dictating, role. It's no surprise that many students list these classes among their favorites and even devote much of their free time to doing extra work in these areas. You've probably heard the band practicing enthusiastically well before school starts or seen students in the woodshop classroom after school, working to complete a project. Without question, we all have a great deal to learn from these teachers and their students about creating powerful learning situations.

Everybody in education is catching up to us. We've always had hands-on activities; we've always incorporated different learning styles. My classes are all interactive, with students working together on projects, and we produce things. The students see a product at the end of each learning experience. I see teachers of more "academic" subjects doing things the way I've always done them in my classes, because that's what turns kids on!

Cynthia Dudley, Home Arts Teacher, North Middle School, Aurora, Colorado

Unfortunately, these vital disciplines are sometimes treated as second-class citizens in many traditional schools and are often the first victims of district and state budget cutting. Accelerated school communities realize that powerful learning happens all the time in these experiential classrooms, and they prioritize the teaching of these subjects.

When Rancho Milpitas first drafted its vision statement, the introduction read as follows: "We the students, with our parents, and staff of Rancho Milpitas Middle School envision academic excellence through an enriched, varied, challenging, innovative curriculum supplemented by a wide variety of electives and activities." The electives department, headed by Jackie Saffold, an art teacher, felt that this wording created an artificial separation between the "academic" disciplines and electives. After all, she argued to the steering committee, electives are part of what makes a curriculum "enriched, varied, challenging, and innovative." The steering committee eagerly passed the department's recommendation on to the school as a whole, and it was unanimously accepted. Rancho now views electives as integral, not extra.

Rancho Milpitas Middle School, Milpitas, California

Many of the vignettes that you've read so far in this chapter (and will read in the rest of the *Resource Guide*) incorporate music, art, cooking, sewing, building, and physical activities. Students at Hollibrook Elementary School continued their learning about ancient Rome in P.E. class, studied Roman recipes and toga fabrics, and even learned about the construction of steam tables. Joan Moss's class built tipis, sewed bead necklaces, created collaborative works of art, listened to Sioux music, and danced Sioux dances. Humanities teachers at Burnett Academy are working with the art teacher to integrate art into each humanities lesson. When thinking about integrating what you teach your students across disciplines, don't forget to include these subjects!

In addition to being crucial components of any integrated approach, these subjects are also particularly powerful when taught as self-contained courses. In middle schools, these types of classes are often organized into an electives department or taught as "exploratories" (in contrast to elementary schools, where all subjects may be taught by the same teacher), and they're the source of incredibly powerful learning in accelerated middle schools. We show here several examples of elective teachers' creativity and importance to the school community:

Industrial Arts

At North Middle School in Aurora, Colorado, Martin Choquette's eighth grade industrial arts class becomes a manufacturing corporation once a year. Each student in the class takes on a different role in the "company," such as quality-control officer, production-line worker, engineer, or sales-team member. Students have to interview for their jobs, and on the day of the interviews, students and teacher come to school in professional attire. One student heads each "division" of the company, and these students make up the management team, directly responsible to Mr. Choquette. Once everyone has a job at the "plant," the student company goes to work, turning out a real product, such as yo-yos, bed trays, or folding stools, which the students then sell to others in the school community. One year the Parent-Teacher-Student Association put in an order to the company for picnic tables for the school's courtyard. These ten tables are now coveted spots during lunch, as well as useful places for teachers when they hold class outside. The company's profits go back into the class, benefiting both the student "employees," who usually get a pizza party, and the students who take the class the following year, who get to work with state-of-the-art materials.

Physical Education

The physical education program at Rancho Milpitas Middle School in Milpitas, California, was named the best in California for its creative and rigorous approach to P.E. The program's philosophy builds on student and parent strengths by emphasizing personal fitness rather than

competition. In addition to sports and fitness, all types of dance are incorporated into the classes' activities. One of the program's most notable innovations is a weekly written health/fitness assignment sent home for parents and students to do together. Recent assignments have focused on the Olympics, nutrition, and keeping in shape. Parents are required to sign the assignment after they complete it with their child. When some students pointed out that their parents didn't read English, the P.E. department had the assignments translated into three different languages. The teachers developed this curriculum themsleves, and it's been so successful that they're now marketing it to other schools. P.E. teacher Nancy Turner, "Teacher of the Year" at Rancho last year, stresses, however, that other departments and schools should really come up with their own activities and lessons to fit the needs of their communities, as she and her colleagues did at Rancho.

Music

Zachary Bonilla, a professional musician in San Jose, California, will tell you that he got his start in Burnett Academy's band, led by Dave Anderson. Anderson's teaching was so powerful, so motivating, that Zachary continued his study of piano and keyboards throughout high school and even graduated early so that he could begin his musical career. His band, which consists of himself and a saxophone player, has been extremely successful around the Bay Area. They recently completed their first recording, and they play local gigs almost every night. Zachary hasn't forgotten the "little people," though. Members of the Burnett school community recently participated as facilitators and speakers at an Accelerated Schools Project training session, and they invited him to play as the evening's entertainment. He cut short another performance just so he could be there and support the school that had given him so much.

Home Economics

The foods class at Rancho Milpitas played an integral role in that school's vision celebration. One of the vision celebration's activities was an Accelerated Cookie Bake-Off, with categories such as "biggest cookie," "tastiest cookie," and "most accelerated cookie." Anyone in the school community could make an entry, but students in the foods class made this project the focus of their work. The class worked for weeks coming up with recipes, practicing them, and finally preparing their masterpieces. In the end, every cookie in the "competition" won a prize, but the real reward was the sense that these students and their teacher had of being a living part of their school's vision.

Aerospace

Burnett Academy in San Jose, California, received a grant to turn its industrial arts program into an aerospace/aviation center. Every

student in the school takes at least two classes in this center, learning about engineering, drafting, and designing by working with incredibly high-tech materials such as computer software to design cities, hydroponic gardens, and flight simulators. Students also build hot-air balloons and model rockets with everyday materials. Students love these classes which incorporate many different learning centers and opportunities for student collaboration into each day's activities.

What's to Come

We hope that you've enjoyed reading these exciting stories from accelerated schools around the country. The next two chapters, which address the *how* and the *context* of powerful learning situations, include the same type of vignettes; but we analyze these with an eye for instructional and organizational innovations. Unavoidably, there's a great deal of overlap of these elements of powerful learning in each story you read, and this is as it should be. It's impossible to create powerful learning with only one or two of these elements. So as you read on, recall these vignettes that represent the *what* and think about how they also illustrate powerful *hows* and *contexts*. Then go on to conduct powerful learning in your own classroom every day!

CHAPTER 8

The *How* of Powerful Learning

Instructional Innovations and Rediscoveries

At Hollibrook Elementary School in Houston, Texas, a group of third graders has turned their classroom into a replica of an ocean vessel that travels each week to explore and study different continents around the globe. Their teacher completely redecorates and reorganizes her classroom as they go from place to place. This week they're in Antarctica. There's a giant simulated continent on the floor, complete with icebergs, stuffed penguins, and seals. All subjects have been taught this week with an emphasis on Antarctica and its characteristics. The teacher has filled a trunk in the room with artifacts that might be found on the continent: gloves, snow goggles, a parka, a compass, a short-wave radio, books written by explorers, some freeze-dried foodstuffs, and cooking utensils. These third graders are all actively engaged in various academic tasks related to their exploration. Some are working in small groups with a student as the facilitator, while others are working with the teacher or teacher's aide.

If the *what* of powerful learning is the content or curriculum, then the *how* may be thought of as instructional strategies and techniques. In the stories that follow, we present powerful learning experiences from accelerated school communities. In this chapter, we focus on *how* staff in accelerated schools have orchestrated learning situations for children that build on their natural curiosity and high energy levels. What accelerated school communities are discovering is that as they challenge the natural talents and abilities of students and work alongside them, using interesting materials and supportive means of instruction, remediation approaches become obsolete.

In the classroom described above, we see how students learn actively through instruction that capitalizes on the natural ways of learning that all children have developed prior to entering formal school systems. We all know that children are natural scientists; they love to explore and inquire about the nature of their world. This is something that we saw evidence of in the previous chapter, in the students who studied Pompeii, and it's a theme that we see time and again in accelerated schools. There's a basic principle involved here—one that underlies most of the *hows* that we'll explore in this chapter: *when children actively participate in a real-life event that builds on their previous knowledge and experiences, the learning that occurs is much more meaningful.*

This principle has important implications for the choices that educators make when selecting educational materials and methods of instruction.

> **I think teachers are learning to view the textbook as just one small part of the entire lesson. Whereas before, you had the textbook, the desks, and the pupils, and that was your lesson, now teachers are using more selectivity and judgment and saying, "Well, we can do this part from the textbook and this from a film I have, and I have an activity for this, and oh, this would be great for a cooperative learning activity. This is something they could interview their parents about." Teachers are a lot more creative. At the beginning of each year, I ask myself, "Which topics am I most excited about teaching?" I've been developing about one new unit a year and building it into my repertoire. You're limited only by your creativity.**
>
> Amy L. Meyer, Teacher, Hoover Elementary School, Redwood City, California

Although most educators would probably agree with these ideas, the traditional goals, values, methods, and assumptions about the nature of instruction put forth by "the system" often make it difficult to utilize our creativity and put these principles into practice. With a mandated curriculum to teach and a fixed schedule to follow, it often seems that we don't have enough time to fit in the real-life activities that produce powerful learning, such as group work, hands-on activities, field experiences, research, and peer tutoring. However, many of us have found that children aren't highly engaged by traditional instructional environments, where the teacher is the transmitter of knowledge and the children are passive recipients. Although we know that strategies for dealing with this challenge exist, it's often difficult for a solitary teacher to take the time to design and use a variety of creative teaching strategies while having to deal with the demands and expectations of traditional schools.

Instead of focusing on external demands of the system (mandates and short-term testing goals), an accelerated school community focuses on a shared vision. The members of the school community work toward this shared vision *collaboratively*. The entire school community works together to create situations in which teachers become facilitators and students become discoverers.

In this chapter, we'll share some of the *hows* that have made learning powerful for children in accelerated schools across the country.

Parents as Teachers

All children have had powerful first teachers—their parents—who know best the variety of ways in which their children can learn. They've taught their children to dress themselves, count, do chores around the house, and play. Parents also think about and plan powerful learning experiences for their children—everything from taking them to the local planetarium and zoo to reading with them at night. As you consider ways to expand your repertoire of strategies for engaging students in what they're learning, be sure to include parents. They'll undoubtedly have some great ideas!

8.1. Big Wheels and Little Wheels of the *How*

Throughout this *Resource Guide*, you've seen references to "big wheels" (the formal processes of accelerated schools) and "little wheels" (the innovations that you can try today, either alone or with others in your school). Successful instructional innovations occur as a result of *both* big-wheel and little-wheel activities. Two examples of innovations in the *how* of powerful learning follow: a little-wheel example from the classroom and a big-wheel example of a cadre's inquiry into the broad area of instruction.

8.1.1. Little Wheel: "Banking Days"

The following is an example of a powerful learning situation constructed by Jackie Dolan, a fourth-grade teacher in an accelerated elementary school. Here Dolan describes her own creative instructional design process to us. What's most striking is how much of the instruction in her classroom emerged out of the challenges that the situation itself presented. While the learning experience began as a way to improve the social environment of the classroom, it became much more. Dolan created a series of powerful learning opportunities by creating an instructional context that allowed for such flexibility. Learning occurred as both the teacher and the children successfully met the challenges that arose out of the various learning experiences. The example illustrates nicely the way in which *what, how,* and *context* are necessarily integrated.

My students sit in groups of four, each group is a team, and I'm always looking for ways to get them to function cooperatively as a group. I was trying to come up with an incentive system to get the kids to behave well and understand that their behavior anywhere in the classroom is a reflection on their team.

Setting the instructional goal. Dolan has a learning goal for her students: to create a cooperative social environment in her classroom. Before thinking about instruction—about *how* she's going to facilitate their learning—she reflects on what she wants her students to learn.

I decided upon giving them points toward some reward every time they do anything positive: bringing in a homework project, working quietly, helping another student, whatever. At first I just got myself some stickers and a bingo stamp. Each child had a card on his or her desk, and every time someone would do something right, I'd give them a sticker or a stamp. You could be across the room from me doing something really neat, and I'd walk over and stamp your card.

Creating an experience. Here Dolan is on the brink of transforming a simple classroom management strategy into something more powerful. The focus is on actions and behavior, and as Dolan moves silently to reward students, she's modeling the idea that actions are what's important here. In the learning process, the experience of being rewarded for positive behavior has become fun, something interesting.

At the end of two weeks, everybody totaled up their points, and each point was worth $600. You multiplied out how many points you had individually and then added that to the points of the other three people on your team to come up with your group total. Then you divided that amount by four, since it was a team effort. It was amazing to watch the children's response to this system. They were really encouraging each other to do well and live up to expectations. They can put a lot of pressure on one another!

Facilitating grass-roots instruction. By making rewards contingent on an entire group's behavior, she shifts much of the instructional responsibility to the students themselves. She creates the learning situation, empowering the students to motivate and teach each other.

So each student ended up with a certain amount of points, or dollars, to start with. Naturally, for the incentive system to work, they had to have something to "buy" with their "money." I brought in pencils, but this wasn't really enough, and I was spending too much of my own money on pencils! So I decided we'd start a checking system. Kids need to learn about the banking system. Boy, did they start appreciating their parents! One of them asked his mother, "How do you get all that money, Mom? How do you pay the rent?" I made up little checks for each student. They were very official-looking, with personal account numbers (their birthdates) and everything. I taught them how to fill out checks and how to endorse them. They had to sign the back just as their name appeared on the front. I was the bank, and I had a little stamp, and when the checks came to me, I stamped them. They got their original back to check against their account. We set up a balance sheet for everyone. It was wonderful. There was so much learning going on!

Seeing opportunity in a challenge. We can see that Dolan is confronted with a problem: the personal financial burden of her new incentive system. Yet rather than focusing narrowly on that personal challenge, she broadens her thinking, looking for further learning opportunities present in the situation that she's constructing. She thinks about the real world outside the classroom, about what her children need to learn about math and money. She then expands the learning situation so that it becomes a simulation of a more complex real-world experience—banking.

The kids wanted to buy things with their checks, so they started bringing in old toys and things from home that they didn't want anymore. I got letters from parents saying, "Thank you! Thank you! He's cleaned out his closet!" They brought in some nice items, and they'd price them. There was a lot of bargaining going on. It just got more and more sophisticated. I set up a rule that each time you cashed in your points for dollars, you had to pay the IRS—or the Internal Room Service—6 percent of what you'd earned. The first question that came up was, "Why do some people pay more than others?" I said, "You figure it out." "Oh, you mean he made more, so he has to pay more?" "Right!" I said. They thought that was fair. Then I added more cost-of-living kinds of expenses. They each had to pay $1,000 rent plus $15 for electricity to Daniel Webster Elementary. Then I also fined them for certain things, like $.99 for wasting water. They really started

watching each other! If you made mistakes in your checking account, I'd fine you as your accountant. I had to keep a lot of records, but it was worth it.

Letting reality set in. Using the real world as a guide, Dolan slowly adds more and more complexity to the "situation" in her classroom. As the children are challenged by the demands of the situation, they're asking and answering questions that they would never have thought of if they'd simply read about banking, taxes, or water conservation in a textbook. They are acquiring knowledge and developing skills while also understanding how to apply those skills and knowledge.

All of the kids loved banking, and because we were making it up as we went along, each one was able to take it as far as he or she could. One day Joshua, a boy in my class, came up and told me that he was going to be my competition; he was going to open his own accounting services. I said, "Great, go right ahead!" I gave him a desk over to the side of the room, and an In and Out box. He made a sign, "J. B. Accounting." He offered a $5 discount to whoever used him. So if the kids were lazy and didn't want to do the math on their own, they could pay him to do it. Of course, they still had to do it themselves over the weekend; if Joshua made a mistake on his calculations, I still fined them $20. But he did a pretty good business.

Building on strengths and interests. Because of the student-centered nature of the instructional situation, Dolan is able to respond flexibly to Joshua's challenge to her "authority." In a traditional classroom, Joshua's strength and interest might have been ignored. Instead, he's given an opportunity to play a greater role and take on a larger challenge. This in turn increases the excitement and "realness" of the experience for everyone!

I used my computer to keep a spreadsheet of everyone's account. The kids had to keep a written copy, and once a month, I'd give them a computer printout, just like a bank statement. It took me hours, but once it got rolling, it wasn't so bad. The whole project really worked. There were all kinds of higher-order thinking going on; the kids were processing complex math in their heads, learning about bartering and trading and the concept of value. Some learned some lessons about themselves. One boy wouldn't spend a dime, and he was quickly becoming a millionaire, but when we finally ended the project, he was left with nothing but pieces of paper. He was furious! He asked me, "What do I get for all this money I saved?" "Nothing," I said. "When you finally decided to buy, the bank was closed." "But that's not fair!" he insisted. "I sold all my things and I saved and saved." I said, "You were great at making money, but you should have spent a little too.

You can't be a miser." He learned a very important lesson, which he'll carry far beyond the fourth grade.

Jackie Dolan, Teacher, Daniel Webster Elementary School, San Francisco, California

Recognizing unexpected and powerful learning. From such a rich and complex instructional experience, the children learned powerful lessons. There were some specific understandings that all the children acquired, and there were also unique lessons that individual children took home—lessons that addressed their particular beliefs, attitudes, and actions in the simulated world of economics and money.

The previous example demonstrates how the learning experiences in accelerated classrooms can differ from those in traditional ones. Constructing a powerful instructional situation requires creativity and a willingness to take risks and share responsibilities with students. As you build on your own strengths and the strengths of your students, powerful learning situations will unfold in your own classroom.

8.1.2. Big Wheel: Using Inquiry to Examine the *How—* A Case Study

In setting priorities at Burnett Academy, a public inner-city middle school in San Jose Unified School District, the staff decided to have a cadre for instruction/achievement because of a sizable gap between their taking-stock findings and their vision for the future. Specifically, they found that students entered Burnett scoring below the district average on standardized tests and left the school scoring even lower. Although most of the cadre members felt satisfied with their own teaching, they also realized (through the taking-stock reports) that lectures and worksheets were the most frequently used instructional techniques at Burnett at the time. These findings were far from the school's vision, which aimed for success for all students through active and meaningful learning experiences.

The following case study, "narrated" by one of the cadre members, outlines how the Instruction Cadre has begun to address the long-term challenge of improving instruction throughout the school by using the Inquiry Process. You'll note that the broader the challenge area, the more challenging it is for a cadre to apply the Inquiry Process.

Stage 1: Focus in on the Challenge Area

1a: Explore the challenge area informally and hypothesize why it exists. Because we chose to tackle the entire area of "instruction," rather than a single aspect of it, our cadre had a difficult time focusing in on the challenge. After some discussion, we began with a general analysis of the taking-stock report with respect to achievement. Our first reaction to the low test scores was to blame the students. After all, they came to us from elementary schools with their study habits already established. They don't come prepared to school. They don't bring their binders. They don't bring pencils. Most of them don't do homework. They don't care about learning. They don't have respect for each other. And they don't respect the teachers. For all of these situations, we found immediate solutions: detention, a stricter homework policy, call in parents and let them see how their children act, don't allow students into the building if they don't come prepared, and many more in that same vein. Finally, one of our members pointed at the inquiry chart on the wall and reminded us that we were jumping to solutions before we'd even defined the problem. She suggested that we try to think in a less negative way as well.

After some discussion, we all agreed that if children had fun learning or had some intrinsic satisfaction when they learned something, they'd come prepared and they'd actively participate. We had an excellent example for this at our school: the music teacher had an amazing jazz band and jazz choir. Students who participated in these groups came to school early on their own, many lugging their instruments along because they'd been practicing at night. These kids weren't our "best" students. In fact, some of our more problematic students were in his jazz band and in his jazz choir. And yet here they came prepared, they practiced innumerable hours, repeating the same pieces over and over until they were satisfied with their performance; they learned to improvise and be creative. Why couldn't this commitment and dedication to learning carry over into the classroom?

Based on our own collective experience as teachers and learners (students were members at several of our cadres meetings), we developed a broad hypothesis about powerful learning. Since we chose such a broad challenge area, our hypothesis was also broad. The steering committee tried to get us to make a list of hypotheses for one aspect of instruction, but we all felt that we wanted to tackle the whole thing under the umbrella of powerful learning. Our "umbrella" hypothesis was that learning can occur only when students are interested in the subject or topic, when what they learn is somehow relevant to their lives, and when they can use all their abilities building on their strengths.

Some of us felt that we'd jumped from an implicit understanding of our problematic situation (*Our students don't want to learn*) to a conclusion about what powerful learning is. They urged the rest of us to make the logical connection between the two statements explicit: *Our students don't want to learn*, because *the school doesn't provide enough powerful learning experiences*. This was indeed a more appropriate hypothesis.

1b: Test hypotheses to see if they hold water. In order to confirm or disprove this hypothesis, we decided to ask our students what powerful learning was to them. We developed a survey instrument and used it as an assignment in all our classes. We felt that this was a good research design, since our cadre membership represented each grade level and subject area. Each of the teachers in our group asked his or her students to respond to the following web of questions:

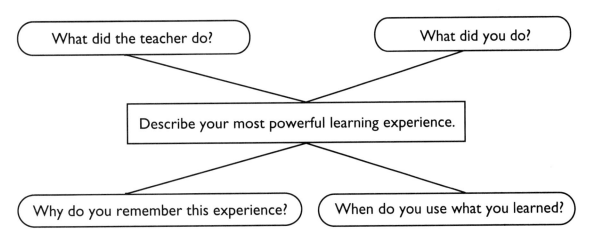

In some classes, the students helped to summarize the data and to calculate percentages; in others, the teacher prepared the summary. In our next cadre meeting, we analyzed the data of each teacher, and we came to the following set of results about what made learning powerful.

Student Activities

Individual	*Group*	*Group/Individual*
Role playing	Hands-on activities	Hands-on activities
Written and oral repetition	Active learning	Active learning
	Dramatizations	Computer use
	Role playing	Research activities
	Games	Projects
	Competitions	
	Debates	
	Field trips	

Teacher Actions and Attitudes

High expectations and belief in students
Supportive and motivating and insistent
    (i.e., "The teacher made me do it")
Caring for each individual student
    and for the group

Individual help
Demonstration of expected behaviors
Modeling of learning processes
Be a facilitator of learning
Give rewards

Characteristics of the Lessons

Fun
Novel, different
Clear relationship to the outside world
Important to current student concerns
Involves students actively
Interesting

Useful
Challenging and difficult, but within
    the reach of all students
Dramatic/shocking
Related to rewards

Most teachers felt that we hadn't learned anything that we didn't already know deep inside but that it was good to have these results from our own students and to make our students aware that we as teachers and support staff are concerned with their learning and want to satisfy their learning needs. A member of the cadre also pointed out that it was important to actively acknowledge what *really* works in teaching.

1c: Interpret the results of testing and develop a clear understanding of the challenge area. After we finished tallying the survey, our first school year as an accelerated school came to an end. We hadn't yet introduced any school-wide changes, but we felt that we had a clearer understanding of our problem: when students don't want to learn, we must motivate them and not punish them. We agreed that students need to be actively involved if learning is to reach its greatest potential. And we thought that a way to help students learn would be to build on our findings of the active student survey above. Specifically, our focus areas were to make learning relevant and interesting, to build on students' experiences, and to build on their best ways of learning.

We shared our findings with the school as a whole, and they seemed impressed with what we'd done. Their interest in the findings and eagerness for us to link them to a plan of action contributed toward our impetus to move forward.

Stage 2: Brainstorm Solutions. As we began our second year as an accelerated school, we had a 47 percent rise in student population, which greatly increased class size—a challenge that was exacerbated by the unusually small classrooms in our school. All of us were desperate for effective instructional and classroom management strategies. Rather than ignoring these immediate concerns and continuing with our focus from last spring, we asked the entire staff their areas of greatest concern so that we could plan relevant staff development. We found that most people were concerned with discipline. Several members of the cadre, who were certified trainers of a classroom management approach by Fred Jones, offered that as a solution and volunteered to train the rest of us.

Once this training had begun, we returned to our exploration of powerful learning strategies to address the results of the student survey. We began searching for solutions and strategies to make teaching more in line with our findings from our powerful learning survey. Throughout the late fall, we looked at the most recent education literature. We all shared and read articles from professional journals about innovative instructional techniques and discussed their merit.

In searching for solutions, we also explored a number of instructional strategies that had accompanying training. One that we were particularly interested in was called the Program for Complex Instruction, a cooperative learning approach by Elizabeth Cohen at Stanford University. A few of us attended an orientation session to explore the program. We were so impressed that we also organized an orientation for our entire staff at our own school site. After the orientation, people broke off into cadres and discussed whether we should pursue the program. There was definite interest. Our cadre followed up on the interest by visiting schools that already were using Complex Instruction. We kept the school community in touch with our continued findings in this area.

In our continued search for solutions, we sometimes found ideas when we weren't even looking. The seed for many of our favorite ideas came to us as we reflected back to our retreat at the beginning of our second year as an accelerated school. At that time, we'd participated in a building-on-strengths exercise, where all members of the Burnett school community interviewed each other in pairs, writing out our strengths, our interests, and what we'd like to share with others in the school. Our cadre remembered liking this exercise and introduced the ideas into our cadre meetings. We knew it was important to keep looking outside the school, but we thought that there were a multitude of strengths *inside* the school that we could tap. Many of these strengths would address our list of powerful learning elements. For example, one of our support staff members has her own cake-decorating business; she could come into the home economics classes and help do a special unit on cake decorating for the holidays.

Stage 3: Synthesize Solutions and Develop an Action Plan. As I said, the classroom management situation was most pressing, so we focused first on implementing Fred Jones. The cadre presented the Fred Jones approach to discipline at a school-as-a-whole meeting and received approval to begin voluntary classes for interested staff, presented by our own certified trainers.

The broader work of our cadre stemmed from the results of the student survey about powerful learning, the teacher-needs survey we conducted at the beginning of the year, our interest in the Program for Complex Instruction, and the idea we liked about accessing our own strengths inside the school. We synthesized these ideas into a series of action plans. We were able to flesh out and move forward with the first two components of our plan. We planned to do the following:

- Publish a periodic teacher newsletter with "pearls of wisdom," in which teachers would present advice on specific successful teaching experiences that related to our study of powerful learning. For this, we arranged how to collect these "pearls," who would be responsible for their collection and dissemination, what they should consist of, how to present them on a regular basis to the rest of the school community, how to keep track of them, and how to assess their influence.

- Move forward with the Program for Complex Instruction. For this, our cadre arranged a visit to a nearby middle school utilizing Complex Instruction. Teachers from other cadres and our student representatives came with us to further explore the program and report back to the SAW. We were most impressed with the cooperation and collaboration, individual accountability, thematic approach to studies, emphasis on self-esteem, critical thinking skills, incorporation of ESL students, and strategies for evaluation. We felt that these issues were all relevant to our cadre's focus areas, our powerful learning survey results, and most important, our school vision. After this, we identified partial funding and participants from each subject area to participate in formal training so that the program would have the potential for schoolwide implementation in the future.

We didn't get to flesh out the other components of our action plan. When we return next year, we plan to do the following:

- Organize short sample lessons for our monthly school-as-a-whole meetings.

- Set up a master calendar and get substitute teachers so that teachers can visit each other and develop peer-coaching relationships.

- Initiate a catalog of strengths. We plan to survey all staff—asking them about their interests, their strengths, what they do best in the classroom, what instructional strategies they'd like to share, in which areas they'd like to grow. Using the HyperCard program on a Macintosh, we're going to develop a catalog with all our strengths so that we have access to our in-school resources.

- Organize a group of students to videotape teachers by request. Staff can use these tapes either privately (for self-assessment) or for "exemplary lessons" that will be kept on file in the media center for everyone to check out.

Stage 4: Pilot Test and/or Implement the Action Plan. In response to the staff concern with student discipline, the Fred Jones seminars have taken place weekly in an afternoon and morning class due to great interest. Teachers walked around with Fred Jones videotapes, discussing successful and failed implementation efforts.

We also piloted the pearls of wisdom in Burnett's *Daily Bulletin* for the last four weeks of school. We divided responsibility for ensuring that at least one pearl of wisdom appeared each day in the *Bulletin*, our school community's daily news sheet. The pearls came from personal conversations and interviews with our colleagues in each cluster of the school.

We also moved forward with the Program for Complex Instruction. After SAW approval, the cadre prepared a grant to obtain funding and finalized arrangements with staff members who would attend the training during the upcoming summer months.

Stage 5: Evaluate and Reassess. In regard to the Fred Jones training, discipline problems have diminished in the school. Staff feel that the Fred Jones approach is useful and want to have a half-day refresher course in September.

In our assessment of the pearls of wisdom, we found that concrete suggestions of activities and organizational ideas were more useful than some of the quotes and anecdotes that were submitted. We came up with the idea for thematic pearls of wisdom that would be most appropriate for full implementation at the beginning of the school year. We're planning to save the pearls of wisdom on a data base, compile them in a notebook in the media center, and post them on bulletin boards around the school as well.

In terms of assessing some of the other components of our plans, we intend to include an assessment procedure for each of our pilot plans so that we can see which parts of the plans get effective use and which parts make a difference in student learning and achievement.

Because the Instruction Cadre described in the preceding case study chose such a broad challenge area, members had trouble following the first stage of the Inquiry Process systematically. With an area as broad as "instruction," developing a list of ten or more hypotheses using the words "I think _____ is a challenge because . . ." became difficult. Still, you can see how the cadre tried to stay true to inquiry by embarking on a research project with the students to define the challenge area.

The instructional issues uncovered by this cadre are ones faced by the entire school community. Realizing their responsibility to the school as a whole, cadre members took time to adequately explore the challenge and to craft solutions that would positively affect everyone in the school. At the same time, this case illustrates how the Inquiry Process must accommodate immediate, pressing concerns at the school. The dramatic increase in class size and subsequent influence on instruction and classroom management couldn't be ignored by the cadre. Once the immediate need was assuaged, however, the big wheels of the accelerated school continued to turn—more slowly than the little wheels, but in a more structured way that addressed the underlying causes of the challenge area and began to lead to systematically improved instruction across the school community.

8.1.3. Big Wheels and Little Wheels Interacting

We often emphasize that the acceleration of learning requires that both approaches to solving problems—big wheels and little wheels—occur side by side. That is, individuals and small groups are encouraged to be creative, take risks, and explore new forms of instruction. One Burnett teacher, previously quite traditional in her instructional approach, was so inspired by what she was learning while working on the Instruction Cadre that she began to try some cooperative, active, and thematic learning approaches in her own classroom long before the SAW got involved in any major changes:

> Based on the research findings from their cadre's inquiry, Gloria Luna and two other seventh grade humanities teachers, Lynn Pickering and Lynne Mahan, worked together to incorporate some creative cooperative learning projects into their unit on archaeology and geography. Luna brought into her classroom a bag full of trash from her own home and spilled it out onto the floor. Like archaeologists on a dig, groups of students were to analyze each piece of trash and come up with a valid hypothesis as to the characteristics and makeup of her household. This project led into another on time capsules. Imagining that at some future date the United States will no longer exist and that the only remnant of our civilization will be a time capsule, students worked in groups to choose the seven items that would best represent our society. In one group, a boy sketched a representation of the Constitution; in another, a girl explained to her peers why she thought a photo of her family should be included.

Burnett Academy, San Jose, California

8.2. Instructional Innovations and Rediscoveries from Accelerated Schools

When we teach children to ride a bike, we don't sit them down in desks and say, "Okay, this is a handlebar. This is a pedal. These are reflectors." We just put them on it and say, "Go!"

Suzanne Still, Former Principal, Hollibrook Elementary School, Houston, Texas

In the rest of this chapter, we present instructional innovations designed by teachers and other staff in accelerated schools; these teachers share the powerful *hows* that they use to enrich their students' learning. In the course of these pages, we use the term *active learning* to describe all kinds of hands-on, experiential, cooperative, and participatory learning experiences. With active learning, the whole child is involved and is asked to play an active role in his or her own learning. The instructional situation brings crucial information and knowledge alive so that children can construct understandings for themselves. Active learning simultaneously engages a child's senses and abilities with real and meaningful learning experiences.

8.2.1. Seizing the Moment

We have already seen a good example of active learning in Dolan's Banking Days project. In the following example, we see how formal studies can be brought alive and made more meaningful when children have a real situation to which to apply their studies.

One morning in late May, a group of fifth grade boys brought a piece of whale skin, wrapped in plastic, to school. They told their teacher, Vira Lozano, that they'd taken it from a huge whale that was lying dead on a beach several miles away. At first Lozano thought that they were pulling her leg, bringing her a strip of rubber. Closer examination (and the smell!) convinced her that their story was true. The class had been studying marine life, so Lozano felt that this opportunity to see a real whale warranted an emergency field trip. As they set out on the three-mile journey, the mood was anxious and excited. It was a long walk, and this was the last week of school. But a whale—wow!

Addressing a learning emergency! A discovery made by a group of children sparks immediate action, and it seems clear to Lozano that this is one learning experience that must not be missed. By her actions, she demonstrates to her students that she trusts them totally and that their firsthand learning takes priority over scheduled activities. And, as we shall see, this spontaneous field trip provides a meaningful closing chapter for a year-long learning experience.

Last December the class visited the local Marine Science Institute, where they took a voyage on a boat and examined some marine life from San Francisco Bay. They also studied oceanography in the classroom, and together the class read the book *Stranded*, by Ann Coleridge. This story deals with the mystery facing a community when whales begin washing up on their beaches. The vocabulary was difficult for some of the kids, but the class tackled it together, and the details and meaning of the book were understood by everybody. Class members used this book and the field trip to explore the anatomy of ocean mammals and understand how they lived. Now suddenly, during the last week of school, they had the opportunity to see a real whale.

Seeing how real life reinforces previous learning. Here's a chance to connect the children's previous studies to a real-life dramatic event! It's an opportunity to build on the students' knowledge and allow them to see how their mental images and beliefs correspond to reality.

Upon their arrival at the fifty-foot male whale lying dead on the beach, the group switched from excited chatter to respectful whispering. In

small groups of five or six, the children went down to see the whale close up and talk with the scientists who were there observing it. The mood was reverent and serious. Lozano describes the class's reaction: "I think that the fact that they'd just studied whales, and it wasn't just a circus show, made it something for them to see. I think they felt good because they knew a lot of the terminology. When a scientist told them about counting the baleen, they knew what he was talking about. At one point, a scientist started to explain to them about the skin, but they already knew it was insulation. They knew that the animal was a mammal. When they saw the blowhole, they knew that it doesn't blow water out; it actually blows air out, and whatever water is there is moved out too. They knew that it would have lungs and not gills. I think for them it was like seeing the results of a test that they'd passed and done really well on. When we finally had to leave, there was this neat feeling, like a peaceful feeling. I know that I felt it, and I'm sure that they felt it too. It was sort of like being fulfilled; something really major had just happened. It was like they respected the fact that this was another life form. It was almost as if they had gone to the whale's funeral."

Achieving personal connections and deep emotional understanding. This experience transcends the normal realm of what we refer to as "education." This is learning that touches children's hearts as well as minds. The richness of such an experience may never show up on a multiple-choice test, but it shows itself in changed attitudes and feelings about nature. Such learning is indeed powerful, for it may influence these children for the rest of their lives.

There was a reporter there also, and she interviewed some of the kids. She called Lozano later and told her that her class had acted very mature around the whale compared to a group of kids from another school—a pretty well-off school—who'd come to see it. "The other kids were just really complaining about the smell, saying, 'Just get me away from this thing.' The reporter really noticed the difference in the interest levels. The other kids didn't want anything to do with it. Our kids wanted to be there with the whale. Their knowledge made them respect and honor it."

Vira Lozano, Teacher, Hoover Elementary, Redwood City, California

In the Banking example, the teacher used a simulation of real life to ground children's knowledge in their experiences. In the Pompeii example, the teacher was able to plan her instructional activities so that they led up to the museum visit. In this whale example, the dramatic event was unplanned, but when the opportunity to make practical use of their knowledge, interests, and experiences emerged, the teacher and students were able to seize the moment.

Brainstorm with your students or with a group of fellow teachers some of the powerful natural or human phenomena that either exist or sometimes occur in your community. (Examples: winter, spring, animal migrations, tornadoes, hurricanes, earthquakes, pollution problems, economic problems, political events, museum exhibits, births, deaths, regional celebrations.) Do any of these connect with some of the topics that you plan to cover this month or year? How might you design instructional experiences now that will prepare you and your students for powerful real-life learning if the opportunity arises?

8.2.2. Creative Use of Everyday Objects and Events

Innovative instructional experiences don't always require dramatic activities and complex preparations. As the following example demonstrates, teachers in accelerated schools are often able to create truly exciting and powerful learning activities simply by approaching objects and events in our everyday world in a different way:

> **Last October I had each child bring in a relatively small pumpkin. First we wrote poetry about them, to get in a little language arts. We gave each one a name, and then we washed them down and started our math and science experiments. I was using the AIMS curriculum, which has them guessing the circumference, and then measuring it for real, and comparing the two figures. We graphed these. A neat activity was predicting which one would have the most seeds, the bigger one or the smaller one, and why. Of course, to find out, we had to carve them up and actually count seeds. They absolutely loved it. And we ended up with some great jack-o-lanterns. You can pick up any piece of fruit and do those activities. I never fully realized how many learning resources just go untapped.**

Seeing that Halloween isn't just about candy. Here Amy Meyer adds new meaning to a basic holiday ritual. A jack-o-lantern-carving experience gives the children an opportunity to write poetry and apply their math and science knowledge in a practical way. As Meyer describes it, creating a mini-lesson that connects instruction to objects and events in the real world isn't really that difficult. Part of the secret is to make use of children's innate curiosity about things unknown, weaving the elements of surprise and discovery into their activities.

> **It's just a matter of pulling a bunch of materials together and then telling the kids, "Here are our experiments for the next two weeks." They get to explore instead of just being told. That's what's exciting. They get to say why they think something is going to happen. It's an unknown, and I don't know the answer either. I don't know which**

pumpkin is going to have more or fewer seeds, and I don't know why. I don't know why the seeds are different sizes. It's just so fun to try to figure these things out in different ways. You can get into some pretty sophisticated concepts too, like how does circumference relate to weight? Concrete activities lead to more abstract thinking. When you present questions in this way—that their mission is to find out—they get so excited. They really want to find the answers.

Amy L. Meyer, Teacher, Hoover Elementary School, Redwood City, California

When we stop and look, we can find educational value in a variety of everyday events, objects, places, and topics. Another fertile resource from which powerful instructional experiences can be constructed is the numerous physical and historical locations in your community. In this next example, we see how a teacher built on the hidden strengths and services that her children's community had to offer:

Jennifer Spotorno and her third grade class took many field trips within their school's local community last year. Their destinations included the firehouse, a local port, and historic homes. But by far the most exciting trip was the one that they took to Union Cemetery, the oldest cemetery in their community of Redwood City, California.

Before the trip, the children looked at old records of people buried in the town graveyard. These records told them what people's countries of origin had been, what jobs they'd held, how they'd died, and how old they'd been when they died. These records had been obtained from the archives at the local library by a former teacher, who'd put together a unit based on the people buried in the graves in Union Cemetery.

As they discovered individuals' places of origin, they constructed a map of the world, using yarn to connect their community to Asia, Europe, and South America. The individualized records sparked some interesting discussions and helped the children get a picture of what life was like for people in their town in the past. Some of the jobs that the people had held were rather interesting. For example, in Redwood City, there was once a barber who also took out tonsils!

Discovering history. We see how topics come alive when Spotorno gives the children an opportunity to explore the hidden stories and connections that exist in their real lives. Here the children explore the present and the past of their communityand sense the very real way in which their local history connects them to people in the past and the rest of the world.

On the day of the field trip, the children were really excited. Spotorno asked them to do a scavenger hunt: to find particular individuals who'd died at a certain age, who'd come to the United States from specific countries, or who'd held specific jobs. While scavenger hunting, the kids became more interested in the stones themselves, the ornaments on them, and the names of the particular people buried under each stone that they came upon. They really enjoyed doing rubbings of the stones, and these were later hung in the classroom. (In retrospect, Spotorno feels that it might have been better to let the children do rubbings first and then walk slowly through the graveyard together, rather than starting off with a scavenger hunt.)

Practicing flexible planning. Things don't always go smoothly when we begin to ground instruction in events, places, and life experiences. Sequence and timing become as important for teachers as they are for directors of any creative activity, from filmmakers and writers to orchestra conductors! Yet like Spotorno, with patience and self-reflection we can learn directly from our experiences, honing and developing our skills from year to year.

After the visit, a woman from the local library came to speak to the children about what life was like in their community in the past. She told them about what school was like: what the rules were and how things were done. She brought old photographs of the land in the days when logging was an enterprise (before the land was developed and cleared of many trees). Spotorno remembers that "she had the kids in awe." The students followed up her visit with thank-you notes.

Jennifer Spotorno, Teacher, Hoover Elementary School, Redwood City, California

Following up and following through. We see again the role that personal contact with other adults from the community can play. These face-to-face interactions confirm for students the value and utility that knowledge and learning hold in our society. As they're able to connect their knowledge with larger events in the world, learning itself becomes more and more exciting. History becomes an active learning experience when writing, art, and photography are incorporated into the lesson.

8.2.3. Experiencing the World Wearing "Others' Shoes"

Actively researching and discovering our natural and social environments is one exciting way to find out about the world around us, but we also gain valuable knowledge by putting ourselves in others' shoes—in other words, by reflecting on or actually participating in another's experiences. Students in the following examples have been given an opportunity to learn about human experience in all its complexity: how we relate to ourselves, each other, and the plant and animal kingdoms. Their own life experiences become the medium through which they learn about the lives of others.

I was trying to figure out how I could make Martin Luther's story interesting to seventh graders, and the theme of standing up for something you believe in just jumped out at me. After all, what did Luther do? He was a rebel; he took a stand. So I designed a writing assignment in which the kids get to write about some time in their lives when they took a stand for something they believed in. They can really express themselves; it's not another library assignment where they have to write about something irrelevant to their lives. This time they get to write about *their* identities and *their* lives. That's phase 1 of the lesson. Next, I'm going to give them copies of a Matt Groenig cartoon (you know, he's the one who created the Simpsons) called "My Fifth Grade Diary," in which the main character takes a stand against his friends who are cheating. It's a very realistic cartoon, and I think the kids can really relate to the story. After reading and discussing it, the kids will create their own cartoon versions of their "taking a stand" stories. I've found that combining writing and art is very successful in getting kids to write more. When their artistic creativity is sparked, their writing becomes more creative as well.

Kris Estrada, Teacher, Burnett Academy, San Jose, California

Seeing oneself in history. Estrada transforms a possibly mundane and distant subject into something intensely relevant to students' lives. By encouraging them to reflect on a personal experience of their own, she paves the way for them to connect with Luther and understand his personal motivations and beliefs. History springs forth from the written page and is all of a sudden about people just like us!

Continuing to build on the students' experiences, Estrada incorporates a popular cartoon (which most students would assume has nothing to do with learning) into the lesson and makes it a powerful learning tool. Children learn about communicating through multiple channels: writing, discussing, and drawing. "Artistic creativity" is stressed, and students learn that art can be a powerful messenger.

Reflection on one's own situation is as important for self-understanding as thinking about someone else's situation is for an understanding of the world. At Burnett, one of the emphases of the Culture Cadre was to infuse the variety of cultures represented at the school into the curriculum, instruction, and daily life of the school. Burnett middle school students reflected on their own cultures through writing poems in their humanities classes—the poem at right is one example. A variety of parents commented about how meaningful it was for them and their children to have an opportunity to celebrate their culture together.

Of course, the world we live in isn't exclusively made up of humans; animals and plants also share our earth. It's possible (and fun!) to contemplate what it must be like to be another species, although that task is more difficult than thinking about other humans' experiences. The following vignette highlights the excitement of students in an elementary school class as they imagine that they're plants. The teacher, Luz Aguilar, invited a graduate student from Stanford University, Christopher Chase, to teach a lesson. (Accelerated school communities actively recruit visitors to their classes to give their students a broad perspective on the world. For more on inviting the community into the classroom, please refer to Chapter Ten, "Family and Community Involvement.")

Hispanic Culture

Hispanic culture is ...

The Mariachi bands playing at Cinco de Mayo.

Hearing the taco shells sizzle in the frying pan.

Hitting a piñata at a child's birthday party.

Making tortillas with your grandmother

Listening to stories about the yorona

Having pride and being proud of who you are.

By Andrea Santiago

Chase began the first lesson by reading to the children a traditional Russian children's story called "The Turnip." This illustrated story is about the cooperative efforts of a farmer, his family, and his animal friends to pull a huge turnip from the ground. The children loved mimicking the movements of the story characters as they "pulled, and pulled, and pulled" in their efforts to lift the turnip out of the ground. After that, Chase and the children drew cartoonlike pictures of different vegetables and fruits. He then presented the children and their teacher with a gift of radish seeds (the fastest growing of plants), which the teacher later helped the children plant in small cups.

Achieving active learning through listening. By getting the children on their feet "pulling, and pulling, and pulling," Chase transforms the traditional idea of reading a story to children. Instead of sitting quiet and

still, the students use their bodies to understand the situation of the book's characters. To further stress the real-life themes of this activity, Chase provides the class with real seeds, which will grow and ignite their curiosity about plants, leading to another powerful learning situation.

The second lesson took place the following week. The children were excited to show Chase the neat little radish plants that had sprouted. After looking at the plants, he asked the children if they'd like to make believe they were plants. They all formed a circle and dramatized the different stages of a plant's growth. He taught the children how to sing the song "You Are My Sunshine" while playing the role of plants with their bodies.

Channeling powerful learning through multiple forms of expression. The children are able to use their imaginations, their bodies, and their voices to express their understanding. Nothing about this learning is rote, dull, or "drill and kill." On the contrary, students learn that the information that they observe and read can be expressed in as many different ways as they have senses.

The classroom teacher then divided the children into groups of four and asked them to stand side by side as each child represented one stage in a plant's growth. After the children had all done this successfully, they drew pictures of plants in these four stages. This was an important part of the lesson, because it showed that the kids really understood that they were representing plants with their bodies. For example, one of the non-English-speaking children hadn't drawn leaves on one of his plants. Chase asked him, "What about the leaves?" and he simply looked at Chase with a blank expression. Chase then raised his arm and pointed to it while repeating the question. This time the

child's face glowed with comprehension, and he quickly drew in the leaves.

Letting understanding and communication shine through. In addition to being a fun, creative activity, pretending to be plants *works*; it enhances the children's understanding of a complex natural phenomenon! And this kind of powerful learning experience works well with *all* children, regardless of their English-language proficiency. By structuring your lessons in an active and imaginative way, you can instruct children from very diverse backgrounds side by side.

When the children were pretending to be plants, Chase asked them how they got their nourishment and water. Either they didn't know or they didn't understand the question. Some kids mimicked the gesture that he'd used when asking the question and made gestures toward their mouths. Then suddenly the classroom teacher, who'd been participating in the exercise with them, said, "Ooh, I feel something! Something's coming up through my roots. There's *water* coming up through my roots!" The children laughed and looked down at their legs and feet, pretending that they could feel the water coming up through their legs. After that, when the children drew pictures, most included water going into the roots.

The next week, when Chase was doing this lesson with another class, he forgot to ask the children about nourishment and water during the drama exercise. Instead, he illustrated the idea of root feeding on the blackboard while they were drawing their pictures. He noted that the concept didn't seem to evoke the same kind of "*aha!*" that it had during the dramatic instruction, when the kids were making believe they were flowers.

Hoover Elementary School, Redwood City, California

Putting oneself in another's shoes. These children are putting themselves in a very different kind of shoes—those of plants! As Chase discovers, learning is always much more powerful when you *feel* rather than only *see* it. Through this simulated role-playing activity, these children are able to imagine what it must be like to be a plant, and they therefore develop a conceptual understanding of the methods plants use to live and grow in their natural environment.

8.2.4. Providing Special Opportunities

While all children have unique gifts and an innate ability to learn, some individuals face unique educational challenges. The challenge that *we* face is how to provide these children with special opportunities that build on their strengths without remediating their learning or treating them as if they were fundamentally deficient or "different" from other kids. Coming up

with such strategies isn't easy, but teachers in accelerated schools have developed a number of innovative ways of approaching the special needs that remedial programs such as Chapter I were originally designed to address:

> **The in-class approach became our alternative to the Chapter I pullout program for remedial math and reading. I really like having the Chapter I teachers come into my classroom; it's like team teaching. They work with all of the students on whatever activity we're doing so that not a single first grader would think that he or she was a "remedial" student. As a result of having two teachers in the classroom, we could provide more hands-on activities in math. We could break the class up into groups, instead of whole-class instruction every day. We did the same type of activities in reading. In this way, all of the students get the benefit of two teachers, and no students feel stigmatized.**
>
> Lavon Horton, Teacher, Fairbanks Elementary School, Springfield, Missouri

Taking a risk. This innovative approach shows us how much easier it is to transform problems when we let go of our traditional beliefs about how things should be done. Clearly, this is a situation in which everyone wins, and it came about because the best interests of the children were put first. Yet because personalities and circumstances differ from school to school, we don't present this (or any of the other vignettes in this book) as *the* solution, *the* way that accelerated schools deal with Chapter I. Each community must carefully examine the unique circumstances it faces using inquiry and then come up with appropriate solutions.

Another group whose needs educators must consider are students who crave more challenging or complex learning opportunities than most of their peers. We saw an example of this in the banking story: Joshua, the student who wanted to open an accounting firm that would compete with his teacher's. Fortunately, as several of our examples demonstrate, when teachers create flexible instructional environments, it becomes easier to empower students to take on greater responsibility in the context of any class assignment. Children are thus able to pursue their interests in a way that adds to the opportunities for learning that they (as well as other children) have.

In the following example, we see great emphasis placed on the idea that learning is something natural and fun; no one worries about everyone learning the same thing at the exact same time.

> **I find that math and science are more fun for everyone if you use activities and experiments—hands-on learning with real student**

involvement. When we're working as a whole class, I'll explain a new idea, work a few examples on the board, and get people going on their own. Then I go over to the rug and sit down, and everyone knows that they can come to me for more help if they still haven't got it. Usually a small group forms over on the rug, but it tends to be different kids each time. It's not like I'm over there with the "low" group, because the group depends on the task we're doing, not on who the kids are. It's always voluntary to come over to the rug. Sometimes I'll invite someone to come join us in a very friendly way. I tell all my kids, "Don't worry if you don't catch on the first time you see something. You're just not ready yet. If you don't get it now, you'll get it next week, or next month. Just keep trying."

Amy L. Meyer, Teacher, Hoover Elementary School, Redwood City, California

Taking the time to learn. Amy Meyer values student effort and learning, and her instruction is structured so that it recognizes that children learn things at different paces and in different ways. To create a flexible learning environment such as hers isn't always easy. With our traditional emphasis on teaching ideas sequentially at a set pace, we often unconsciously place a priority on knowing the right answers by a specific time. To make students comfortable with learning things at their own pace, Meyer creates multiple opportunities for learning in her classroom.

8.2.5. Children Teaching Each Other

Another creative way to provide children with increased learning opportunities is to get them to teach one another. Adults teach each other all the time—at work, in families, while playing sports. So why do we assume that only adults can teach children? In fact, children learn well from their peers, older children, and younger children. Just think about when your oldest child taught your youngest how to hold a baseball bat, or remember when you taught your own younger sibling how to drive. Inevitably, when working together, both parties learn a great deal (and become closer to each other in the process). The next few vignettes highlight the successes of peer- and cross-age tutoring programs at accelerated schools. They remind us not to forget a critical element of the *who* (our students) when we think about the *how* of powerful learning.

At Fairbanks School, we believe that all students can learn well. Since one of the major components of accelerated schools is building on strengths, we wanted to create a project that would allow students to demonstrate their individual strengths as well as help other students develop their own. FAST stands for Fellow Achievers/Student Teachers. It's a program that another teacher, Ms. Monroe, and I created to give sixth grade students the opportunity to apply for positions as student teachers to our first grade students.

Taking the initiative. Leslie McIlquham and her colleague seize upon a core accelerated schools principle and come up with a way to bring it to life in their school. They create an instructional situation that embodies the ideal of building on strengths. Cross-age tutoring builds on the natural position of older children as role models for younger students.

We started the process by putting together a "real" job application. This wasn't only to find out their qualifications but to give the students the opportunity to see what it's really like to apply for a job. Each student needed to have three adult references, complete with addresses and phone numbers. Once the application was completed, we interviewed students to find their strengths and areas of interest. Sixth graders again had a chance to show responsibility by keeping the appointment and being prepared to answer questions. We discussed eye contact, personal appearance, and well-composed answers.

Giving the older students a taste of "real" life. All children are intensely curious about the adult world and enjoy participating in it meaningfully. Having the prospective tutors "apply" for the privilege of interacting with the first graders gives the older students a chance to learn something about adult life at the same time that it encourages them to take the role of tutor very seriously.

Students were then chosen for the area in which we felt they could most benefit the first graders. The sixth graders committed to a period of training and designing lessons for the first graders. All participating sixth grade students stayed after school once a week for three weeks, learning to cooperate with one another and planning the lessons. Five centers—reading, math, writing, art, and discovery—were set up by sixth graders with our assistance. Finally, the program was ready to begin. First graders were divided up into five groups to be rotated every week for five weeks. Sixth graders' spirits were high right before the start of the program. They were excited to show what they knew and to help the younger students to "be smart."

Blending careful planning and unbridled excitement. Peer- and cross-age tutoring programs require advance planning to be successful. Knowing this, McIlquham and her colleague orchestrate a complex set of training and planning sessions, requiring a great deal of commitment from themselves as well as from the student tutors. As is the case with most powerful learning situations, the students' "pre-service" training is fun, challenging, and worthwhile. The sixth graders are all willing (even eager) to give up some of their free time to participate in this experience.

We all learned so many things together! Sixth graders found out that things don't always go as planned. They had to immediately revise and adjust their plans to meet the needs of the first graders. First graders

found out that learning was indeed fun and much easier with their own individual teachers (the tutors!). Both sixth and first grade students enjoyed hugs, praise, and admiration.

Creating opportunities for students to interact and care about each other. Cross-age tutoring brings a multitude of rewards for both the older and younger children. Tutoring gives the student helpers a sense of responsibility, achievement, and importance—valuable feelings for building self-confidence and self-esteem. The younger children bask in the attention of the knowledgeable older students, and the tutors discover that the best way to learn something is to teach it. If their students aren't catching on, the young tutors learn to try different approaches or ask the teacher for help.

Each week sixth graders evaluated in their journals and through discussion what worked and what would be of more use if changed. They learned that it's necessary to be well organized, because teaching the lesson and maintaining first graders' attention took all of their energy. It was amazing to see how much the sixth graders were learning by teaching the younger students. They took on responsibilities that they never would have otherwise. Sixth graders realized that the degree of satisfaction in personal accomplishment is directly related to the investments made (especially in time and effort). They all saw dignity and value in hard work. There were many comments about feeling challenged and needed.

Reflecting on life lessons. These students are learning and internalizing lessons that some adults never do! McIlquham and Monroe treat the sixth graders with a great deal of respect, allowing them to reflect on their own strengths and challenges instead of automatically taking over and correcting them when a lesson doesn't go as planned. The children are empowered and pushed to take responsibility for what they and their peers learn. As a result, they develop a new understanding and appreciation of the complexity and excitement of the learning process.

First graders became very attached to the older students and referred to them as *their* teachers. They not only learned academic skills; they felt good about themselves, because they had these special teachers taking an interest in each of them. One first grader had never had the nerve to speak aloud in class, but when presenting a play spoke louder and more clearly than any of the other children. Her sixth grade teachers weren't aware of her usual shyness; they just told her she could do it, and she did!

Presenting role models and high expectations. What better way to interest children in learning than for the older students to demonstrate that it's a wonderfully rich experience? Children often have a special way with one another—one that's particularly encouraging and trusting; older children genuinely believe in the abilities and potential of younger children to succeed. This belief pushes younger students to overcome their doubts and believe in themselves.

During the final session, sixth graders were given a set of questions to evaluate the program and help us make it better in years to come. To show their appreciation, the first graders threw a party for the sixth graders. They made thank-you notes and shared them along with refreshments. The first graders wanted to teach their teachers something, so they taught them several games. There were many hugs and all of the kids asked, "When can we do this again?"

Leslie McIlquham, Teacher, Fairbanks Elementary School, Springfield, Missouri

Enjoying happy endings (or is it beginnings?). The end of the FAST program for the year is a blend of celebration and serious reflection. Involving the sixth graders in an evaluation not just of their own teaching but of the program itself is an amazing source of empowerment and responsibility for the students. Their opinion *counts*! The warmth of the first graders' gestures lets the sixth graders know that they count as people too. The lessons learned by these children about caring, planning, reflecting, and interacting with others will last them for the rest of their lives.

Peer tutoring can be a special way for students to get to know others who are very different from themselves. Working closely with someone whose experiences you don't fully understand builds caring, appreciation, and trust. At Hoover Elementary School, fourth graders are learning these skills, as well as practicing maturity and commitment.

My fourth grade class works with students from the special education classrooms as peer tutors. It started out with just a few kids taking an interest at recess or lunch, and then it expanded into something a lot of kids in my class do. I went around to each teacher and asked if she'd be interested in having a few of my kids come in for a certain part of the day to tutor or work with her kids. All of them were interested, so I sent two or three students to each of them for half an hour in the morning, which turned out to be half of my class. I did the same thing with the rest of the kids for half an hour in the afternoon. That freed me up to work specially with just half the class for a whole hour a day! Usually we'd read during those times, and sometimes we'd bring in some of the special education students to read with us. It was kind of like an exchange program. It created such an attitude of acceptance and valuing each other, helping each other, and supporting each other.

The kids from my room who went over there have really benefited from having that responsibility. As it turns out, the kids in my class who

are having the most trouble behaviorally and academically are the ones about whom I get the most compliments from the special education teachers. It's been a great self-esteem builder for those kids, who are so hungry for responsibility. I don't mind that they're missing class at all. I figure, if they're spending half an hour focused on a task and seeing those kids through an activity that they normally wouldn't be able to concentrate on long enough to do on their own, they must be learning something.

Amy L. Meyer, Teacher, Hoover Elementary, Redwood City, California

Learning about caring. Indeed, the students in Amy Meyer's class *are* learning something! In addition to the responsibility and sense of pride that come from doing a serious job well, these fourth graders are learning about tolerance, sensitivity, generosity, and caring for those who are different from them. Childhood is sometimes characterized as a "mean" time, when individuals tease and make fun of those who are different or less fortunate than they are. While ignorance can lead to these responses, the response of loving, caring support comes even more naturally to children. Because children are used to interacting with and helping their peers in many different situations, those in your classes may already possess informal tutoring skills that you weren't aware they had. Peer- and cross-age tutoring are the natural ways that children learn all over the world, from sessions in one-room schoolhouses to afterschool basketball and baseball games.

8.2.6. Technology: A *How*, Not a *What*

Schools are bombarded these days with offers of new technologies that will make the job of teaching easier and the quality of learning better. Unfortunately, in many schools, useful technologies are treated as ends in themselves instead of as means to achieve powerful learning. Classes in computers or keyboarding are making a *how* into a *what*. They fail to show students that technology is a tool to *enrich* our lives; it shouldn't be the *focus* of our lives. The following examples from accelerated schools illustrate the ways in which various technologies, from word processing to flight simulation, can be harnessed in the creation of powerful learning situations for all students.

Our school now has a great facility, Lab 2000, for teaching aerodynamics, engineering design, and computers, which we've developed from a grant. The classroom is stocked with state-of-the-art technology: Macintosh computers, a flight simulator, robotics equipment. The kids love to come in here. In a lot of schools, this kind of technology might be available only to the "advanced" or "gifted" kids, but here we want all of the kids to have access to it. My second-period class consists of all non-English-proficient students. Several of them are new to the school and have been in this country only a few months. Some of them have attended only one or two years of any type of school. I don't even speak any Spanish (although I'm learning!), and this class is one of my best! Right now they're working on building tetrahedral kites, which we'll go out and test-fly at the end of the month.

I've organized the kids into working groups, which they seem to enjoy a great deal. You know, we talk about building on strengths, and I believe one strength of these students is knowing how to work cooperatively in groups. They really support each other and work together. I've recruited some bilingual eighth grade students to help translate, and they've been super; they're real leaders. The experience has helped a lot of students come out of their shells. You know, just because a student doesn't speak English doesn't mean he or she can't be a leader and a role model for other students. One boy, Sevandro, had to be sent to the office on the first day of class. Now he's become my best student. He's a whiz at the computers, and moreover, he loves to teach the other students how to use them. He's especially helpful with the newcomers. Here's a kid a lot of people might have written off as a loss, but he's a very talented individual. It just took the right setting for him to blossom.

Steve Novotny, Teacher, Burnett Academy, San Jose, California

Using high technology as a means to unexpected ends. Many children are fascinated by all forms of technology. Real hands-on experiences with exciting media tools and modern technological devices can spark children's interest in learning and provide them with the tools and skills they'll need in order to develop their potential and meet the educational and career demands of the twenty-first century. If the goal of an accelerated school is to bring students in at-risk situations into the mainstream, then you must do all you can to bridge any technology gap that might exist for your students. In Steve Novotny's classroom, one such student becomes the class expert, surprising his teacher (and perhaps himself). As he works with his peers, he's also developing valuable leadership skills, which will spill over into his other life experiences. Novotny is learning Spanish, and his students are undoubtedly learning English— and a great deal more—as they interact with him and their eighth grade tutors. In his classroom, technology is being used as it should be—as an instructional *means* rather than an *end*. It's a means to learning a variety of skills: the English language; leadership and communication skills among peers; complex science, engineering, and math skills; and computer literacy skills that will be valuable both to the students and to their future employers.

Students aren't the only ones who can benefit from the effective use of technology in schools. As you recall from Jackie Dolan's story about banking in her fourth grade classroom, she used a computer to generate spreadsheets for her students' "checking accounts." This example demonstrates the usefulness of relatively simple technologies (such as the personal computer) that many people now have in their homes in the creation of powerful learning experiences for children. Dolan spent a considerable amount of time setting up a system that she could use to balance their accounts, but once this front-end work was done, her weekly job was greatly simplified.

Kris Estrada, a teacher at Burnett Academy, also referred to the use of technology in her classroom in her stories about Burnett's Writing Lab. Her classroom, filled with word-processing terminals connected to a mainframe that she controls from her own large-screen terminal, is never the site of lessons in typing or programming; these skills are built into each humanities lesson she teaches. These days, when almost all jobs require computer literacy and almost all writing is done with a word processor, these students are learning real-life writing skills at the same time that they're learning powerful information about our social and historical world.

In the next vignette, we see how two sixth grade science teachers from an accelerated middle school made use of modern video technology in their design of an instructional unit on the weather. By giving their students a chance to collaboratively research, write, direct, and film TV weather reports, they enabled their students to approach the subject matter as it's often presented in real life.

As with many of our previous examples, this vignette shows how well-designed instructional activities often go beyond traditional subject-area curricular goals, becoming vehicles for learning about oneself and others.

> **Before we started our weather unit, I told the students, "You all are going to be on camera; you all are going to make your own weather report in front of the whole class, and your tape will be seen next year just as you're going to see last year's videos. However, in order to do the weather video, you need to know what weather is, what makes up weather, what the most important weather concepts are. So before we do the videos, we'll have to do certain experiments so that you have knowledge of what meteorologists are talking about, and how they get that data."**

Establishing a powerful incentive for learning. By letting the students know about the videos up front, Glenda Coching-Yap and Jack DiCarlo are able to provide them with a meaningful reason for studying the scientific concepts and participating in the class experiments. The incentive not only motivates them to learn; it contextualizes what

they're learning (meteorology) in an everyday experience—watching the news on television. The teachers' planning and creativity are exhibited in the way the different phases of instruction are set up to take place smoothly and sequentially.

First I showed them my own video with myself, and I did everything wrong, reading the paper really scrunched up, and fiddling around. The kids really liked that. That's to show what not to do in the video. Then I had segments of real live meteorologists—TV personalities—doing weather reports. Then I showed them last year's student videos. They see the videos both at the beginning and as they go along to give them reinforcement. Because a lot of times they'll forget what they've seen. If you show it midway, while they're working on their own project, they might be at a spot where they're not sure about what to do, and then they can get an idea of how to do it from another video. They improve in that way. And they just keep getting better each year.

Building on the strengths and experiences of others. The students aren't expected to reinvent the wheel. By having actual examples of what to do and what not to do, they're better able to steer clear of common pitfalls. In this way, the students experience science and technological development as they actually work in the world. Practical science has little to do with memorizing formulas or answering questions on multiple-choice tests. It involves collaborating with others, learning from the work of the past and building on its strengths, and coming up with innovations that work even better than the old ways.

We have a mixture of people in the class—Hispanics, Caucasians, Vietnamese. When they do this weather report, I encourage them to tap into their resources. Why can't it be a bilingual weather video? Why can't it be a *trilingual* video? If a group wants to do a video in just

Spanish—go ahead, fine. If they have a Spanish video with an English translation, that's okay too. Not only do they have to speak that language, but they have to write their scripts in that language. When English-speaking kids work with Spanish-speaking kids to translate their English into a bilingual weather video, they really get to like each other. They see each other in a different light. "Hey, you've got a talent for speaking another language to help us make this weather video just another step ahead of anybody else's, different from anybody else's."

The weather report was like a carrot. We did the experiments and studied the concepts prior to doing the weather videos. The video was a culminating project, designed so that the ideas will stick in their brains a lot more. This way they're enjoying themselves, and they get to use the knowledge.

Glenda Coching-Yap and Jack DiCarlo, Teachers, Burnett Academy, San Jose, California

Teaching language and science through technology. As we saw in Steve Novotny's Lab 2000, working with sophisticated equipment is a powerful way to learn language and communication skills. These students will take home an awareness, appreciation, and understanding of meteorology, video making, group dynamics, different languages, public speaking, presentation writing, and (above all) each other.

8.3. Assessment of Student Learning— A Critical *How*

Figuring out how to present the *what*—or the content of learning situations—to students requires thinking about how you'll assess what learning has taken place and evaluate how effective (or *powerful*) a learning situation has been. As we all know, assessment is usually handled through tests that follow each unit of curriculum. Many educators agree, however, that this approach hides or distorts as much information as it tests. Children's knowledge is too complex to be represented on a multiple-choice or essay test. In addition, there are many more aspects of your teaching besides factual content that deserve feedback. How did the students *feel* about the lesson? Were they challenged by the curriculum and instructional environment? Do they want to learn more about a particular topic because of an idea or question that your lesson sparked for them?

Assessment ideally involves both the learner and the teacher, as whole beings, complete with strengths and challenges, feelings and experiences. In accelerated schools, teachers are just beginning to venture into creative ways to assess the powerful learning situations that they've created. This is an area that we're starting to learn more about, but we still have a long way to go.

The examples that follow are some of the first steps that staff in accelerated schools have taken in the area of "authentic" assessment. They may spark your thinking about all the assessment opportunities that abound in your classroom.

One of our teachers, Meg, started using portfolios with her kids. She'd have the students keep a portfolio with every piece of work they did, and once a week, she asked them to choose one or two items from it that they wanted to share with her. She'd set up little appointments with each child and ask them, "Why did you select this piece to show me? Why are you proud of this one? Where do you want to go from here?" She really got them to talk about what was important to them; it was neat! She placed these student-selected works in a smaller, long-term portfolio that she kept for the children. She used these portfolios when she'd talk with the parents. She told me that at first she didn't realize what an incredible resource the portfolios would be for parent conferences—she'd started them to give the students a say about what they liked in their own work and about their goals and ideas—but as soon as she started using them, she was really pleased with the parents' responses. Meg really got to the heart of it. She said to me, "If you just put aside all of your notions about teacher-directed instruction—you know, the teacher chooses what to show parents, and what to assess— and take a risk and let the students choose, you can learn so much from them!" She kept notes on what the children would say about their work, and she said that often their reasons for having selected something were things she never would have thought of.

Getting to the heart of assessment. By taking a risk and trying something completely new, this teacher is opening the doors to powerful learning for her students *and* for herself! Not only is Meg collecting information about her students' academic skills; she's getting to know the kids as people in a way she would not have through tests and graded assignments. The caring that she shows toward the children is obvious to their parents, who get to find out how their children feel about themselves in school and what they're most proud of.

In the Language Arts Cadre, we were very excited about what Meg was doing, and we wanted to bring the idea to the school as a whole. As a cadre, we researched inside and outside the school about different types of portfolios and alternative assessments, discussed our findings, and finally we presented before the SAW. Our principal loved the idea, and in fact, the district was just gearing up to help schools move toward performance-based assessment, so some of us attended a district meeting. At first our principal said, "I want everyone to keep portfolios next year!" but I reminded him that he couldn't just mandate that kind of change; it had to be voluntary. So then we presented it to the school

as a whole by asking, "Who would like to participate in a portfolio group next year?" Half of our staff volunteered! We've gotten together a few times to plan what we'll do, and we're all going to be experimenting with different methods. Some will be doing just writing portfolios; others will include everything.

Enjoying an empowering governance structure that makes it happen. A "little wheel" conceived by an individual teacher becomes the basis for a powerful "big wheel"—schoolwide change. But the change isn't mandated from above. Rather, the entire school community considers an idea that might move the school toward its vision, and enthusiastic teachers volunteer to take on the project. Empowerment comes to life!

At first some people said, "Oh, this is just one more thing we have to do." And yes, it *is* "one more thing," but it may be *the* "one more thing" that really makes a difference for the kids and helps us too. It will take us that much closer to authentic assessment, and that's so important. Traditionally, assessment is so competitive and comparative between students. This way, you give the child a chance to say, "This is where *I* stand in relation to *me*."

Barbara Ruel, Resource Teacher, Hoover Elementary School, Redwood City, California

Heading toward authentic success through authentic assessment. These teachers have their vision clearly in mind as they make decisions regarding their interactions with children. What could be more important than helping a child gain self-confidence, build academic skills, and authentically express herself?

Portfolios are one type of alternative assessment that has been widely discussed in the education literature. Alternative assessments aren't limited to ideas that others have had, however; you can create your own unique ways of assessing your students' learning and your teaching. In the next example, Jackie Dolan has done just that:

I don't give standard spelling tests—you know, when you read a list of words and the kids have to write them down. What I do is have the kids write a spelling story sometime during the week for homework. We brainstorm in class about how to write it, and I give them all week to work on it. They bring their stories in, I read them, we read them to each other, and we pick one story from someone in the class to use as the basis for the dictation test.

Designing assessment as a powerful learning experience. Dolan fully incorporates assessment into the planning of her spelling lesson; it's not an afterthought, or an unconnected add-on after the lesson has been taught. Because she contextualizes the new spelling words into a multi-faceted language lesson, students understand that spelling is important for effective reading and writing. An informal assessment of students' writing takes place before any spelling words are dictated: the *students* share their work with each other and then choose which story they want to use to continue their learning. Through this process, students receive invaluable feedback from the teacher and their peers about their writing skills—but in a safe, low-stakes situation. A "routine" spelling test is transformed into a powerful learning experience for all the children.

After the kids decide which story they like best, I sit down with the author and we edit and shorten it to no more than three paragraphs, making sure to get all the spelling words in. The revised stories are concise, but the point is that I'm using that person's ideas as the basis for the test. So on test day, I dictate the shortened story to them, and the class writes it down—the whole thing. We always begin by writing the title of the story and then "by" whomever. The kids love it, and the "author" for that week's story always shines on that particular test, because it's *his* story. They feel such ownership!

Stressing ownership, empowerment, and building on strengths. The students in Dolan's class are in charge of their own learning. By honoring and building on their ideas and abilities, Dolan creates an atmosphere in which each student is responsible for his or her own success; and in such an environment, students shine!

I can work on skills other than spelling too. As I dictate the stories, the kids get really good about listening. By the end of the year, we even use dialogue. If I teach punctuation of dialogue during the year, then they have to use it during the spelling tests. Handwriting counts too. Also, at the end of every test, I always have them write me a brief paragraph about how they felt about that particular test. That free writing gives me an idea about how they can assimilate their thoughts quickly, put an idea down on paper, and see how much sense they could make of it. My spelling units last two weeks, and the second week I run the test differently. I put the spelling words up on the board in three sections, corresponding to the three paragraphs in the previous week's story. They have to use the words to recreate the story as best they can. In this way, I find out about their listening comprehension and their writing skills. I get a great deal of information for the children's portfolios from these spelling tests.

Seeing how powerful learning leads to powerful assessment. Every situation is used as an opportunity for both formal and informal assessment of a wide variety of knowledge, skills, and feelings. In addition to gaining crucial knowledge about spelling, dialogue, punctuation, writing, handwriting, and listening comprehension, Dolan is assessing how the children feel about the assessment experience. When students are given an opportunity to provide the teacher with feedback about learning activities, a more open line of communication is established. As you demonstrate your willingness to listen to assessments, you model the idea that honest feedback need not be threatening and that we need such feedback in order to learn. Dolan reinforces this idea by using portfolios instead of strictly quantitative test scores to formally assess students' growth.

There were some kids who came to me and said they just couldn't do it; they couldn't write the stories. So we came up with this other little group that formulated their own spelling tests. My aide and I would help them to write their own sentences for each word, and they'd be tested using these sentences. They knew exactly what they'd be asked to write for the test, and they had a lot of success. They had a hand in what they were going to be doing; they were making the decisions. *All* of the kids are given the chance to be successful, and it really works well. I like it much better than just giving a standard spelling test, because the children are using all of the skills you want them to learn. It goes back to the idea that good writers make good readers. And I saw it happen with these kids. They really learned how to communicate.

Jackie Dolan, Teacher, Daniel Webster Elementary School, San Francisco, California

Achieving success and learning for all *children.* Dolan provides a great example of the ways in which the classroom can be set up to satisfy the needs of all students while holding them all accountable for their own learning. Instead of reinforcing certain students' feelings that they can't participate by refusing to be flexible or by reverting to a remediation approach—Dolan shows them that they *can* be just as creative as they want to be and that they have responsibility for and ownership of their own success. The end result, for *all* of Dolan's students, is growth in their skills and abilities through powerful learning experiences.

As you've seen, creative assessment takes advantage of resources that are already in your classroom or your experience. Another teacher used simple technology—a tape recorder—with her primary students:

One teacher at Hoover Elementary School uses audiotapes to document her first graders' reading development. She makes a tape of each child reading at the beginning of the year, in February, and again in May. These tapes allow her to say to the parents, "Here's your child reading to me in October, and here's your child reading to me in May." She uses tapes mainly for "a proud moment to show off to the parents," but they're also valuable records of a student's progress. Tapes let kids say, "Yeah, Mom, yeah."

Hoover Elementary School, Redwood City, California

What's to Come

How we teach our students has a great impact on *what* they learn in school. It is our hope that, as you work collaboratively with others in your school community, you'll begin to discover the interdependence of the *how* and the *what* and the power that comes when your teaching incorporates the very *best* that you know about these elements of powerful learning situations. In the next chapter, we turn to a discussion of the final component of powerful learning—the *context* in which it occurs.

The *Context* of Powerful Learning

Supportive Organizational Elements

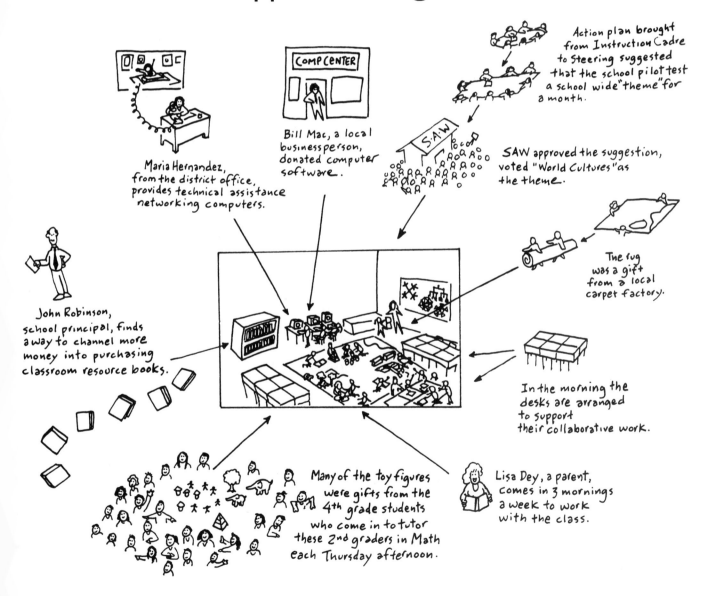

Action plan brought from Instruction Cadre to Steering suggested that the school pilot test a school wide "theme" for a month.

Maria Hernandez, from the district office, provides technical assistance networking computers.

Bill Mac, a local businessperson, donated computer software.

SAW approved the suggestion, voted "World Cultures" as the theme.

The rug was a gift from a local carpet factory.

John Robinson, school principal, finds a way to channel more money into purchasing classroom resource books.

In the morning the desks are arranged to support their collaborative work.

Many of the toy figures were gifts from the 4th grade students who come in to tutor these 2nd graders in Math each Thursday afternoon.

Lisa Dey, a parent, comes in 3 mornings a week to work with the class.

249

You may recognize the centerpiece of the preceding drawing from Chapter Six; it depicts students recreating various societies of our world. Here we've enhanced that drawing to include the factors and conditions that enabled such a learning experience to occur. As the base of our powerful learning triangle, *context* supports the *what* and the *how*. Contextual factors operate at many different levels, from one-on-one interactions in the classroom to decisions about funding at the district office. For example, notice in the drawing how the Instruction Cadre proposed to the steering committee and the school as a whole that the school pilot test a schoolwide theme; how the principal found some money in the budget that could go toward historical resource books; how the district office provided technical assistance in networking the computers in the classroom; and how a local computer shop donated the software that students are using to simulate different societies. These are all enabling *contextual* factors that support powerful learning.

As you read the vignettes in the previous chapters, you probably noticed how much the organization of physical factors and attention to learning environments affected children's learning. All of the powerful learning experiences we've seen so far involved the careful organization of physical settings, people, resources, and time, all within a larger social environment that encouraged and supported risk taking and discovery. By drawing on a wide range of resources and expertise available in the school and in the community (which ranged from going on meaningful outings to using household items as classroom materials), the teachers and students found themselves free to learn much more than they could have in the context of a traditional remedial classroom.

Traditional school contexts were designed to support traditional beliefs about the abilities of children and the nature of learning. Members of accelerated school communities, on the other hand, consciously organize learning environments in ways that support their school's vision, learning goals, and methods of instruction. By focusing on creating powerful learning situations rather than on delivering information, accelerated school communities are flexible and creative; they're therefore able to attend to the contextual factors that contribute to the learning environment.

The following example illustrates an accelerated context. Two teachers detail the way in which they were able to create an enriched bilingual instructional environment for their students—an environment that they felt would greatly accelerate their students' learning. In this instance, the teachers are meeting the students' particular needs by creating special opportunities and providing special attention and care.

> **We'd been trying for a long time to get full-day kindergarten for our kids, because that's what we feel serves them best. Each time we brought it up, our principal would tell us that we couldn't afford it.**

There wasn't enough in the Chapter I budget to hire a new teacher full-time. Eventually, one half-day kindergarten teacher was transferred, and we proposed to the steering committee that she not be replaced and that the Chapter I funds for her salary go toward funding two of us to team-teach a full-day program. We wanted to combine the bilingual and English-speaking kids into one class of about forty kids.

Gaining big-wheel support for little-wheel innovations. Here we see how the new governance structures of an accelerated school create a *social context* that supports innovation and the creative use of financial resources. There's now a social forum and a process in place for presenting to the community new ideas that keep the best interests of the students in mind.

The proposal was accepted by the school, and this is the first year of the program. So far, it's going great. You can see that Lynne's class is right over on the other side of the room; we're always together, and our kids are taught every subject together except language arts, when I work with the Spanish-speaking kids and Lynne works with the English-speaking group. Otherwise, they're taught math, science, social studies, everything side by side. Our rooms are set up that way: on my side we have the playhouse, and on her side is the science area. The kids travel freely from side to side, and they know that both Lynne and I are their teachers. Both rooms are labeled with English and Spanish words everywhere: Spanish is in red; English is in black. Lynne's kids are learning a lot of Spanish from me!

Unleashing the power of context. With the school community behind them, these teachers begin to shape the *social, physical, and informational contexts* in their classroom. The children are surrounded by two languages in both their social and physical environments. They learn about science in a physical context that's designed for experimental and discovery activities. They have frequent social contact with two adults, who model cooperative behavior throughout the day.

Lynne and I planned everything about the class ourselves, even down to when we eat lunch. After all, we know our kids and ourselves best; we know when is the best time for us to eat. We decided it would be helpful for our kids if they had older students in the school as their "buddies"—really, it's cross-age tutoring. Right now, during naptime, the fifth graders come in and rub their backs to help them fall asleep. During other periods, the fifth graders help them learn the alphabet or counting. Also, a third grade transitional bilingual class comes in and reads to the kindergarteners three times a week. They're a big help; and it helps them too. They learn responsibility and caring.

Maria Eugenia Fernandez, Teacher, Hollibrook Elementary School, Houston, Texas

Creating a supportive environment. With control over *time*, these teachers schedule experiences so that they best meet their students' needs. Frequent interactions with older children create a supportive *social context* for their kids and have a strong impact on the social development of the older children as well.

The kindergarten teachers in the preceding vignette designed this learning context by influencing the use of school funds, creatively planning their own schedules (thereby affecting the schedule of the entire school), creating an inviting and stimulating physical environment in their classroom, and surrounding the students with a warm and supportive social environment. This vignette highlights four of the most important elements of building contexts that enable powerful learning to occur:

- *The availability and use of material, financial, and informational resources.* This element includes providing access to quality literature, using computer and media technologies in innovative ways, creatively finding and using funding, working with art materials.

- *The physical environment.* This element includes organizing and using furniture, placing artwork and murals, designing learning centers, utilizing community locations and outdoor settings, making creative use of school space, using music to create ambience.

- *The creative organization and use of time and timing.* This element includes finding time for meetings, allowing for flexibility in scheduling, setting priorities, involving students in goal-setting activities, providing time for full-day learning experiences.

- *The social environment.* This element includes collaborating and sharing decision making among members of the school community, setting school standards and expectations, grouping students creatively, encouraging high levels of student and parent involvement in big-wheel and little-wheel activities, ensuring responsiveness of adults to children's interests and concerns, providing for peer- and cross-age interactions.

All of these contextual factors play a role in student learning, whether or not we're aware of them. They support and structure *what* students learn and *how* they learn it. Learning becomes more powerful as we take responsibility for designing learning environments that address the real needs, interests, and abilities of all members of our school communities.

In the following sections, we'll briefly explore these four contextual elements, highlighting organizational strategies and learning environments related to each that accelerated schools have developed for the classroom. We'll also discuss schoolwide contextual and organizational issues, including structure and scheduling. Then we'll move to a discussion of the roles played by different individuals at the school site and in the larger school community. In considering all these issues, remember that the way in which we structure and organize contexts has a tremendous impact on the lives and learning of everyone who enters the school environment.

9.1. The Four Critical Elements of Context in the Classroom and Across the School Community

9.1.1. Material, Financial, and Informational Resources

Accelerated school communities find many ways to make creative use of materials and other resources at their fingertips and beyond. Powerful learning materials go far beyond paper, pencil, and textbook, but they're not necessarily expensive or out of the reach of most schools. In Chapter Eight, we read how one teacher used pumpkins and pumpkin seeds as the focus of an interdisciplinary unit. Another teacher collected many different bugs that were discussed in a book she was teaching and kept them in a terrarium so that the students could examine them. In Chapter Seven, the former principal of Hollibrook Elementary School described how she discovered a wealth of materials for

her unit on Roman history—many of them from other teachers' classrooms. Your colleagues can be a tremendous source for ideas and actual materials, but don't stop there! Enlist parents and the local community in your search too, as this teacher did:

> **Eugene's dad is a custodian for IBM, and he saw all of the stuff that the executives threw away, like bubble wrap, cardboard, blank paper, Styrofoam chips, all sorts of stuff. Well, he started bringing it to the school every week. You should see our workroom—it's piled to the ceiling with materials! He asks us what we want, like if we're doing a special project. In my class, we constructed the San Jacinto monument out of little Styrofoam sponges. The teacher next to me had her class make castles out of cardboard and Styrofoam.**
>
> Mary Dwight, Teacher, Hollibrook Elementary School, Houston, Texas

Utilizing the treasures that our communities discard recalls the story in Chapter Eight of Gloria Luna's class sorting through her trash to find clues to history. Even your school's garbage can become part of a powerful learning experience! What does your staff do with all the boxes that come to school? What about all the extra sheets of paper that come off the copy machine? Is your school recycling aluminum, paper, plastic, or glass? At Burnett Academy, the student council proposed to initiate a totally student-run recycling program. The steering committee and the school as a whole approved the proposal and the students now operate a recycling program that has in itself become a powerful learning experience for everyone at the school, including the administrators.

As you begin to explore the material resources within (and outside) your whole school, you'll find that simple materials can lead to wonderful student creations; you might also find some items at your fingertips that you didn't know existed!

> **In our humanities classes, we've done several art projects. The students made cave paintings out of paper bags and colored chalk. Also, we made paddle dolls, which are figures of servants and other significant people that the ancient Egyptians would place on their tombs as companions in the afterlife. Gorette's class made kartushes, a type of amulet, with hieroglyphics spelling each child's name. Next year I want to work with clay, because the Neolithic period is the time when humans started to use clay. One of the special education teachers knows how to make pottery, and I just found out we have a kiln that no one uses tucked away in one wing of our school, so it should work out!**
> Kathy Hoffman and Gorette Cardosa, Teachers, Burnett Academy, San Jose, California

Like hands-on materials for use by students and teachers, informational and technological resources are also important elements in the learning environment. In Chapter Eight, you read about Burnett's Lab 2000, a former industrial arts classroom turned into a high-tech aviation and aeronautics workshop. Anthony Jackson, a teacher in Los Angeles, whom you read about in Chapter Seven, turned his students into reporters, editors, photographers, and desktop publishers responsible for a school newspaper. In putting the newspaper together, he used the community around the school as an informational resource and the technologies available within the school—cameras and computers—as powerful learning tools. If your school doesn't have "fancy" technology or strong informational resources (such as a good library), take your students to them! There are businesses with computers and other high-tech equipment in almost every community. And as we saw in the story about Jennifer Spotorno's class trip to the neighborhood graveyard, there are archival and historical resources everywhere. Think of these resources as field trips waiting to happen!

Several of the vignettes in the previous two chapters referred to the pursuit and use of grant money to fund special projects. Joan Moss's Native American museum and year-long curriculum were funded in this way, as was Burnett's Lab 2000. In addition to outside grant funds, districts often provide small grants to individuals or groups of teachers who wish to create curricular or instructional innovations. Indeed, your school itself may have discretionary funds available. In fact, such funds helped send Hollibrook students to the planetarium during their space unit (which you read about in Chapter Seven). To create a powerful learning environment for children, we can often get by with financial flexibility rather than more money. For example, Burnett's principal made it possible for humanities teachers to plan together by having the flexibility to hire substitutes for a few days, using funds already allocated for the general purpose of curriculum development.

9.1.2. Physical Environment

Throughout this guide, we've seen how accelerated school community members make use of contexts outside school to provide their students with powerful learning experiences. From museums and boats to graveyards and forests, our communities offer myriad settings for powerful learning; it's up to us to design contexts to take advantage of these opportunities.

The physical environment *within* a school offers a somewhat different challenge. Creative use of the space available at a school enhances the opportunities for staff and students to learn and grow. Even the hallways can become avenues for learning! The walls of the cafeteria, the windows in the office—wherever there's space, there's an environment that can be used for learning. Remember the Native American unit at Daniel Webster? The three teachers and their classes turned the school library into a Native American museum that other students and teachers could visit. And one teacher at Burnett uses her classroom walls as a timeline of student work so that the kids can visually reflect on their learning process. At Hollibrook, the hallways and stairwells house giant, colorful banners reading, "SWEAT!" to remind them that "genius is 1 percent inspiration and 99 percent perspiration."

The way we set up our classrooms also sets the tone for the learning that will take place. For that reason, it's a good idea to give students an active part in the setup of the classroom.

> **Our desire to build on student strengths in the classroom led to some changes in the way we designed seating plans. Our students worked in cooperative groups, which we rotated about every six weeks. For one cycle, we asked the students to identify their own strengths. (Their observations were, perhaps not surprisingly, very accurate!) They then worked cooperatively to form seating groups that had students with complementary strengths, such as in math, language arts, second-language skills, and so on. The children really felt proud of their self-**

appointed roles as leaders in a particular area, helped their group willingly, and respected the other students' strengths and knowledge as well.

Francesca Bertone, Teacher, Roseland School, Santa Rosa, California

We transform learning environments as we find space for innovative student groupings, corners for storage, and places for thinking, reading, and writing. Learning centers are a particularly effective way of organizing classrooms (and student studies). Each center creates a context for interactions with different material and informational resources. The key is to provide an environment in which students feel comfortable learning, thinking, and being creative!

When the Native American museum was finished, each class signed up for a time to go visit. My class hadn't studied Indian culture formally, and I wanted them to have an appreciation of what they were going to see. So I prepared a three-day mini-lesson, using learning centers, to give them some exposure to the ideas represented in the museum.

At the first center, we listened to a story on tape called "The People Shall Continue," which talks about Native American culture and what happened to the Indians in this country. The kids listened to the story in small groups and then they'd come to me for discussion. Everyone gave his or her opinions about the story, or what they'd felt while listening. We had some really great discussions.

In the meantime, a group at another center was making mini-murals celebrating their lives. They were to put themselves in the center of the mural, and all around it they were to draw or write all the things they could think of to celebrate in their own culture, or life, or family.

When a group finished that center, they went on to the game center, where I'd put shells and beans and sticks and rocks and all kinds of things out on the table. First the students had to read a short article on a hoop game that Indian children used to play; it described how they made the materials for the game, and how they'd made up the rules. Then, with a partner, you'd devise a game together using all of these things from nature. The next day, after everyone had been to that center, the whole class paired off with their partners, and they had to write down the rules of their game and show the class how to play it. In this way, it turned into a language arts activity.

The next station was run by my aide. I'd given her some examples of poetry about nature, and she also had things from nature at her table, like leaves, sand, rocks, etc. She had the kids write their own poetry about nature and then illustrate it. At the next center, I just put out books having to do with Native American culture; some were fiction,

some were historical. They could read to each other or just do silent readings by themselves—whatever they wanted to do. Some sat on the couch, some on the rug. It was a very comfortable place for them to be.

The last center they went to was watercolors. I told them to think again about something beautiful in nature and just paint. The whole thing was very easy to organize. I prepared them for the lesson on Monday; I walked them through each station so they'd know what to expect. Then Tuesday, Wednesday, Thursday they went to two centers a day for about half an hour at each, and Friday was our trip to the museum. Every day before we started, we talked about what we were doing, what we'd learned the day before. At the end of each activity, I'd wrap it up and give them some things to think about. By the time they got to the museum, they had a very high respect for what the kids had done to make that museum. They really appreciated what they were seeing.

Jackie Dolan, Teacher, Daniel Webster Elementary School, San Francisco, California

Integrating learning through creative physical organization. Dolan creates a truly integrated learning experience for her students by creating a physical environment free of the constraints of a traditional classroom. Through the learning centers approach, she exposes the children to concepts from the disciplines of art, science, mathematics, language, literature, and social studies, all focusing on a common theme of Native Americans. Each center varies in its physical set-up and instructional style: some are reflective, some are active, some involve interaction among students, and all build on children's natural creativity.

Her mini-lesson is also beautifully integrated with the work of her colleague, Joan Moss. Not only do the students learn facts and information that make their tour of the museum richer; they also learn that their school is an integrated whole: their teachers communicate and collaborate with one another to support *every* child's education, and their fellow students, even younger ones, have important learning to share. All of the crucial elements of a supportive context are present here.

Physical space is also crucial to school staff and parents. As you take stock and create or revisit your vision, think about how the physical environment of your school serves the needs of adults as well as children. Community members at one accelerated school reorganized their campus to support their professional development by creating special meeting rooms for accelerated school staff.

Several accelerated schools have devoted physical space for parent rooms as a result of their Inquiry Process in the area of family involvement. In

Chapter Four, "The Inquiry Process," we described how Burnett Academy created a family room; it shares its space with the student council, which sets a tone for other collaborative student and parent activities.

There may be spaces in your school that can be converted into student, parent, and staff centers without too much energy or money. Getting a group of students, parents, and school staff together to plan their space through the Inquiry Process can produce amazing results!

9.1.3. Time and Timing

In addition to finding ways to move beyond the physical constraints of your classroom, reorganizing the way you use time during the day, week, months, or year with students also contributes to creating an environment for powerful learning. Though time itself can't be changed, our use and organization of it can. In Chapter Five, "Group Dynamics and Meeting Management," we suggested some ways to "capture" time for meetings. An accelerated school community can also capture and reorganize time for powerful learning.

Instead of focusing on perceived constraints, accelerated schools look for opportunities to meet their needs by building on the strengths of their communities. By applying the principles and values of the Accelerated Schools Project, using the Inquiry Process, and openly communicating the schools' needs to the central office, accelerated schools are often able to achieve scheduling flexibility that they hadn't known was within their reach. That flexibility may extend to the length of classes, the order of classes, and even who's teaching the classes. Teachers at Burnett Academy, for example, reorganized their curriculum, spreading reading across the subject areas and freeing up a period for electives:

> **Before accelerated schools, the way the curriculum was structured for the seventh and eighth graders was into separate periods of social studies, language arts, and reading. Sixth graders took a full year of reading and then a semester each of social studies and science. In the Curriculum Cadre, some of us were pushing for more elective classes for the students—we'd surveyed the students about what they wanted us to teach, and they'd requested more electives—but we didn't have enough room in the day for all the classes we wanted to offer the kids. So we were willing to compromise and combine language arts, reading, and social studies into a two-period humanities core. This change freed up a whole period for an elective course. The idea was proposed by the cadre to the school as a whole and was accepted. The social studies and**

language arts departments were combined into the humanities department, and each grade level had the responsibility to create its own curriculum for the coming year.

Kathy Hoffman and Gorette Cardosa, Teachers, Burnett Academy, San Jose, California

In the following example, we see how the Fairbanks school community in Missouri finds useful instructional time even in small bits.

First thing in the morning, while other students are getting organized and figuring out milk and lunch counts and attendance, is an especially good time to use cross-age tutoring for a specific skill that a student hasn't yet mastered. Shawn was having trouble remembering his numbers from 1 to 100, so a very patient Laura worked with him for ten minutes each morning. After a week (with Laura celebrating every accomplishment along the way), the two proudly reported to the teacher that Shawn knew his numbers and he wanted to recite them.

Using a minute here, a minute there. A very valuable and largely untapped resource in most schools is the "free time" of students. This time can be structured and organized, often quite informally, in such a way that children are empowered to take responsibility for many of the learning needs of their peers.

We've used cross-age tutoring in one instance to help with a management problem. Many of our students have breakfast at school and then must wait around in the multipurpose room to be picked up for class. They tend to become pretty noisy if they have nothing to do. To alleviate this problem and to give first grade students some extra practice reading, we came up with a system so that when a first grade student has finished breakfast, he or she may choose an upper grade (second to sixth) student to listen to him or her read. Both students come to the first grade classroom and the first grader chooses a book to read. We've really seen results from this program. Eric, a student in the Chapter I program, asked if he could read to his teacher during free time. He read from an advanced book with words such as *whispered, temperature, fever, thermometer,* and *scared.* When asked how come he was so smart, Eric said, "Stuart (his third grade reading buddy) read it with me and helped me with the words I didn't know."

Leslie McIlquham, Teacher, Fairbanks Elementary School, Springfield, Missouri

Creating win-win situations. In any school, staff, students, and parents have many goals to satisfy all at once. They need to provide a safe environment for students; they want to advance student learning; and they want students to get along well with one another. Finding the time to manage such important demands simultaneously is tricky, but McIlquham and her colleagues have done a masterful job! At Fairbanks, everybody wins: teachers, school staff, parents, administrators—and especially students.

A whole school can be rearranged to enable *everyone* to participate in exciting, enriching, powerful learning experiences.

Fabulous Friday is run like a mini-university. Students register for courses, listing a first and second choice. Students from all grade levels are integrated into these classes. The older students go to the kindergarten and first grade classrooms to pick up their "little buddies" and escort them to their Fabulous Friday class. The course offerings are extensive, and every adult in the building teaches one. Classes include beginning swimming, bowling, scuba diving, the history of rug making, art, counted cross-stitch, babysitting, tumbling for tots (for the pre-K classes), camping, mystery writers, eating around the world, sign language, secret codes and spy stories, and book making. At a given signal, students pass quickly and quietly through the hallway to their classes. Vans wait outside to take the bowlers and swimmers to their destination. The rest of the afternoon is spent in these special classes, which are four weeks in duration. All have an academic focus as well as an activity base.

Hollibrook Elementary School, Houston, Texas

As school community members become comfortable in their new roles as collaborators and begin to feel that their vision can be a reality, they begin to experiment with new ways to schedule classes and meeting times across the school, plan and coordinate the various uses of school facilities, and provide the necessary materials for the entire school. In the next section, we'll explore how the social environment changes in accelerated schools and how *people* bring about schoolwide changes in organizational structures and conditions.

9.1.4. The Social Environment

Throughout this *Resource Guide*, we've discussed how the accelerated schools philosophy and process include all members of the school community: the students, parents, teachers, support staff, administrators, central office staff, and local community. In conventional schools, initiative and authority flow from the central office to the principal, then to the teachers and support staff, and finally to the students and their parents. Those at the "top" monitor the compliance of those at the "bottom." Accelerated schools not only reverse this organizational flow but change the entire social paradigm as well.

In fact, in accelerated schools, we refer to the school as a "school community." By interacting and utilizing the strengths of each individual in that community, the focus of the school shifts, creating a schoolwide social environment that nurtures collaboration, innovation, and learning through experience rather than meeting compliance standards set by individuals in institutions far removed from the school community.

By participating in the accelerated schools transformation process, the adults in a school community model collaborative behaviors and high expectations; in so doing, they create a new social climate for the students.

> **As a staff, we believe that the best way to teach something is to live what we believe. With this in mind, we're often seen using peer- and cross-age "tutoring" among ourselves. Students regularly see the principal, teachers, and other school staff working together and brain-storming a way to solve a problem in the school as a whole or in a particular class. Cross-age tutoring is really about individuals with different types of experiences working together to solve a common problem. I see this same theme in our work to coordinate our activities with junior high and high school teachers, former students, parents, and central office administrators.**
>
> Leslie McIlquham, Teacher, Fairbanks Elementary School, Springfield, Missouri

As we noted in Chapters Seven and Eight (covering the *what* and the *how* of powerful learning), the schoolwide governance structures—the SAW, the steering committee, and the cadres—and the Inquiry Process provide the mechanism for decision making within accelerated schools and directly influence the context in which powerful learning occurs throughout the school. This intensely collaborative decision-making structure leads to an ever-evolving social context.

Like the decision-making process, the principles of accelerated schools are designed to facilitate the development of a positive social context. By keeping these principles in mind while you work, you can go a long way toward creating an environment that's stimulating and healthy for you and your students. By using the accelerated schools principles and values as a starting point, you can provide students with social experiences in which they learn the rewards of collaborating with others.

> **The first ten days of school you're waiting for an official student count, and the kids in your room are changing every day. It's difficult to start curriculum then, so what I like to do is to get the kids to know each other so that they'll be ready for cooperative learning once we really get under way. One activity that works well is an activity in which I put different pieces of colored paper into a bag. After the students come in and settle down, I greet them and we make a circle on the floor. We sit around the circle and we talk and do a few activities. Then I pass the bag around, and everybody takes out a piece without looking. The tables are already labeled with those colors, so the kids who have blue go to the "blue" table, etc.**

I give them an activity, such as "How many different ways can you use a feather?" Everyone at the table brainstorms about this question, and then they write down their answers on one sheet of chart paper. They have to decide who's going to record the information and how they'll record it. Then we go around the room and hear from each group. I do this every single day, and the kids get to draw a new color each day. Sometimes they'll be with different people, sometimes the same. They regroup and we do another kind of activity. I always use that as a beginning way of getting the kids to know each other, so I can start curriculum-based cooperative learning with them as soon as possible. It's a process similar to the experimentation stage in using math manipulatives. You give the kids materials just to fool around with, so they become familiar with them. Later you can use the same materials productively and much more efficiently. I do the same process, only the kids are getting familiar with each other, so they can use each other's strengths more productively and efficiently later on. It's a very good way of getting cooperative groups formed.

Jackie Dolan, Teacher, Daniel Webster Elementary School, San Francisco, California

Laying the groundwork for powerful learning. This vignette provides an excellent example of the way in which the *what, how,* and *context* of powerful learning are interrelated. In this case, *what* the students learn is group roles and cooperative behavior. *How* they learn it is by working together at tables with very simple creative materials. Finally, as a result of learning the group roles and cooperative behavior, they create a cooperative *social context*!

Experiences such as these prepare students to engage productively in heterogeneous groups and to respect the contributions of all members of the class. Another teacher explains why she doesn't separate students by ability:

When you first mix the kids up, the kids who are farther behind won't participate as much at first. They probably won't be able to come up with the answers as much. I put kids into pairs and small groups all the time, and they help each other. They somehow start coming up with the answers. They may not understand exactly how or why they came up with that, but eventually, through working with other kids and me, they do. They'll certainly never come around to these answers if you pull them aside and put them in a lower group. If they're being challenged to find the answers themselves, first they'll look toward their buddies for a clue. Other students become models for them, and pretty soon they're getting it. If they were separated from the rest of the group, they'd never get anywhere.

Amy L. Meyer, Teacher, Hoover Elementary School, Redwood City, California

Showing that two heads are better than one. By teaming children, Meyer creates a social context that both challenges students and provides them with a one-on-one resource for learning. *What* they eventually learn is thinking strategies and knowledge about a particular area. *How* they learn is by being challenged and given a model from which to learn. (*For a more in-depth look at heterogeneous and homogeneous grouping, refer to the discussion at the end of this chapter.*)

One method of creating a social context supportive of collaboration among students is to establish a sense of what you expect from your students and what they can expect from you and their peers. Teachers who carefully plan the classroom environment with their students at the beginning of the year are often most successful in terms of student learning. Building on strengths and empowerment coupled with responsibility can mean involving the students in setting the routines and boundaries of the classroom and setting up a supportive environment that leads to learning gains for the rest of the year. A few basic, positively phrased guidelines that reflect how you and your students will interact often go a long way:

> **I don't use the word *rules*; I use *expectations*. I say, "I have some high expectations for you, and these are the things that I'd like to see." Then I ask them, "What would you like your classroom to be like?" and we discuss these issues. They have a chance to give their input, but I also tell them, "We work as a group. We're a family, but ultimately there's one boss in here. I'm the big boss. If I make a decision, it stands, unless you can find a reasonable way of having me change that decision." They understand that. Once we settle on our mutual expectations for the classroom, I type the list up and have each student sign it, and I sign it, and then it goes home for mom and dad to sign it. Everything is phrased positively: for example, instead of writing, "Don't run in the hallways," we write, "We walk in the hallways." The consequences for not living up to the expectations are also clear to them. If you're doing something you're not supposed to be doing, you receive a check in my notebook. You then owe me half of your recess, and we sit down and talk about the problem. If you receive a second check, you have to write down the problem, what you did, and what you could have done instead. This approach ties in to what we're learning in the classroom about writing and reading: what's the problem, what's your response, what action do you take, what's the outcome? I have them do this writing during recess or lunch. I don't like for them to take problems home. It doesn't usually go much further than that. I really don't have that many problems in my room.**

Jackie Dolan, Teacher, Daniel Webster Elementary School, San Francisco, California

Creating clear expectations. Here's a wonderful example of empowerment and responsibility at work. When rules are transformed into expectations, everyone becomes involved in creating and maintaining them. Expectations are also more meaningful to children when they recognize that the adults in their social environment really care about them.

Schools and home can help each other by communicating their expectations clearly to one another and by establishing some commonality. When the entire staff, students, and parents share the same standards and expectations, consistency becomes the norm.

BEFORE

9.2. New Roles in Accelerated Schools

As a school community collaboratively works toward a shared vision, the conventional roles that the various members have played in the past inevitably undergo a transformation. All of these role transformations happen over time and require compassion, caring, and a good sense of humor. As we grow into our new roles, we also transform the social context within which teaching and learning occur. Let's take a look at some of these roles and how they've evolved.

9.2.1. Students

As we've already emphasized, students are at the center of accelerated schools. In addition to being the focus of all the school's efforts, they're also increasingly recognized as valuable participants in helping to move the community toward its vision. Students begin to play many different roles as they become involved in all aspects of the accelerated schools process. They actively participate in the big-wheel activities of taking stock, developing a vision, setting priorities, serving as part of the governance structure, and using the Inquiry Process. Students make significant contributions to the acceleration of their schools by providing useful insights at cadre meetings, steering committee meetings, and meetings of the school as a whole. Students provide an essential perspective on the challenges that face a school.

Several students from Rancho Milpitas Middle School participated in the formal training program when the school started its process of becoming an accelerated school. Julia Wilhelmsen, a seventh grader, became so interested in transforming _her_ school that she got several of her friends to attend some of the training, on their own time, and eventually to join some of the cadres. At the vision celebration, Julia shared her version of the accelerated schools philosophy and process

with the other 650 middle-grade students. At the end of her very articulate presentation, she said, "This describes the process of how an accelerated school is run, but an accelerated school is really what the students, staff, parents, and community make it. An accelerated school is a way of pulling a school together so that everyone has a say. It's a way of running the school so it can be the best it possibly can be. An accelerated school is like a piece of clay. It can be molded by anyone to make the school just right for the people it affects. Most of all, an accelerated school is the students that go there. Acceleration is distance divided by time squared. It's the measure of how fast we're getting faster, or for Rancho, how fast we're getting better."

Julia Wilhelmsen, Seventh Grade Student, Rancho Milpitas Middle School

AFTER

We had several sixth graders involved last year, and I remember quite vividly Andrew and Crystal very often contributing comments that were invaluable to our work. They were applauded often. With their involvement, we never lost sight of our real purpose for participating in the Accelerated Schools Project—the children and providing them the very best education we can deliver.

Alison Beskin, Principal, Sheppard Elementary School, Santa Rosa, California

Keeping your students actively involved in the accelerated schools process requires communicating with them about schoolwide decisions as well as scheduling meetings so that students can easily participate.

The participation of students in the decision-making process and within the classroom creates a social context that facilitates the development of a sense of responsibility in children. Traditional schools may not provide enough real-life opportunities for students to develop the basic social skills and understandings that lead to responsible behavior. Accelerated school communities develop most fully when students are challenged with the responsibility to participate in the school transformation. In one school, the inclusion of students as stakeholders in the development of schoolwide expectations transformed enforced "rules" into collaboratively agreed upon guidelines and standards.

After months of inquiry, the School Interactions Cadre at our school presented the school as a whole with a proposal for a set of schoolwide

expectations. The word *respect* was a central part of their plan. As an English teacher, I believe you can't make people respect one another, but you can make them treat each other with *courtesy*. We debated this in our SAW meeting. Since the School Interactions Cadre had been working collaboratively with the student council, I had to take my case to them (and I'm an English teacher!). The students wanted to use the word *respect*. We all took this very seriously.

Connie Posner, Teacher, Burnett Academy, San Jose, California

With student input into the school's expectations and rules, one can imagine that the students will probably have more commitment to upholding them.

In addition to big-wheel involvement, students can play a leading role when it comes to taking responsibility and assuming leadership within classrooms each day, thereby providing the positive peer interactions needed to make accelerated schools a reality. As many of the vignettes in this guide illustrate, empowerment of students (both within the classroom and within the whole school) requires time and attention, but the rewards to the students and the rest of the school make the effort extremely worthwhile.

Many students love to tutor and teach other children. This is a role that children always play in some cultures and used to play more frequently in ours, back in the days of the one-room schoolhouse. As we again share this teaching responsibility with children, our classroom learning environments are often totally transformed.

Some older students help in the kindergarten and first grade classrooms teaching students how to begin the day, how to work independently, how to use the learning centers, how to care for their areas, and how to take care of their work when it's completed. Veronica was especially pleased when a younger student she'd coached for almost a month came into the classroom one morning, checked in, sharpened his pencil, and got right to work without having to be reminded of anything. She reported his accomplishment to the classroom teacher and said, "I guess he's finally growing up!"

Leslie McIlquham, Teacher, Fairbanks Elementary School, Springfield, Missouri

9.2.2. Teachers

As we've seen throughout this guide, the role of teachers also changes within accelerated schools. In the classroom, teachers begin to share many of their instructional responsibilities with students. In addition, they become more conscious of being role models for children in everything that they do. One of the most important things that they model is the way in which they take on new responsibilities outside the four walls of their classroom. As they become active, involved participants in the process of transforming their school into one that accelerates the learning of all children, their attitudes as well as behaviors undergo a significant shift. Instead of carrying out mandates from above, they're empowered to collaboratively make decisions and take the responsibility for carrying them out. Their responsibility is no longer only to the students in their classrooms but to the entire student body—indeed, the entire school community.

> **Two years ago, I never would've cared what the math department was doing or how they were doing it. Now I feel it's within my realm to find out what's going on and let them know what I think about it. I care about how the school as a whole is operating. That's what empowerment coupled with responsibility means to me. Now if someone told me I had to go back into my classroom and be quiet, I'd scream and holler.**
>
> Steve Novotny, Teacher, Burnett Academy, San Jose, California

The collaborative environment created by accelerated schools not only empowers teachers; it also facilitates greater cooperation and interaction among them. Instead of working in isolation, teachers are reaching outward and building on the strengths of their colleagues toward a common purpose. In their new roles as members of a community, they're able to develop and transform the very environments of which they're a part.

> **Two third grade teachers, two fourth grade teachers, and two fifth grade teachers have joined together to form a giant team. We'll still be part of our various grade-level teams, but we'll also form a big block, in which we'll try to cross-group and do things within those six teachers, six classes. And what we've done is the following: the fourth grade teachers are moving up with their classes, and the fifth grade teachers (whose classes have gone on to middle school) are moving down to teach third grade. So we'll be with these kids for three years. The way we decided on this was that a couple of us teachers were talking toward the end of the school year about how we were only now feeling that we were really getting to know these kids. It takes teachers something like twelve weeks in the beginning of the school year to really get to know their kids' learning styles. And so it takes a while to really get going. By moving up with our kids, we figured that we could save a lot of introductory time and so have a lot more quality instruction time to really accelerate our kids' learning. And among the six teachers doing this, each has a special strength; so the students won't see only one teacher for three years. They'll see more than just one teaching style. We'll trade off or work together whenever we think it would be good for our kids. And also, the stability of having the same teacher for three years might be good for these kids, because lots of them don't have the most stable lives.**
>
> Valerie Johnson, Teacher, Hollibrook Elementary School, Houston, Texas

I'm more involved in things now. I work more closely with the teachers. I didn't know what they were doing in their classrooms before, and they didn't know what I was doing in the lab. I see us pulling together more for the children now.

Marilyn D. Chinnis, Lab Proctor, Memminger Elementary School, Charleston, South Carolina

9.2.3. Support Staff

Other school community members whose roles have greatly expanded are the support staff. The office personnel, instructional assistants, yard-duty supervisors, maintenance personnel, special services personnel, and so on all find their roles expanding. In one accelerated school, for example, a paraprofessional now chairs the steering committee. In another school, an instructional aide has the primary responsibility for coordinating the family newsletter. In yet another school, we find the school secretary serving on a staff in-service planning team. The support staff find that as they actively participate in the cadres, they're treated with respect and seen, for the first time, as equals, with strengths to value and incorporate into the school's transformation.

As teachers and support staff are brought together by a shared vision, staff communicate frequently with one another on issues important to the school's mission. Staff members are no longer just "the teacher's aide," or "the guidance counselor." Instead, they become a group of professionals working together with others in team meetings, cadres, staff development, and coaching.

> **I see leadership developing in the staff—the whole staff. The paraprofessionals are taking the lead. They have the opportunity now. The paraprofessionals and the teachers meet together and support each other. They look at the whole picture through the eyes of curriculum; they use the Inquiry Process.**
>
> Kathy Shimizu, Principal, Sanchez Elementary School, San Francisco, California

Their mutual communication and support lead to increased camaraderie, more effective problem solving, and improved education for all students in their school. One accelerated school has in the teacher's lounge a wall of strengths on which all faculty and staff are represented. The principal jokingly relates how it was "vandalized": each day someone added a new strength to someone else's card.

9.2.4. School-Site Administrators

When we look at conventional schools, we find that principals often wield the greatest formal power at the local school site. Although many invite the assistance of faculty or parent advisers, they typically spend a great deal of time making decisions that affect the day-to-day functioning of the school and ensuring that their school is in compliance with district, state, and federal guidelines.

The accelerated schools philosophy and process transform the traditional role of the principal. Instead of being the one who implements programs, initiates change, coordinates the activities of the teachers, and disciplines students, the principal of an accelerated school is one of the *many* creative, caring, collaborative individuals who focuses on the students. While the principal is commissioned by the district or school board with the ultimate responsibility of the proper running of the school, he or she now *shares* this responsibility and works as a member of the school team.

> **Now the school is the responsibility of all, because it's our family. All can see their role in the community. The whole staff has a say in everything—budget, curriculum, parents. They're very much empowered. I have my opinions and get feedback—and so do they. We come to consensus. Staff involvement in the decision-making process has made it easier and more efficient. Accountability is easier because it's a team.**
>
> John Baker, Principal, Hoover Elementary School, Redwood City, California

Principals (like the teachers, support staff, students, and parents) participate on the cadres, on the steering committee, and in school-as-a-whole meetings. In addition to issues and ideas brought from the cadres, to the steering committee and the school as a whole, the principal raises other questions and concerns that affect the entire school. The decisions are shared, and so is the responsibility for implementing the decisions. The principal, along with the entire staff, acts on the decisions and recommendations of these bodies and puts them into practice.

With the entire community taking responsibility for making and implementing decisions, the principal can focus on other duties. The principal is often the one who's in the best position to identify and cultivate talents among staff, influence the beliefs that members of the community hold about themselves, and keep everyone focused on the vision.

The principal's organizational and people skills are crucial in accelerated schools as he or she works to inspire the staff to engage in the many ongoing activities and initiatives of the school, while also helping to prevent burnout among the staff. In addition, he or she must work effectively with students, parents, and the community to help maintain the motivation of all actors in the school community and to marshal the resources needed for the school to move toward its vision.

Above all, the principal helps keep the dream alive, working with staff to overcome temporary disappointments or setbacks by maintaining the vision and reinforcing the unity of purpose at every step of the process.

9.2.5. Parents and Families

Providing a more active role for families in the accelerated schools process is absolutely essential for its success. We've devoted Chapter Ten ("Family and Community Involvement") to this topic. There we explore some of the

There's been a dramatic shift since we began this process a year ago. Staff are much more willing to challenge my ideas, dispute a position, and share responsibility. The staff have observed me relinquish power yet still work as hard as before.

Ken Saltzberg, Principal, Roseland Elementary School, Santa Rosa, California

We have to help people find their identity—to find themselves, their self-concept. Being a school administrator is not about being a boss, not about power. It's about influence and learning how to recognize the belief that everyone can succeed.

Michael O'Kane, Principal, Burnett Academy, San Jose, California

269

Teachers have a lot on their plates. It's sometimes difficult for them to step out of their role and see the big picture. But the parent can see the intent of her child's education. I can think about her really going to college.

Kathy Lynn, Parent, Madison Middle School, Seattle, Washington

successful partnerships that have been formed between schools, families, and communities.

Accelerated schools get parent and family members involved from the beginning by inviting them to play an active role in taking stock, creating the vision, setting priorities, and forming the cadres. From these experiences, collaboration begins, friendships form, and little-wheel activities spin off. Parents who feel welcomed and valued at the school often begin to look around for an area to which they can contribute, an area in which their strengths can make a difference. Some parents begin to work with teachers and staff in the office, in the classrooms, or in the schoolyard.

A lot of parents want to get involved, but they don't have the background. Once they do get involved, they begin to see how the school works. This [involvement] can begin as simply being an extra pair of hands. At first you might be there just for your child's benefit, not for the benefit of the school. Then you begin to see what's going on. If you're open-minded and share in the process, you become a part of the school just by being there. You see that the value of change isn't just that it helps your kid but that it helps every kid.

Kathy Lynn, Parent, Madison Middle School, Seattle, Washington

Open communication, recognition, and flexible scheduling are some of the keys to the active participation of families. Just making sure that families feel welcome and that their contributions are valued goes a very long way.

At our PTA meetings this year, we gave awards to the parents instead of the kids. Awards for their child's academic achievement or for their volunteer work. You should have seen the looks on those parents' faces. Three years ago, we were lucky if we had a PTA meeting and forty people showed up, most of whom were teachers and a few Anglo parents. So what we did was to pick up our coffee pots, our chairs, and our bodies, and we walked into the community, to anyplace we could find to meet. We set up over there. We knocked on doors; we sent out flyers; we let everyone know that we were there because we love and care about your children. Now how can we help you? Now when we have PTA meetings, we have between 600 and 800 people show up. It was so packed that we had to get a new cafeteria built to accommodate more people. We had to redefine PTA. What did we want it to be? Now it's a really dynamic group that can get things accomplished.

Suzanne Still, Maria Eugenia Fernandez, and Mary Dwight, Staff, Hollibrook Elementary School, Houston, Texas

The role that parents and guardians play at home may be the most critical. Family support and encouragement of a child's learning often sets the tone for how a child thinks about and approaches education. The structures that families can provide—such as creating quiet times (and places) for study, limiting television, and enforcing bedtimes—are often just as important as those that schools provide. As we've seen throughout this chapter, the contexts (social, physical, time, and material) that support learning extend far beyond the four walls of the classroom.

Active family involvement is a cornerstone of any successful accelerated school. Without the support and participation of family members, we miss a vital link in developing the kind of schools that will be most beneficial for our students. As we build on family members' strengths, we begin to recognize the essential role that their personal expectations, love, support, and confidence can have on the educational path that their children will take.

9.3. Creating a Context for Learning Beyond the School Site

Just as accelerated schools create powerful learning situations through the creative use of organizational strategies within the classroom and throughout the school, they also address how the learning environment is further enriched by looking beyond their school walls to the rest of their school's community. Central office staff and community members have the ability to directly influence the kind of learning situations your school decides to provide for the students, whether by supplying needed funds or materials or by supporting, say, an innovative schoolwide reading program.

Accelerated schools also build on the strengths of the *entire* school community, drawing on the many valuable strengths that exist at other schools in the district, within the district office itself, and within the local community. By keeping the district and other schools apprised of your school's efforts and involved in the process of acceleration, you not only build on their strengths but also give them a stake in ensuring your school's success. Through open communication and interaction among staff, students, parents, community members, and district personnel, the school will be better equipped to meet its challenges and develop meaningful and lasting solutions to any problems that arise.

9.3.1. The District

Note: *While we've interacted with district and state education offices since the inception of the Accelerated Schools Project, we've worked most intensively and directly with accelerated schools. But because schools clearly operate within the context of districts and states, we're now moving in the direction of collaborating with districts and states to initiate and support accelerated schools themselves. As our work with districts and states progresses, we'll share our experiences. At this point, we'd simply like to offer information on how current accelerated schools and their district offices have collaborated; the role of the state is beyond the scope of this edition of the* Resource Guide.

All accelerated schools are situated in the context of the school district. And as much as people joke about "downtown," we all know many central office staff who are eager to have greater interaction and share their expertise with school community members. Many of them are excited about the potential of the Accelerated Schools Project, because they agree with the philosophy and feel that the process will allow real change to occur.

> **The Accelerated Schools Project has provided Memminger Elementary School with a wonderful framework to undertake a comprehensive school improvement effort. Through the inquiry and data collection processes, the staff has been empowered to restructure their school building upon their strengths and unique characteristics. The enthusiasm and commitment demonstrated by the faculty and staff has been inspiring. Everyone—the principal, teachers, parents, students, and community—has become involved in *their* plan to create a first-class school. We welcome the chance to work with Memminger to facilitate the changes *they* want to make. I think that Memminger will demonstrate that schools should lead rather than just follow directives.**
>
> Marian Mentavlos, Executive Director, Curriculum and Instruction, Charleston County School District, Charleston, South Carolina

Central office staff members can share a different perspective on educational concerns and provide access to information about individual schools as well as districtwide issues. The district office is also a source of varied expertise and funding for schools. In addition, the district office has responsibility for a number of federal and state programs, which gives them a good overview of the options available to schools and the different strategies that can be employed to accomplish common goals.

As accelerated schools communicate with their district offices, they find that district representatives can also help create a climate for collaboration by using their strengths to provide support for the many efforts going on at the school site.

> **It used to be that someone in the central office would divine that everyone in the entire district had to take the same in-service course, so we'd all have to spend our in-service days at a central location. Now, after talking a lot with that person, he's enabling us this year to build our staff development around what our needs are and what we want to hear about. He also helped us last year to allocate about $10,000 of our budget, that's almost half, for the teachers to go to all sorts of staff-**

development conferences on their own and then come back and report to the rest of us. Now, instead of having a course catalog offered by the district, we have one of courses offered by Hollibrook teachers. If you want to learn about running a writer's workshop, you sign up for the "Donald Graves Writing Workshop" course taught by Mary Wright, a teacher here, on Thursday afternoons for six weeks in the spring. Central office people have helped make these things happen.

Suzanne Still, Former Principal, Hollibrook Elementary School, Houston, Texas

Offering opportunities for the central office to become involved in the process of acceleration helps ensure district support and encouragement of that process. By involving central office representatives in your efforts, you can be more confident of their participation and support in the implementation of schoolwide projects that move you toward your vision. The district can participate right from the start in the taking-stock and visioning processes: the district staff can add their unique perspectives to help build a unity of purpose, to identify the strengths of the school, and perhaps to contribute information on the strengths of the district as a whole. In addition, having the district involved in creating the vision can be a good way for the district to support accountability to *the school's vision* (and not something else), particularly for long-term-planning purposes.

Once the district office staff become *part* of the accelerated schools transformation process, they're likely to become partners in helping accelerated schools achieve their goals rather than regulators of compliance standards. We all learn experientially!

At Rancho Milpitas Middle School, the district's director of curriculum attended several of the initial accelerated schools training sessions. He was so interested in what was going on that he later served on the Curriculum Cadre. He was impressed with the school's efforts (especially with the way the cadre was using the Inquiry Process), and he shared his enthusiasm back at the district office. The director of maintenance and safety was intrigued by his co-worker's excitement and asked to join the Facilities and Safety Cadre.

Rancho Milpitas Middle School, Milpitas, California

Districts (and individuals within any given district office) have different styles of supporting accelerated schools. While some representatives participate actively and regularly in cadres, on the steering committee, and at school-as-a-whole meetings, others work behind the scenes to support the accelerated school's new endeavors by communicating with others in the district office and on the school board to protect the school's risk taking.

I've tried mostly to stay out of the way and help them as much as I can. I'm not talking necessarily about financial support, because everyone has a problem with that. What I'm talking about is support to experi-

ment, to try new approaches, and to support the school even if what they try initially doesn't work perfectly. I never expected immediate results, and in this business, we usually do. But district administrators, just like school staff and faculty, have to understand that this is a process. It takes a lot of district support for a school to live with uncertainty. I helped give them the courage to experiment, and at the same time, I had to muster a lot of courage to justify this experimentation to the board of education. It's hard to stick your neck out like that, but we were able to get a number of early-release days for Burnett that the other schools don't have. Teachers will use these days for school-as-a-whole meetings, cadre meetings, or further training. This is the kind of support I'm talking about.

Claire L. Pelton, Director of Educational Services, Cluster I, San Jose Unified School District, San Jose, California

While the district can help support an accelerated school by giving the school greater discretion in the kinds of decisions that can be made on-site, it can also assist the school in its efforts to find creative ways to develop programs and allocate resources based on its own goals rather than on federal, state, and district mandates. Historically, time and funding are resources that have been controlled to a large extent by the district. Most schools receive funds from a variety of different sources, all channeled through the district office: in addition to the general funding available from state and local property taxes, schools receive funds from both state and federal sources for special or categorical purposes. Many children who are caught in at-risk situations are eligible for multiple programs; for example, migrant students are typically eligible for educational assistance through migrant, bilingual, and compensatory education funds—and sometimes special education funds as well. Despite the fact that all these funds reach the school through one conduit—the district—each program is designed and administered separately; thus the child is the recipient of three or four relatively independent programs, often conducted as "pullout" classes.

This approach has a number of consequences, all of which work against school acceleration. First, this approach means that school sites must devote considerable resources to meeting separate compliance and reporting requirements. Second, this approach tends to undermine the unity of purpose of schools. Instead of exploring how all students can be provided with experiences that build on their strengths, comprehensively employing all funding sources for which they're eligible, schools expose children to a number of different programs with little integration. All in all, the approach takes attention away from student needs by focusing school efforts on meeting separate program compliance demands.

Recognizing that these challenges exist within school funding, accelerated schools accomplish greater resource efficiency by applying unity of purpose to the use of funding from different sources (see also the discussion of providing special opportunities in Chapter Eight). School districts can assist accelerated schools in developing an integrated and comprehensive program that will benefit *all* students, as the example below illustrates.

> **One way that our district has been supportive is by helping us to become a Chapter I school, under the new federal guidelines, so that we don't have to conduct a separate Chapter I program for those students. This was recommended to us by the district staff because they recognized that we had relatively high numbers of Chapter I–eligible students at Hoover, which makes it more sensible to become a Chapter I school. Under this approach, the focus was more on the plan (as developed by the school and the district) and the associated monitoring and evaluation of the plan versus the specific uses of the categorical funds within a separate program.**
>
> John Baker, Principal, Hoover Elementary School, Redwood City, California

Another means by which the district office can help support creative resource allocation is by allowing flexible use of time. In order for the accelerated schools process to be truly effective, each school needs to build time into the schedule for school community members to collaboratively work together to reflect on, develop, implement, and evaluate school decisions. For a school to maximize the amount of time available, the district must be open to and flexible about the various strategies the school may employ to capture time efficiently. As you read earlier, Claire Pelton helped Burnett Academy maneuver the system to allow early-release days for cadre meetings and other accelerated school activities. Now all schools that plan to become accelerated schools request full and half release days from their districts *before* they receive training to begin the accelerated schools process.

As you read about ways that the district can directly influence the context of learning in accelerated schools, keep in mind that a good relationship between the district and the accelerated school requires communication and an exposure to activities at the accelerated school site. This communication and sharing of experiences builds understanding, mutual respect, and collaboration. If you can't get your district to the school often enough, you can bring your school to the district!

> **At Madison Middle School, the principal, Marella Griffin, sends *all* documentation on her school's acceleration efforts to all board members and key people in the district. By seeing the results of the school's taking-stock data and its cadre, steering committee, and school-as-a-whole meeting agendas and minutes, the district and board get a sense that "something's happening" at Madison. And the school doesn't limit what's sent to the district office to documents: during the school's vision celebration, all 900 students marched from the Seattle Center to the district office!**
>
> Madison Middle School, Seattle, Washington

As an accelerated school becomes more focused on its vision and proficient in using the acceleration process to reach that vision, a trusting relationship develops between the school and the district that can result in greater autonomy for the school. In turn, the district feels more confident calling on the school to provide services to the rest of the district's schools to improve the workings of the overall school community.

9.3.2. The Community

Accelerated schools stay in close contact with their local communities and create avenues for community participation in their schools. By arranging meetings and activities at times that accommodate the schedules of community members as well as family and school members, the resources of the school community are enhanced tremendously.

We suggest a two-way exchange between the community and the school site—a true partnership with mutual contributions. This means that students go out into the community, and the community comes into the school. Remember the various lessons mentioned in Chapters Seven and Eight that made use of neighborhood libraries, parks, and museums? In addition to resources such as those, communities include businesspeople, doctors, artists, and other professionals who can provide invaluable contributions to the learning experiences of the students and teachers.

> **El Toro Elementary School staff and parents invited various members of the local community of Morgan Hill to participate in their vision celebration. They asked representatives to talk to the students in small groups about their professions and to show the students how important it was to continue their education so that they could do whatever they wanted when they grew up. The future would be possible only if the youngsters started today on the road of a successful education.**
> El Toro Elementary School, Morgan Hill, California

Chapter Ten, "Family and Community Involvement," will give you a far richer picture of the many contributions that the local community can make to your school (and vice versa).

9.3.3. Other Schools

As much as we grow to love our students, we know they all move on. As they leave, new students enter our schools. For now, most of the schools that our students graduate to and come from aren't accelerated schools and therefore operate in a very different manner. Communication between members of the various schools within the district may help make the transition smoother. Establishing bonds between teachers, staff, parents, students, and administrators of all district schools may ease some of the adjustments that students are forced to make when they enter a new school, and provide a more supportive and enriched learning environment. Some of these schools may even consider becoming accelerated schools as they become more familiar with the concept.

In order to make the transition from an accelerated elementary school to a conventional middle school easier, elementary schools must learn about the expectations and the course offerings at the middle school level. Elementary schools must also make clear to middle schools the educational expectations and achievements of their own students. Conventional middle schools must be aware of the strengths and skills that students bring to the school and respond to these with challenging and stimulating learning experiences that enhance and support continued development.

> **At Hollibrook Elementary School, the students had made such incredible achievement gains that the principal wanted to ensure that her colleagues at the middle school level would meet the Hollibrook students with the high expectations they deserved. Among other means of communication, she wrote the middle school principal a friendly letter celebrating the Hollibrook students and their achievements, hopes, and goals.**
>
> Hollibrook Elementary School, Houston, Texas

Because middle school students enter from elementary schools and depart to high schools, middle schools must articulate and coordinate their programs with both elementary schools and high schools; they must collaboratively determine the skills and qualities that students bring with them and those that they'll need when they leave middle school. Middle schools should play an aggressive role in setting out educational expectations and communicating them to conventional elementary schools. For example, as algebra becomes a standard part of the middle school curriculum for all students, accelerated middle schools (along with their districts) must jointly plan with elementary schools to prepare students to be ready for algebra by the end of elementary school. Middle schools should also communicate with high schools about both the curriculum and instruction expected at the high school level.

Districts can provide assistance in this communicaton, to help ensure that many of the powerful learning experiences offered in an accelerated middle school extend to the high school level.

At Burnett Academy, all students take algebra by the eighth grade. To prepare for these students, their receiving high school had to increase the number of high-level mathematics classes they offer.

Burnett Academy, San Jose, California

What's to Come

We hope that you've enjoyed reading these three chapters on powerful learning as much as we've enjoyed researching and writing them. As we noted in the Introduction, these are just the first set of vignettes. As you transform your own school, you'll discover new ways to create powerful learning by experimenting with different *whats*, *hows*, and *contexts*. Please let us know of your efforts so that we can continue to serve as a clearinghouse for creating and supporting accelerated schools.

Postscript: Some Thoughts on the Grouping of Students

Until recently, teachers judged the intellectual ability of their students almost exclusively on their performance on standardized tests in reading, writing, and arithmetic. Ability grouping was therefore limited to two general approaches: homogeneous or heterogeneous ability in the students' subject matters. In the first approach, students who test at the same ability level are grouped together either in the same classroom or within the classroom in same-ability groups. This practice of homogeneous grouping is built on a view of intelligence that's been challenged by research on learning and intelligence. Intellectual ability is no longer seen as an unchanging, unidimensional gift but as a multiplicity of talents—a broad range of many different abilities that change through involvement in the teaching/learning environment. In the second approach, students of differing ability levels are deliberately grouped together.

Problems with Homogeneous Grouping

One of the main justifications for segregating students into classrooms of similar, tested ability is that this is the best way to provide for individual differences. In this way, the theory goes, "fast" students grouped together will have no "slower" classmates holding them back. Likewise, "slow" students won't be intimidated, excluded from classroom interaction, or left behind by the quicker learning pace set by "faster" students. Segregating each student with his or her "ability peers" theoretically ensures that each student will receive an appropriate level and speed of instruction. Another supposed benefit of homogeneous grouping is that it makes the teacher's task much simpler. No longer will it be necessary to tailor the lesson to different levels at once. When all students are of the same ability, one approach is all that's needed.

Unfortunately, homogeneous ability grouping works well with only some students—those who are considered "fast learners" or "gifted" because the tasks they are given are challenging, and they are allowed to use all their abilities to solve these tasks. Teachers expect them to be self-motivated, to help each other, and to come up with creative answers. While these students may thrive, most so-called average or slow learners generally slow down in homogeneous groups. The tasks generally assigned to them aren't demanding, and they don't allow students to use those intellectual abilities in which they excel. For example, students who are "slow" readers may be allowed only to read and fill in the blanks on a worksheet; they're rarely given the chance to benefit from interesting literature, peer input from more proficient readers, or allowed to use strengths that might help them understand the text (such as dramatic performance or the translation of the text into movement or pictures).

Furthermore, it's now generally recognized that most standardized tests used to measure ability are culturally biased, inadequate measures of what students know and can do. Because of this, it's likely that same-ability grouping will turn out to be grouping by similarity of cultural background rather than by students' potential for learning. This may lead to a morally and legally questionable internal classroom resegregation of students within an apparently integrated school. Studies have shown that same-ability grouping tends to stratify students by family income as well.

When students are grouped by ability level, they quickly figure out whether or not they're in a "slow" or "fast" class or track. Studies concerned with students' self-image and social relationships have found that ability classification tends to isolate students in determinate castes that affect their attitude toward themselves, toward school, and toward students of other ability groups. Those in low-ability groups tend to have low opinions of themselves and of the importance of schooling. Those in higher-ability groups are self-confident and tend to have low opinions of those in low-ability groups. Students tend to like school less and perform less well in low-ability groups than in heterogeneous groups. Because homogeneous grouping severely limits the range of learning alternatives in the classroom, students assigned to low-ability groups are, in effect, given an anchor to impede their progress.

Benefits of Heterogeneous Grouping

Given that the United States is the most heterogeneous nation on earth and given that the entire modern world offers great diversity and intercultural contact, schools should take every opportunity to prepare children to flower in the midst of diversity. Learning to achieve within an environment of difference is essential. Mixed-ability grouping can teach students to perform cooperatively in a diverse environment, thereby contributing to their social growth and understanding as well as their academic growth.

In fact, academic performance of all types of students in heterogeneous groups has been shown to rise especially when teachers use a variety of innovative and powerful teaching techniques that tap *all* students' abilities and apply them to relevant situations.

In addition to gains in academic achievement, many successful programs using heterogeneous grouping over the last decade have shown that student self-image is higher and peer acceptance is greater in mixed-ability classes.

Students don't bear the stigma of being assigned to a low-ability group when heterogeneous grouping is used; instead, social contact, cooperation, and friendship are fostered among classmates of different abilities, ethnicities, and socioeconomic backgrounds. In heterogeneous groups, students find a learning environment that allows for greater diversity and individual development. Additionally, higher achievers have a positive effect on lower achievers (and an increase in their own self-image).

Even within "homogeneous" groups of children, there's considerable diversity of ability, achievement, interest, learning styles, and engagement with schooling. Therefore, even same-ability classes don't allow the teacher to provide students with only one approach to a lesson. Differences in approach are likely to be necessary even with students who score in the same percentile of a particular standardized test. It seems, then, that all teachers are faced with the task of educating a classroom full of different individuals.

Because we believe that *each* individual child is intelligent and possesses unique gifts, and because we want to build on the strengths of *each* student, we suggest that you heterogeneously group your students; using their multiple intellectual abilities, they can then help each other to accomplish their academic tasks. This suggestion presupposes that what you teach demands the use of a broad range of intellectual abilities. As we've noted, curricular and instructional strategies complement each other. Heterogeneous grouping is facilitated if the curriculum encourages students to be creative and critical and allows them to use many different abilities in addition to reading, writing, and computation. Heterogeneous grouping, together with a multiple-ability curriculum, allows students to use their various types of expertise and accomplishments.

Family and Community Involvement

Families and local communities, vital to children's success and well-being, are key members of an accelerated school community. This chapter is divided into two sections, one on family involvement and one on community involvement, and it highlights the benefits to schools and children themselves that result from bringing families and communities into the accelerated schools transformation process.

10.1. Family Involvement

All of us probably agree that parent involvement is a key ingredient in creating successful schools and successful students; however, pinning down exactly what we mean by that involvement is more difficult. In every school a few parents are involved in some fashion, whether it be through regular parent-teacher conferences, as classroom volunteers, or through an organized PTA. But accelerated school communities extend their conception of parent involvement far beyond these traditional modes: they strive to include all parents as vital participants in the daily life of the school and as the most crucial supporters of their children's education at home.

> Involving parents in the education of their children in accelerated schools isn't just important; it's crucial. We can't do it without them.
>
> Henry Levin, Director, Accelerated Schools Project

In the accelerated school, family involvement is both a means to an end and an end in itself. The goal of making parents full partners in the education of their children is to provide the maximum support and opportunity for the children, both at home and at school. When defined in this way, family involvement means much more than just a periodic PTA meeting.

Jesse Tello has nineteen children, three of whom attend Daniel Webster Elementary School. Jesse is as much a part of Daniel Webster as any teacher, administrator, or student. He brings his children to school in the morning, volunteers his time all day, every day, and many days

Stemming from the principles of unity of purpose, empowerment coupled with responsibility, and building on strengths, communication between parents and staff in accelerated schools is equal and mutual and takes into account the unique strengths and perspectives both parties bring. School staff and families both have useful information and advice for each other concerning the children they care so much about. Open communication between staff and families lets parents know how their children are experiencing school each day, what strengths children are displaying, and what challenges exist. Parents can let teachers know what's going on in the life of their child at home and what interests and hobbies their child displays.

Open communication can be difficult at first. Yet by using the accelerated schools philosophy and process, accelerated school communities slowly begin to create an environment in which families and school staff can come together and communicate effectively. Accelerated schools begin by recognizing that parents know and love their children more than anyone else. In addition to knowing and loving their children, many parents have a great deal of expertise to share with the school; for example, a parent may be a craftsperson, a nurse, a coach, an artist, a storyteller, fluent in several languages, adept at computer technology, or simply wonderful with children. By collaboratively supporting the education of their children, families and schools together can accomplish much more than either group can alone.

As we mentioned, family involvement extends far beyond the school grounds. In many cases, the most important family involvement goes on at home, as a grandfather helps his granddaughter with an art project or a mother listens to her son describe what happened in science class that day. Support of a child's education at home means everything from setting a reasonable bedtime, imposing constructive restraints on television viewing, and helping with homework, to giving plenty of love, affection, and attention. If the partnership between the school and the home isn't forged, it's the child's learning that will suffer. Creating that bridge is therefore one of the most important things a staff can do. The gains that this key partnership brings are phenomenal.

We took one classroom and turned it into what we call the parent center. Through the Inquiry Process, we'd decided to pilot test this idea

to see if it would draw more parents into our school. Then we went out and gathered all sorts of materials to stock the room and make it a comfortable place. When you walk into the parent center, some things you might see are magazines and sewing machines.

We have a crib and a playpen in there, for mothers who need to bring their babies with them. That works great. We've found that many moms who want to volunteer can't because they can't afford a babysitter. Well, if we can bring in five moms with five babies, one mom can stay in the parent center with the little ones and that frees up four moms to work in the office, the classrooms, or anywhere. We've found that it frees up dads too.

Most of our parents are very poor, and some have extra time on their hands, so we provide clothes and material to sew for their kids. When it was time for kindergarten graduation (a ceremony requested by the parents!), guess who sewed the robes? The mothers did, right there in the parent center. So all of our little kindergartners got to march down the aisle in beautiful robes.

The parents have created a parent advisory committee that meets with the school social worker for a luncheon every week. They talk about what they like and don't like about the school, just any issue that comes up.

Our dads repair all of our tricycles and wagons out in the nursery yard. If we need benches built, they know how to build them; if we need sidewalks poured, they know how to pour them. One man was working on a landscaping crew during the day, and one day he pulled up in front of our school with a whole truckload of shrubs that were just going to be thrown away. He didn't speak a word of English. Thank goodness we have bilingual people everywhere in our school to make everyone feel welcome, because that man had hundreds of dollars worth of shrubs. They're planted out front of our school now.

Suzanne Still, Maria Eugenia Fernandez, and Mary Dwight, Staff, Hollibrook Elementary School, Houston, Texas

We all have stories about wonderful parents who fuel their kids' enthusiasm for learning and help them succeed, but more than anecdotal evidence exists to prove the strength of this relationship. Research clearly shows the power of family involvement in children's education. (For more information on this research, refer to the References and Resources at the end of the book.)

Before

10.1.1. The Big Wheels of Family Involvement

Accelerated schools view the task of involving families as a *process*. No school can move quickly from a few isolated parents volunteering in the office once a week to a dynamic community of mothers, fathers, aunts, uncles, and grandparents interacting in all areas of the school and with their

---

Involving Families in Acceleration

Here are some tips from accelerated schools on ways to get families involved in accelerated schools efforts up front. (Notice that they all involve personal contact.)

- Invite families to accelerated schools training sessions.

- Have students interview their parents about their vision ideas.

- Persuasively invite parents to participate in the vision celebration. (It's an event that creates meaning for people.)

- Have teachers and other school staff make personal phone calls to families.

- Encourage those parents who are already involved to form telephone trees.

- Call families ahead to remind them about meetings they've been invited to.

- Translate all materials as needed.

After

children at home each night. Accelerated school communities begin by building bridges of communication between homes and schools, thereby developing mutual trust and respect and a shared sense of purpose.

One of the most important ways an accelerated school can begin this process of partnership and communication is by involving parents in each step of the accelerated schools process. As you recall from Chapter Three, it's vital that you include parents in the getting-started stages—taking stock, forging the vision, and setting priorities—as well as in the formal Inquiry Process in cadres, on the steering committee, and in the school as a whole. Through participation in these stages of the development of an accelerated school, family members will begin to feel a sense of empowerment and ownership of their child's school—feelings that will facilitate their support of their child's education.

The following examples illustrate how schools have included parents in some of the big-wheel accelerated schools processes.

Deciding to Become an Accelerated School. The decision to begin the accelerated schools process is one that's best made by everyone in the school community, including parents. This process of "exploration and buy-in" is the first opportunity for a school community to begin to build unity of purpose among all its members.

> **Members of the Madison Middle School community spent over one year thoroughly exploring whether they wanted to become an accelerated school. A group of six Madison representatives, a third of whom were parents, even traveled to San Jose, California, to visit Burnett Academy. When the whole school community voted on**

whether or not to become an accelerated school, the parent group unanimously approved. And at the first training session, one-fourth of the eighty participants were parents.

Madison Middle School, Seattle, Washington

Taking Stock. Because parents offer a unique perspective on the learning going on in their child's life, they should be included in the entire taking-stock process. In addition to asking parents to respond to taking-stock surveys, schools should encourage parents to attend training, serve on taking-stock committees, and design taking-stock questions. This parental involvement will lead to research questions that might not have been asked otherwise and ensure a thorough assessment of the current state of a school community.

Although many parents in Las Vegas work long night shifts, they found ways to rearrange their schedules to participate in their chlidren's school's taking-stock process. The parents involved helped to decide which questions parents needed to be asked and to design those questions in a way that would ensure the greatest response rate. They also pointed out which questions they felt would be too intrusive or value-laden. For example, the parents participating suggested looking through school records to find out which students were on free lunch, instead of asking the parents such a sensitive question via a survey. The dialogue between staff and parents was crucial to the school's highly successful taking-stock process.

Helen Herr Elementary School, Las Vegas, Nevada

Creating a Vision. When teachers and staff in an accelerated school begin to forge their vision of a dream school, their guiding question is, "What kind of school would I want my own child to attend?" Who better to pose this question to than a parent? A parent's vision for his or her child's school is a moving testimony of pride, hope, and love. Thus all efforts made to include parents in the process of creating a vision will enrich the power of the collaborative vision constructed.

Parents were involved at every step of the creation of Burnett Academy's vision. At the San Jose middle school's back-to-school night, which drew record attendance due to warm written invitations to parents to "come be a part of our vision," each parent was given a sheet of paper and asked to write down two things that he or she wanted for the children at Burnett. Parents excitedly wrote their dreams for their children in all different languages. Mike O'Kane, the principal, explained that a vision-writing committee would take this information, combine it with the written hopes of the students, staff, and teachers, and develop a document that represented the vision of the entire school community. (Parents who couldn't attend the meeting could offer their input on the taking-stock survey, which was mailed to each parent.) He then stressed to the crowd that parents had to have equal representation on the vision-writing committee. Before the end of the evening, several mothers and fathers had volunteered to be a part of this process. As a result, Burnett's vision statement is a rich, moving document that's meaningful to all members of the school community.

Burnett Academy, San Jose, California

Setting Priorities. Once parents have participated in researching the school's current state through the taking-stock process and shared their dreams with the school through the creation of the vision, it's only natural that they then participate in setting priority challenge areas. Parents may view a particular discrepancy between the status quo and the vision in a different light than other members of the school community, and their thoughts must be heard and valued.

During setting priorities, members of the Sheppard Elementary School community used information that they'd gathered during interviews with non-English-speaking parents in order to gain the insights of those members who traditionally wouldn't be able to participate.

Sheppard Elementary School, Santa Rosa, California

Creating Governance Structures. In an accelerated school, parents help create the governance structures that run the school, and they serve on each of its component parts: parents serve on each cadre, parents have a representative on the steering committee, and parents (as many as possible) attend school-as-a-whole meetings. Only through such continuing input from parents and all members of a school community can an accelerated school move toward its shared vision.

I just arrived back at school after summer break today, one week early. Already, three parents have contacted me wanting to find out when their first cadre meeting was scheduled. Now the parents are seeking us out rather than the other way around.

Gene Chasin, Principal, Edison Elementary School, Sacramento, California

The Inquiry Process. As full participants on cadres, parents and family members become partners in a school's collaborative inquiry into problems. Families bring their own insights and strengths (which in some cases include lots of time and energy) to the task of researching why a challenge area exists and then proposing and implementing solutions to the problem. Their unique and varied perspectives on the school, combined with those of the school staff, lead to wonderfully creative outcomes.

Arnold Astrada, the father of an eighth grader at Burnett Academy, became a vital member of that school's Family Involvement Cadre. In

287

addition to being able to draw more parents into the process through personal phone calls, his outlook was especially helpful in generating the most accurate hypotheses about why so few parents were involved at the school.

Burnett Academy, San Jose, California

10.1.2. Creating Opportunities for At-Home Support Through the Inquiry Process

It's likely that your school will identify at least some priority challenge areas that involve exploring family involvement. Perhaps you'll decide to have a Family Involvement Cadre, for example, or maybe your Curriculum Cadre will eventually decide to focus on homework issues. Through the formal Inquiry Process, your school will generate different ideas that meet your school's particular needs in the area of family involvement.

All of the examples that follow stem from different accelerated schools' processes of inquiry; and as you can see, they range from major interventions to simple communication. The solutions that each of these schools generated are based on their *own specific challenge situations and strengths*. It's important that each accelerated school use the Inquiry Process to understand and address its own unique situation rather than simply adopting ideas that relate to another school's specific set of circumstances.

During taking stock, Whitney Elementary School in Las Vegas, Nevada, identified student hygiene as an area of challenge. Specifically, they discovered that many of their students, through no fault of their own, were living in the back of campers, sharing beds, and doing without running water. Children in these situations were coming to school without having had the opportunity for basic hygiene. A cadre was eventually formed that developed a pilot program for one of the school "families"—a group of five primary and intermediate classes—to collaboratively implement and assess. Their pilot consisted of a year-long thematic unit on "healthy living," with academic, social, and personal components. The family developed a number of projects for students and their parents. For example, they did role playing and skits in which parents and children acted out healthy living, and they studied the chemistry of toothpaste and shampoo. Using a donated washer and dryer, the students learned math by sorting and counting their laundry as they washed their own clothes (and took advantage of an unembarrassing opportunity to launder their clothes). Finally, the school held a parent-child health fair at which local community agencies provided free health screenings and materials.

Whitney Elementary School, Las Vegas, Nevada

We'd been offering ESL and amnesty classes for our parents, and they were very popular, but eventually the parents came to us and said, "This is great, but we don't need this anymore. We want something more." So a group of teachers and parents explored other needs parents might have, and we came up with the idea of a "parent university." Basically, the idea is to offer short-term classes, taught by teachers, to parents on various topics ranging from computer literacy to parenting tips. At first we thought that the teachers wouldn't want to have the extra burden, but they were really excited about it. We spread the responsibility around so that different teachers teach from session to session; no one person is always responsible. We come up with topics by surveying teachers about their strengths and what they'd like to teach and by surveying parents and finding out what they want to know. A lot of parents have requested a class on how to help their children with their homework, so I think that one will be pretty popular this session.

Juanita Brewer, Social Worker, Hollibrook Elementary School, Houston, Texas

We decided through our Inquiry Process we needed to have some kind of parent newsletter to let parents know what goes on at our school on a daily basis. We wanted it to be more than just a rule book or school calendar, although that information is important; we wanted to convey a feeling for what's happening in the classrooms so that parents really know what their children are doing every day. We examined other schools' newsletters and finally came up with a neat one-page design; we send it out weekly. It consists of brief blurbs about activities going on that week, such as cadre meetings or basketball games, and anyone in the school can submit an article about what he or she is doing in class. Last week one of the ESL teachers submitted a story about what her curriculum will be for the coming week, and we translated it into Spanish to make sure all of the parents would be informed. Each week we translate about half of the stories and also include a phone number that Spanish-speaking parents can call for more information. We also profile a student, teacher, or staff member in each issue so that parents can get to know the people who interact with their children every day.

Fran Laplante, Counselor, Burnett Academy, San Jose, California

Hoover Elementary School set up a voice-mail system for parent-teacher communication. Each teacher has a phone in his or her room with a separate extension, and each can leave a unique voice-mail

message. Parents simply call the school, dial their child's teacher's extension, and then listen to whatever announcements the teacher has. For example, a parent could find out what the child had for homework that day, when the next test is, or that the class will be going on a field trip, or a parent could simply leave a message setting up an appointment with the teacher.

Hoover Elementary School, Redwood City, California

Because so many accelerated schools have formed cadres to tackle the larger issue of why parents aren't more involved with their children's education, we've included a case study at the end of this chapter that details one elementary school's use of the Inquiry Process to address the issue of family involvement.

10.1.3. The Little Wheels of Family Involvement

Moving from very little family involvement to a full partnership of parents and school staff on behalf of students results from collaboration on big-wheel activities, but it also requires a great deal of creativity, spontaneity, and willingness to reach out. Inevitably, as the big wheels of the accelerated schools process are turning, certain smaller initiatives and ideas will spin off. These little wheels might include parents volunteering in classrooms, a parent-student-teacher talent show, a parent negotiating a corporate partnership between her company and the school, or a parent-organized, parent-run support and discussion group. Such initiatives are telltale signs of healthy family involvement. Not so obvious will be the little wheels happening in many students' households. Perhaps a father will read more with his son or a mother will organize a corner of the living room as her daughter's study area. These small events, often interactions between just two people, weave the fabric of strong, successful family support for children's education.

Teachers can provide opportunities for family involvement in the schoolwork of the children. Fun games and competitions work nicely. Although the number of formal winners may be limited, the team work at home pays off for everyone!

The Egg Drop Contest (a schoolwide competition that involved students creating containers sturdy enough to preserve several eggs when dropped from two stories) unexpectedly became a vehicle for family involvement. Some students banded together and designed containers on their own, but I saw a lot of parents working with their kids too. There were a lot of "little wins" in that way—a lot of parents who got closer to their children. The student who won the overall competition, a special education student, had worked with his dad, and boy, was his dad proud when the awards were given out. You could tell something special had happened between them.

Steve Novotny, Teacher, Burnett Academy, San Jose, California

Involving more parents in the education of their children is a multifaceted process that deserves exploration. Through collaborative inquiry, each school discovers specific, unique challenges in this area. While the challenges are likely to be unique, all schools' visions of family involvement are likely to include strong bonds between parents and teachers and parents and students—bonds that are a source of unwavering emotional, academic, and social support for the students' lifelong pursuit of education.

An additional vital source of this support can be found in the larger community surrounding the school. As you read the following section on involving the community in the life of the school, begin to envision the powerful potential of a system of parents, teachers, administrators, support staff, students, and community members working together.

10.2. Community Involvement

It was when the community got involved that the Egg Drop Contest took off. The idea behind the whole thing was that students were to design and build a contraption that held eggs and protected them from breaking when the container was dropped off a two-story building. We started walking around to local businesses and asking for their support. I found out that there's tremendous community support for teachers out there. I'd never gone door-to-door before, but I went with the attitude that these kids deserve support. To my surprise, when I said, "I'm a teacher at Burnett Academy," people's eyes lit up. As more and more people began buying into the project, we all had more and more responsibility to make it great. Neighborhood restaurants donated free dinners to give as prizes, General Electric representatives served as judges, and community businesses and organizations donated a total of $3,000 toward prizes and materials. It was kind of like surfing: if you ride the wave until the end, there's a huge rush, but there's always the risk of falling flat on your face if you lose your focus for a minute.

Accelerated schools provided the theme—unity of purpose—I adopted to make the Egg Drop Contest what it was. This principle made me consciously aware that I needed to go out and include people that I wouldn't have normally. Now we have a base of involvement to build on. Last year it was just me getting the whole thing going. This year there are so many people who're excited about doing it again that the burden won't be entirely on my shoulders.

I look at other projects going on around the school now, and I ask, "What are you doing to get other teachers involved? How about

We have parents involved on committees and through cadres. One parent who's always worked closely with El Toro, even prior to our involvement with the Accelerated Schools Project, told me that it's been going through the accelerated schools process that's helped her to justify her support of El Toro.

Doris Cross, Principal, El Toro Elementary School, Morgan Hill, California

parents and the community?" If you don't open the door to that involvement, it stays shut.

Steve Novotny, Teacher, Burnett Academy, San Jose, California

We've talked about utilizing the strengths of the entire school community—administrators, teachers, parents, students, support staff, and central office representatives—to enhance the school environment. Beyond the immediate school lies another area of largely untapped resources: the local community. Community involvement is a widely discussed topic among people concerned with improving our schools. Community members—whether business leaders, librarians, artists, welders, doctors, or ministers—have numerous strengths that your school community can utilize. In addition to drawing on people, involving the community means recruiting institutional agencies and organizations such as the Department of Health, the Department of Social Services, universities, museums, police athletic leagues, boys' and girls' clubs, Girl Scouts, Boy Scouts, the YMCA, the YWCA, and fire and police departments.

Although the methods for involving different community representatives or organizations in the accelerated schools process will vary—you might ask a retired teacher to help tutor, for example, and ask the local manufacturing plant to donate materials or monetary resources—central to any successful collaboration, however small or large, is the need for cooperation and a *shared mission.* While some schools want to ask community members to take part in the initial processes of taking stock and developing the vision, others may find it more beneficial to assess their needs and desires as a school community before recruiting local community members as active participants in their accelerated schools transformation process. (The second case study at the end of the chapter illustrates how one cadre reached outward to its community in searching for solutions to its challenge area.)

Community involvement not only draws on an extensive network of experience and resources; it also helps the students link what they learn in the classroom with their experiences outside of school. In traditional education, a separation has often existed between schools and the world in which skills and knowledge are used. Instead of encouraging this isolation, the accelerated schools philosophy and process emphasize active and challenging learning experiences that are relevant to the students' current life challenges, interests, and cultural values.

When a connection between the school and the community is created, we can also provide children with opportunities to understand how they're supported by a world that extends beyond their daily lives and concerns.

One very interesting thing that happened at Memminger Elementary School last year was the partnership that grew between the school and the City Housing Authority. In addition to helping Memminger become

a hub for community activities, Irene Harvey, the program coordinator for the Housing Authority, works closely with Memminger. Ms. Harvey and Ms. Oplinger, the principal, decided that one of the students who was having some behavior difficulties would spend a few days with Ms. Harvey at her workplace. Once he returned to school, his behavior improved greatly—in fact, he was on the honor roll by the end of the year. He recognized that people inside and outside of the school cared about him.

Memminger Elementary School, Charleston, South Carolina

For some children, these experiences in the community may be just as important as any math or science lesson. They teach children that rooted deep within their community is a sense of pride and an interest in its members' accomplishments and successes. Members of the community who recognize the long-term benefits of providing an enriching and challenging learning environment to children and youth are often willing and eager to lend a hand to schools.

In the process of including community members in the daily life of the school, many accelerated schools have discovered that community involvement is a two-way relationship. While there are many strengths that you can build on within your local community, your school can also serve as a valuable community resource. Making your school available for community events as well as involving your students in community projects or activities can help to build a greater sense of trust and collaboration between you and the community.

Cindy Dudley's home arts class at North Middle School concludes its child-development unit each year by actually setting up a preschool in the classroom and taking care of a room full of preschoolers from a local day-care center. The students set up several different learning centers, in such areas as reading, music, art, and counting, with activities that they plan themselves. They also prepare and serve lunch to the young children. The middle school students are so wrapped up in the project that they keep asking for more and more preschoolers to teach.

North Middle School, Aurora, Colorado

10.2.1. Individuals and Organizations as Resources for the School

On the pages that follow, we describe a few of the opportunities that might be available in your community. This is just a beginning, however; you can add opportunities and build your own list. The key is to tell your story and discover how important each specific group is to reaching your vision and how compatible your vision is to the goals of each outside group.

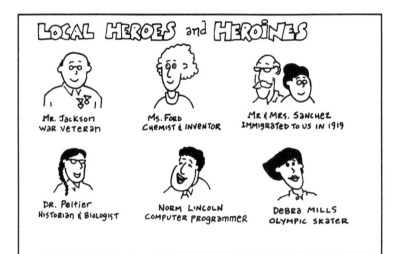

Local Clubs and Organizations. Local social and civic clubs or organizations can be excellent resources for a school. Men's clubs, women's clubs, senior citizens' groups, grassroots self-help organizations, and civic organizations are just a few of the many types of organizations that may exist in your community. Many of these local groups have a philanthropic purpose and are eager to provide assistance. Local organizations, which often include people who've already garnered local trust and have established credibility, may be able to offer tutors, school volunteers, speakers, and scholarships.

Local Heroes and Heroines. Community members from a wide variety of jobs and careers are often regular visitors to accelerated schools, where they talk and work with the students. All communities have individuals with rich personal histories—people who've been engaged in fascinating endeavors and can serve as role models and instructional resources in the schools. These local heroes and heroines rarely advertise themselves, but they can be located by an enterprising principal, teacher, parent, or student. Local ministers and other community leaders often know these people. And sometimes they're the parents, aunts, uncles, and grandparents of the students in your school!

Arranging for these people to come and share their life stories or explain their vocations and hobbies is extremely important for children. All children need role models—people with whom they can relate. Community members are visible and accessible and give the students a chance to know people who have succeeded up close.

Career Day at Rancho Milpitas took on a special slant this year. The Curriculum Cadre worked with the student council to arrange for speakers from a variety of careers in the local community. A track star, a local politician, several people from various medical professions, a firefighter, law enforcement officials, airline pilots, a seamstress, and many other interested, dedicated members of the local community volunteered the afternoon.

Student council officers contacted these various individuals and asked them to come and talk about their profession, bring examples or

illustrations related to their profession, identify how their work related to what was taught in school, and discuss the specialized education they needed for their careers.

When Career Day arrived, student council representatives—one assigned to each guest—were out in front of the school to meet the speakers and escort them to a luncheon that they'd prepared. After lunch, each speaker addressed three different classrooms during the course of the afternoon, enabling the students to learn about three different careers of their choice.

Rancho Milpitas Middle School, Milpitas, California

Local Artists and Craftspeople. There are often local artists (musicians, painters, dancers, singers, poets) and craftspeople (seamstresses, welders, woodworkers, and other people who make things) who'd love to conduct workshops or demonstrations for students about their art and work.

Bob Tyson, an independent fine arts photographer, maintains his studio and darkroom at Hoover Elementary School. In return, he teaches photography to Hoover students. His workshops take several forms, depending on the ages and interests of the children. In one, the students make pinhole photographs using tea tins as the cameras and photographic paper as the film. In another, students check out cameras and film to take home; then they return to print their photographs in the darkroom under his supervision. In addition to structured workshops, students encounter the photographer at work in his studio. Students are welcome to come in and watch an actual artist at work.

Hoover Elementary School, Redwood City, California

Religious Organizations. Religious organizations are communities within communities. Schools can collaborate with their community religious organizations in a variety of ways, often receiving contributions of time, talents, and materials. These partnerships aren't of a religious nature; rather, they support the academic and social goals of the school.

You can share information about your school and its successes, new programs, new personnel, and activities by distributing school newsletters to these organizations or posting announce-

Because Daniel Webster Elementary School didn't have a school counselor or psychologist, the principal persuaded a local pastor to come talk with and encourage some of the children in her school who had behavior and discipline problems.

Daniel Webster Elementary School, San Francisco, California

ments in their bulletins. Administrators and teachers from the school can also ask for opportunities to speak to congregations on behalf of the school.

Religious organizations may be able to contribute physical and material resources to your students or their families. For example, many congregations have food pantries and clothes closets for individuals in need. They can also serve as convenient meeting places for school and/or parent meetings. Religious organizations that operate day-care centers may be willing to provide an after-school or Saturday program for your students. Retired teachers, senior citizens, and other interested persons can be located through these organizations to serve as tutors for students or as assistants to teachers, office personnel, or yard-duty supervisors.

Museums and Libraries. Museums and libraries are great places to supplement the resources found within your own school. Museums commonly offer special programs and activities for student groups, while libraries often enable students to do further research on reports and class topics. Libraries often offer special latchkey programs for children as well. You can contact representatives from your local library to see what kinds of programs are already offered or could be easily coordinated. For example, librarians and museum personnel may be willing to meet with a class of students at your school, identify resources for your class, set up a special program for your students, or create an active partnership or information network with your library staff.

Jennifer Spotorno and her third grade class from Hoover Elementary School enlisted the help of the local librarian in researching information about the people buried in the community's oldest graveyard. The librarian not only sent records of the people in the cemetery before the students went on the field trip but also brought articles and photographs about the history of the area to the classroom for the students to review after the trip. Those supplemental materials helped round out the field trip.

Hoover Elementary School, Redwood City, California

Memminger Elementary School's Facilities and Resources Cadre decided to draw on the expertise of the College of Charleston in transforming old buildings and maintaining beautiful grounds. The head of grounds maintenance at the college is now a member of that cadre.

Memminger Elementary School, Charleston, South Carolina

Universities and Colleges. Community colleges and universities are good institutions with which to form partnerships. They can provide (1) tutors, (2) faculty who can offer technical assistance to the school and expertise for staff development in academic areas as well as in pedagogy, (3) partners for collaborative research (for example, a university might assist the school in researching and responding to its own needs), (4) university activities for students and staff (for example, special programs for students designed to

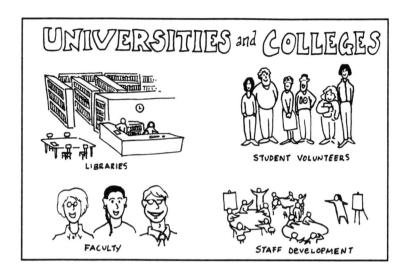

UNIVERSITIES and COLLEGES

LIBRARIES

STUDENT VOLUNTEERS

FACULTY

STAFF DEVELOPMENT

Suder School has developed a partnership with the University of Illinois, Chicago, which offers a six-week Summer Scholars Program and a Saturday Scholars Program for twenty-five or thirty upper-grade students. If a student commits to the program through high school, the university provides a free college education.

Henry Suder School, Chicago, Illinois

inspire them to consider future careers that require college preparation), and (5) an invitation to visit labs, studios, research facilities, the gym, and dorms.

Many universities and colleges are interested in forming formal collaborative relationships with other institutions in the community. Some have become very active partners with the accelerated schools in their area.

College students seeking meaningful ways to help the community in which they live may be willing to spend several hours a week assisting at local schools. If they have special talents or skills in areas such as math, science, athletics, writing, drama, or fine arts, they could conduct a workshop or offer a guest presentation in the classroom. College students are also prime candidates to be tutors, of course.

Health and Human Service Agencies and Local Government. Collaborating with local governmental agencies may be complicated, yet the resulting partnerships can provide comprehensive services to your students and their families—services for which many of them may unknowingly be eligible. Families as well as your students may be able to receive a wide range of assistance at the school site, from eye exams to psychological counseling. The types of services most needed are often best supplied when schools form partnerships with health and human service agencies. Burnett Acad-

Health and Human Service Agencies

JOB TRAINING

SCHOOL CLINIC

PRESENTATIONS

COUNSELING

emy, for example, has a school-based health clinic built on such a partnership. Such clinics are growing in number around the country. Many are able to provide a variety of services, including medical services and job counseling.

As a school nurse, my focus is on how a student's health is linked to his or her education. Obviously, a healthy child learns better than a sick child. Our school-based clinic provides affordable, accessible, and acceptable primary health care for children who wouldn't get it otherwise. Many of these children have no regular physician and have either never had a physical or have not been seen in a well-child exam for three to five years. Students are screened for vision, hearing, and scoliosis at designated grade levels, and all students must be immunized. At the clinic, acute illnesses can be diagnosed and treated, reducing the amount of time a child may be out of school because of illness and doctor appointments.

Often, children who are having difficulties at home or adjusting to school will come to the health office repeatedly with various somatic complaints. We need to rule out a real health problem first. Once an underlying illness has been ruled out, our school may then begin the process of finding out what is really bothering these students and help them. The school does this through Student Study Teams. The teams are made up of the student and his or her parents, the school counselor, the student's teacher(s), the school nurse, and any other support personnel deemed necessary. We start by looking at the student's strengths and talk about what we know about the student. We look at the problems and discuss them. Finally, we brainstorm solutions that might include referral for services or new ways to focus on school. The student is encouraged to participate in all aspects of the process.

Susan Lake, San Jose District School Nurse, Burnett Academy, San Jose, California

Schools with a wide range of needs might want to arrange for the delivery of a wide variety of services at a common site—perhaps even your school—for both students and their families. The establishment of school-based services by community providers may help schools immeasurably in achieving their vision.

The Caring Communities program was started with the idea that through the joint efforts of four state agencies—the Departments of Health, Mental Health, Social Services, and Education—we could help our children succeed by helping families who were in need of support. The program started with two pilot sites, one at an inner-city elementary school and one in a more rural area of Missouri. Through the help of caseworkers, referrals, and after-school programs, we've seen real success in terms of higher attendance and higher achievement in the schools.

There was one case where a six-year-old hardly ever came to school. When he did, his clothes were in tatters. It was a situation where the

**next step usually would have been to report the parent to the author-
ities. But because we had this program, the boy was referred by a
teacher, and a caseworker was sent out to the home. What she found
was a parent who wanted to do all she could for her children but didn't
know where to turn for help. She was a young single parent with three
other children under the age of six receiving $350 a month in welfare.
She washed her clothes every night with a scrubbing board. The electricity in her apartment had been turned off. Through interagency
collaboration, the electricity was turned back on, the children were
placed in day care, and the mother was helped to find a part-time job.
It was a real success story.**

Joan Solomon, Director, Missouri Accelerated Schools Network, Jefferson City, Missouri

Productive school-community partnerships can be initiated by coordinating a meeting of all of the community agencies that work with children and
families. The steering committee or a designated cadre could meet with
representatives from public and private agencies in order to set out a list of
needs as well as an inventory of all of the community resources that might
work together on behalf of children in the school and neighborhood.

Local Businesses. Businesses often have a special interest in the schools in their community.
First, they have a civic interest in supporting
the community at large; second, they have a
self-interest in helping to ensure that the youth
of the community are employable and productive in the future. Thus they're natural partners
for working with schools. Unfortunately, many
school-business partnerships don't fully exploit
the possibilities of this relationship.

Successful relationships between schools and
businesses are usually based on clear and realistic goals supported by a common vision. Setting
clear goals and planning together can ensure a relationship that's both
productive and rewarding. Potential partnership areas include the provision
of guest speakers, the hosting of field trips, and the acquisition of special
library materials, furniture, or supplies. Businesses might also share helpful
managerial insights on how to set up information systems. The more
concrete each partner can be about its needs and expectations, the more
likely the relationship is to be successful.

**Our district had instituted an "adopt-a-school" program, and General
Electric adopted us. We celebrated the event and then didn't know
what to do with each other. But that was before we became an
accelerated school. Now that we at the school know what our priorities**

are and we have a vision of where we're going, the *quality* of our interactions with GE has improved dramatically. Since then, we've had a Science Adventure Day, when GE employees taught all of our afternoon classes a science lesson, many science field trips, for which GE provided not only chaperones but also docents, and most notably, our last Egg Drop Contest, to which GE contributed judges, engineering and packaging specifications, guidance, gifts, and a great deal of time, effort, and encouragement.

Connie Posner, Teacher, Burnett Academy, San Jose, California

Our principal approached a local company that's based around here and worked out a plan so that their employees can volunteer one hour a week at Hollibrook. You'll see them everywhere around the school. Sometimes they work with one student in a class, sometimes the whole class. I remember last year one man, a geologist, brought in rocks and minerals from all over the world and actually taught several classes on geology. He talked to the students about different types of rocks and earth formations in South America and Africa, places where he'd visited. In this way, students also get to hear about different careers: some of them probably had no idea what a geologist was before they met him.

Maria Eugenia Fernandez and Valerie Johnson, Teachers, Hollibrook Elementary School, Houston, Texas

We've talked in this chapter about how the accelerated schools philosophy and process help create an interactive environment for involving family and community members, primarily through the model's emphasis on collaboration by building on the strengths of all involved and shared decision making of the *entire* school community. Family and community members, integral participants in the school community, offer numerous strengths and talents and are often the greatest sources of support for improving the students' learning environment.

One of the greatest keys to getting parents and members of the community fully involved in the accelerated schools philosophy and process—whether through direct participation on a cadre or through less formalized initiatives such as speaking to a classroom—is working together to build bridges of communication among the home, the community, and the school.

As Estelle Robinson and Aleta Mastny note in *Linking Schools and Community Services* (1989), "The collaboration process is a challenging experience because it involves weaving through a myriad of interpersonal relationships. Many partnerships that do succeed, do so with the understanding that in the interconnection of fragile human relationships, each linkage developed is crucial to the development of the whole." Through the development of a shared sense of purpose and by building on everyone's strengths, the entire school community—teachers, support staff, administrators, students, parents, and community members—can collaboratively work together toward similar goals.

Let's turn now to two case studies that illustrate how schools, with the help of the Inquiry Process, can increase school-family-community collaboration.

10.3. Case Study: An Elementary School's Family Involvement Cadre

This first case study follows an elementary school's Family Involvement Cadre as members use the Inquiry Process to address their problem area. (You'll recall a case study of a middle school's Family Involvement Cadre in Chapter Four, "The Inquiry Process.") We present this case study to illustrate both the difficulties and the rewards that the process can bring. We use the five stages of the Inquiry Process as a framework for describing the school's actual experience.

Stage 1: Focus in on the Challenge Area

1a: Explore the Challenge Area Informally and Hypothesize Why It Exists. The first cadre meeting of the year began with a discussion of the existing level of family involvement in the school. Inspired by this discussion, one cadre member suggested that the group might want to spend time planning and hosting an international dinner for which all of the parents would cook foods from their home countries. Other members became excited by this idea, and additional solutions began to emerge from the group. At this point, the cadre facilitator asked cadre members to put the international dinner idea on hold for the moment, reminding them that at this stage of the Inquiry Process they needed to try to better understand their challenge area by immersing themselves in all its details and ambiguities. Only then could they search for solutions. While some cadre members weren't especially pleased to stop their discussion of new ideas, others were anxious to refocus and begin practicing the Inquiry Process.

In order to gain a broader understanding of their challenge area, cadre members decided to conduct informal interviews with the various members of the school community—students, parents, aides, teachers, community members, and administrators. They felt that this would help them to see their challenge area from the perspective of all the actors involved. In addition, they planned to gather information about parent involvement in general. They hoped that these explorations would help them understand the complex set of issues that surrounded the challenge area of family involvement and enable them to hypothesize knowledgeably why that challenge area persisted.

After a couple weeks of interviewing, the members began sifting through all the evidence and information that they'd just gathered, looking for recurring patterns or themes. One of the first hypotheses posed by a cadre member was that many parents didn't come to school events or parent conferences because they weren't the child's parents; perhaps "nontraditional" parents—grandparents, aunts, older sisters, or friends of the family—weren't as committed as biological parents might be. Several other members agreed and began thinking about the kids in their own classes who they knew lived with grandparents. This led to the idea of having a grandparents' program, and a few of the cadre members started planning out themes, dates, and times. At this point, another member of the cadre commented that the idea of a grandparents' program might be useful but suggested that the cadre think about other hypotheses before designing a pilot program.

As the cadre returned to hypothesizing, one teacher volunteered a story from her own past regarding parents who'd been called by the school only for disciplinary reasons. Stating her idea as a hypothesis, she suggested that another reason that parents of the school's poorly behaved students may not be involved is that those parents are embarrassed to show up.

This sparked another hypothesis: maybe parents don't get involved if their kids don't get good grades. Cadre members thought that perhaps parents were embarrassed about their children's achievement or that low achievement was associated with parents' not being involved in the first place. The facilitator summarized all these hypotheses, as well as several more that the group came up with, and the cadre was ready to proceed.

1b: Test Hypotheses to See If They Hold Water. As a first step, cadre members conducted more interviews to get an initial sense of which of their nine hypotheses they should invest the most time formally testing. Then they began to think about how they could test their hypotheses to see if they were truly indicative of their school's situation. The cadre decided to look at test scores of students whose parents had been substantially involved with their children's education, interview parents by phone, check on office referrals from each teacher's class, and check with the school secretary about available records on primary guardianship. Each cadre member took responsibility for accomplishing one of the various hypothesis-testing tasks.

The group also decided to undertake a major data-gathering effort in the form of a teacher survey. Cadre members felt that since it was already January, individual teachers would have considerable knowledge about their own students—whom they lived with, their general achievement, and how well behaved they were. Two teachers and a community volunteer put together a survey for all teachers. The first column provided the teacher's class list, the second column asked with whom the child lived (one parent, both parents, aunt, and so on), the third column asked about the student's overall achievement (high, medium, or low), and the last column asked about the student's behavior (very good, average, often misbehaves). Although the cadre members knew that this method of research was "quick and dirty," they felt that it was sufficient (especially given the size of the student population) to answer the general question of why certain families weren't involved. Two cadre representatives presented this research plan at the next steering committee meeting.

The steering committee approved the cadre's plan and sent it on for a vote at the following school-as-a-whole meeting. At this meeting, the entire staff agreed to participate by filling out the survey. Later, as the surveys began to come in, two cadre members and a community volunteer designed a spreadsheet for analyzing the data on a computer. As the teachers turned in their surveys, two cadre members entered the data into the spreadsheet and then analyzed the data together. This information was presented at the next cadre meeting.

1c: Interpret the Results of Testing and Develop a Clear Understanding of the Challenge Area. The surveys revealed that the nature of the relationship between a student and the adult(s) with whom that student lived didn't determine the level of family involvement; in fact, the average level of the primary caregiver's involvement in school activities and of the quality of the child's work was found to be similar whether a child lived with two biological parents, a grandparent, an aunt, a parent and an aunt, or some other combination. The data also showed that student behavior was somewhat associated with family involvement, but not enough to plan a whole program around that issue. What the survey found to be most important was the strong correlation between student achievement and family involvement. The high-achieving students had an extremely high rate of family involvement; the middle- and low-achieving students had very low levels of family involvement. The survey also revealed that the overall involvement level dropped from kindergarten to sixth grade regardless of a child's achievement. These findings are displayed in the following bar charts, created by the cadre's resource person.

At the next meeting, cadre members decided that their focus area should be *how to involve the families of the school's lowest-achieving students in the academic work of their children.* This conception of their focus area stemmed directly from their findings. Many of the cadre members believed that simply having parents come to dinner or sign weekly folders wouldn't be enough; they believed that families needed help in learning strategies to support their children's efforts in school.

By working through stage 1 of the Inquiry Process, cadre members had tailored their broad challenge area of how to involve more families at the school into a well-defined focus area. Had they jumped into planning an

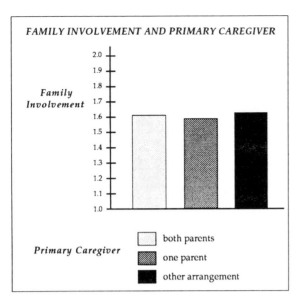

FAMILY INVOLVEMENT AND PRIMARY CAREGIVER

Family Involvement

Primary Caregiver

both parents
one parent
other arrangement

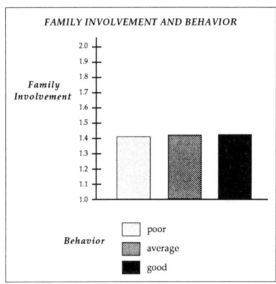

FAMILY INVOLVEMENT AND BEHAVIOR

Family Involvement

Behavior

poor
average
good

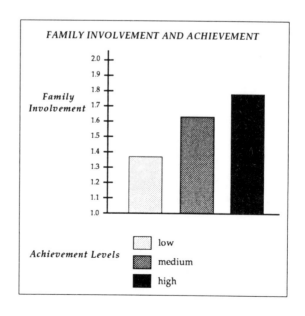

FAMILY INVOLVEMENT AND ACHIEVEMENT

Family Involvement

Achievement Levels

low
medium

international dinner and a grandparents' program, they would've missed a much more thorough understanding of their situation. Although truly understanding a challenge area is time-consuming, it ensures that a cadre's efforts in the following stages go toward designing meaningful programs that address the most pressing problems, cover ground, and take the cadre closer to the school's vision. (The international dinner idea could always occur as a little wheel!)

In this case, a single hypothesis seemed to best explain the forces underlying the cadre's challenge area: that there was a relationship between student achievement and family involvement. In many other cases, however, cadre members find that a combination of their tested hypotheses turn out to hold water and explain the forces underlying their challenge area. When this is true, a cadre must broaden its single focus to multiple focus areas in order to account for the complex combination of accurate hypotheses.

It seems worth noting that at the end of the first stage of the Inquiry Process, the members of this cadre had revised their original mind-set about family involvement. Cadre members no longer thought of successful family involvement as simply "parents coming to the school"; now they were thinking of ways to involve families directly in their children's school achievement at home and at school—to make parents more aware of school and classroom expectations, help parents know how to help their children academically, and assist parents in becoming more involved with their children's homework.

One of the nice outcomes of the hypothesis-testing stage for this group was the feeling of accomplishment and empowerment that cadre members gained by "creating" knowledge through a new technology. Although members of the cadre had read research reports about the relationship between family involvement and student achievement, they felt extremely proud of discovering this fact within the context of their own school setting. After taking the time to digest their data and define a clear focus area, the cadre members moved on and began to brainstorm potential solutions.

Stage 2: Brainstorm Solutions

Although brainstorming solutions seems like a rather simple and straight-forward task, cadre members found the structure of the Inquiry Process helpful, as it urged them to look first inside and then outside their school community for ideas and expertise. The process also emphasized that in brainstorming, creativity is essential; anything goes. Later on, in stage 3 of the process, cadre members would decide which solutions to keep and which ones to eliminate.

Cadre members began brainstorming by thinking about which of their school community's current strengths they could build on in addressing the focus area. They discussed the different programs already being implemented at their school, such as the six-week program for parents of kindergarten children and the program they used to help make parents aware of their children's homework. They talked with teachers who seemed to have successful strategies for communicating with parents, and they noted a number of ways that parents were already involved in positive ways with their children's academic work.

In searching outside the school for ideas, cadre members read articles, spoke to district representatives, talked to colleagues in other schools, and talked to parents. They found a school that sent a calendar of important dates home with each student, for example, and a school system that had produced a multimedia drug prevention series for elementary school students and their parents. By talking with the district and reviewing the research literature, they learned of many other programs that dealt with parent education, and they added these "outside" ideas to their in-school brainstormed list.

Stage 3: Synthesize Solutions and Develop an Action Plan

At this point, cadre members moved on, attempting to synthesize their potential solutions and develop an action plan. They assessed each idea in terms of whether it addressed both their focus area and ultimately their school vision. They discussed the likely outcomes of each idea and the potential obstacles they might encounter in implementing each. After much discussion and reflection, cadre members came up with a multifaceted plan to present to the steering committee and the school as a whole. The plan that they drafted for steering committee approval follows:

1. *Initial orientation for parents.* At back-to-school night, the principal would be joined by a few fourth, fifth, and sixth graders to convey to families the school vision and schoolwide expectations. The school's successful drill team would also perform. Cadre members felt that having students deliver much of the message would both entice the parents to come to the scheduled event and empower the students. The event, delivered in several languages, would be videotaped and sent home with students whose parents had been unable to attend. Parents who didn't have a VCR would have the opportunity to come to school and view the tapes.

2. *Orientation to individual classrooms.* In addition to this schoolwide video, each classroom would make an instructional experience out of creating its own video. Students and teachers would present the information together, conveying the school vision as it related to their class and their classroom expectations. The cadre felt that this would empower students and motivate parents to watch.

3. *Monthly parent workshops related to achievement.* Each month three teachers (one from kindergarten, one from first through third grades, and one from fourth through sixth grades) would put on a workshop for parents on something related to student academic performance. Possible areas could include reading, math, hands-on science, self-esteem, and dinosaurs. The cadre's objective here was to help parents assist their children in ways that build on what's going on in the classroom. Teachers planned to rotate responsibility for putting on the workshops and would receive payment for their time. Each session was to be videotaped for inclusion in a video library that parents could use. Cadre members hoped that videotapes would also be sent home with kids.

4. *Other components of the proposed action plan.* In his regular newsletter, the principal would positively recognize parents who were substantially involved with their children's education.

A team of teachers planned to come in over the summer and create a calendar for parents that would include important information about school that parents could use to actively help their children. For example, although the calendar would include important school dates (such as staff-development days and report card dates) it would also include the vision statement, instructions on understanding report cards, and lots of other useful information.

Parents would be invited to staff-development days so that they could understand what was going on in the classroom, hear about innovations, and gain an understanding of the importance of staff-development release days.

Cadre members would publicize the school vision in a number of different ways. For example, two teachers took responsibility for creating posters to hang in all the halls.

After the steering committee and the school as a whole approved the Family Involvement Cadre's action plan proposal, the cadre set a clear timeline and allocated responsibility for implementation. Cadre members and the staff enthusiastically took on the challenge of organizing the multifaceted program and outlining responsibilities of who will do what when, as well as a plan for assessment.

Stage 4: Pilot Test and/or Implement the Action Plan

In order to support teachers in their implementation efforts, the principal searched for some money to pay the teachers for their work over the summer and during evenings for the following school year. During the next year, cadre members implemented their plan.

Stage 5: Evaluate and Reassess

The workshops with parents blossomed into popular and heavily attended events. On family workshop evenings, the school bustled with parents, students, teachers, and aides working together on a variety of stimulating projects. The calendars were also a great success: they adorn many a refrigerator in the school community. Unfortunately, the videotaping proved to be more involved and therefore more difficult to fully implement.

Even while cadre members were implementing their action plan, the assessment stage of the Inquiry Process had already begun. Cadre members constantly worked on formative as well as summative evaluations of their efforts. They asked themselves, "Was this experimental plan useful? Did we address the focus area for which it was designed?" As members of the Family Involvement Cadre finished their first year of piloting the plan, they began to talk about returning the next year with ideas for improving the videotaping component. They also planned to review the achievement of the students whose families participated in the workshops.

10.4. Case Study: An Ad Hoc Committee's Outreach to the Community

Stage 1: Focus in on the Problem Area

1a: Explore the Challenge Area Informally and Hypothesize Why It Exists.
An elementary school community found from a general survey of staff and teachers that an average of five to six children in a typical class needed considerable individual attention beyond what could be provided by teachers and classroom aides. The principal was told by the central office that because of budget cuts, available resources in the fall would permit a classroom aide for only three hours a day (instead of the current five). Teachers worried that this limiting of resources would only add to an already overwhelming situation. After discussing the problem, the steering committee formed an ad hoc committee to look more carefully at the specific issues involved.

The first several meetings of that committee were spent trying to gain a better understanding of the problem. The group looked closely at the staff survey and at statistical information from the past several years on class size, student population, and other factors. Several members of the committee offered to interview teachers and classroom aides informally.

After gathering and analyzing information and reading related research, the committee came up with several hypotheses explaining why so many of the children seem to need special attention:

1. Classes are characterized by children of many different educational abilities and linguistic and ethnic backgrounds. Classroom makeup of the younger grades has become increasingly more diverse: over the last five years, the Hispanic population has more than doubled, some children entering the school without any formal education experiences.

2. Classes are large and overcrowded; many of them have more than thirty students.

3. There's a high turnover rate among students—as much as 67 percent one year.

4. Many of the parents are working ten to fourteen hours a day and aren't able to provide the educational and emotional support the children need at home.

Committee members felt strongly that all four of these hypotheses might indeed contribute to the problem, but they realized that they needed to find ways of validating these hypotheses before proceeding any further so as not to wander down the wrong path.

1b: Test Hypotheses to See If They Hold Water. The committee decided that the best way to find out why so many students needed extra attention in class was to design two surveys, one to send to teachers and classroom aides and one to send to families. The teacher/staff survey was intended to elicit the specific needs of both students and teachers; the family survey focused on examining the kinds of support the children received at home and the level of involvement the family members felt in their children's education.

During these initial steps of exploring the problem, committee members presented progress reports at steering committee meetings. After approval of their surveys by the steering committee, they presented the surveys at a school-as-a-whole meeting and received unanimous approval. Surveys were then distributed to staff and parents. After two weeks, the cadre received back 92 percent of the staff surveys and 72 percent of the parent surveys.

1c: Interpret the Results of Testing and Develop a Clear Understanding of the Challenge Area. The committee carefully compiled and analyzed the data from the surveys and came up with several interesting results. First, teachers of the younger students identified more children needing additional attention than did teachers of the older students. These former teachers had, on average, 17 percent more students in their classrooms than their counterparts in the upper grades did, and they identified "lack of communication" and "not following directions" as their primary frustrations in getting children involved in a lesson or activity. Another interesting discovery was that students who routinely failed to follow instructions and to successfully participate in classroom activities didn't fall into any specific category, such as a gender or ethnic grouping. The committee also found that only 24 percent of the parents and guardians spent two hours or more a week working with their children on homework or reading to them. More than 80 percent of the parents and guardians cited "lack of time" as a reason for not spending more time with their children, primarily due to their work situation. After carefully discussing these findings, the committee decided to focus on finding ways to provide more individual attention to the younger students—both in the classroom and the home—to help facilitate instruction.

Stage 2: Brainstorm Solutions

The committee brainstormed potential solutions, drawing on ideas, programs, and expertise from within the school community. The committee searched for ways to enable the teachers to spend more time as facilitators rather than instructors and to ensure that the lessons/activities could be understood by a diverse student population. With that in mind, the committee looked at some of the programs already being implemented at the school, such as the peer-tutoring program. Although that program was seen as successful, teachers were eager to find a way to help students from within the classroom instead of by pulling them out of class and disrupting their day. One committee member suggested that parent-student lesson nights might be a way to help, but others in the group argued that the majority of parents wouldn't have time for such an activity. Another member suggested having more culturally diverse homework assignments with directions translated into other languages.

Remembering numerous conversations with overworked teachers and classroom aides about their limited resources, one committee member reminded the group that it hadn't pursued resources outside of the school. One parent on the committee then mentioned that employees in her husband's office worked closely with a high school in the area. The group discussed this idea further and agreed that another option might be developing a classroom assistance program for the younger students—a program in which adults (ideally bilingual or at least familiar with another language) could help out in the classroom so that students could get needed adult supervision and attention.

Note: True brainstorming allows all ideas to be brought forth without any discussion. Discussion takes place later, when the group looks at the brainstormed ideas and evaluates and synthesizes them.

Stage 3: Synthesize Solutions and Develop an Action Plan

As committee members informally presented some of their ideas to other cadres and to the steering committee, they learned that some of the ideas were already being explored and developed within other cadres. The groups worked together to allocate responsibility without duplicating efforts: the Curriculum Cadre agreed to take over the responsibility of looking more carefully at the cultural diversity of curricular materials used in the classroom, and the Parent Involvement Cadre planned to continue pursuing ways to involve the parents in their children's education. That left the ad hoc committee free to concentrate on developing the classroom assistance program.

One of the first things that the ad hoc committee did was collect information and ideas from each classroom teacher and aide about how a classroom assistance program should be developed. One of the biggest concerns cited by the staff was that classroom volunteers have flexible hours and be available primarily in the late-morning and early-afternoon hours. The committee also solicited (and incorporated) ideas on available resources and support from the principal and from other organizations using tutoring or volunteer programs. That input suggested that many people within the community would be willing to contribute some of their time and talent toward helping the school. In fact, the school had been contacted occasionally by churches, senior citizen groups, community organizations, and members of the local community college with offers of help, but there had been no opportunity for the school to coordinate this assistance in the past. The committee identified the following potential sources of adult volunteers: senior citizen residences and organizations, colleges and universities, churches, businesses, and voluntary agencies (such as the YMCA, the YWCA, Big Brothers, and Big Sisters).

After initial research, the committee found that senior citizens and college students have the most flexible schedules available. Many retired teachers, engineers, doctors, businesspeople, craftspeople, and others are especially interested in working with young people. The committee decided to have an awareness session at which interested volunteers could learn about the accelerated schools philosophy and process and meet some of the teachers, staff, parents, and students. The committee planned that the school community would provide a short presentation on the school, its students, and their needs, artwork and messages from the children would decorate the room, and students would serve as hosts and hostesses. Invitations made by the students were sent out to all the community organizations identified by the cadre.

The awareness session proved to be a big success, with more than forty potential volunteers attending. During the question-and-answer period, a representative from one of the larger local businesses suggested that her company might be willing to allow employees to use an hour of work a week for a community service project such as this. Spirits were high, and the committee members eagerly began developing their action plan.

Once the committee had explored all the options, members developed a detailed and well-thought-out action plan that specified how responsibilities would be delegated and included a plan for assessment.

Stages 4 and 5: Pilot Test and/or Implement the Action Plan; Evaluate and Reassess

They then shared their action plan with the steering committee and the school as a whole for approval. Upon approval, the committee began planning for implementation and evaluation. Even as they progressed with implementing the program, they informally started gathering information for assessment.

CHAPTER **11**

How Will I Know
If My School Is
Accelerating?

The vision that your school community so enthusiastically and carefully created is much more than words on a piece of paper; it's a living document that's ever present in your hearts, minds, and actions. Collaboratively and individually, your school community is working to make your vision a reality. But how do you know if you're really accelerating? In this chapter, we provide you with a sense of how to assess your accelerated school efforts. Although a small part of the chapter is aimed specifically at beginning accelerated schools, the majority of the text and reflection questions should be useful to all accelerated schools at any stage. (We're in the process of creating self-reflection tools tailored for schools in the intermediate and advanced stages of acceleration.)

On a regular basis, accelerated school community members ask themselves whether their individual and collective actions reflect the accelerated schools philosophy and process and whether these actions lead to their vision. They reflect not only on the big wheels of acceleration but also on the little wheels that result as members of the school community use the accelerated schools philosophy and process to transform themselves.

Accelerated school communities recognize that self-assessment is the on-going responsibility of the entire school community rather than an annual event accomplished by outsiders or committees. They know that it's the responsibility of the school community itself to ascertain how well it's doing in its quest to bring students into the productive educational mainstream. An accelerated school's vision is the yardstick against which the success of that quest is measured.

11.1. A Way of Thinking About Assessment

Since the 1970s, school assessment has been the province of people outside of the school—often people involved in district and statewide testing and evaluation programs. These outside organizations frequently use standardized assessment tools not based on the curriculum of the local school, and they often limit their assessment to only a few dimensions of school life. Not surprisingly, then, these assessments usually tell school communities little about the effects of their teaching and learning processes. Because of this, school communities are rarely able to use test results and other outcomes or recommendations as guides to improving their practices. Instead, the outside evaluation encourages school communities to work toward meeting predetermined compliance standards.

We believe that the insensitivity of this remote-control approach to particular student and school needs is at the heart of the present failures that beset schools attended by students in at-risk situations. Accelerated school communities require assessment techniques that they can use comfortably, systematically, and for all educational activities and that they can apply to their own school as a whole, individual classrooms, specific programs, particular groups of students, and even individual students.

The Accelerated Schools Project views the school site as the center of expertise not only in the areas of instructional, curricular, and organizational decisions but also in the area of assessment. Only by assessing the consequences of our own decisions can we obtain the information that we need in order to develop as professionals and to create the accelerated experiences that we seek for our students.

A central goal of the Accelerated Schools Project is to create the kinds of schools for students in at-risk situations that each of us would want for our own children. As we work with our school community to build our collective capacity to establish accelerated educational practices, we should look carefully at our school at every moment of the day and ask ourselves if this learning environment is one that we'd want for our own offspring. If it's not good enough for our own children, it's not yet good enough for any child.

When we use this criterion, we begin to recognize certain problems inherent in conventional approaches to school assessment. Standardized test scores don't begin to tell us whether our schools are good enough, and they say nothing about why our students are having difficulties or what life experiences they may already have had in a certain area. Test scores are limited both in the domains that they cover and in the methods used to test those domains. Although accelerated schools have witnessed dramatic increases in standardized test scores (often experiencing the largest test-score gains in their districts and successfully bringing all students to grade level and above), it's important to emphasize that these results are by-products of successful accelerated school activities rather than the principal focus of acceleration. Other means of evaluating schools, such as the PQR (California's Program Quality Review) and regional accreditation association procedures, look at specific, prescribed areas at a certain point in time. While helpful, these aren't sufficient for true ongoing self-assessment.

The accelerated schools process is based on ongoing self-assessment and school improvement. In fact, the process begins with a self-assessment as accelerated school community members take stock of their present situation (see Chapter Three, "Getting Started"). Then, in inquiry, school community members study the nature and underlying causes of their challenge areas (see Chapter Four, "The Inquiry Process"). Accelerated schools staff have found that the self-assessments inherent in the accelerated schools process are far more thorough and fulfilling than state- or district-mandated evaluations. At the same time, they view the "outside" evaluations as a resource for their own taking-stock and inquiry efforts.

In addition to using the accelerated schools process to evaluate success systematically, accelerated school community members can make important use of a very simple assessment question that reflects the central goal of the entire Accelerated Schools Project: Is this school good enough for my own children and therefore for *all* children? Most of us want schools for our own children in which students are provided with warmth and caring, with activities that build on their experiences and cultural backgrounds, with opportunities for independent study and research, and with activities that enable children to work together and learn from each other. We want schools in which rich learning experiences throughout the curriculum provide students with themes and activities appropriate to their personal interests and motivation, with arts and creative opportunities, with frequent problem-solving challenges, with opportunities to engage in meaningful discussion and expressive activity, and with an abundance of extracurricular and cocurricular possibilities. Indeed, this is just a short list of what most of us would want for our *own* children.

By assessing our daily practices, we're able to tell instantly whether a program or set of school experiences or the entire school environment meets our expectations for our own children. We can evaluate the experiences of a single child or a group of children, becoming increasingly sensitive to how situations may be experienced from their perspective. We can meet with other members of the school community and evaluate how well we're implementing the accelerated schools process.

We can evaluate our own schools and activities by becoming "educational connoisseurs" (Eisner, 1991)—developing a taste and evaluative expertise for what is good education. We can share our expectations and observations with one another and sharpen our sensitivity to what's happening in our schools. *We're* the experts on what we want for our own children; *we're* the educational "insiders" who can tell whether these standards are being met.

Consider the power that this informal assessment provides to us as educators. Instead of waiting until the end of the year or the beginning of the following year to receive the test results that are supposed to tell us whether our schools are good enough, we can make our own expert observations at any time, using a far richer set of information and a more personal set of criteria. (And we already have in place the process by which to implement needed changes!)

Assessment and the Three Principles

In an accelerated school, self-assessment embodies our three central principles of unity of purpose, empowerment coupled with responsibility, and building on strengths.

- Assessment builds on the collective dream or vision on which the entire school is based—a vision derived from working together and sharing a common perception of the kind of school that would work for our own children and for all children.

- Assessment draws on our responsibility for the consequences of the learning opportunities and situations that we create, providing us with information on whether these environments are aligned with our vision or need to be modified in some way.

- Assessment builds on our strengths as educational professionals to evaluate our own activities and to use our combined expertise to alter those activities if necessary. It also builds on the strengths of our students and parents to make assessments of their schools' experiences and student progress. Finally, it provides feedback and assistance in improving school practices and outcomes.

11.2. Assessing the Progress of an Accelerated School

In this section, we discuss the kinds of questions that accelerated school communities ask themselves in order to assess progress in their transformation from a traditional institution into a vibrant and creative learning community. While the informal assessments just described will guide your interactions on a daily basis, we now offer more formal, long-term assessments that will help you to reflect on and then fine-tune the progress you're making as an accelerated school. In the following pages, we describe a systematic way of ascertaining how your community has internalized and implemented the accelerated schools philosophy and process. Even if a school has had training in the accelerated schools philosophy and process, it doesn't *become* an accelerated school until it's begun to successfully incorporate the accelerated schools philosophy and process into its daily life as a community. To do this, school community members *continuously* assess whether they're using the accelerated schools philosophy and process effectively. They need not be overly concerned with outcomes at first; rather, assessing the *process* that they're using to accelerate their school is the first order of business. *Only after the processes have been implemented and the philosophy internalized does it make sense to see if the accelerated practices are producing the desired results (such as those described in the introduction of this chapter and those set out in the school's vision).*

11.2.1. Three Interrelated Stages of Becoming an Accelerated School: Assessing Big-Wheel Processes

One of the strengths of the Accelerated Schools Project is that it provides a philosophy and process for long-lasting school change. We've all had disappointing experiences with educational packages that were supposed to work quickly. What we've learned is that deep and meaningful change occurs over time.

We see three *interrelated* stages or aspects involved in producing such long-lasting change in an accelerated school. The first stage of a school community's transformation involves *building the capacity to collaboratively make decisions*. The second stage involves *implementing the results of collaboratively made decisions*. The third stage involves *the emergence of accelerated school outcomes*, such as strong academic performance by students and high parental participation, which your school should be able to trace to the use of the accelerated schools process. Assessment is central at all three stages and helps the school determine its progress.

It's important to note that these stages are not strictly linear. Indeed, school communities first need to build the capacity to make and implement collaborative decisions, but outcomes inevitably occur early on in the process. As your school begins to internalize the philosophy and process, little-wheel activities might, for example, result in parents feeling more welcome on campus, staff feeling free to take risks in their teaching, and students being more engaged in their schoolwork. In fact, sometimes even test scores go up early on as a result of a school's transformation efforts. Keeping a record of all of these successes will be important in helping your school community trace the evolution of your long-term schoolwide achievements.

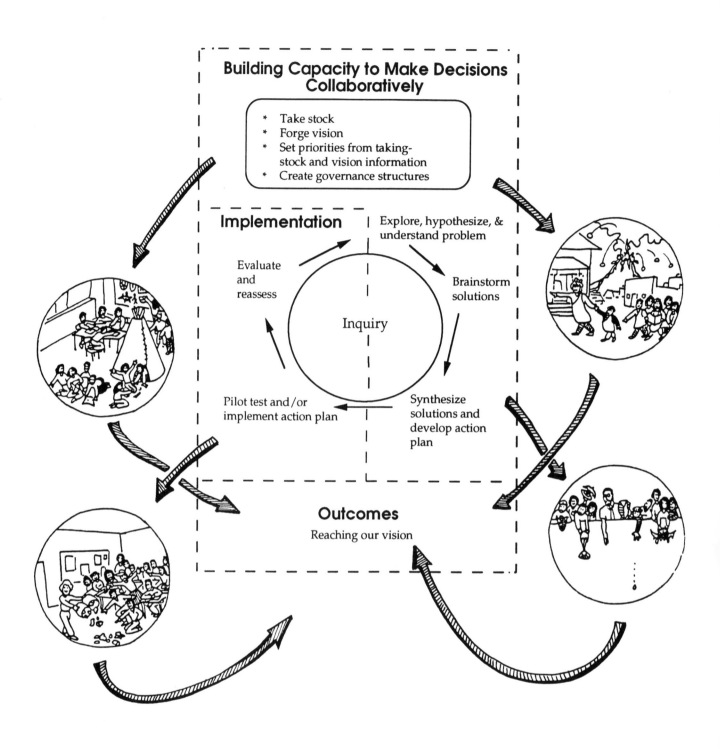

Building Capacity to Make Decisions Collaboratively

* Take stock
* Forge vision
* Set priorities from taking-stock and vision information
* Create governance structures

Implementation

Explore, hypothesize, & understand problem

Evaluate and reassess

Brainstorm solutions

Inquiry

Pilot test and/or implement action plan

Synthesize solutions and develop action plan

Outcomes

Reaching our vision

Accelerated schools need not relegate assessment to a mechanical checklist of procedures. As they focus on the implementation of the accelerated schools philosophy and process, their tools can include observations, impressions, discussions, interviews, reviews of reports, and minutes of meetings. Attempts to answer the type of reflection questions set out at the end of this chapter should be part of a continuing schoolwide discourse.

Planning for Self-Assessment

As a school community, think of ways that you could use the reflection questions at the end of this chapter to help guide you in implementing the accelerated schools philosophy and process. **To ensure that self-assessment actually occurs, all governance groups should set specific times for self-assessment at the beginning, middle, and end of the school year.** Other activities that will support your more formal assessment efforts include the following:

- Selecting a person or team responsible for maintaining important documentation of the school's journey toward acceleration. This includes not only historical information on the acceleration process but also documentation on agreed upon indicators for assessment of outcomes (such as test scores, teacher and student turnover rates, absentee rates, and grade retention and student discipline figures), which should be collected from the start and regularly updated. Your school community should decide what kind of data collection is needed to give you a yardstick for measuring later progress and actual outcomes.

- Keeping a log of the major activities involved in the accelerated schools process (via calendars of training sessions, bulletins, agendas).

- Maintaining a multimedia portfolio or library of all important powerful learning experiences and community events that happen each year (composed of photo albums, news clippings, essays, videos, television coverage).

- Developing an accelerated schools portfolio of minutes, reports, and various activities of all meetings and stages of the process (taking-stock surveys and survey results, a record of the visioning process, the list of priorities, cadre names and membership, cadre agendas and minutes, steering committee membership, steering committee agendas and minutes, and SAW agendas and minutes).

- Maintaining a centrally located place to house your school's acceleration portfolio and a general bulletin board for all agendas and minutes.

- Keeping a copy of the curriculum offerings and class schedules from year to year.

- Updating an organizational chart and a copy of the decision-making process and governance structure that your school decides to use.

- Setting up a formal opportunity for the entire school community to reflect on its progress toward becoming an accelerated school by having an end-of-the-year reflection day.

Rancho Milpitas Middle School had an end-of-the-year reflection day. Each cadre reported where it was in terms of the Inquiry Process, and each individual shared the successes and challenges of the big and little wheels that had spun during the year. One of the teachers summarized the afternoon well: "Our successes indicate that we're on our way to the vision. Our challenges show our frustration in not being there yet!"
Rancho Milpitas Middle School, Milpitas, California

Building the Capacity to Make Decisions Together. Traditional schools don't involve *all* members of the school community in decision making to nearly the extent that accelerated schools do. To work together in a totally collaborative manner, accelerated school communities must develop the capacity to make decisions together. They do so through the collaborative processes of taking stock of their current situation; forging a shared vision; setting priorities; creating a governance structure made up of cadres, a steering committee, and the school as a whole; and using the Inquiry Process to make informed decisions that are responsive to the problems of their specific school. They also begin to work together collaboratively on a number of the little-wheel innovations.

Assessment at this first stage focuses on how the process of decision making has changed in the school through building capacity to make collaborative decisions. In seeing how well a school community is collaborating, members should begin by reflecting on how well they're using each of the three principles. We urge you to develop your own reflection questions to assess your school community's internalization of each of the three principles and all other aspects of the accelerated schools philosophy.

In the sections that follow, we set out the interrelated stages of the accelerated schools process, a summary of each area, and sample reflection questions. The growth and development of your accelerated school depends on your ability to assess yourself in each of these areas. Throughout the guide and at the end of this chapter, we've presented some specific reflection questions that we encourage you to use. You'll also create your own questions specific to your community, of course.

- *Taking stock.* Your school begins the accelerated schools process with an extensive endeavor to take stock of its present situation by exploring all of the important dimensions of the here and now. Teachers, support staff, administrators, students, as many parents as possible, district office representatives, and community members participate in taking stock.

  As your school pursues and completes taking stock, it's important to assess thoroughness. Were all of the important dimensions of your school community covered? Did everyone in the school community share in setting out the dimensions of the taking-stock process, formulating questions, gathering data, interpreting data, and reaching conclusions about the taking-stock findings? Did the taking-stock report and process build a sense of ownership of and responsibility for the school? Did it acknowledge strengths as well as challenges? (*Please refer also to the end-of-chapter reflection questions on taking stock.*)

- *Forging a shared vision.* Concurrent with the taking-stock phase, your whole school community develops a collective picture of the school that it desires to create over the next five to six years—a dream school that will work for *all* children. This process requires detailed answers to specific questions regarding what parents and staff want for their own children, what kind of school children want, what children should know and be able to do, and what kind of school would enable all members of the school community to fully put their talents to use. The process of developing this vision must be done collaboratively and thoughtfully and involve *all* members of the school community.

  When the school community reflects on the visioning process, members ask themselves, Have all the participants in the school community (parents, teachers, support staff, students, administrators, and community members) contributed to the vision? Is the vision sufficiently cohesive, concrete, rich, and inspirational that it can become the goal toward which all of our actions will focus? Are all members of the school community represented in the vision? (*Please refer also to the end-of-chapter reflection questions on forging a vision.*)

- *Setting priorities.* After reporting the taking-stock findings and forging the vision, your school compares the vision with the current situation (as reflected in the taking-stock report). From this comparision, you develop a comprehensive and concrete picture of all the areas in which your taking-stock data fall short of your vision. The full school community discusses these "gap" areas fully to ascertain their relative importance and select a limited number of challenge areas as initial priorities. These areas of focus will be the basis for your school's cadres, which will use the Inquiry Process to address the priority challenges and move toward the school's vision.

  In assessing the setting-priorities process, the school community asks itself, How well do the priority areas reflect the whole school's concerns? How thoroughly did the school community study the taking-stock and vision data in order to determine priority challenges? How was the entire school community involved in selecting priorities from the full list of challenges identified? (*Please refer also to the end-of-chapter reflection questions on setting priorities.*)

- *Utilizing accelerated governance structures and beginning the Inquiry Process.* Your school forms cadres around the priorities determined during the setting-priorities stage. A steering committee, composed of representatives of each cadre, parents, students, administrators, and others as determined by the school, serves as a clearinghouse for ideas and potential decisions that are then refined, if need be, before being recommended to the school as a whole (all staff and representative students, parents, and community members). The steering committee also helps to ensure that the cadres and the school as a whole are using the Inquiry Process to move toward the vision. The school as a whole comes together regularly to discuss and approve major decisions that affect the entire school. All of these accelerated schools governance groups meet regularly and follow a systematic and collaborative Inquiry Process. Decision-making structures work best when meetings are well organized and managed. Communication channels are most effective when information and minutes are made readily available to all members of the school community and regular opportunities are provided for feedback and group discussion.

Assessment needs to be built into each part of this phase to ensure that it's thoughtful and complete. Accelerated school communities ask themselves, Is *everyone* involved in the cadres (all staff and administrators, with representative parents, students, district workers, and community members)? Are cadres, the steering committee, and the SAW meeting regularly, following the first stages of the Inquiry Process, and employing effective group processes? Does the SAW meet regularly to discuss and approve major decisions suggested by the cadres and the steering committee? Are the steering committee and the SAW helping to keep the cadres on track with the school's vision and with the Inquiry Process? Does the SAW set new priorities as solutions to earlier priorities are implemented? How do the entire school's activities embody the school's vision through the SAW's emerging unity of purpose, empowerment, and building on student, staff, parental, and community strengths? (*Please refer also to the end-of-chapter reflection questions on governance structures and the Inquiry Process.*)

Implementing the Results of Collaboratively Made Decisions. Once problems are well understood and solutions have been carefully researched, cadres develop pilot (or full) action plans using the Inquiry Process. Clearly, if the decisions aren't implemented effectively, we can't expect much change in school outcomes. In this area, we assess whether the decisions recommended by cadres to the steering committee and the school as a whole are being followed and applied fully to the school setting. Pilot testing and implementation include not only getting the staff involved in adopting the ideas but also creating the logistical support for building the capacity of the school to implement the changes. This latter effort is often facilitated if responsibilities for particular implementation tasks are clear and are assigned a timeline.

It's helpful to trace the implementation process to the classrooms and to overall school programs and practices to see if the initial challenge area determined in stage 1 of the Inquiry Process is being addressed. This may require careful observation and assessment of educational practices from the perspective of each of the three dimensions of powerful learning (*how*, *what*, and *context*). It's important to know whether the anticipated changes are actually occurring in terms of observable school practices. This phase of assessment provides feedback for improving and refining implementation of specific school decisions. The school community can ensure that the implementation of decisions leads toward the vision and encompasses the unity of purpose of the school, the empowerment and active participation of staff, students, and parents, and the building on strengths of all of these groups. (*Please refer also to the end-of-chapter reflection questions on the Inquiry Process.*)

Examining School Outcomes. In implementing the accelerated schools philosophy and process, your school should assess whether the outcomes of collaboratively made decisions are producing the desired results and whether these outcomes stem from the first two stages of long-term change, discussed in the preceding paragraphs: building capacity to make collaborative decisions and implementation. Your school's detailed vision can provide the framework by which you assess actual outcomes. You can also ask whether or not you're creating the kind of learning situations that you'd want for your own child. In order to successfully determine whether these outcomes are a result of the accelerated schools process, your school must collect data from the beginning of acceleration, and on a regular basis thereafter, to assess progress and actual outcomes. The data that your school collected in the taking-stock process serve as a valuable source of information for subsequent discussion and evaluation of school outcomes. In addition, your school community should collect documentation on agreed upon indicators for assessment of outcomes, such as test scores, teacher and student turnover rates, absentee rates, and grade retention and student discipline figures. Assessment of the outcomes and the process for achieving those outcomes will become the basis for reconsidering strategies and priorities and for providing input into the Inquiry Process so that improvement is continuous.

Let's see how a school could use its vision statement as an assessment tool. Below are excerpts from two accelerated schools' vision statements. After each are sample reflection questions that might be addressed to assess whether the outcomes are producing the desired results.

Burnett Academy is a cooperative partnership of students, parents, staff, and community working together to create an environment in which:

- **All students develop a love of learning, inquisitiveness about the world around them, and resourcefulness in meeting life's challenges; they are problem solvers, critical thinkers, and communicators.**

- **All students connect the past, the present, and the future by applying their academic knowledge to the world around them and learning through experience.**

- **All students appreciate and build on the strengths of many cultures.**

- **All students find opportunities to express their individual needs and talents through a variety of artistic, musical, technological, athletic, social, and intellectual outlets.**

Burnett Academy, San Jose, California

With this excerpt of the vision as their standard, Burnett community members might now ask questions such as these: Are all the members of the school community—students, parents, staff, and community members—actively and collaboratively working together to make decisions and implement them? How has the expectation level of students, parents, and staff changed? How much and in what ways is critical thinking emphasized in the school's curriculum and instruction? How problem-centered are the school's curriculum and instruction? How much of the learning in the school is generated by the students themselves? How much of the learning centers around textbooks? What evidence is there that the curriculum and instruction invite active student involvement and incorporate students' prior knowledge and experience? In what ways does the curriculum incorporate and draw on the experiences of many cultures? In what ways are students now more engaged in following individual pursuits, such as artistic or musical projects, reading and writing, and involvement in after-school activities? What improvements in student self-esteem have been seen? How has the quality of student work improved in writing, analysis, creativity, and problem solving? In what ways and in what areas has student achievement improved? What percentage of students who graduate are accomplished and competent enough to move on with their continuing education? In what ways are parents working more closely with their children to develop and support their learning? How has the school climate changed?

At Hoover Elementary School, students take responsibility for themselves and their learning. The staff and students use active, thematic approaches to explore meaningful curriculum and cultural and linguistic diversity.

Hoover Elementary School, Redwood City, California

Based on that one component of the vision statement, Hoover community members might now ask questions such as these: How much of the learning in the school is generated by the students themselves? What evidence is there that the classrooms are places where all teachers and students are engaged in building on their knowledge and sharing important issues and ideas? How does the school's curriculum invite active student involvement that uses students' prior knowledge and experience? In what ways does the curriculum build on the diversity of the student body? How much and in what ways is the curriculum integrated between subjects and grade levels? In what ways and in what areas has student achievement improved? What improvements in student self-esteem have been seen? Are students more engaged in their school activities, as reflected in student excitement, completion of homework assignments, and student attendance? Are staff using more creative and integrated, thematic approaches in their instruction? What percentage of students who graduate are accomplished and competent enough to move on with their continuing education?

Many of these questions might look like taking-stock questions—questions that attempt to draw a picture of the here and now. Indeed, they *are* trying to draw a picture of the here and now, but that here and now is a *new* "present" situation—one that reflects how you're bringing your vision statement to life after several years of acceleration. (*Note:* Another way to see how far you've progressed since taking stock is to retake your taking-stock surveys and compare the answers to your original taking-stock data! Indeed, utilizing both the vision and taking-stock data are excellent tools for on-going assessment.)

11.2.2. Assessing Little-Wheel Processes

In moving toward its vision, the school continuously follows and assesses its progress. As we said earlier, outcomes will indeed emerge as a result of your big-wheel efforts, but they'll also most certainly occur along the way as a result of the little-wheel initiatives of each individual member of your school community.

Keeping track of little-wheel events and activities and how they help lead to the vision can be very rewarding. It can also provide the community with information that will feed into big-wheel processes. In addition, providing community recognition or award ceremonies for powerful learning advances at the little-wheel level can be an inspiration to everyone.

In order to keep track of and assess little-wheel activities and innovations, you may want to keep a video or media archive that people could regularly refer to. Assessment questions that you might ask could include the following: Who was involved in setting up little-wheel activities? What responsibilities did the different parties have? What did they do? Were they successful? If not, what was their assessment of what went wrong? What was learned from the experience? How did a particular innovation promote powerful learning? How did the three principles underlie the innovation? How did it involve all the actors in the community? What were the students' roles? How did people feel about the activity? Did it have an impact on big-wheel processes? What big-wheel processes helped give rise to the various little-wheel activities and innovations?

11.2.3. Assessing the Overarching Issue

Ultimately, the entire school staff and all parents and students must ask themselves if this is the school that they'd choose for their offspring or themselves. Many of the questions that address that issue are unique to each person. They might include the following: Is this a school that challenges all learners (children and adults) and builds on their strengths? Does the school imbue both students and adults with the excitement of learning? Is this a school that provides the best opportunities for advancing professional practices? Is it a place where ideas count? Does the school provide a supportive environment for students, staff, and parents? Is this a school in which all the stakeholders responsibly participate in decision making and governance? Is this a school in which parents contribute to the unity of purpose and are assisted in supporting accelerated practices in the home?

If our school doesn't yet meet our own personal and shared standards, we must continue to work at the process until the schools that we want for our own children and those that we provide for students in at-risk situations are one and the same.

11.3. Reflection Questions

As mentioned at the beginning of this chapter, the first part of the following reflection questions (repeated from Chapters Three and Four) are aimed specifically at beginning accelerated schools. Even so, all the questions—especially those on governance, the Inquiry Process, and school outcomes—are applicable to all schools.

11.3.1. Taking Stock

Were *all* members of the school community meaningfully involved in all aspects of the taking-stock process? How did the committees generate questions? What areas of school life were investigated? What were your taking-stock committee names? How was the taking-stock information gathered? How effective was the taking-stock coordinating committee at fulfilling its tasks and communicating with the rest of the school? What was the response rate on the master surveys for the various groups? How did the taking-stock committees follow through on the nonsurvey research? Were the reports generated by each taking-stock committee thorough and clear? How did the school community feel about the findings? Was there widespread agreement among the members of the school community about the big picture of the here and now? What strengths were found in the school community through the taking-stock process? What challenges were identified? Did the taking-stock process yield some surprising information? How did the taking-stock process and report build a sense of ownership of and responsibility for the school? What evidence is there that the school community has begun to develop a unity of purpose, collective empowerment, and recognition of strengths and the opportunities to build on them?

11.3.2. Forging a Shared Vision

Creating the Vision. Were all members of the school community meaningfully involved in the visioning process? How did the various members contribute to the vision? How did your school community synthesize all the ideas of the various constituents into the vision statement? How does the vision address the dreams of parents, staff, and students? How about the district and community? How was the vision made known to all staff, students, parents, and local community members? Did the whole school community celebrate the vision? How so?

Keeping the Vision Alive. How is the vision being kept alive? What connection do individuals within the school community have with the vision? How does this play out in their actions? What connection does the vision have with group decisions? Are decisions evaluated in terms of how they will lead to achieving the vision? How does the vision continue to address the dreams of the entire school community? How does the vision contribute to a framework for action? What goals does the vision suggest for the school community?

For more mature accelerated schools, how often have you revisited the vision to see if it continues to address your dreams? How have you incorporated the views of new members of your school community into the vision?

II.3.3. Setting Priorities

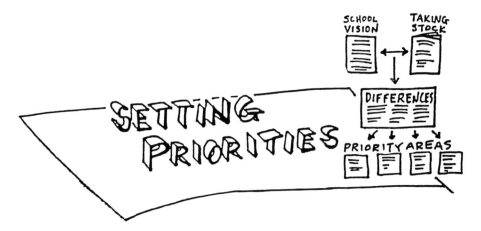

What process did your school community use to compare its vision with all of the information gathered in the taking-stock process in order to set priorities? Were all participants in the school community involved in this process? How thorough was the process of identifying challenge areas? How did the school select initial priorities from the full list of challenge areas? Was there widespread agreement among the members of the school community as to the priorities? In what ways will these challenge areas eventually lead your school community to the vision? How were the challenge areas not included in the initial priorities recorded for future action?

For more mature schools, how are you assessing which priority areas have been addressed and shifting emphasis toward other challenge areas that need to be addressed?

II.3.4. Governance Structure

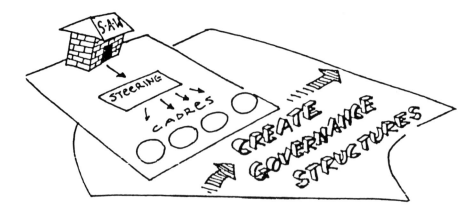

Cadres. What cadres were formed? What is the membership of each? How does the membership reflect the total school community? Are teachers, support staff, parents, students, administrators, and the community represented on each cadre? Are the cadres meeting weekly? If not, are they meeting at least biweekly so that they can thoroughly address their challenge areas and develop an action plan? Are all the cadres following the Inquiry Process? Are they having any difficulties? Are they incorporating the participation of all members? Do all members take responsibility? How well are they using productive group processes to ensure continuity from meeting to meeting? How are participants prepared for their roles as facilitator, recorder, closure person, and so on? How are agendas created? Do the cadres report on how they're doing and where they are in the Inquiry Process at least twice a month to the steering committee and once a month to the school as a whole? Do cadres seek ratification from the steering committee and the SAW on decisions and proposals? Do all participants receive agendas and minutes in a timely manner? Are agendas and minutes also posted regularly in a public place? How well do cadres follow through with implementing and assessing decisions or plans of action? How do the cadres keep in touch with the district and obtain district assistance or advice on implementation? How do the members build on the strengths of the school community, work toward a unified purpose, and provide a real opportunity for shared decision making coupled with responsibility?

Steering Committee. What is the membership of the steering committee? Are all cadres represented? Are teachers, support staff, parents, students, administrators, the district office, and the community represented? Was the whole school involved in determining the composition of this group? How often does the steering committee meet? Does it meet at least twice a month so that it can discuss schoolwide issues and make sure that the cadres and the SAW are using the Inquiry Process in moving toward the vision? Is the steering committee using the Inquiry Process? Do all steering committee members actively participate? Do all members take responsibility? Are they using productive group processes to ensure continuity from meeting to meeting? How are participants prepared for their roles as facilitator, recorder, closure person, and so on? How are agendas created? Are ad hoc committees formed in response to short-term problems? If so, how are they coordinated through the steering committee? Do all participants receive agendas and minutes in a timely manner? Are agendas and minutes also posted regularly in a public place? How does the steering committee keep in touch with the district and obtain district assistance or advice on implementation? How do the members build on the strengths of the school community, work toward a unified purpose, and provide a real opportunity for shared decision making coupled with responsibility? For more mature accelerated schools, is the steering committee helping cadres set new priorities as solutions to earlier priorities are successfully implemented?

School as a Whole. Is there full participation of all teachers, support and classified staff, administrators, and representative parents, students, district office, and community members in SAW meetings and decisions? How often is the SAW meeting to discuss schoolwide issues and approve major decisions? At least once a month? How are SAW decisions made? How are members of the school community informed about the activities of the steering committee and cadres? Is the communication between cadres, the steering committee, and the SAW smooth, regular, and effective? Do cadres regularly report verbally to the SAW? Does the SAW use the Inquiry Process? Do all SAW members actively participate? Do all members take responsibility? Does the SAW use productive group processes to ensure continuity from meeting to meeting? How are agendas created? Do all participants receive agendas and minutes in a timely manner? Are agendas and minutes also posted regularly in a public place? How does the SAW follow through with implementing and assessing decisions? How does the SAW keep in touch with the district and obtain district assistance or advice on implementation? How do the members build on the strengths of the school community, work toward a unified purpose, and provide a real opportunity for shared decision making coupled with responsibility?

II.3.5. The Inquiry Process

The questions supplied for each stage of the Inquiry Process should be asked by each cadre and ad hoc committee as it works to achieve the school's vision.

Stage 1: Focus in on the Challenge Area.

1a: Explore the challenge area informally and hypothesize why it exists. What was the cadre's initial understanding of its challenge area? How did the cadre explore its challenge area informally? How did cadre members make use of the taking-stock data? How did they explore the challenge area outside of the cadre? With whom did they talk? What questions did they ask? Did they invest adequately in understanding the challenge and hypothesizing why it exists? What were the cadre's hypotheses? Were there at least fifteen hypotheses? Did the cadre report its research to the steering committee and the SAW and obtain their input?

1b: Test hypotheses to see if they hold water. How did the cadre look for evidence to see which hypotheses held water? Did cadre members adequately test each hypothesis? How did they test each? With whom did they talk? What did they do (surveys, interviews, and so on)? Which hypotheses held water? Were the hypotheses that held water relevant to the cadre's initial understanding of the challenge area? Did the cadre report its research to the steering committee and the SAW and obtain their input?

1c: Interpret the results of testing and develop a clear understanding of the challenge area. How did cadre members interpret their findings? Did they look at all the evidence gathered? How did they communicate with the steering committee and the SAW about their findings? What is their clearest understanding of the challenge area—the focus areas for which they plan to

The Inquiry Process

1. **Focus in on the Challenge Area**

   Explore the problem informally and hypothesize why challenge area exists

   Test the hypotheses

   Interpret the results of testing and develop a clear understanding of the challenge area

5. Evaluate and Reassess

INQUIRY

2. Brainstorm Solutions

   Look inside and outside the school for ideas

4. Pilot Test and/or Implement the Plan

3. Synthesize Solutions and Develop an Action Plan

brainstorm solutions? Did the cadre's final understanding of the challenge area affirm or redefine their initial understanding of the challenge?

Stage 2: Brainstorm Solutions. How did cadre members search for solutions to address the focus areas—that is, the hypotheses that they found to hold water? Were all members of the school community included in compiling ideas? Did cadre members incorporate any solutions that surfaced in stage 1? Did they look both inside and outside the school for potential solutions? How did they obtain input from the school community? How did they look outside the school for possible solutions? How did they communicate their brainstormed ideas to the entire school community, including students and parents?

Stage 3: Synthesize Solutions and Develop an Action Plan. How did cadre members synthesize their brainstormed solutions before pilot testing? Did they ask themselves what the consequences of implementing each solution might be? Did they make sure that the consequences of the various solutions would address their final understanding of their challenge area (focus areas) and lead toward the vision? If the recommended plan is implemented, will the actions of the entire school change, or just the actions of a single teacher? Will the plan lead to the vision? Will the resulting change be sustained over the years? Were all three major dimensions—*what* (curriculum), *how* (instructional strategies), and *context* (school organization)—considered during this stage? Is the plan feasible? What obstacles might arise if the plan is implemented? What resources will be needed to implement it? Did the cadre modify the solutions to fit the realities of the students, classrooms, and school? Did the cadre attempt to refine, reorganize, or restructure current school policies or classroom practices to fit its proposal? Does the plan actively involve all members of the school community? Are all members who are part of the challenge (teachers, support staff, parents, students, the district office, school administrators, and the community) part of the action plan as well? Did the cadre obtain the approval of the steering committee and the SAW? What goals and objectives were set out for the action plan? Did the cadre carefully plan implementation and assessment strategies before pilot testing the action plan? Are all the elements of the pilot plan present (*who* will do *what* by *when*, and *how*, as well as details about how the plan will be evaluated)?

Stage 4: Pilot Test and/or Implement the Action Plan. How was the action plan approved? Were the steering committee and the SAW appropriately involved? If the cadre submitted a pilot action plan, did the school pilot test the plan thoroughly before recommending schoolwide implementation? If the cadre proposed a full implementation plan, how was it implemented? How was it determined to go with a pilot test? full implementation? Did the action plan specify who was responsible for doing what, and by when? Were all members of the school community (teachers, support staff, administrators, parents, students) involved in implementation? In pilot testing and/or implementing the action plan, did the cadre, the principal, the steering committee, the SAW, and central office personnel work together productively? Was a time set for evaluating the pilot plan? If that time has come, has the cadre taken steps to evaluate the action plan? Who was involved in its evaluation? Did all the people involved in the plan participate in its evaluation? What were the actual evaluation plans? What checkpoints were built into the implementation process to assess progress toward the intended goal? Did the cadre routinely report its progress to the steering committee and the SAW and obtain their continued input?

Stage 5: Evaluate and Reassess. Is the cadre formally and informally evaluating the success of its action plan? How? Did the activities proposed in the action plan and then implemented directly address the problem as finally defined in stage 1? Did the action plan help move the school toward its vision? How did the action plan build on the strengths of all members of the school community? Were all members of the school community involved in implementation? Did everyone take responsibility for his or her role? How were the areas of curriculum, instructional strategies, and school organization addressed? Did the cadre report its research to the steering committee and the SAW and obtain their input?

11.3.6. School Outcomes: Long-Term and Intermediate

Reexamine your school's vision and determine how far toward it you've progressed. How do school outcomes reflect that vision? How does the school meet the standards that staff members would set for their own children's schools? How is the Inquiry Process seeping into the classroom, the office, the schoolyard? What special projects have been undertaken as a result of the school's journey toward acceleration? What evidence is there that the classrooms are places where all teachers and students are engaged in building on their knowledge and sharing important issues and ideas? What percentage of students who graduate are accomplished and competent enough to move on with their continuing education? Are all the members of your school community—students, parents, staff, central office representatives, and community members—working collaboratively to reach decisions and implement them? How has the community built on the strengths of the teachers in order to provide students with powerful learning experiences? How has the community built on the strengths of the administration (and the community, the support staff, students' families, and the students themselves) in order to provide powerful learning experiences?

Provide specific examples of how the school community has changed *what* students learn, *how* students learn, and the *contexts* (social, material, time,

physical) in which students learn. How have the expectation levels of students, parents, and staff changed? Has there been a change in students' attitudes toward learning? Toward their teachers? Toward themselves? Toward their future educational or career path? How are parents involved in supporting their children's education? In what ways are parents working more closely with their children to reinforce the unity of purpose of the school by supporting school goals and practices? How is the entire staff working more collaboratively and productively? What other changes have you noticed since becoming an accelerated school?

The Inquiry Process: A Note-Keeping Device

Once you get into your cadres, we suggest that each cadre create a cadre notebook which includes this or your own version of a note-keeping device (as well as your vision, a chart of the Inquiry Process, and a copy of your school's meeting standards). Since the Inquiry Process (outlined in Chapter Four) is so long, we created this note-keeping device to serve as a tool you and your fellow cadre members can use in two ways: (1) to quickly reference the stages of the Inquiry Process, and (2) to keep track of your cadre's progress using inquiry. It is not a replacement for reading the inquiry chapter and going through training; rather, it is a supplement. While there is some space for notes on these pages, we encourage you to create your own systematic method of note keeping and to use this appendix as a guide. Finally, remember to report your cadre's progress throughout each stage of your inquiry at every steering committee and school-as-a-whole meeting.

Stage I: Focus in on the Challenge Area

1a: Explore the Challenge Area Informally and Hypothesize Why It Exists

Set out an initial view of the challenge area. *We perceive our challenge area to be:*

Consider possible reasons why the challenge area exists. Don't expect to discover any single correct explanation. Instead, think about any and all possible reasons for the challenge at hand. To get yourselves started in developing hypotheses, use the following format but beware of solutions dressed in hypotheses' clothes:

I think _____ *is a challenge for our school,* **because***:*

• Hypothesis 1:

• Hypothesis 2:

• Hypothesis 3:

• Hypothesis 4:

• Hypothesis 5:

• Hypothesis 6:

• Hypothesis 7:

• Hypothesis 8:

• Remember to develop at least 15 hypotheses!

How is the challenge area experienced from the perspective of the many different actors involved? Explore outside your cadre to learn about the hypotheses of others.

Who might we talk with?

What questions might we ask?

What materials might we look at?

1b: Test Hypotheses to See If They Hold Water

Cadres can use a variety of research methods to test their hypotheses. Your cadre should think about how you want to test each of your hypotheses and then split up responsibility for testing. Among the strategies that cadres in accelerated schools have used successfully are these:

- Observe each other's classes.

- Survey each other and/or other relevant groups.

- Interview each other and other relevant groups.

- Review test scores and achievement data.

- Analyze curriculum materials.

- Discuss and meet.

How have we tested our hypotheses?

Try out certain ideas as little wheels, but remember to wear bifocals when you implement a mini-solution! *How do the results of any of our mini-solutions inform our understanding of the challenge area?*

1c: Interpret Results of Testing and Develop a Clear Understanding of the Challenge Area

Which of our hypotheses held water?

Which ones didn't?

What is your cadre's understanding of your challenge area now? What does the combination of accurate hypotheses lead you to believe you must look for in brainstorming solutions? *Our cadre's focus areas are:*

Stage 2: Brainstorm Solutions

2a: Look Inside the School for Ideas and Expertise

Remember to ask all members of the school community for ideas and to look at ideas suggested during stage 1 that were put on a "waiting list." *What things are already being done within our school to address this challenge?*

How might we build on our school community's present strengths and interests to address this issue?

2b: Look Outside the School for Programs, Ideas, and Expertise

Explore potential programs and alternative approaches in other schools, with the district office, at the state level, in the education literature, in libraries, in museums, at universities, and wherever else your looking-outward efforts lead. (This can be accomplished during release days, during individual planning time, as a staff-development activity, or as a departmental effort.) *Places and ideas that we want to pursue include:*

Ensure follow-up on all brainstorming activities. For each follow-up activity, indicate who's responsible for doing what activity and by what time.

Stage 3: Synthesize Solutions and Develop an Action Plan

3a: Synthesize Brainstormed Solutions

Look critically at the list developed in your brainstorming sessions and try to prioritize your ideas and determine their feasibility. You can use the following criteria to help evaluate your solutions and decide which direction to go. For *each* proposed idea ask:

- *Will the implementation of this solution address the focus areas that we discovered in stage 1c of the Inquiry Process?*

- *Does this solution move us toward our vision?*

- *What obstacles might arise if we try to implement this?*

- *Is everyone who's part of the challenge part of this solution?*

- *How might we modify this solution to fit the realities of our students, their families, our classrooms, and our school?*

- *How might current school policies or classroom practices be refined, reorganized, or restructured to fit this proposal?*

- *What resources do we need to implement this?*

- *How might others (district representatives, school administrators, aides, parents, students, or university personnel) assist in designing and implementing this proposed program?*

- *Will the actions of the school change, or just the actions of a few individuals? Will the change be sustained over the years?*

- *What will happen if we implement this solution successfully? What will the consequences be?*

3b: Develop an Action Plan

After synthesizing your ideas, weave your best solutions into an action plan. In designing your plan, make sure all types of members in your school community are involved. Also, determine the resources you will need. Submit that plan, with an accompanying assessment plan, to the steering committee and school as a whole. Keep in mind the major components of the plan: *who* will do *what* by *when*, and *how*, as well as details about how the plan will be evaluated.

Our program goal is:

Our program objectives are:

You might want to use a chart such as the one that follows to keep track of your action plan.

TASK: *(List major title of task here.)*

Steps necessary for implementation:	By when:	By whom:
1. *(Break down the major task into individual steps—*		
2. *what needs to be done first, second, third, and so on.)*		
3.		
4.		
Etc.		
How will we monitor the program? *(This is for keeping track of program along the way.)*		
How will progress be evaluated? *(This is to see how successful the program was. Did it address your focus areas and goals?)*		

Stage 4: Pilot Test and/or Implement the Action Plan

Each week or so, the facilitator of each cadre presents his or her cadre's progress to the steering committee for discussion. When it's time to present an action plan proposal, the cadre needs to get steering committee and school-as-a-whole approval. The steering committee may request modifications before sending the proposal to the school as a whole for consensus. After the SAW approves the pilot program, the cadre begins implementation. Remember, teachers, administrators, aides, parents, district and community representatives, and students themselves can assist in implementing new programs.

Although the next stage calls for formal evaluation of the program, the cadre should begin assessing it upon implemention, keeping careful records of successes and difficulties encountered. If the cadre implements a pilot test, ongoing assessment of the pilot plan is important in determining whether to go to full implementation. The cadre may decide to fully implement it in its original form, modify it where necessary, or drop it and start over.

In the case of full implementation, ongoing assessment is important in determining whether to continue with the implementation. It's critical that the cadre look thoroughly at the implemented program to see whether there are areas for improvement or refinement.

Stage 5: Evaluate and Reassess

In this final stage, cadre members evaluate and assess the usefulness of the pilot program in addressing the major challenge for which it was designed. Cadres can use quantitative and qualitative evaluation tools to assess the strengths and weaknesses of the pilot program. Qualitative assessments seek out the opinions of all those affected by the program. Quantitative assessments may look at changes in achievement levels, attendance, how much something was liked, and so on. Cadres can use the results of the evaluations as a springboard for discussion about possible modifications of the pilot program or for discussion of full implementation. If cadre members have totally addressed their broad challenge area, they can move on to a new priority area. If not, they can continue working on other facets of their challenge area.

Strategies you can use to evaluate your plan include:

- Observations

- Tests

- Interviews

- Portfolios

- Videos

- Surveys

- Anecdotes

Did the plan address our focus area determined in stage 1c? How?

Did the plan help move us toward our vision?

Did the plan build on the strengths of all members of our school community? How?

Did the plan incorporate the three principles? How?

What are the successes of the plan? The challenges?

These are only some of the questions you can use to evaluate your action plan. Your cadre needs to develop its own assessment plan that uniquely fits your situation.

References and Resources

Introduction: **A Guide to the Guide**

Levin, H. M. (1985). *The educationally disadvantaged: A national crisis.* Philadelphia: Public/Private Ventures.

Levin, H. M. (1986). *Educational reform for disadvantaged students: An emerging crisis.* Washington, DC: National Education Association.

Levin, H. M. (1987a). Accelerated schools for disadvantaged students. *Educational Leadership, 44*(6), 19–21.

Levin, H. M. (1987b). New schools for the disadvantaged. *Teacher Education Quarterly, 14*(4), 60–83.

Levin, H. M. (1988). *Towards accelerated schools.* New Brunswick, NJ: Center for Policy Research in Education.

Levin, H. M. (1991). *Building school capacity for effective teacher empowerment: Applications to elementary schools with at-risk students* (CPRE Research Rep. No. RR-019). New Brunswick, NJ: Center for Policy Research in Education.

Chapter 1: **Children in At-Risk Situations**

Anyon, J. (1980). Social class and the hidden curriculum of work. *Journal of Education, 16*(2), 67–92.

Anyon, J. (1981). Social class and school knowledge. *Curriculum Inquiry, 11*(1), 3–42.

Austin, S., & Meister, G. (1990). *Responding to children at-risk: A guide to recent reports.* Philadelphia: Research for Better Schools.

Berlin, G., & Sum, A. (1988). *Toward a more perfect union: Basic skills, poor families, and our economic future* (Occasional Paper No. 3, Ford Foundation Project on Social Welfare and the American Future). New York: Ford Foundation.

Brodinsky, B. (1989). *Students at risk: Problems and solutions.* Arlington, VA: American Association of School Administrators Critical Issues Report. (ERIC Document Reproduction Service No. ED 306 642)

Carnegie Council on Adolescent Development. (1989). *Turning points: Preparing American youth for the 21st century* (Report of the Task Force on Education of Young Adolescents). New York: Carnegie Council on Adolescent Development.

Carnegie Foundation for the Advancement of Teaching. (1988). *An imperiled generation: Saving urban schools.* Lawrenceville, NJ: Princeton University Press.

Comer, J. (1988). Educating poor minority students. *Scientific American, 259*(5), 42–48.

Committee for Economic Development. (1988). *CED and education: National impact and next steps.* New York: Committee for Economic Development.

Cuban, L. (1986). Another look at constancy in the classroom. *Phi Delta Kappan, 68*(1), 7–11.

Cuban, L. (1988). A fundamental puzzle of school reform. *Phi Delta Kappan, 69*(5), 341–344.

Feldman, S., & Elliot, G. (1990). *At the threshold: The developing adolescent.* Cambridge, MA: Harvard University Press.

Fine, M. (1988). Deinstitutionalizing educational inequity: Contexts that constrict and construct the lives and minds of public school adolescents. *School success for students at risk: Analysis and recommendations of the Council of Chief State School Officers.* Washington, DC: Council of Chief State School Officers. (ERIC Document Reproduction Service No. ED 305 150)

Fiske, E. B. (1991). *Smart schools, smart kids: Why do some schools work?* New York: Simon & Schuster.

LeCompte, M. D., & Dworkin, A. G. (1991). *Giving up on school: Student dropout and teacher burnout.* Newbury Park, CA: Corwin Press.

Levin, H. M. (1986). *Educational reform for disadvantaged students: An emerging crisis.* Washington, DC: National Education Association.

Levin, H. M., & Rumberger, R. (1989). Schooling for the modern workplace. In *Investing in people: Vol. 2* (Report of the Commission on Workplace Quality and Labor Market Efficiency, U.S. Department of Labor). Washington, DC: U.S. Government Printing Office.

MDC, Inc. (1988). *America's shame, America's hope: Twelve million youth at risk.* Chapel Hill, NC: Author.

Muller, T. (1985). *The fourth wave: California's newest immigrants.* Washington, DC: Urban Institute Press.

National Center for Education Statistics. (1989). *Dropout rates in the United States: 1989.* Washington, DC: U.S. Department of Education, Office of Educational Research and Improvement.

Natriello, G., McDill, E., & Pallas, A. (1990). *Schooling the disadvantaged.* New York: Teachers College Press.

Pallas, A., Natriello, G., & McDill, E. (1989). The changing nature of the disadvantaged population: Current dimensions and future trends. *Educational Researcher, 18*(5), 16–22.

Phelan, P., Davidson, A. L., & Cao, H. T. (1991). *Students' multiple worlds: Negotiating the boundaries of peer, family, and school cultures.* Stanford, CA: Center for Research on the Context of Secondary Teaching, Stanford University.

Timpane, M., & McNeill, L. M. (1991). *Business impact on education and child development reform.* New York: Committee on Economic Development. (ERIC Document Reproduction Service No. ED 337 514)

Waggoner, D. (1991). *Undereducation in America: The demography of high school dropouts.* New York: Auburn House.

Chapter 2: What Are Accelerated Schools?

Note: Because the Accelerated Schools Project is constantly evolving, some of the concepts you encounter in the Project's earlier papers have been and continue to be transformed.

Accelerated Schools Newsletter. (1992, Winter). *2*(1).

Accelerated Schools Newsletter. (1991, Winter). *1*(1).

Brophey, J. (1987). Synthesis of research on strategies for motivating students. *Educational Leadership, 45*(10), 40–48.

Brunner, I., & Hopfenberg, W. S. (1992). *Growth and learning in accelerated schools: Big wheels and little wheels interacting.* Paper presented at the annual meeting of the American Educational Research Association, San Francisco.

California State Department of Education. (1987). *Caught in the middle: Educational reform for young adolescents in California public schools* (Report of the Superintendent's Middle Grades Task Force). Sacramento: California State Department of Education.

Carnegie Council on Adolescent Development. (1989). *Turning points: Preparing American youth for the 21st century* (Report of the Task Force on the Education of Young Adolescents). New York: Carnegie Council.

Carnoy, M., & Levin, H. M. (1985). *Schooling and work in the democratic state.* Stanford, CA: Stanford University Press.

Dewey, J. (1902). *The child and the curriculum.* Chicago: University of Chicago Press.

Dewey, J. (1915). *The school and society.* Chicago: University of Chicago Press.

Dewey, J. (1916). *Democracy and education.* New York: Macmillan.

Dewey, J. (1929). *Experience and nature.* New York: Norton.

Dewey, J. (1938a). *Experience and education.* New York: Macmillan.

Dewey, J. (1938b). *Logic, the theory of inquiry.* Troy, MO: Holt, Rinehart & Winston.

Dewey, J. (1940). Democracy in education. In J. Ratner (Ed.), *Education today.* New York: Putnam.

Dewey, J. (1984). The public and its problems. In J. A. Boydston (Ed.), *John Dewey: The later works, 1925–1953: Vol. 2. 1925–1927.* Carbondale: Southern Illinois University Press. (Original work published 1927)

Dewey, J. (1988). Creative democracy: The task before us. In J. A. Boydston (Ed.), *John Dewey: The later works, 1925–1953: Vol. 14. 1939–1941.* Carbondale: Southern Illinois University Press. (Original work published 1940)

Egan, T. (1992, August 2). Accelerating poor achievers. *The New York Times*, Section 4A, p. 34.

Finnan, C. (1992). *Becoming an accelerated middle school: Initiating school culture change*. Paper presented at the annual meeting of the American Educational Research Association, San Francisco.

Freeburg, L. (1989). Don't remediate, accelerate: Can disadvantaged students benefit from fast-forward instruction? *Equity and Choice, 5*(2), 40–43.

Goodlad, J. (1984). *A place called school*. New York: McGraw-Hill.

Goodlad, J., & Oakes, J. (1988). We must offer equal access to knowledge. *Educational Leadership, 45*(5), 16–22.

Guskey, T. M. (1990). Integrating innovations. *Educational Leadership, 45*(5), 11–15.

Heckman, P., Oakes, J., & Sirotnik, K. (1983). Expanding the concepts of school renewal and change. *Educational Leadership, 40*(7), 26–32.

Hopfenberg, W. S. (1991). *The accelerated middle school: Moving from concept to reality*. Paper presented at the annual meeting of the American Educational Research Association, Chicago.

Hopfenberg, W. S., Levin, H. M., Meister, G., & Rogers, J. (1990a). *Accelerated schools*. Stanford, CA: Center for Educational Research, Stanford University.

Hopfenberg, W. S., Levin, H. M., Meister, G., & Rogers, J. (1990b). *Toward accelerated middle schools*. Prepared for the Project to Develop Accelerated Middle Schools for At-Risk Youth. Stanford, CA: Center for Educational Research, Stanford University.

Levin, H. M. (1988). Accelerating elementary education for disadvantaged students. *School success for students at-risk: Analysis and recommendations of the Chief State School Officers*. Washington, DC: Council of Chief State School Officers. (ERIC Document Reproduction Service No. ED 305 150)

Levin, H. M. (1989a). Accelerated schools: A new strategy for at-risk students. *Policy Bulletin* (6). Bloomington, IN: Consortium on Educational Policy Studies.

Levin, H. M. (1989b). Financing the education of at-risk students. *Educational Evaluation and Policy Analysis, 11*(1), 47–60.

Levin, H. M. (1989c). *Learning from accelerated schools*. Stanford, CA: Center for Educational Research, Stanford University.

Levin, H. M. (1990a). *Accelerated schools after three years*. Stanford, CA: Center for Educational Research, Stanford University.

Levin, H. M. (1990b). At-risk students in the yuppie age. *Educational Policy, 4*(4), 283–295.

Levin, H. M. (1991). *Building school capacity for effective teacher empowerment: Applications to schools with at-risk students* (CPRE Research Rep. No.

RR-019). New Brunswick, NJ: Consortium for Policy Research in Education.

Levin, H. M., & Hopfenberg, W. S. (1991). Don't remediate: Accelerate. *Principal, 70*(3), 11–13.

Levin, H. M., & Hopfenberg, W. S. (1991). Accelerated schools for at-risk students. *Education Digest, 56*(9), 47–50.

Lieberman, A. (1992). The meaning of scholarly activity and the building of community. *Educational Researcher, 21*(6), 5–12.

Lipsitz, J. (1984). *Successful schools for young adolescents*. New Brunswick, NJ: Transaction Books.

McCarthy, J. (1991). *Accelerated schools: The satellite center project*. Paper presented at the annual meeting of the American Educational Research Association, Chicago.

McCarthy, J. (1992). *The effect of the accelerated schools process on individual teachers' decision-making and instructional strategies*. Paper presented at the annual meeting of the American Educational Research Association, San Francisco.

Sirotnik, K., & Clark, R. (1988). School-centered decision making and renewal. *Phi Delta Kappan, 69*(9), 660–664.

Stallings, J., & McCarthy, J. (1990). Teacher effectiveness research and equity issues. In H. P. Baptiste Jr., H. C. Waxman, J. W. de Felix, & J. E. Anderson (Eds.), *Leadership, Quality, and School Effectiveness*. Newbury Park, CA: Sage.

Stout, H. (1992, July 30). Remedial curriculum for low achievers is falling from favor. *The Wall Street Journal*. p. 1.

Chapter 3:   Getting Started

Accelerated Schools Newsletter. (1991, Spring). *1*(2).

Accelerated Schools Newsletter. (1993, Winter). *2*(3).

Merriam, S. B. (1988). *Case study research in education: A qualitative approach*. San Francisco: Jossey-Bass.
This guide gives advice on conducting effective interviews, being a careful observer, and employing other, similar data collection techniques that are often employed during the taking-stock stage of the acceleration process.

Patton, M. Q. (1982). *Practical evaluation*. Newbury Park, CA: Sage.
This popular and practical book provides helpful hints on preparing and administering questionnaires, interviewing, and data collection and analysis—techniques often employed during the taking-stock stage of the acceleration process.

Chapter 4:   The Inquiry Process

Accelerated Schools Newsletter. (1991, Summer). *1*(3).

Brunner, I., & Hopfenberg, W. S. (1992). *The interactive production of knowledge in accelerated schools*. Paper presented at the annual meeting of the American Educational Research Association, San Francisco.

Polkinghorn, R., Bartels, D., & Levin, H. M. (1990). *Accelerated schools: The Inquiry Process and the prospects for school change.* Paper presented at the annual meeting of the American Educational Research Association, Boston.

Sirotnik, K., & Oakes, J. (1986). Critical inquiry for school renewal: Liberating theory and practice. In K. Sirotnik & J. Oakes (Eds.), *Critical perspectives on the organization and improvement of schooling.* Boston: Kluwer-Nijihoff.

Chapter 5: Group Dynamics and Meeting Management

Bradford, L. P. (Ed.). (1961). *Group development.* San Diego, CA: University Associates.

Bradford, L. P. (1976). *Making meetings work.* San Diego, CA: University Associates.

Doyle, M., & Strauss, D. (1982). *How to make meetings work.* New York: Jove.

Fox, W. M. (1988). *Effective group problem solving: How to broaden participation, improve decision making, and increase commitment to action.* San Francisco: Jossey-Bass.

Jones, J. E., & Pfeiffer, J. W. (Eds.). (1971–1987). *The annual handbook for group facilitators.* San Diego, CA: University Associates.

LeTendre, B., Funderberg, J., & Wippern, D. (1989). *Teaming with excellence: Skills for collaboration.* Joplin, MO: Author.

Palmer, P. J. (1983). *To know as we are known: A spirituality of education.* San Francisco, CA: HarperCollins.

Purnell, S., & Hill, P. (1992). *Time for reform.* Santa Monica, CA: Rand Corporation.

Stech, E., & Ratliffe, S. A. (1985). *Effective group communication.* Lincolnwood, IL: National Textbook Company.

Zander, A. (1982). *Making groups effective.* San Francisco: Jossey-Bass.

Chapters 6 and 7: Creating Powerful Learning Experiences *and* The *What* of Powerful Learning

Books and Articles

Barell, J., Liebmann, R., & Sigel, I. (1988). Fostering thoughtful self-direction in students. *Educational Leadership, 45*(7), 14–17.

Connolly, P., & Vilardi, T. (Eds.). (1989). *Writing to learn mathematics and science.* New York: Teachers College Press.

Eden, D., & Shani, A. B. (1982). Pygmalion goes to boot camp: Expectancy, leadership, and trainee performance. *Journal of Applied Psychology, 67*(2), 194–199.

Graves, D. (1983). *Writing: Teachers and children at work.* Portsmouth, NH: Heinemann.

Harste, J., Short, K., & Burke, C. (1988a). *Creating classrooms for authors: The reading-writing connection.* Portsmouth, NH: Heinemann.

   The Authoring Cycle is designed to organize interdisciplinary units, or units in science, social science, and math, and thus create a general learning cycle. Starting with the life experiences of each individual student, the units first engage the children in an uninterrupted personal study of materials related to the unit. Then, in small study circles, students explore meaning constructs, comparing their personal experiences and what they've read with the learning experiences of the other group members. Individually or in small groups, students revise their insights and prepare for the sharing of their learning. This may take the form of a research report, a drawing, a diorama, a mural, a story, a poem, an exposition, a play, an experiment, or any other form that communicates meaning. Finally, study-group members examine how they created meaning and which of their communication vehicles were most effective in sharing that meaning with the rest of the class. Full lesson plans for thirty-two of the strategies discussed are included in the second section of the book.

Humphreys, A., Post, T. R., & Ellis, A. K. (1981). *Interdisciplinary methods: A thematic approach*. Santa Monica, CA: Goodyear.

Jacobs, H. H. (1989). *Interdisciplinary curriculum: Design and implementation*. Alexandria, VA: Association for Supervision and Curriculum Development.

Kleiman, G. M. (1991). Mathematics across the curriculum. *Educational Leadership, 49*(2), 48–51.

Resnick, L. B. (1987). *Education and learning to think*. Washington, DC: National Academy Press.

Russell, S. (1977). *An interdisciplinary approach to reading and mathematics*. San Rafael, CA: Academic Therapy Publications.

Shor, I. (1987). *Critical teaching in everyday life*. Chicago: University of Chicago Press.

Shor, I. (1992). *Empowering education*. Chicago: University of Chicago Press.

Sperling, M. (1991). Toward an interactive model of writing instruction in the accelerated school. *Accelerated Schools Newsletter. 1*(4).

Watson, B., & Konicek, R. (1990). Teaching for conceptual change: Confronting children's experience. *Phi Delta Kappan, 71*(9), 680–685.

Wiggins, G. (1987). Creating a thought-provoking curriculum. *American Educator: The Professional Journal of the American Federation of Teachers, 11*(4), 10–17.

Organizations and Programs

De Avila, E. A., & Duncan, S. E. (1980). *Finding Out/Descubrimiento*. Corte Madera, CA: Linguistics Group.

Finding Out/Descubrimiento (FO/D) is a bilingual math and science curriculum. In FO/D, more than 100 group learning activities are organized around seventeen science themes, such as change and measurement, balance, structures, probability, estimation, magnetism, electricity, and sound. Children are assigned specific roles of the sort one might expect to find on any scientific research team. This program is often used in conjunction with the Program for Complex Instruction from Stanford University (see References and Resources for Chapter Eight).

Gray, J. (1974). *The Bay Area Writing Project*. Berkeley: University of California.

This program was developed on the University of California, Berkeley, campus through the School of Education. Its purpose is to improve the teaching of writing across the curriculum from kindergarten through college. "Teachers teaching teachers" has been the key focus of the project since its beginning. The project gathers successful teachers of writing together to share their experiences and build a core of strategies. These teachers become consultants and provide hands-on writing workshops to other teachers. The project, now known throughout California as The California Writing Project, has expanded across the country to become The National Writing Project.

The National Writing Project
5627 Tolman Hall
School of Education
University of California
Berkeley, CA 94720
(510) 642-0963

Harste, J., Short, K., & Burke, C. (1988b). Family stories. In *Creating classrooms for authors: The reading-writing connection*. Portsmouth, NH: Heinemann.

"Family Stories," one of the curricular components developed in the Authoring Cycle, offers a good way to connect children's current experiences to the past. Students are asked to record stories that families repeat over and over at family gatherings or when children ask for a story. Students in heterogeneous classrooms have the opportunity to come to know their peers through these family stories and glimpse a cultural environment that may be very different from their own. In the process of gathering family stories, students learn many research strategies used by social scientists: they learn interviewing techniques, note taking, storytelling, and the written reconstruction of orally presented stories based on their field notes. After a successful collection of family stories, students may want to research and write community stories told by elderly people who've lived in the community for a long time.

Makler, A. (1991). Imagining history: A good story and a well-formed argument. In C. Witherell & N. Noddings (Eds.), *Stories lives tell: Narratives and dialogue in education*. New York: Teachers College Press.

Makler has developed a highly motivating history curriculum framework in the form of a set of open-ended scripts. Each student is presented with an outline of a fictional character's vital statistics, such as age, occupation, place of residence, family status, religion, and race. "The students' task [is] to use this information to develop a personal life history connecting the character to the events and issues of the historical period under study. Developing these narratives (entries in diaries, letters, expository essays) [is] a means for students quite literally to write themselves into the historical record" (pp. 29–30).

Open Doors Program. (1990). New York: Scholastic Text Division.

The Open Doors Program focuses on developing children's problem-solving abilities, social skills, and language skills (in reading, writing, listening, and speaking) and their conceptual understandings of subject areas. The interdisciplinary units are organized around a common theme, employing activities in many discipline areas. Lessons are designed to build children's knowledge of a topic by constantly relating it to their own personal lives and experiences. Students are given opportunities to actively participate in hands-on cooperative learning experiences, enabling them to learn from their peers.

Open Doors Program
Scholastic, Inc.
730 Broadway
New York, NY 10003

The Private Eye. (1989). Seattle, WA: Kerry Ruef.

The Private Eye is a program designed to develop higher-order thinking skills, creativity, and scientific literacy through a carefully designed process of looking closely at the world, thinking by analogy, and changing scale. It offers a teacher's seminar, a resource guide, and the Private Eye kit of hands-on investigative materials to stimulate interest in art, writing, science, math, and social studies.

The Private Eye Project
7710 31st Avenue
Seattle, WA 98117

Project Read. (1980). Stanford, CA: Stanford University.

Project Read is a collection of teaching/learning techniques that facilitate student learning by utilizing organizing structures and strategies that are especially effective in helping students understand, learn, and use information. The project also focuses on developing critical literacy and responsive instruction and building an inquiring school community. The elements of an inquiring school community include increased classroom practices, professional collaboration, and shared decision making.

Calfee Projects
Project Read
School of Education
Stanford University
Stanford, CA 94305-3096

Project Wild. (1983). Elementary activity guide. Boulder, CO: Western Regional Environmental Educational Council.

Project Wild is a commercially available interdisciplinary program for environmental and conservation education and problem solving from kindergarten to high school. Its purpose is "to motivate youngsters to take intelligent and constructive action to conserve wildlife and natural resources" (p. *ix*). It provides students with information and helps them evaluate choices and make reasonable decisions.

Project Wild
Salina Star Route
Boulder, CO 80302
(303) 444-2390

Stenmark, J. K., Thompson, V., & Cossey, R. (1986). *Family Math*. Berkeley: University of California Regents.

This program was developed by researchers at the Lawrence Hall of Science at the University of California, Berkeley, to help parents help their children learn mathematics. The Family Math program focuses on parents and children (from kindergarten to eighth grade) learning mathematics together by introducing fun activities directly related to everyday situations and events. Topics included in Family Math are part of the domains of arithmetic, geometry, probability and statistics, measurement, estimation, calculators, computers, logical thinking, and careers.

Family Math
c/o Lawrence Hall of Science
University of California
Berkeley, CA 94720

Chapter 8: The *How* of Powerful Learning

Sources for Active Learning

Brown, D. (1976). *Learning and teaching*. Los Gatos, CA: Lamplighters Roadway Press.

Chase, C. (1992). *Learning in accelerated schools: The power of collaborative experience*. Paper presented at the annual meeting of the American Educational Research Association, San Francisco.

Gardner, H. (1985). *Frames of mind: The theory of multiple intelligences*. New York: Basic Books.

Gardner, H. (1991). *The unschooled mind: How children think and how schools should teach*. New York: HarperCollins.

Hansen, K. L. (1989). Tombstones as textbooks. *Learning, 18*(3), 27–29.

Kavalik, S. (1986). *Teachers make the difference*. Village of Oak Creek, AZ: Susan Kavalik and Associates.

Lotan, R. A., & Benton, J. (1989). Finding out about complex instruction: Teaching math and science in heterogeneous classrooms. In N. Davidson (Ed.), *Cooperative learning in mathematics: A handbook for teachers*. Reading, MA: Addison-Wesley.

Sheingold, K. (1990). *Restructuring for learning with technology*. Rochester, NY: National Center on Education and the Economy and the Center for Technology in Education.

Wigginton, E. (1989). Foxfire grows up. *Harvard Educational Review, 59*(1), 24–29.

Sources for Alternative Assessment in the Classroom

Alternative assessment in mathematics. (1989). EQUALS, Lawrence Hall of Science, University of California, Berkeley, CA 94720. ATTN: Assessment Booklet.

Educational Leadership. (1989, April). *46*(7). This issue includes a series of articles on assessment.

Educational Leadership. (1992, May). *49*(8). This issue focuses on the use of performance assessment.

Jongsma, K. S. (1989). Portfolio assessment (questions and answers). *Reading Teacher, 43*(3), 264–265.

Learning by doing: A manual for teaching and assessing higher-order thinking in science and mathematics. (1987). National Assessment of Educational Progress. Princeton, NJ: Educational Testing Service.

Meyer, C., Schuman, S., & Angello, N. (1990). *Aggregating portfolio data.* Lake Oswego, OR: Northwest Evaluation Association.

Nahrgang, C., & Peterson, B. (1986). Using writing to learn mathematics. *Mathematics Teacher, 79*(6), 461–465.

Randall, C., Lester, F., & O'Daffer, P. (1987). *How to evaluate progress in problem solving.* Reston, VA: National Council of Teachers of Mathematics.

White, E. M. (1985). *Teaching and assessing writing: Recent advances in understanding, evaluating, and improving student performance.* San Francisco: Jossey-Bass.

Wiggins, G. (1989). A true test: Toward more authentic and equitable assessment. *Phi Delta Kappan, 70*(9), 703–713.

Sources for Cooperative Learning

Books and Articles

Aronson, E., Blaney, N., Stephan, C., Sikes, J., & Snapp, M. (1978). *The jigsaw classroom.* Newbury Park, CA: Sage.

Bossert, S.T.C. (1977). Tasks, group management, and teacher control. *School Review, 85*(4), 552–564.

Cohen, E. G. (1986a). *Designing groupwork: Strategies for the heterogeneous classroom.* New York: Teachers College Press.

Cohen, E. G. (1986b). On the sociology of the classroom. In J. Hannaway & M. E. Lockeed (Eds.), *The contributions of the social sciences to educational policy and practice: 1965–1985.* Berkeley, CA: McCutchan.

Educational Leadership. (1989, December–1990, January). *47*(4). This issue focuses on cooperative learning.

Johnson, D., & Johnson, R. (1989). Social skills for successful group work. *Educational Leadership, 47*(4), 29–33.

Johnson, D., Johnson, R., & Johnson Holubec, E. (1987). *Structuring cooperative learning: Lesson plans for teachers.* Edina, MN: Interaction Book Company.

Johnson., D., Johnson, R., Johnson Holubec, E., & Roy, P. (1986). *Circles of learning: Cooperation in the classroom.* Alexandria, VA: Association of Supervision and Curriculum Development.

Kagan, S. (1989a). *Cooperative learning resources for teachers.* San Juan Capistrano, CA: Resources for Teachers.

Kagan, S. (1989b). A structural approach to cooperative learning. *Educational Leadership, 47*(4), 12–15.

Lewis, C. C. (1988). Japanese first-grade classrooms: Implications for U.S. theory and research. *Comparative Education Review, 32*(2), 159–172.

Lotan, R. A., & Benton, J. (1989). Finding out about complex instruction: Teaching math and science in heterogeneous classrooms. In N. Davidson (Ed.), *Cooperative learning in mathematics: A handbook for teachers.* Reading, MA: Addison-Wesley.

Sharan, S., & Sharan, Y. (1976). *Small group teaching.* Englewood Cliffs, NJ: Educational Technology Publication.

Sharan, Y., & Sharan, S. (1989). Group investigation expands cooperative learning. *Educational Leadership, 47*(4), 17–21.

Slavin, R. E. (1985). *Learning to cooperate, cooperating to learn.* New York: Plenum.

Slavin, R., & Madden, N. (1989). *Effective classroom programs for students at risk.* Needham Heights, MA: Allyn & Bacon.

Slavin, R. E., Madden, N. A., & Stevens, R. J. (1989). Cooperative learning models for the 3 R's. *Educational Leadership, 47*(4), 22–28.

Organizations and Programs

Program for Complex Instruction
Dr. Elizabeth Cohen
Center for Educational Research at Stanford
Stanford University, Stanford, CA 94305

> The Program for Complex Instruction is a cooperative learning approach that incorporates a unique classroom management strategy specifically aimed at developing higher-order thinking skills in academically and linguistically heterogeneous classrooms, delegating authority and responsibility for problem solving to students, dealing with status differences among students, and helping children from mixed language backgrounds and with different abilities to work together and learn from each other.

Resources for Teachers
Structured Approach
Spencer Kagan, Ph.D.
Paseo Espada #202
San Juan Capistrano, CA 92675

Team Assisted Individuation
Center for Research on Elementary and Middle Schools
Johns Hopkins University
North Charles Street
Baltimore, MD 21218

Sources for Educational Technology

Books, Journals, and Articles

The computing teacher. The International Society for Computers in Education, 1787 Agate Street, Eugene, OR 97403-9905.

Dunn, S., & Larson, R. (1990). *Design technology: Children's engineering.* New York: Falmer Press.

Electronic learning. Scholastic, Inc. P.O. Box 3025, Southeastern, PA 19398.

Howe, S. F. (1989). Rubbing elbows with reality. *Learning, 18*(3), 48–50.

Rhodes, L. (1986). Using the sticks we have. *Educational Leadership, 43*(6), 3.

Sachse, T. P. (1989). Making science happen. *Educational Leadership, 47*(3), 18–21.

Sheingold, K. (1990). *Restructuring for learning with technology.* Rochester, NY: National Center on Education and the Economy and the Center for Technology in Education.

Tyson, H., & Woodward, A. (1989). Why students aren't learning very much from textbooks. *Educational Leadership, 47*(3), 14–17.

U.S. Office of Technology. (1988). *Power on! New tools for teaching and learning* (GPO Stock No. 052-003-01125-5). Washington, DC: U.S. Government Printing Office.

Organizations and Programs

Apple Computer Clubs
Mailstop 36AA
Apple Computer, Inc.
20525 Mariani
Cupertino, CA 95014

Association of Supervision and Curriculum Development
Curriculum/Technology Resource Center
1250 North Pitt Street
Alexandria, VA 22314-1403

Computer Learning Foundation
PO Box 60007
Palo Alto, CA 94306-0007

Computer Using Educators, Inc.
PO Box 2087
Menlo Park, CA 94025

Kids' Network
Geography Education Programs
National Geographic Society
17th and M Streets
Washington, DC 20036

Sources for Expressive Modes

Best, D. (1974). *Expression in movement and the arts: A philosophical enquiry.* London: Lepus Books.

Dewey, J. (1934). *Art as experience.* New York: Capricorn Books.

Eisner, E. (1972). *Educating artistic vision.* New York: Macmillan.

Eisner, E. (Ed.). (1985). *Learning and teaching the ways of knowing* (National Society for the Study of Education, 84th Yearbook). Chicago: University of Chicago Press.

Herman, N. (1989). *The creative brain* (rev. ed.). Lake Lurie, NC: Brain Books.

Houston, J. (1982). *The possible human: A course in extending your physical, mental, and creative abilities.* New York: J. P. Tarcher.

Kupfer, J. (1983). *Experience as art: Aesthetics in everyday life.* Albany, NY: SUNY Press.

Madeja, S. (Ed.). (1978). *The arts, cognition, and basic skills.* St. Louis, MO: CEMREL.

Van Oech, R. (1990). *A whack in the side of the head* (rev. ed.). New York: Warner Books.

Van Oech, R. (1986). *A kick in the seat of the pants.* New York: Warner Books.

Sources for Peer Tutoring

Fitz-Gibbon, C. T. (1988). Peer tutoring as a teaching strategy. *Educational Management and Administration, 16*(3), 217–219.

Goodlad, S., & Hirst, B. (1989). *Peer tutoring: A guide to learning by teaching.* New York: Nichols.

Topping, K. (1989). Peer tutoring and paired reading: Combining two powerful techniques. *Reading Teacher, 42*(7), 488–494.

Chapter 9: **The *Context* of Powerful Learning**

Books and Articles

Bailey, C., & Bridges, D. (1983). *Mixed ability grouping: A philosophical perspective.* London: Allen & Unwin.

Barth, R. S. (1990). *Improving schools from within: Teachers, parents, and principals can make the difference.* San Francisco: Jossey-Bass.

Braddock, J. II. (1990). Tracking in the middle grades: National patterns of grouping for instruction. *Phi Delta Kappan, 71*(6), 445–449.

Bryan, M. (1971). *Ability grouping: Status, impact, and alternatives.* Princeton, NJ: ERIC Clearinghouse on Tests, Measurements, and Evaluation. (ERIC Document Reproduction Service No. ED 052 260, Clearinghouse No. TM 000 770)

Christensen, G. (1992). *The changing role of the administrator in an accelerated school.* Paper presented at the annual meeting of the American Educational Research Association, San Francisco.

Cotton, K., & Savard, W. G. (1981). *Instructional grouping, ability grouping: Research on school effectiveness project* (Topic Summary Report). Portland, OR: Northwest Regional Educational Lab.

Cunningham, L., & Mitchell, B. (Eds.). (1990). *Educational leadership and changing contexts of families, communities, and schools.* Chicago: University of Chicago Press.

Educational Leadership. (1992, October). 50(2). This issue focuses on tracking in America's schools.

Lake, S. (1988). *Equal access to education: Alternatives to tracking and ability grouping.* Sacramento, CA: California League of Middle Schools.

Levin, H. M. (1991). *Building school capacity for effective teacher empowerment: Applications to schools with at-risk students* (CPRE Research Rep. No. RR-019). New Brunswick, NJ: Consortium for Policy Research in Education.

Lieberman, A. (1992). *The changing context of teaching.* Chicago: University of Chicago Press.

Oakes, J. (1985). *Keeping track: How schools structure inequality.* New Haven, CT: Yale University Press.

Rosenthal, S., & Jacobson (1968). *Pygmalion in the classroom: Teacher expectation and pupils' intellectual ability.* Troy, MO: Holt, Rinehart, & Winston.

Wehlage, G., Rutter, R., Smith, G., Lesko, N., & Fernandez, R. (1989). *Reducing the risk: Schools as communities of support.* New York: Falmer Press.

Wheelock, A. (1992). *Crossing the tracks: How "untracking" can save America's schools.* New York: New Press.

Organizations and Programs

Fred H. Jones & Associates, Inc.
103 Quarry Lane
Santa Cruz, CA 95060
(408) 425-8222
FAX (408) 426-8222

Fred Jones offers both seminars and videos on positive classroom discipline and positive classroom instruction. The classroom discipline course teaches limit setting and responsibility training in the classroom, the use of low-key sanctions, and a synthesis of classroom management techniques. The positive classroom instruction course teaches techniques in corrective feedback, lesson design, and lesson presentation for maximizing students' learning and performance.

Chapter 10: Family and Community Involvement

Books and Articles

Education Commission of the States. (1988). *Drawing in the family: Family involvement in schools.* Denver, CO: Author.

Educational Leadership. (1989, December–1990, January). 47(4). This issue has a section on corporate influence on public schools.

Epstein, J. (1985). Home and school connections in schools of the future: Implications of research on parent involvement. *Peabody Journal of Education, 62*(2), 18–41.

Epstein, J. (1986). *Parent involvement: Implications for limited-English-proficient parents.* In C. Simich-Dudgeon (Ed.), *Issues of parent involvement and literacy.* Proceedings of the symposium held at Trinity College, Washington, DC. (ERIC Document Reproduction Service No. ED 275 208, Clearinghouse No. FL 016 192)

Epstein, J. (1986). Parents' reaction to teacher practices of parent involvement. *Elementary School Journal, 86*(3), 277–294.

Epstein, J. (1987). Parent involvement: What research says to administrators. *Education and Urban Society, 19*(2), 119–136.

Epstein, J. (1988). How do we improve programs for parent involvement? *Educational Horizons, 66*(2), 58–59.

Epstein, J. (1991). Paths to partnerships: What can we learn from federal, state, and district school initiatives? *Phi Delta Kappan, 72*(5), 344–349.

Henderson, A. (1986). *Beyond the bake sale. An educator's guide to working with parents.* Washington, DC: National Committee for Citizens in Education.

Henderson, A. (1988). Parents are a school's best friends. *Phi Delta Kappan, 70*(2), 148–153.

King, A. (1987). *Learning together: Examples of school/business/community partnerships.* Austin, TX: Southwest Educational Development Laboratory.

The National Alliance of Business. (1989). *The compact project: School business partnerships for improving education.* Washington, DC: Author.

Rigden, D. W. (1991). *Business/school partnerships.* New York: Council for Aid to Education.

Robinson, E., & Mastny, A. (1989). *Linking schools and community services: A practical guide.* New Brunswick, NJ: Center for Community Education, School of Social Work, Rutgers University.

Seeley, D. (1989). A new paradigm for parent involvement. *Educational Leadership, 47*(2), 46–48.

Shelton, C. W. (1987). *The double dozen: A checklist of practical ideas for school-business partnerships.* Alexandria, VA: National Community Education Association.

Sprinzen, M. (1989). *Business response to education in America: A study conducted among the largest U.S. companies.* (ERIC Document Reproduction Service No. ED 309 226, Clearinghouse No. UD 026 891)

Swap, S. (1987). *Enhancing parent involvement in schools.* New York: Teachers College Press.

Swap, S. (1990). Comparing three philosophies of home-school collaboration. *Equity and Choice, 6*(3), 9–19.

Swap, S. (1991). *Can parent involvement lead to increased student achievement in urban schools?* Paper presented at the annual meeting of the American Educational Research Association, Chicago.

Organizations and Programs

Family Math
c/o Lawrence Hall of Science
University of California
Berkeley, CA 94720

School Based Youth Services Program
Assistant Commissioner for Intergovernmental Affairs
Department of Human Services
Capital Place One
222 South Warren Street
Trenton, NJ 08625

Support Center for School-Based Clinics
Sharon Lovick, Director
5650 Kirby Drive, Suite 242
Houston, TX 77005

Chapter 11: How Will I Know If My School Is Accelerating?

Accelerated Schools Newsletter. (1991, Fall). *1*(4).

Accelerated Schools Newsletter. (1993, Winter). *2*(3).

Alternative Assessment in Mathematics. (1989). EQUALS, Lawrence Hall of Science, University of California, Berkeley, CA 94720. ATTN: Assessment Booklet.

Davidson, B. M. (1992). *Building school capacity to accelerate learning: A study of restructuring processes in four elementary schools*. Unpublished doctoral dissertation, University of New Orleans.

Educational Leadership. (1989, April). *46*(7). This issue includes a series of articles on assessment.

Educational Leadership. (1992, May). *49*(8). This issue focuses on using performance assessment.

Eisner, E. (1991). Taking a second look: Educational connoisseurship revisited. In M. McLaughlin & D. C. Phillips (Eds.), *Evaluation and education at quarter century*. Chicago: University of Chicago Press.

Fetterman, D. M., & Haertel, E. H. (in press). *A school-based evaluation model for accelerating the education of students at-risk*. New York: Falmer Press.

Finnan, C. (1992). *Becoming an accelerated middle school: Initiating school culture change*. Stanford, CA: Center for Educational Research, Stanford University.

Gardner, H. (1991). *The unschooled mind: How children think and how schools should teach*. New York: HarperCollins.

Jongsma, K. S. (1989). Portfolio assessment (questions and answers). *Reading Teacher, 43*(3), 264–265.

Learning by doing: A manual for teaching and assessing higher-order thinking in science and mathematics. (1987). National Assessment of Educational Progress. Princeton, NJ: Educational Testing Service.

McCarthy, J. (1992). *Assessing the progress of an accelerated school: The Hollibrook Elementary School project*. Paper presented at the annual meeting of the American Educational Research Association, San Francisco.

McCarthy, J., Hopfenberg, W. S., & Levin, H. M. (1991). *Accelerated schools: Evolving thoughts on the evaluation of an innovative model*. Paper presented at the annual meeting of the American Educational Research Association, Chicago.

Meister, G. (1992). *Assessment inside two accelerated elementary schools: Summary.* Paper presented at the annual meeting of the American Educational Research Association, San Francisco.

Merriam, S. B. (1988). *Case study research in education: A qualitative approach.* San Francisco: Jossey-Bass.

Meyer, C., Schuman, S., & Angello, N. (1990). *Aggregating portfolio data.* Lake Oswego, OR: Northwest Evaluation Association.

Morton, J. L. (1991). *What teachers want to know about portfolio assessment.* (ERIC Document Reproduction Service No. ED 336 728, Clearinghouse No. CS 010 710)

Nahrgang, C., & Peterson, B. (1986). Using writing to learn mathematics. *Mathematics Teacher, 79*(6), 461–465.

Patton, M. Q. (1982). *Practical evaluation.* Newbury Park, CA: Sage.

Phi Delta Kappan. (1989, May). *70*(9). This issue contains several articles on alternatives to standardized tests.

Randall, C., Lester, F., & O'Daffer, P. (1987). *How to evaluate progress in problem solving.* Reston, VA: National Council of Teachers of Mathematics.

Shepard, L. A. (1989). Why we need better assessments. *Educational Leadership, 46*(7), 4–9.

Tierney, R. J. (1991). *Portfolio assessment in the reading-writing classroom.* Norwood, MA: Christopher-Gordon.

White, E. M. (1985). *Teaching and assessing writing: Recent advances in understanding, evaluating, and improving student performance.* San Francisco: Jossey-Bass.

Wiggins, G. (1989). A true test: Toward more authentic and equitable assessment. *Phi Delta Kappan, 70*(9), 703–713.

Wolf, D. P. (1989). Portfolio assessment: Sampling student work. *Educational Leadership, 46*(7), 35–39.

Index

Ability grouping. *See* Grouping

Accelerated schools: assessment of, 313–334; as centers of expertise, 33, 95, 116–117, 172; definition of, 2; extent of, 1–2; goal of equity in, 16, 20, 314, 315, 326; initial steps for becoming, 57–92; involvement of, in resource guide, 6–7; philosophy of, 17–37, 161–162; principles of, 20–30, 86, 164–167, 188, 261, 316; principles of, exercise in, 167; process in, 161; process of becoming, 37, 55–60, 285–288, 327–337; reflection in, 32; versus remedial education, 17–18, 211–212, 234–235; role transformations in, 264–271; stages of, 317–326; successes of, 18–19; transition from, to other schools, 276–277; values of, 31–33; visits to, 37–54. *See also* Powerful learning experiences

Accelerated Schools Newsletter, 7, 37, 54

Accelerated Schools Project: assessment of, 8; philosophy/process of, 20–37, 55; state involvement and, 271–272. *See also* Accelerated Schools

Accountability, district-school collaboration for, 26

Accreditation association evaluation procedures, 315

Achievement: gains in, 18–20, 41, 44, 46; and parental involvement, 301–302, 303, 306; strategies for improvement of, 217–224. *See also* Assessment; Test scores

Acting-out, in traditional schools, 14

Action plans: assessment of, 322, 331–332; case examples of, 125–134, 183–189, 217–224, 301–308, 308–312; chart for, 121; develop-

ment of, 120, 305–307, 310–312, 339–340; evaluation/reassessment of, 121–122, 188–189, 224–225, 307, 312, 341–342; pilot testing/implementation of, 121–122, 187–188, 307, 312, 340–341; reflection questions for, 124–125, 331–332

Active learning, 31, 41, 181, 182, 206–207; definition of, 224; examples of, 224–247; in mathematics, 185–186; seizing the moment in, 225–227; through listening, 231–232. *See also* Hands-on learning; Powerful learning experiences

Administrators: role of, 268–269; and steering committee, 90; in traditional systems, 98, 268–269; utilizing strengths of, 29–30, 165-166, 179. *See also* Principals; Support staff

"Adopt-a-school" program, 300

Adults, "at-risk," 10; and academic failure, 11; demographics of, 11

Aerospace classes, 51–52, 209–210, 239–240. *See also* Space unit

Agenda: importance of, 91; sample of, 151–152

Aguilar, L., 231

AIMS curriculum, 227–228

Archaeology, cooperative learning projects in, 224

Art: for active learning, 232–233; for communication, 230–231; creative materials for, 253, 254; for cultural studies, 256–257

Artists/craftspeople, local, 295

Assessment: and accelerated principles, 316; of accelerated schools, 7–8, 313–334; authentic, examples of, 244–247; of big-wheel processes, 317–325; of cadres, 328–329; of collaborative deci-

sion making, 320–322; conceptions of, 314–316; criterion for, 314; data collection for, 319–320, 322–323; documentation for, 319, 323–324; of forging a vision, 321, 327; formal processes of, 316–325; of governance structure, 328–329; of implementation, 322; of Inquiry Process, 330–332; of little-wheel processes, 326; of outcomes, 322–324, 332–334; by outside organizations, 314–315; of overall accelerated schools goal, 325; planning for, 319–320; portfolios for, 319–320; qualitative versus quantitative tools of, 123; reflection time for, 320; responsibility for, 319; of school as a whole, 329; self-, 313, 315–316, 317–334; of setting priorities, 321–322, 328; of steering committee, 329; of student learning, 243–247; of taking stock, 321, 326; tools for, 319; traditional, 314–315; and vision statement, 323–325. *See also* Evaluation; Reflection; Test scores

Astronomy class, 52. *See also* Aerospace classes; Space unit

At-risk situations, children in, 9–16; accelerated schools goal for, 16, 20, 314, 315, 326; demographics of, 10; failure of educational system for, 10–12; funding for, 274–275; and language development, 191; positive view of, 16; versus at-risk children, 9, 29; special programs for, 274–275; stigmatization of, 11, 167; in traditional schools, 12–13; utilizing strengths of, 27–28. *See also* Chapter I Students; Students

At-risk students, 9. *See also* At-risk situations; Students

229, 242, 257, 261–263; modeling of, 260–261; of staff, 22–23; as value, 32, 169–170. *See also* Inquiry Process; Meetings

Colleges, partnership with, 297

Commitment, group, 142

Committees: for forging a vision, 78–79; for taking stock, 63, 67. *See also* Steering committee

Communication: and consensus building, 150; and governance, 91; and group dynamics, 141; holistic approach to, 53–54; about meetings, 147; with parents, 282, 285, 289–290, 301, 307; and participation, 45; and steering committee, 89–90; as value, 31–32, 169–170

Community involvement: in accelerated schools, 276, 291–293; of artists/craftspeople, 295; in brainstorming solutions, 117; of businesses, 298–300, 312; of clubs/organizations, 294; examples of, 38–39, 54; in forging a vision, 79; of health/human services agencies, 297–298; Inquiry Process for, 308–312; of libraries, 296–297; of local government, 297–298; of museums, 296–297; of religious organizations, 296; of role models, 294–295; in traditional systems, 98; as two-way exchange, 276, 293; of universities/colleges, 297; utilizing resources of, 30, 166–167, 228–230, 292, 293–301; volunteers and, 312

Community spirit, as value, 32

Computers: for cataloging strengths, 224; for teachers, 217; and writing instruction, 194, 206, 241. *See also* Technology

Conflict: and consensus building, 149–150; in setting priorities, 85–86

Consensus building, 149–150

Context, of powerful learning, 35, 36, 161, 162, 249–277; elements of, 252–264; levels of, 250; and role transformation, 264–271; beyond school site, 271–277; and social environment, 251–252, 260–264; supportive, 251–252; in traditional schools, 250; types of, 251. *See also* Funding; Physical environment; Resources; Social environment; Time

Context questions, for challenge area hypothesis, 105. *See also* Context, of powerful learning

Cooperative learning. *See* Active learning; Collaboration; Team learning

Cross-age tutoring. *See* Tutoring

Cultural bias, 11, 279

Cultural studies: curriculum for, 192–193, 200–206; and reflection, 230–231; writing and, 231

Curriculum: broadening of, 28–29; and challenge area hypothesis, 104; child-centered, 181, 194, 203–204; integrated, examples of, 179–183, 191–193, 207–208, 257; integrated, research on, 190–191; interdisciplinary, 180, 189; for language arts, 191–196; for powerful learning experiences, 35, 177–209; planning for, 180; for scientific/quantitative understanding, 196–200; thematic, 191; in traditional schools, 12, 13, 189. *See also What*, in powerful learning; Powerful learning experiences; Thematic learning

Daniel Webster Elementary School (San Francisco, California): alternative assessment in, 245–247; cooperative learning in, 261–262; cultural studies in, 202–206, 256–257; innovative instruction in, 36, 213–217; integrated curriculum in, 191–192; parental involvement in, 167, 281; physical environment in, 255; reading instruction in, 194–195; risk taking in, 172; shared vision in, 82; using substitute time in, 155, 166

Day-care centers, in community, 296

Decision making: assessment of, 320–322; examples of, 48–50; group, 45–46, 143–144; informed, 38, 49–50; principal's role in, 269; school-based, 25; through voting/consensus building, 149–150. *See also* Collaboration; Forging a vision; Governance structure; Inquiry Process; Meetings; Setting priorities; Taking stock

Democracy: versus consensus, 150; education in, 33

Dewey, J., 33

Discipline. *See* Classrooms

Disciplines: experiential, 206–209; integration of, 189–209. *See also* Curriculum

District office: involvement of, in decision making, 25–26; involvement of, in forging a vision, 79, 273; involvement of, in making meeting time, 152; involvement of, in planning, 57; requirements of, 174; and resource allocation, 274–275; roles of, 271–276

Diversity, through heterogeneous grouping, 278–280, 308. *See also* Grouping

Drama, for active learning, 233

Early release days, 154, 275

Ecology instruction, 197–199

"Educational connoisseurs," 315

Eisner, E., 315

El Toro Elementary School (Morgan Hill, California), 276, 291

Elective courses, 207–209

Elementary schools, accelerated: genesis of, 3; transition from, to middle schools, 277–278

Empowerment coupled with responsibility: and assessment, 316; in classroom, 245–246, 262–263, 265–266; and cross-age/peer tutoring, 257–258, 265–266; and governance, 86, 244; principle of, 24–26, 164–165; of students, 26; of teachers, 26, 53, 267

English proficiency: and bilingual instruction, 240; and dramatic instruction, 233; expectation of, in conventional schools, 11; and parents, 289, 306; webbing method for, 206. *See also* Bilingual instruction; Language-centered instruction

Equity, as value, 31, 167. *See also* Accelerated schools

Evaluation: of accelerated schools projects, 8; of action plans, 121–123, 125, 134, 188–189, 224, 307, 312, 332, 341–342; qualitative versus quantitative, 123. *See also* Assessment

Exercises: in accelerated school principles, 167; for building on strengths, 30–31; for develop-